FLYING TO VICTORY

CAMPAIGNS & COMMANDERS

GREGORY J. W. URWIN, SERIES EDITOR

Flying to Victory

Raymond Collishaw and the Western Desert Campaign, 1940–1941

Mike Bechthold

University of Oklahoma Press | Norman

Library of Congress Cataloging-in-Publication Data

Name: Bechthold, Michael, 1968– author.
Title: Flying to victory : Raymond Collishaw and the western desert
  campaign, 1940–1941 / Mike Bechthold.
Description: Norman : University of Oklahoma Press, 2017. | Series:
Campaigns and commanders ; volume 58 | Includes bibliographical references and index.
Identifiers: LCCN 2016034806 | ISBN 978-0-8061-5596-8 (hardcover : alk. paper)
Subjects: LCSH: Collishaw, Raymond, 1893–1976. | World War,
  1939–1945—Campaigns—Africa, North. | Great Britain. Royal Air Force.
  Desert Air Force. | World War, 1939–1945—Aerial operations, British.
Classification: LCC D766.82 .B328 2017 | DDC 940.54/4941092 [B] —dc23
LC record available at https://lccn.loc.gov/2016034806

Flying to Victory: Raymond Collishaw and the Western Desert Campaign, 1940–1941 is Volume 58
in the Campaigns and Commanders series.

The paper in this book meets the guidelines for permanence and durability of the Committee on
Production Guidelines for Book Longevity of the Council on Library Resources, Inc. ∞

1 2 3 4 5 6 7 8 9 10

Interior layout and composition: Alcorn Publication Design

In Memoriam

Beverly E. Bechthold
1943–2011

Jeffrey Grey
1959–2016

Contents

Illustrations

Figures

Maps

Acknowledgments

For many years the issue of tactical air support has been a topic of great interest to me. While reading an article on British and American airmen in North Africa by the late Vincent Orange, I stumbled on a short section where the New Zealander described the unappreciated efforts of Raymond Collishaw in 1940 and 1941. It struck me that this might be a topic worth further investigation, so I tucked the idea away. I met Orange in 2004 at a conference in Wolverhampton, where I shared my curiosity for Collishaw. He agreed that there was much left to learn and encouraged me to explore the Second World War career of a Canadian known mainly for his First World War exploits. So I owe my first thanks to Professor Orange for setting me on this path of discovery, having taken his one page of musings and spun it into an entire book.

This project originated as my PhD dissertation, and I was fortunate to have Drs. Jeffrey Grey and Eleanor Hancock as my co-supervisors. Dr. Grey quickly and positively responded to my initial email enquiry seeking a PhD advisor and ably guided me through this complex process, offering key advice and direction as needed. Dr. Hancock's fine editing skills and insightful comments have helped make this a much stronger work. I must also mention the essential support provided by Dr. Craig Stockings, who was crucial in facilitating the completion of my degree.

I was lucky to spend twenty years working at the Laurier Centre for Military Strategic and Disarmament Studies at Wilfrid Laurier University. The center has influenced and enriched my study of history in innumerable ways. Prof. Terry Copp guided me through my undergraduate and master's degrees and first cultivated my academic interest in military aviation in general and tactical air support in particular. As the director of the Laurier Centre, Terry provided me with unparalleled opportunities for travel and research. I have benefited greatly from the sage advice of Dr. Roger Sarty, with whom I worked closely over the past decade on *Canadian Military History* and other similar projects.

A work of this nature is always collaborative, and I have received great support from my friends and colleagues. Dr. Lee Windsor has long been a fellow traveler down this path of discovery. We first met when he returned to Kitchener-Waterloo in 1994, and since then he has provided me with untold support and encouragement. His wife, Dr. Cindy Brown, is a more recent friend, but her support has been no less important. Dr. Tim Cook suggested

xi

that I approach Dr. Grey in Australia about my PhD. He has remained a good friend and source of inspiration throughout this project. In completing this project I have profited from the advice and linguistic skills of Drs. Oliver Haller and Kirk Goodlet, who helped me interpret German and Italian sources. I have also benefited from numerous individuals who have provided research support, including Dr. Douglas Delaney, Dr. Geoff Keelan, William March, Caitlin McWilliams, and Cathy Murphy. There are a number of individuals who have kindly shared their knowledge to help me understand various facets of this subject. They include Lt. Col. (ret.) David Bashow, Dr. John Buckley, Owen Cooke, Dr. Guy Finch, Dr. Richard Goette, Dr. David Ian Hall, Gary Komar, Dr. Ross Mahoney, Allan Snowie, Dr. William Stewart, Dr. Randall Wakelam, and Thomas Wildenberg. Amy Menary of the Interlibrary Loans office at the Wilfrid Laurier University Library deserves a special thanks for her efforts to find the many obscure titles I have requested. Over the years I have placed dozens of requests, and she has never failed to find me what I needed.

Financial support for this project has come from a number of sources. I need to recognize the University of New South Wales at the Australian Defence Force Academy and the Laurier Centre for Military Strategic and Disarmament Studies for providing research and travel funds, the Canadian Forces Aerospace Warfare Centre for providing a research grant, and the Brick Robb Memorial Scholarship, awarded by the Ontario Secondary School Teachers' Federation.

Special thanks to Gregory Urwin, Charles Rankin, Adam Kane, Stephanie Evans, Kevin Brock, Amy Hernandez, Mette Flynt, and the rest of the team at the University of Oklahoma Press for their professional support and guidance throughout this project. This book is much stronger as a result of their efforts.

My parents have always been tireless supporters of my efforts. Without their love and encouragement I would never have enjoyed so many opportunities.

Finally and most importantly, I must thank my wife, Paula, and my children, Addison and Alexander, for their support, encouragement, and understanding during this project. There is no way this work could have been completed without their patience. I dedicate this book to them, with all my love.

Note on Conventions

The question of individuals' ranks is a confusing matter as many of the officers mentioned in this text were regularly promoted during the period under consideration. An officer's ultimate rank will be used when referencing his overall career, but officers will be identified by the rank they held during the events under consideration. Thus, it is Group Capt. Arthur Longmore in chapter 1, when discussing his role in Iraq in 1923, and Air Chief Marshal Longmore in chapter 4, when he was the senior RAF officer in the Middle East at the time of Operation Compass.

The spelling of towns and places in Egypt and Libya varies widely depending on the source. For example, the British official history refers to Rabia, Maktila, and Tummar; the German official history contains Rabiyah, Maqtalah, and Tummayr; while original documents contain an even wider variety of different spellings.[1] For the purposes of this narrative as well as the original maps created for this book, spelling has been standardized as it is found in the British official history; the only exception is the usage found in direct quotations.

FLYING TO VICTORY

CHAPTER 1

INTRODUCTION

"I feel that my days of command in North Africa, when we had to outwit and outfight a numerically superior enemy by a combination of deception, superior tactics and fighting spirit, represent by far my best effort."[1] Raymond Collishaw, one of the top aces of the Great War, referred not to his skill and success flying Sopwith Triplanes and Camels, but rather to his command of 202 Group, Royal Air Force (RAF), in the Western Desert in 1940 and 1941, when his small, obsolete force kept a much larger Italian opponent off balance until Operation Compass routed them in the first decisive British victory of the Second World War. As remarkable as this victory was, Collishaw's statement is even more noteworthy coming from an officer who spent twenty-eight eventful years in the air force, fought in two major wars and numerous minor conflicts, and was credited with sixty-one kills over the western front. Having accomplished so much in his career, what led Collishaw to value his command in the Western Desert over everything else?

Through the lens of Raymond Collishaw, this book explores the evolution of RAF–army relations and the development of tactical-air-support doctrine in the Western Desert from the start of the Second World War to the eve of Operation Crusader (November 1941). Allied tactical air support was an issue of fundamental importance in the defeat of Nazi Germany. In the Mediterranean and Northwest Europe, British and American aircraft worked closely with ground forces to destroy the Luftwaffe, obstruct the movement of reserves and supplies to the front lines, and on occasion destroy tanks and other targets in direct support of the army. Without effective Allied air support, the war in Europe would have lasted much longer than it did. The Second Tactical Air Force of the RAF and the Ninth Air Force of the U.S. Army Air Forces emerged from the war as sophisticated organizations that worked closely, if not always harmoniously, with their army groups to defeat the Germans.[2] The situation was much different at the start of the war, however, when the British Army and the RAF held conflicting views on air support. The May–June 1940 campaign in France ended with the expulsion of the British Expeditionary Force from the Continent and much recrimination by the army over inadequate RAF participation.[3]

Differing circumstances in the Middle East resulted in more-harmonious interservice cooperation. Close personal and working relationships between army and RAF officers in Egypt, the distance from Great Britain, and a paucity of theater resources facilitated better cooperation than occurred in France. It was during this period that the basic principles of an effective air-support system were first successfully employed. Operation Compass, launched in December 1940 as a five-day raid, expelled the Italians from Egypt and the eastern region of Libya (Cyrenaica) in a well-orchestrated offensive during which the army and the RAF worked closely to destroy and capture a much larger enemy force. This air campaign demonstrated the fundamental features of the formal Allied tactical air doctrine that would emerge later in the war. The central figure in this success was Air Commodore Raymond Collishaw, who directed his small force to overwhelm the Italian air force, dislocate enemy logistics, and make a substantial contribution to the success of Operation Compass. His accomplishments were guided by his First World War experience, as one of the first specialists in close air support, and years of imperial postings, especially in the Middle East, where he learned to work closely with the other services and operate with minimal resources at the end of a long supply line.

Unfortunately, the early détente in army-air relations was lost soon after the conclusion of Operation Compass. A series of defeats in Greece, Crete, and Cyrenaica led the army to blame the RAF for failing to provide the necessary air support. The next major operation in the Western Desert, Operation Battleaxe (June 1941), an attempt to relieve the trapped British garrison at Tobruk, became a test of the army's view of air support. Political intrigue at the highest levels in London forced the RAF to adopt the army's plan for Battleaxe or again risk being held responsible for any setback. Collishaw advocated against the army's ill-conceived demand for the close fighter protection of its troops, but he was overruled by his commander, Air Marshal Arthur Tedder. The subsequent failure of Battleaxe spurred a wide-ranging reappraisal of the methods of cooperation between the army and the RAF.

Battleaxe was the catalyst for an attempt by General Claude Auchinleck, the army's senior commander in the Middle East, to assume control of all air resources in his region. British prime minister Winston Churchill was forced to remind him that "the Air Force has its own dominant strategic role to play, and must not be frittered away in providing small umbrellas for the Army."[4] Churchill reinforced this statement with a comprehensive directive that fundamentally changed the dynamic of British army-air cooperation and established parameters that guided the provision of air support at the operational level for the remainder of the war. This directive, based on the earlier pattern of air operations in the Western Desert, did not end interservice bickering, nor did it solve any technical problems, but it confirmed the RAF view of mission and target selection. By explicitly endorsing the RAF view of air power, Churchill effectively ended the debate regarding the future form of air support and allowed the army and air force to concentrate on refining the command-and-control elements of support missions.[5] The pattern of operations outlined by Churchill rejected the army's preference to use warplanes for the close defense of its troops and the attack of enemy targets on the battlefield, treating air power in the same manner as the artillery. Rather, his directive reflected the only successful British joint campaign up to that point in the war—Operation Compass and the defeat of the Italians in the Western Desert between December 1940 and February 1941.[6]

Scholarship on the development of Allied tactical air doctrine in the Second World War has largely overlooked this early period. The origins of the air-support system are generally traced to the arrival of Air Vice-Marshal Arthur Coningham in the desert in late 1941. He is said to have transformed the RAF into an effective organization that worked well with the army and resulted in the defeat of the Axis in North Africa. In the aftermath of Battleaxe, significant progress was made at the tactical level on improving the command-and-control aspects of air support as well as improving the mobility and logistics of RAF squadrons. Coningham introduced important improvements to the air-support system, especially in the areas of communications, intelligence, mobility, logistics, and repair, but these changes were effective because Churchill had settled the higher-level debate regarding the RAF's role in land battles.[7] Coningham was an effective commander, but his role was to refine and improve the effectiveness of the Desert Air Force (the successor to Collishaw's 202 Group) using the vastly greater resources at his disposal. This system was later adopted by the Allied air forces in Northwest Europe and served as the template for both American and British tactical air operations in support of the D-Day landings and through the rest of the war.[8] Yet this conventional narrative overlooks the genesis of the Desert Air Force and the fact that Coningham inherited Collishaw's maturing organization, which had already proven itself in battle using exactly the same tenets for which the air vice-marshal would be credited.

The air component of the first British victory was directed by Collishaw, who drew on his considerable personal experience to orchestrate a successful air campaign despite commanding an air force that was obsolescent and outnumbered. His knowledge of ground-support missions from the First World War, combined with his interwar postings to various colonial conflicts, gave him firsthand knowledge of how the air force could best assist a land campaign; he also understood army culture due to his past postings. Collishaw rejected army demands to provide defensive air cover and attack armored fighting vehicles on the battlefield as he knew these types of operations were dangerous, wasteful, and ineffective. To protect the soldiers, it was far more advantageous to take the initiative and destroy the enemy air force through offensive sweeps and airfield interdiction rather than react to their attacks. Having spent nearly five years in the desert starting in late 1935, he understood that the logistical support of the army was vital, and attacks on ports and road convoys affected the ability of enemy forces to fight as surely as destroying them in battle. Most importantly, Collishaw took these principles of tactical aviation and proved that they worked in combat.[9]

At the outset of the Second World War, the British Army and the RAF held very different conceptions regarding the form of air operations required to support the army on the battlefield. Ground commanders considered aircraft an ancillary tactical weapon, like artillery or tanks, which should be used in small numbers, or "penny packets," to attack enemy positions on the front lines to aid the infantry.[10] Army officers believed they should control these air operations locally. Conversely, the RAF viewed air power as a weapon that should be centrally controlled and concentrated to achieve an operational-level effect through the attainment of air superiority and interdiction of enemy forces. Unlike artillery, which acted in a small, defined space, aircraft could operate over a much wider area, perform a variety of tasks, and quickly be redirected against widely separated targets. Only in rare or dire circumstances should air power be applied directly on the battlefield, where targets were fleeting, difficult to find and hit, and severe losses in pilots and aircraft could be expected.

The British Army's experience in Norway, France, Greece, and Crete in 1940 and 1941 reinforced the requirement for its own specialized air force. The RAF countered that air superiority was a necessary precondition for effective support, and without central control, which allowed a concentration of air resources, failure was sure to follow. This acrimonious debate did not end with Churchill's intervention following Battleaxe, but his pronouncement established the army and air force as coequal partners and settled the form of their cooperation at the operational level. Future discussions focused on shaping support operations at the tactical level rather than debate over who controlled the resource.[11]

Collishaw, a Canadian from Nanaimo, British Columbia, was among the top aces of the First World War. He served with the Royal Naval Air Service (RNAS) and the RAF over the western front and was credited with destroying sixty-one enemy aircraft and eight observation balloons.[12] Early in his flying career, Collishaw was identified as a pilot with leadership, command,

and organizational skills, and his confidential efficiency reports consistently remarked upon these talents. In January 1917 Capt. (N) W. L. Elder, his commanding officer in No. 3 Wing RNAS, commented: "Ability to command Very Good Indeed being steady & reliable pilot. Has shown great resource as a fighter pilot. Recommended for promotion."[13] Collishaw combined the rare talents of a great fighter pilot and a capable leader.

Maj. Bertram Bell met Collishaw when he was a flight commander with No. 3 Squadron RNAS and recognized him as "one of the most promising boys in the squadron" when he first encountered the "round, red-faced boy sitting in one corner" of the mess.[14] When Bell was assigned command of No. 10 Squadron RNAS, he brought Collishaw along as one of his flight commanders. Bell was considered an abrasive, "no nonsense" Australian and was not well liked by his pilots, but he was an able commander and turned No. 10 Naval into one of the top Allied squadrons on the western front. He was "completely intolerant" of pilots who did not display his same level of commitment, but he was extremely generous to those, such as Collishaw, who did.[15]

Collishaw, in his first command position, proved Bell's confidence in his leadership ability by quickly putting B Flight in good order.[16] This was the famous "Black Flight," made up entirely of Canadians flying the Sopwith Triplane. Collishaw's aircraft was dubbed "Black Maria"; the other aircraft of the flight were known as "Black Death," "Black Prince," "Black Roger," and "Black Sheep." This unit was one of the most successful fighting groups of the war, destroying eighty-seven enemy aircraft between May and July 1917. Collishaw alone accounted for twenty-seven aircraft destroyed during this period and was awarded the Distinguished Service Cross and Distinguished Service Order for his accomplishments.[17]

Although best known as a fighter pilot, Collishaw was one of the first Allied specialists in low-level attack missions. Little mention is made of this in writings about him, but by Collishaw's own admission, half his missions in the last three months of the war were low-level strafing and bombing attacks.[18] In 1918 he commanded No. 3 Squadron RNAS/No. 203 Squadron RAF, which was dedicated to trench-strafing operations to help stop the German offensive in March, and flew in close support of the army during the "Hundred Days Offensive" in the fall of 1918. Collishaw learned a great deal about flying missions against ground targets, including what air power could be expected to achieve as well as the cost and limitations of such operations.[19]

Collishaw discussed the merits of low-level air support in his autobiography. He noted that during the German March offensives, the vast majority of RFC and RNAS units, including artillery cooperation and day-bombing squadrons, had been devoted to direct attacks designed to blunt the enemy advance.

Though this use of aircraft was controversial, he believed that the effort was justified by the dire situation.[20] Collishaw admitted that it was difficult to assess the effect these attacks had on German forces, but he quoted German regimental histories that discussed the consequences of these strikes on their troops. Based on these Collishaw concluded, "there seems little doubt that our low-level attack resulted in significant German losses."[21]

The Battle of Amiens, the great Allied victory of August 1918, is remembered as the beginning of the end for Germany in the First World War. It was operationally important as the "black day of the German army," but it also featured the greatest air concentration of any First World War battle.[22] Units flew air-superiority, interdiction, and close-support missions. In many respects it was the first thoroughly modern and comprehensive application of air power on the battlefield and set the standard for future air operations in both World Wars.[23] Collishaw was busy at Amiens flying and directing support missions as the commander of No. 203 Squadron.

Collishaw led his men into the air soon after the offensive commenced. His squadron attacked targets on the front of the Canadian Corps and provided crucial support as the infantry advanced beyond the range of their own artillery. The intensity and tempo of air operations on 8 August matched those of the ground forces. No. 203 Squadron was the most active low-level squadron in I Brigade, RAF, dropping 112 25-pound bombs by midafternoon.[24] Collishaw flew four missions that day, and his final flight ended in near tragedy when his Camel was hit by ground fire and forced down.[25] He recalled, "My logbook shows that I put in 11 hours, 20 minutes in the air during the day, all at heights of 100 feet or less."[26]

It is impossible to quantify the effectiveness of close air support on 8 August, but anecdotal evidence suggests the attacks helped the progress of the infantry. Gen. Sir Henry Rawlinson, commander of Fourth Army, stated after the battle that "the action of low-flying machines on 'Z' day, though it entailed heavy casualties, had a serious effect in lowering the enemy's morale and inflicting serious losses, as is shown by captured enemy documents. . . . In no battle had [the RAF] taken part with greater success in dealing with ground attacks."[27] The war diary of the 5th Canadian Infantry Battalion highlighted the importance of aircraft that day:

> In a sunken road between one hundred and fifty and two hundred germans [sic] were caught by Tanks and aeroplanes, and not one got away. The enemy losses must have been terrible. Our planes seemed like things possessed; a plane would streak down from behind to within a few yards of our heads, and with a roar shoot up almost perpendicularly, the cheers of our men following it. Kilometres ahead they could be seen diving at the retreating enemy, and the

merry rattle of their machine guns was heard continuously. The air was thick with them, and never an enemy plane to be seen.[28]

But this type of low-level support was costly to the RAF. On the first day of operations, 45 aircraft were lost, and a further 52 returned to base but were scrapped due to severe damage. In terms of personnel, sixty-one aircrew were killed, missing, or became prisoners of war, and nineteen men were wounded. This meant an unsustainable attrition rate of 13 percent for the approximately 700 aircraft involved in operations that day. The loss rate was even worse for the 300 aircraft involved in low-level operations, which suffered 70 of the 97 aircraft losses, an attrition rate of 34 percent.[29]

The army was aware of the heavy price paid by the RAF but considered the results "well worth the losses incurred."[30] The air force had a different view, especially No. 203 Squadron, which suffered heavily in these attacks. Of the fifteen pilots available for action on 8 August, four were lost on the first day and another a few days later, meaning the squadron suffered losses of over 25 percent.[31] Collishaw recalled of Amiens, "Each time the fighter pilots were launched to assault the infantry, they could see the aeroplane graveyard beneath them, and one was conscious, while passing through a hail of fire, that at any moment the frail shell [of his aircraft], in which the pilot felt poised precariously, might join its kind below."[32] He knew what he was talking about as he frequently flew low-level missions, hit by enemy small-arms fire numerous times and at least twice forced down by the damage.[33] Collishaw much preferred aerial combat, which offered pilots the opportunity to test their skill in a more or less even contest against fellow pilots. He did not like the exposed nature of ground-attack missions:

Air fighting is exclusively an individualist and specialist game, and pilots of outstanding merit require considerable experience before they can be relied upon to engage the enemy successfully. Experienced and talented leaders are required both to achieve results and so that the novices may generate enthusiasm to emulate the exploits of their leaders. Ground strafing eliminates without distinction both the fit and the unfit, and a Commander must beware of embarking upon any project potentially capable of destroying the fighting value of his Air Force. Army Commanders without Air Force experience are sometime inclined to insist upon the employment of an Air Force in close support in a way which might lead to this result, with the consequence that air superiority might be lost at a later stage in the campaign. This lesson was learned in the Roye Road Battle [Amiens], with the result that the ruthless employment of the major part of the Air Force upon ground strafing was not repeated during the Great War.[34]

The fighting ended for Collishaw on 21 October 1918, when he was ordered to London. He amassed over one thousand hours of flying time and sixty-one confirmed kills over the western front. The traditional narrative of Collishaw's career emphasizes his skill and aerial combat as well as his leadership abilities. Less understood is his familiarity with ground-support operations. Collishaw drew lessons from this experience that served him well later in his career. Flying low over enemy trenches exposed pilots to a range of dangers not present when flying at altitude, and the proximity to the ground meant that when something went wrong, there was little time to recover. As shown from Amiens on, the RAF was able to contribute materially to supporting army operations, but it came at a high cost in lost aircraft and pilots.

The RAF was drastically cut at the end of the 1918, but Collishaw was one of the few officers offered a permanent commission. Though the First World War was over, the British were still fighting in Russia. The Bolshevik seizure of power and the subsequent armistice with Germany transformed the Allied intervention into support for the anticommunist side in the Russian Civil War.[35] The British committed ground, naval, and air forces to support the White Russian effort, but the majority of these units, including two infantry divisions, were withdrawn by June 1919. The White Army possessed an air arm of some strength, but it was inexperienced and required substantial British support. No. 47 Squadron RAF was transferred from the Caucasus in the spring of 1919 to join Gen. Anton Denikin's army to fulfill this role.[36] By mid-1919 the RAF detachments in South Russia were war weary. The Air Ministry decided to replace these men with volunteers from England. Collishaw, an experienced squadron leader, was a natural choice to take over No. 47 Squadron, and as an RAF career officer, he accepted without hesitation. After he collected a cadre of volunteer pilots and men, the group arrived in the Caucasus in June 1919.[37]

Historians are mixed in their evaluation of RAF operations in South Russia. One historian has stated: "The RAF had no significant influence upon the course of events in Russia. Its employment was piecemeal, and bore no comparison to the massive deployment of air power on the Western Front. Some of its work had a short-term effect upon military operations, . . . but nowhere could the RAF exert any decisive effect."[38] Another evaluated the campaign more positively: "The British had played a major part in the fortunes of the Armed Forces of South Russia. . . . The RAF squadrons . . . were never very large, but they played a role out of all proportion to their size. They were the only really effective air units available to the Russians. Number 47 Squadron, operating on the Tsaritsin front, played a significant part in [Baron Pyotr] Wrangel's battles to hold onto the city."[39] Collishaw's own appraisal fell somewhere in between. He recognized that his one squadron could not influence the outcome of a war fought over such a vast area. But he believed that his squadron "made a surprising contribution to the White cause, mostly through its attacks on the Red ground forces. The destruction that we were able to wreak on the enemy on numerous occasions boosted tremendously the morale of the White troops in the area and at times caused near-panic in the ranks of the Reds."[40] Conditions were much less formidable than on the western front due to the lack of effective opposition in the air, but for the main ground-support task, the pilots faced intense fire anytime they pressed their attacks home at low level.

Collishaw's time in Russia was an eventful period in his life and had a significant influence on him. He cheated death on a number of occasions: his aircraft was brought down by hostile fire on at least two occasions; he had numerous close calls on his train ride to the Crimea; and he survived a debilitating case of typhus. The importance of this period is reflected in his memoirs, which contain a surprisingly long chapter on his Russian adventures.[41]

Collishaw's experience commanding No. 47 Squadron prepared him for future responsibilities. He was fighting a war in a faraway foreign land at the end of an extremely long supply chain. He worked closely with and depended on allies who might or might not follow through on their plans. Though having limited forces under his command, he was responsible for providing air support over a vast area and faced an enemy who was often larger, better equipped, and in possession of the initiative. Finally, he frequently had to act without reference to his higher chain of command because of the time and distance involved. The very landscape was often more hostile than the enemy; extremes of weather, climate, temperature, and distance were major limiting factors on operations. All these conditions combined to demand a commander who was smart, resourceful, adaptable, flexible, decisive, and fearless. Collishaw demonstrated all of these traits.

In 1923 Collishaw was posted into the middle of rising tensions between Great Britain and Turkey. This placed him at the frontier of the evolving relationship between the three British services. The cost of administering its empire forced Britain to make changes to the conduct of its colonial affairs; the expense of maintaining a large army also needed to be addressed. Winston Churchill, newly appointed as colonial secretary in February 1921, consulted with Air Marshal Sir Hugh Trenchard, chief of the Air Staff, about the future of the RAF. Trenchard saw an opportunity to secure the future of his service by demonstrating that it could effectively police the empire at a fraction of the cost of the army. Churchill facilitated this experiment by convening the Cairo Conference in March 1921. This meeting was approved by the cabinet and brought together the senior civilian and military leadership responsible for the Middle East. The Air Staff, on Trenchard's instructions, had prepared a detailed appreciation of the contribution the RAF could make to imperial defense. Based on experience in Somaliland and Waziristan, it recommended that "the efficiency of the Royal Air Force as an independent arm should be put to proof by the transference to it of primary responsibility for the maintenance of order in some area of the Middle East."[42] After much discussion, this scheme was approved, and all British military forces (army, air force, and navy) in Iraq were placed under RAF command. This significant event in the development of the service marked the first time an air force officer had been given overall command of a theater. In late 1922 Air Marshal Sir John Salmond arrived in Baghdad, where he assumed the role of air officer commanding in Iraq.[43]

In 1923 Collishaw joined an army expedition against Turkish and Kurdish insurgents as the RAF liaison officer. He played a role "of considerable value" during the advance, facilitating cooperation between the army and the air force while acting as the army-column commander's air advisor.[44] The relationship was effective but not perfect. Collishaw's RAF commander, Group Capt. Arthur Longmore, commented in his after-action report that a more senior air advisor should take part in future missions to ensure that "no opportunity should be lost."[45] There was a tendency for the army commander to treat air matters as an afterthought, and a higher-ranking RAF advisor could alleviate this problem. Though the two services needed to work closely to achieve success, and a powerful air force presence facilitated the army mission, there was still tension underlying the operation.[46] This was an important experience for Collishaw as it took him out of the cockpit and allowed him to see air operations from the army's perspective. As a pilot over the western front and during combat missions in South Russia and Mesopotamia, he understood the challenges of ground-support missions. His time in northern Iraq gave him a better understanding of the needs of the army and its view of how air operations were best conducted.

Five years after the end of the Great War, Collishaw finally received a posting away from an active theater. Given command of No. 41 Squadron, based in England in late 1923, he soon after attended RAF Staff College, where he received the doctrinal and institutional grounding to complement his considerable operational experience and prepare him for higher command. The college was established in April 1922 by Air Marshal Trenchard to train the future commanders of the RAF. Its first commandant, Air Commodore H. R. M. Brooke-Popham, a founding father of the Royal Flying Corps, saw the school as an essential preparation for officers aspiring to higher command. It would "'train officers in staff duties' and offer 'a general education which will serve as a sound foundation for the building up of a school of thought in the Royal Air Force.'"[47]

The nascent RAF Staff College was still establishing itself when Collishaw attended the third course, running from 1924 to 1925. Students studied twenty-two topics, including the nature of war; air, land, and sea tactics; history; and science, designed to give them a broad education. Outside the classroom, the officers participated in sports and horseback riding. Visits were made to various military bases and related civilian establishments, army and navy exercises were observed, and student exchanges were conducted with the other service staff colleges at Camberley (army) and Greenwich (navy). Of course, time was also spent flying the school's aircraft.[48]

Collishaw learned a great deal at the Staff College, but he believed the directing staff tended to look for conservative solutions based on practical or historical experience. He found this ironic, considering that the embryonic state of air power meant there was still much to learn about its broader application, for which there was no historical precedent.[49] He came away from his studies as an "air enthusiast" who saw the true potential of air power to act in a manner that was independent of the army and the navy, though he could parrot back the party line when required.[50]

In the mid-1920s Collishaw commanded various squadrons, stations, and wings, also serving for two years as the head of operations and intelligence at the headquarters of the Air Defence of Great Britain (ADGB). He drew two important lessons from his time at ADGB—the impracticality of maintaining standing patrols of fighters waiting to intercept marauding bombers, which was wasteful of resources, and the desirability of having different aircraft types grouped together in the same command.[51]

In July 1929 Collishaw was promoted to wing commander and the following month was sent to serve with the navy. He was appointed officer commanding, flying, the senior RAF officer on HMS *Courageous,* the Royal Navy's most capable aircraft carrier. Collishaw spent the next three years at sea, interrupted only by a brief stint in 1930 to attend a Senior Officers' Technical Course while *Courageous* was in port for scheduled maintenance. By his own admission, he found himself in a "delicate position" during this posting.[52] The birth of the RAF through the amalgamation of the RFC and RNAS in April 1918 meant that the Royal Navy no longer had its own flying service. This created difficulties for the operation of aircraft carriers. The resulting "dual control" policy created the compromise situation where carriers deployed squadrons of RAF aircraft commanded by RAF officers. A "taxi service owned by the RAF, [and] chartered by the Navy" was how one contemporary described the interservice working relationship.[53] This did not change until the navy formally assumed command of the Fleet Air Arm on 24 May 1939.[54]

The convoluted relationship between the navy and the air force caused numerous problems, especially for an aircraft carrier's senior RAF officer. Collishaw described the situation as "ridiculous."[55] He stated that the navy thought its own pilots "could do a better job at sea than those of the RAF." If the senior RAF officer "did not support this thesis he was reactionary and anti-navy. If he did, he was likely to come into disfavor at the Air Ministry."[56] Collishaw relied heavily on his experience to see him successfully through this posting. His six years in the Canadian Fisheries Protection Service prior to the First World War, advancing from cabin boy to first officer, were of great value. So too were his years with the RNAS. Both stints provided him the knowledge necessary to effectively liaise with naval officers and made him less an "outsider"; thus, he was more easily accepted by his naval peers while on the carrier.

Collishaw joined *Courageous* at Malta in early August 1929 and familiarized himself with the ship and its routines during a cruise and fleet maneuvers in the eastern Mediterranean. Soon after the ship returned to the island, trouble broke out in the Middle East. Tensions between Arabs and Jews turned into violence in August 1929, and *Courageous* was dispatched as part of the British response. The carrier arrived on 28 August, and Capt. Studholme Brownrigg, its commanding officer, received a signal that his aircraft were desperately needed.[57] In conjunction with local officials, Collishaw developed a plan to base his aircraft at Gaza and fly missions over Palestine. The force under his command consisted of forty-eight aircraft, forty-seven officers, and 385 other ranks. For the next week, the Fleet Air Arm units were busy flying patrols and reconnaissance missions, cooperating with the army during raids, and distributing proclamations. In total, Collishaw's aircraft logged over 340 hours of operational flying time and another 100 hours of nonoperational flying.[58]

The air contribution to the Palestine emergency was characterized as a failure since it was unable to stop or deter the violence. The conflict could only be ended by the presence of armed troops on the ground. It could not be solved in any other manner in a built-up area where antagonists and innocent parties mingled and could not be identified from the air.[59]

This view of the air contribution applies primarily to the regular RAF units that conducted the majority of air attacks early in the conflict before ground troops and Collishaw's Fleet Air Arm contingent arrived. At that stage there were no other options to deal with the marauders. Attacks on Jewish colonies at Bir Tovia, Haifa, and Beit Alfa were driven off by air action, while looters caught in the act were machine gunned at Khulda, Safed, and Zicheron Jacob. Within a few days, most daylight attacks on Jewish settlements ceased or were confined to nighttime, when aircraft could not operate.[60] Collishaw understood the limitations of his force and required caution from his pilots even when they received army orders to "attack natives alleged to be looters or incendiaries."[61] Captain Brownrigg seconded this view in his covering letter to Collishaw's report:

An interesting point disclosed by these operations is the difficulty aircraft have in carrying out pure police work of preserving order among civilian population, apart from morale effect. An outstanding example is that when aircraft are sent to drive off incendiaries, and arrive on the scene sometime later, it is practically impossible for an airman to know whether the crowd round a burning house are looters, or the legitimate owner and their friends salvaging property.[62]

Collishaw handled his force with much greater restraint in contrast to the regular RAF contingent, which strafed Arab insurgents on numerous occasions. His flight commanders were empowered to conduct attacks on looters only if such hostile action was warranted. Though instructions were frequently received to attack suspected insurgents, in each case the flight commanders determined "the natives under observation were peaceful and not raiders."[63] As such, no Fleet Air Arm aircraft engaged in attacks on inhabitants. Instead, the force was very active during its four weeks ashore flying reconnaissance missions and presence patrols.[64]

The three years Collishaw spent aboard *Courageous* were important in the development of his skills as a commander. This was his first time leading an organization larger than a squadron, and it required him to be equal parts warrior and diplomat. He recalled that the posting placed him in a delicate position in which he needed to answer to two masters with different agendas. During his time aboard the carrier, Collishaw disagreed with the navy's view of air power as a defensive weapon, believing instead that naval air power on its own could be decisive against enemy ships. The experience of the Royal Navy off Norway in 1940, in the Far East in 1941, and in the Mediterranean throughout the Second World War showed Collishaw to be right. His ability to function in a position where he was required to carry out a mission with which he did not fully concur was a testament to his growth and maturity as a commanding officer. The skills he refined aboard *Courageous* served him well during his subsequent appointments.

After a series of postings with Bomber Command in the United Kingdom, Collishaw returned to the Mediterranean in 1935 as the commander of No. 5 Wing, then being formed in the Anglo-Egyptian Sudan. This deployment was in response to Italian ruler Benito Mussolini's aspirations to resurrect the imperial glory of ancient Rome by creating a new empire in Africa, a policy bound to lead Italy into conflict with Britain and France, which had long held sway in that part of the world. British-influenced Egypt was the centerpiece of Mussolini's ambitions. Libya had already been conquered, and it seemed that Abyssinia was next.[65] By 1935 it was clear that Italy intended to invade Abyssinia, and Britain, worried that this Great Power showdown might lead to war, reinforced its Mediterranean forces beginning in the late summer.

On 18 October 1935 Collishaw arrived in Alexandria, where he was briefed by Air Chief Marshal Sir Robert Brooke-Popham, his former commandant at the RAF Staff College and the overall RAF commander for the mission.[66] Two days later Collishaw flew to Khartoum. Three squadrons arrived from England and were in the process of being made flight ready by the time he arrived, joining a fourth already in theater.[67] The primary task of the wing was the protection of trade routes through the Red Sea. As Brooke-Popham described, "Communications through the Red Sea were of great importance because it was the channel along which came the oil for the Fleet, and in the event of passage through the central Mediterranean being rendered hazardous owing to enemy submarines or aircraft, communications through the Red Sea became vital to the Army and to the Air Force as well as to the Navy."[68] Close cooperation with Aden Command as well as the Royal Navy's East Indian Squadron and the Red Sea Sloops was an essential component of this mission. In the event of an Italian invasion of Sudan, No. 5 Wing, in consultation with the governor general, would defend the region and drive out the invaders.[69]

Tensions lasted through the first half of 1936, but ultimately the crisis passed without serious incident. Germany's march into the Rhineland that March shifted the focus of the British government, and the defense of the United Kingdom became the top priority. Italy completed its conquest of Abyssinia, and the immediate threat of a wider conflict in the Mediterranean passed.[70] No. 5 Wing received orders to disband, and Collishaw reported to Egypt, where he took command of the RAF station at Heliopolis in the Nile Delta near Cairo. He spent the next five years as one of the senior RAF commanders in the region, where his main task was to defend Egypt and the Suez Canal.[71]

Collishaw reflected that his experiences in the Sudan "proved most valuable to me ultimately during the campaign in the Western Desert. Many of the lessons learned there were retaught to the enemy to our advantage."[72] It is difficult to overlook the many similarities Collishaw faced. He was working in a desert environment from primitive airfields with aircraft that were not ideal for the task. The theater was large, but the forces at his disposal were small. He commanded a mixed force of fighters and bombers that were employed on a variety of tasks, covering virtually the entire spectrum of operations: air defense, reconnaissance, close support, bombing operations, and maritime patrol. No shots were fired in anger while in the Sudan, but the experience provided many lessons for the future.

Raymond Collishaw left extensive personal documents that form a major source for this study. His main papers reside at the Library and Archives Canada in Ottawa and are augmented by significant holdings at the Canadian

War Museum and at the Directorate of History and Heritage, National Defence Headquarters. The documentary records of the RAF and British Army are largely held by the UK National Archives in Kew. Squadron and formation operational record books, war diaries, and operations orders and after action reports found in the Air Ministry and War Office collections form the primary body of evidence for examining the events in the Western Desert in 1940–41.[73]

Collishaw wrote an autobiography, aided by Ronald Dodds, an historian who worked for the Royal Canadian Air Force during the 1960s. It offers the most comprehensive record of his overall career, from his start in the Canadian Fisheries Protection Service through to the end of the Second World War.[74] It accurately reflects the documentary record and is largely free of the hyperbole found in the memoirs of some First World War aces.[75] Its main drawback is that it was published late in his life. This makes it excellent regarding impressions and recollections, but it lacks the detail and immediacy that would accrue from a narrative written closer to the events.[76] Large sections of this book, however, are drawn from an autobiographical account that Collishaw wrote prior to the Second World War. This narrative also provides important details that are lacking in the published autobiography.[77] Collishaw referred to his time in command of RAF Station Heliopolis in Egypt before the outbreak of the Second World War as "the most pleasant of all those that I spent in uniform."[78] His family was able to join him then, and it is likely that the relative calm of this posting allowed him the time to draft his autobiographical account.

The *Times Literary Supplement* considered that Collishaw's memoirs ably showed both sides of air operations, from the point of view of the pilot and the senior commander, and found the section dealing with the Western Desert to be "the more informative part of the book."[79] Collishaw was quick to criticize problems he identified in the conduct of operations, praised colleagues he admired (like "the very able General Richard O'Connor"), but refrained from criticizing individuals in his memoir.[80] His silence on Air Marshal Tedder speaks volumes about the relationship with his commander.

Significant autobiographies have been published by the two senior air commanders, Air Marshals Arthur Longmore and Tedder. Longmore was Commander-in-Chief, RAF Middle East Command, from April 1940 until May 1941 and worked with Gen. Archibald Wavell and Adm. Andrew Cunningham during this extremely busy year when campaigns were being fought in East Africa, Malta, Greece, Crete, and the Western Desert. His memoirs prominently feature Collishaw as his senior operational commander, and he comments favorably upon his subordinate's performance. Longmore knew Collishaw from previous service together in Kurdistan and trusted him with the operational control of all squadrons engaged in the Western Desert.[81] He reproduced verbatim Lieutenant General O'Connor's glowing tribute to Collishaw's support during Operation Compass. Longmore's memoirs highlight the challenges faced when fighting a numerically superior enemy on numerous fronts while dealing with the difficulties of interservice cooperation.[82]

Tedder's appropriately titled memoirs, *With Prejudice,* serve as the most complete and accessible commentary on Collishaw's time in the Western Desert. Despite Collishaw's overwhelming success in his battles against the Italians and Germans, there is a tendency in the literature to accept Tedder's view that he would not have succeeded at a higher level of command. This conjecture is repeated in most accounts of the first desert air campaign and confuses an assessment of Collishaw's command potential with an honest appraisal of what he actually accomplished.[83] A biographer of Tedder states that Collishaw was "contemptuously dismissed" in the air marshal's memoirs and that it was not surprising that he in turn was "completely ignored" in Collishaw's account.[84] Tedder's first mention of his subordinate offers mild praise for his accomplishments early in the war, but he considered him to be a "bull in a china shop" who had a tendency to "go off half-cock."[85] Collishaw, according to Tedder, may have had success against the Italians, but he was not up to the future challenge of fighting the Germans.[86] This memoir, as well as various letters written by the air marshal during the period, indicate that he held a serious bias against Collishaw formed either before being posted to Cairo in December 1940 or shortly after his arrival.[87]

The air campaigns in North Africa have received less attention than the ground war. This reflects the wider historiography of the former, which highlights strategic air campaigns and, to a lesser extent, air battles over England and continental Europe to the detriment of operations in support of the army. The two volumes of the British official history on the Mediterranean and Middle East by I. S. O. Playfair and his coauthors craft a detailed account of Britain's preparations for war, Italy's first moves, and the successful British counteroffensive.[88] It is an essential, top-down history that does a better job than most of integrating air and land elements into the narrative. The two volumes relevant to the period under consideration here discuss the challenges and mechanics of the system of air support as it developed in the Western Desert but, not surprisingly, do not analyze it in any great detail. The RAF official history provides only a perfunctory examination of the air campaign in the Western Desert.[89] In contrast, the unpublished first volume of the RAF Air Historical Branch's operational narratives, *The Middle East Campaigns,* provides a detailed description of the early battles in the desert. Yet while it is very strong at conveying battle details, it lacks a sophisticated analysis of events.[90]

Two recent books provide the best current scholarship on air aspects of the desert war. David Ian Hall's *Strategy for Victory: The Development of British Tactical Air Power, 1919–1943* presents a strong narrative that examines the development of British tactical air power from its genesis in the First World War to its maturation through the early campaigns of the Second World War.[91] It begins with the state of British tactical air doctrine at the end of the Great War before examining developments in the interwar period. Hall's ability to relate doctrinal developments with real-world experience of tactical air operations is one of the strengths of his book, and its comparison of developments in England and France with the often independent but concurrent evolution of tactical air operations in the Western Desert and North Africa is also useful. Hall briefly covers the early period of fighting in the Western Desert but has more to say on the battles from Operation Crusader onward. Brad William Gladman's *Intelligence and Anglo-American Air Support in World War Two: The Western Desert and Tunisia, 1940–43* also focuses on the air war in the desert.[92] He argues that intelligence (specifically its acquisition and application) was critical to the success of close air support in the Second World War, using the battles in North Africa to prove his point. Yet he goes even further by suggesting that lessons learned by the British and their American partners led to the creation of "the best system of air/land warfare ever seen," which became one of the Allies' "great tools for victory."[93] Like Hall, Gladman concentrates on events starting with Operation Crusader.

Philip Guedalla, a prolific British writer, barrister, and failed parliamentarian, enlisted in the RAF at the start of the Second World War and wrote the first contemporary history of the air war in the desert, published in 1944 shortly before his premature death from a disease contracted in the Middle East while researching his book.[94] Although it is a straightforward narrative of events, it combines the views of one who was there with a first-generation historical account, and it has merit on both counts. Two early histories were written by Roderic Owen. His first, *The Desert Air Force*, chronicles that organization from its origins to the end of the war in Italy, while the second is a biography of Tedder.[95] Richard Townshend Bickers wrote an account of the desert air war that follows the same pattern as earlier studies.[96] Like Guedalla, these books are largely uncritical histories that value narrative over analysis and tend to be quite enamored with their subjects. Christopher Shores has produced a number of important books on the air campaigns in the Middle East. Through meticulous research, he has compiled a substantial amount of important data on day-to-day air operations. Although weak on analysis, his works provide a wealth of information crucial to any in-depth study.[97]

There is much to be learned from a detailed campaign study of the first year of the war in Egypt and Libya. The roots of the British air-support system saw its first operational test during Operation Compass and demonstrated the legitimacy of those methods. Collishaw effectively directed his squadrons to support the ground offensive, which succeeded beyond the expectations of all and destroyed a much larger enemy force. This could not have occurred without the air superiority and interdiction campaign conducted by Collishaw, a pattern of operations that eventually became standard in the Allied air forces for the remainder of the war. There was much work yet to be done on the technical matters of providing effective support, but when relations between the army and the RAF deteriorated, Churchill decisively intervened by advocating the exact methods successfully employed by Collishaw during Operation Compass.

Raymond Collishaw is variously described as a great fighter pilot, inspirational leader, and iconic hero, but he is also characterized as a commander who was promoted perhaps one rank too high and did not possess the skills to manage a large staff. But the ultimate test of a commander's abilities lies in his conduct during battle, and it is by that standard he should be judged. His overall conduct of RAF operations in the Western Desert showed none of these flaws.

CHAPTER 2

THE WESTERN DESERT, 1939–1940

The Middle East was not immediately affected by the start of the Second World War in Europe. Egypt was a secondary but strategically important area for Britain. Its most important feature was the Suez Canal, and the general defense of Egypt could not be separated from that of this important waterway. Its strategic and commercial importance made the Suez Canal a "central tenet of British foreign policy from 1882 to 1954."[1] Viewed as the "lifeline of Empire," the canal offered the shortest trade route to India and the Far East, where the natural resources of the latter, primarily oil, were growing in importance.[2] The Anglo-Egyptian Treaty of 1936 granted Egypt sovereignty, but Britain retained the right to base troops in the country to protect the canal and the British vowed to defend Egypt in the event of unprovoked aggression. Italy was not specifically mentioned, but in the wake of the Abyssinian crisis, Mussolini's imperial aspirations were seen as the greatest external threat to the North African country. Britain did not want to lose the region, but it was stretched too thin to adequately protect it.[3]

Events in Abyssinia had demonstrated the vulnerability of Egypt to an attack by Italy. The Western Desert shielded the country from Libya and its Italian masters, but it was an inhospitable environment that caused problems for attacker and defender alike. Few roads and tracks navigable by modern mechanized forces existed between Libya and Alexandria. The main route followed the coastal highway from the border at Sollum through the Halfaya Pass to Mersa Matruh and on to Alexandria. The wide metaled highway was occasionally interrupted by uneven stretches, but it remained the most direct path into Egypt. Proximity to the coast, however, made the possibility of naval and air interdiction a real concern. The Siwa Oasis, which could be used as a staging point for an advance on Mersa Matruh from the south, was the only other possible line of approach for the Italians.[4]

In anticipation of possible attacks along these routes, the British had moved their forces forward into the desert during the Abyssinian crisis. Air Chief Marshal Sir Robert Brooke-Popham, air officer commanding-in-chief, RAF Middle East, planned to take advantage of his air assets if there was an

Italian attack on British interests. Group Capt. Wilfred McClaughry, the officer commanding RAF at Mersa Matruh (designated Truforce), was instructed to work with the Royal Navy to attack a Libyan port for the first forty-eight hours of hostilities before switching his focus to destroying the ability of the Italian air force to operate in the theater. If the Italians launched a full-scale offensive, McClaughry was instructed to focus on supporting the British Army.[5] The balance of power in the desert was favorable to the British in the fall of 1935; Truforce was composed of five bomber, two fighter, one bomber-transport, and two army-cooperation squadrons, while the Italians had only three fighter and one bomber squadrons in Libya.[6]

As it turned out, the only enemy encountered by the British was the harsh environment. The deployment proved the ability of the air and ground forces to operate in the Western Desert, but it was an unforgiving place. Dust storms, which could last from three days to three weeks, tormented man and machine. Vacuum cleaners were needed to clean the fine sand out of aircraft. Sand and debris on the makeshift airfields took a toll on aircraft engines and other moving parts.[7] The travails of McClaughry's Truforce proved invaluable: "exercises were carried out from the forward landing grounds, a supply system was set up and the experience served as a preliminary canter for the war which was to come."[8]

Following the stabilization of the international situation, the threat posed by Italy was reevaluated. Indeed, two years before the commencement of war in the Middle East, British planning was dominated by the assumption that Italy would be the principal enemy.[9] In July 1937 the Committee of Imperial Defence directed that action be taken to protect Egypt from Mussolini's imperial ambitions. "Italy cannot be considered as a reliable friend and . . . steps should be taken to bring [Mediterranean defenses] up to date and increase their efficiency," stated one note to the cabinet.[10] The rationale for this directive was confirmed in November, when Italy joined Germany and Japan in the Anti-Comintern Pact and withdrew from the League of Nations. The Air Ministry examined the problem in March 1938, confirming that British forces were at a major disadvantage in the theater; steps were taken to better defend against an attack.[11]

Air-staff planners estimated that an Italian offensive would be led by two motorized divisions with strong air support. The close proximity of Italy would allow the Italians to triple the 174 aircraft then in Libya in just two months. Their ability to strengthen and supply their forces in North Africa rapidly contrasted with the prospect of a slow and gradual reinforcement from the United Kingdom. The British planned to counter this threat in the short term by transferring squadrons from Palestine, Iraq, and India. This force of approximately

250 aircraft had some deterrent effect, but it was not believed sufficient to stop an Italian attack. In late 1937 these units were bolstered with the addition of an antiaircraft brigade and a light-tank battalion. In February 1938 the British Army took further steps to reinforce Egypt's defenses and transferred an infantry brigade to Palestine, where it would be available on short notice. The RAF also benefited from this rearmament with the addition of a squadron of Gladiator biplane fighters, twelve medium bombers, and two squadrons of light bombers.[12]

The threat of Italian aggression and the general British weakness in Egypt also led to the creation in 1939 of the Combined Plan, which called for the army and the air force to "co-ordinate their over-stretched resources for a combined defensive effort against Italian forces of vastly superior numbers."[13] This document provided the basis for a close working relationship between the two services, both in planning and operations, and focused all British strength in the theater on the defense of Egypt. This unity of action was judged to be the only practical method of offsetting the numerical and qualitative inferiority of British forces when compared to the Italians.[14] The Combined Plan identified the isolated and outnumbered nature of defenses in Egypt and ensured that the army and RAF cooperated to diminish those deficits. This set relations between the two services on a very different path than was occurring as a result of the Battle of France.[15]

Raymond Collishaw, newly promoted to air commodore, assumed greater command responsibilities as Egypt gained priority in the defensive schemes of the empire. As he recalled, "Heliopolis was one of the RAF's major overseas bases and there was much to do."[16] Changing administrative arrangements in the air force confirmed the increased importance of the region. The commander of RAF Middle East, raised to the rank of air marshal in April 1938, gained authority over units in Iraq, Aden, and Malta as it affected matters in Egypt. A year later the post was given the status of air officer commanding-in-chief when Air Marshal Sir William Mitchell assumed command. The importance of operations in the Western Desert was formally acknowledged on 18 April 1939 by the creation of the Egypt Group, under command of Collishaw. The mission of the organization was to "exercise control over operational units allocated to it by H.Q. R.A.F., Middle East, for operations in the Western Desert, and to exercise operational supervision of such maintenance and administrative units as may be allocated in the field for the servicing of operational units."[17]

Mitchell outlined Collishaw's new responsibilities in a set of operational instructions issued when the Egypt Group was created. The instructions are notable for the close working relationship with the army it established. In peacetime Collishaw maintained operational control over the three main RAF stations in Egypt (Heliopolis, Helwan, and Ismailia) as well as the Advanced Wing and Nos. 1 and 2 Bomber Wings. In time of war the Advanced Wing (composed of two bomber, one army-cooperation, and one fighter squadron) would deploy to the desert. Liaison between the army's Mobile Division and the RAF would be conducted through the commander of the Advanced Wing, who would collocate his headquarters with that of the division.[18] A senior air-staff officer was attached to Mobile Division to ensure effective communications between the army and the RAF. He was instructed to

> keep himself informed at all times of the military situation on the land and of the situation with regard to air forces, in order that he may be able, at any moment, to advise the GOC [general officer commanding] Mobile Division, as to what air support he may be afforded and similarly, he must be able to advise the Advanced Wing Commander as to the existence, or anticipated existence, of suitable objectives for air attack, or vital points calling for air defence.[19]

The instructions further noted that Collishaw and the Advanced Wing commander should not solely rely on the liaison officer and "should take every opportunity possible" to establish personal contact with the Mobile Division commander, who, it was suggested, should endeavor to locate his advanced headquarters near a suitable landing ground to facilitate such communications.[20]

The standing operational instructions for the Egypt Group declared that the first priority in the event of an Italian attack was to provide urgent close support to the army in the face of what was expected to be superior enemy forces. The group would also cooperate with the Royal Navy to attack more-distant land targets. After the initial crisis period had passed, or in the event of no land attack, Advanced Wing operations would conform with the overall RAF Middle East plan. These instructions to Collishaw highlighted the finite resources available in the theater but allowed him the freedom to act when necessary:

> In view of the difficulty, if not impossibility, of replacing wastage in pilots and aircraft, the Air Officer Commanding, Egypt Group, should, as a general principle, economise as far as possible in the use of his aircraft, but bearing in mind always that, if the opportunity offers for striking a severe blow at the enemy land forces or air forces, a successful result might materially contribute to the defeat of the enemy and hamper their continuance of operations.[21]

In other words be careful, but not too careful.

In September Egypt Group was redesignated 202 Group and its war mission was modified. RAF headquarters in Cairo believed that the strength of the Royal Navy in the Mediterranean would prevent the timely resupply of Italian forces in Libya, which would have to rely on existing stocks. This was a major change from earlier assumptions. Commanders also thought that the best method of dealing with the Italian superiority in aircraft was to attack their air bases and repair facilities. This assessment led to a new operational plan that shifted the primary role of Collishaw's aircraft from close support of the army to attacks against enemy air bases and coordinating with the navy to interdict the Italian lines of communications across the Mediterranean. The army was still provided with close support on a priority basis when necessary, but this operational order more clearly established the flexible and wide-ranging nature of land-based air power.[22]

Despite the changed nature of 202 Group's operational plan, Collishaw continued to focus his training on a close working relationship with the army. This pattern of training, which continued from November 1939 until his forces were put on high alert in May 1940, reinforced a longstanding tradition of good relations between the army and the air force in the Middle East and stands in marked contrast to the situation that existed in Britain at this time. Differing doctrine and a competition for resources led to an adversarial relationship between the RAF and the British Army at home.[23] The situation was quite different outside the home islands, however, where operational necessity, scarce resources, and a genuine need to work together fostered a more harmonious bond between the services. Uncharacteristically for an army officer, the senior commander in Egypt in the early 1930s, Gen. Sir Jock Burnett-Stuart, favored close relations with the RAF. He believed that air officers knew how best to employ their resources and an army commander should depend on that knowledge. Joint-training schemes in Egypt in the mid-1930s reflected this attitude.[24]

The senior leadership of the RAF in Egypt was also predisposed to close relations with the army. Air Chief Marshal Mitchell and his successor, Air Chief Marshal Arthur Longmore, had significant experience directing RAF colonial-policing operations, which required an understanding of army-support operations. Collishaw was also very comfortable working in this joint environment.[25]

The command of the army and navy underwent a similar rationalization process on the eve of the war. For the army, Gen. Archibald Percival Wavell was appointed general officer commanding-in-chief, Middle East in July 1939. Previously, there were three separate commands in the region—Egypt, the Sudan, and Palestine and the Transjordan. The War Office recognized that a central authority was needed, however, and ordered Wavell to Cairo, where he took command of those three areas; he also assumed responsibility for Libya,

Iraq, East Africa, and the Persian Gulf. Highly regarded in the interwar army, Wavell excelled as a commander, was an innovative thinker, and was known as an outstanding instructor. He had previous experience in the Middle East, where he commanded in Palestine and the Transjordan during the outbreak of Arab-Jewish troubles from July 1937 to April 1938.[26] Under Wavell was Lt. Gen. Henry Maitland Wilson, "Jumbo" to his friends, who was the general officer commanding British troops in Egypt. Wilson enjoyed the confidence of Sir Anthony Eden, the secretary of state for war, and later earned the respect of Winston Churchill, who described him as "one of our finest tacticians."[27] The large size of Wavell's command was matched by its strategic importance, but it was severely underresourced.

During Operation Compass, the first British offensive in the Western Desert launched in December 1940, the lines of command authority in the army were rather confused. In June 1940 Maj. Gen. Richard O'Connor transferred to Egypt from Palestine with the headquarters of 6th Division. He was a capable battlefield commander who did very well on the western and Italian fronts during the First World War. In the interwar period he served in India and Palestine and was commended for his service. Upon his transfer to Egypt, he was given command of all troops in the Western Desert, relieving Wilson of this responsibility, and his formation was redesignated Headquarters Western Desert Force. In this capacity O'Connor was the primary operational commander of Operation Compass and the author of its success, but he served two masters, Wavell and Wilson.[28]

The principal Royal Navy command for the region was held by Adm. Andrew Cunningham, who was commander-in-chief, Mediterranean, a position he considered "the finest appointment the Royal Navy has to offer."[29] His responsibility to keep the Italian navy in check was significant, but he felt well prepared: "I probably knew the Mediterranean as well as any naval officer of my generation."[30] Naval command of the region was split, and the Red Sea, Suez Canal, and Gulf of Aden were the responsibility of Adm. Sir Ralph Leatham, commander-in-chief, East Indies Station. This division created some liaison problems for Wavell, who preferred to deal with one naval commander with an overlapping area of responsibility.[31]

A series of exercises in October–November 1939 tested the working relationship of the army and the air force. The efficacy of RAF doctrine was largely confirmed, but there was room for improvement. The exercises brought together the Armoured Division and 253 Wing (formerly the Advanced Wing) to test the Combined Plan, which would be executed upon the commencement of an Italian offensive from Libya. Westland, an imaginary force representing Italy, was to launch an invasion of Egypt with two divisions, one moving along

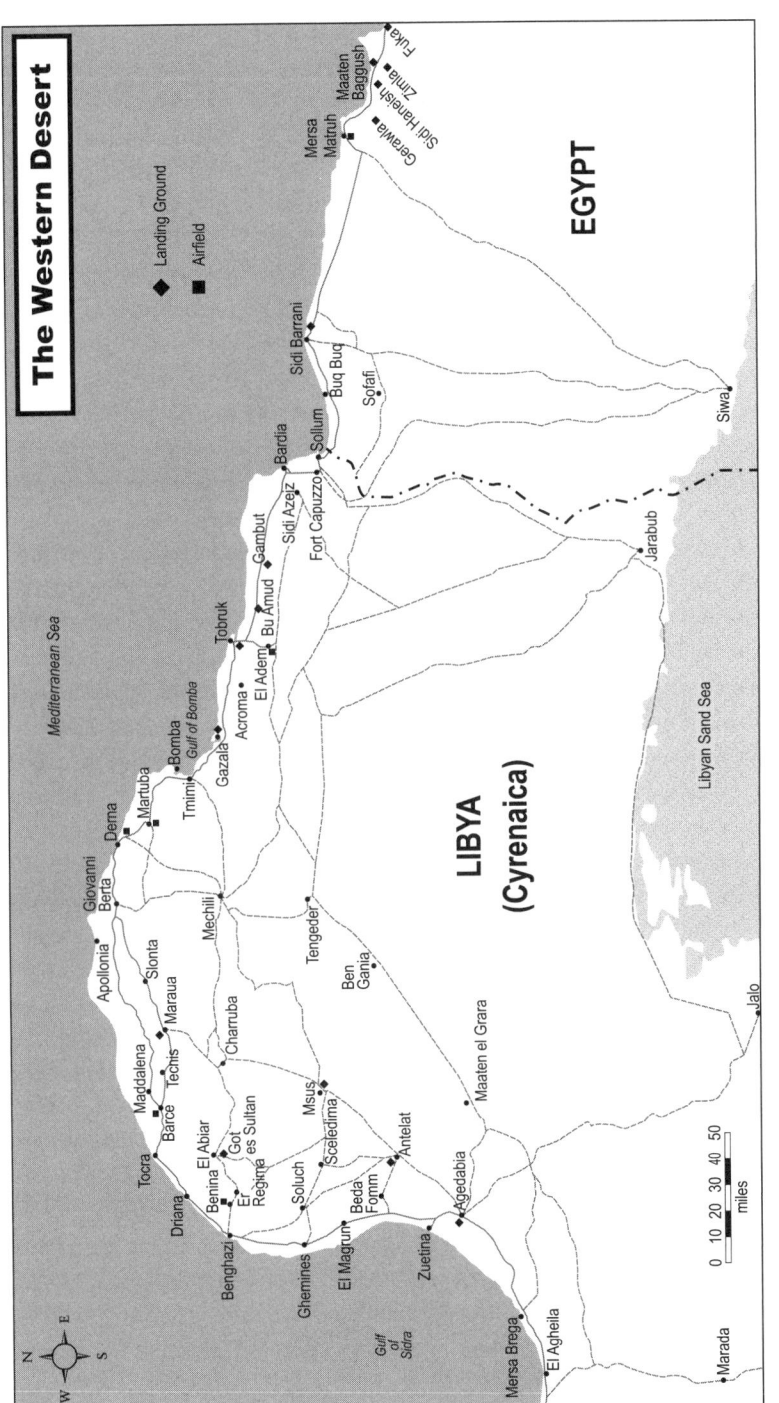

The Western Desert. Map by Mike Bechthold. Copyright © 2017 by the University of Oklahoma Press.

the coast road from Sollum to Mersa Matruh and the second crossing the frontier farther south at Fort Maddalena and moving across the desert to Mersa Matruh. Eastland, represented by the Armoured Division, was to resist the invasion and defend Egypt. The Eastland air force was responsible for reconnaissance tasks as well as bombing targets that might present themselves, such as convoys on the coast road or troop and vehicle concentrations in the desert. If necessary, the Eastland air force would cover a withdrawal of the Armoured Division. A command-post exercise without troops or aircraft was conducted from 23 to 25 October. This was followed by a second exercise from 28 to 31 October in which a fictitious Westland army attacked Eastland, whose forces were represented in the field again by the Armoured Division and 253 Wing. A third exercise postulated a different scenario in which a Westland armored brigade conducted a raid on a defended post located two days' march from its base. A long-range bombing raid would be synchronized with the final attack on the post.[32]

The exercises were a useful training tool for the air force and confirmed air-staff views regarding operations in support of the army. Collishaw wrote an extensive report on the exercises, highlighting a number of lessons learned. The outcome largely confirmed his experience in these types of operations and indicated areas where the army needed to be better educated in the application of battlefield air support. Bombing experiments showed that attempts to destroy moving armored vehicles were not profitable; bombing frontline troops rarely achieved desired results. Instead, attacking targets along the lines of communication proved a better option.[33]

The exercises also revealed a number of RAF vulnerabilities. Aircraft were most exposed, and suffered their greatest losses, during enemy attacks on airfields. Greater use needed to be made of satellite fields to better disburse aircraft. Another failing was the complete vulnerability of the army-cooperation aircraft. The Westland Lysanders were too slow to operate in the face of an enemy air threat. As a result they had to be escorted on all their missions by fighter aircraft. This increased the complexity of operations and prevented the fighters from performing to their full capabilities.[34]

The plan for the Westland attack on Mersa Matruh called for the operational employment of mustard gas by aerial spraying, no doubt influenced by the Italian use of poison gas in Abyssinia four years earlier. A training liquid was released during the exercise, but Collishaw recommended a live trial as "our knowledge of mustard gas for operational employment in tropical climates is extremely limited. We ought to experiment to discover whether daylight conditions will dissipate this gas when released at 3,000 feet, before it reaches the ground. Night releases also ought to be made."[35] Despite the fact that the Italians never employed gas in the Western Desert, Collishaw was right to plan for the worst. Following the capture of Tobruk in January 1941, British troops discovered a cache of poison gas.[36]

Coordination problems between the army and air force were exposed during the exercises. Communications breakdowns were frequent, and in one case Group Capt. Leslie "Bingo" Brown, the commander of 253 Wing, had to personally go forward to learn the position of the Eastland troops so he could then lead a support mission that avoided friendly fire casualties. Collishaw observed that it was essential for the army to maintain fully briefed air-liaison officers at each advanced airfield so that all aircrew could benefit from correct and timely intelligence before each mission. The RAF had difficulty getting timely information from the army to allow them to plan their missions and outfit aircraft with the appropriate munitions. It also experienced problems in the mobility of the squadrons during the exercise. A number of the squadrons had moved forward into the desert from their home bases in the Nile Delta and encountered operational difficulties due to a shortage of mechanics and spare parts. The headquarters staff of 253 Wing found themselves overcommitted due to the extra work needed while engaged in active operations. To overcome these obstacles, Collishaw recommended an increase in the headquarters staff as well as the forward deployment of large detachments from each squadron to facilitate mobile operations.[37]

Collishaw made clear in his report that the army staff officers needed to be better informed regarding the proper employment of air support. There were numerous requests for fighter cover that unnecessarily diluted the amount of available air support. Troops tended to view aircraft in much the same manner as artillery:

> Military Staff Officers seemed somewhat inclined to visualise the proper employment of an Air Striking Force to be the Air bombardment of minor military targets such as strong entrenched positions and dispersed moving armoured vehicles. This type of target is very difficult to hit and there appears to be good reason to suppose that as good or better results could be obtained by the use of artillery. . . . It is important, therefore, that the RAF adviser to the GOC-in-C should resist any tendency to tactical misemployment of our striking force on targets unlikely to achieve vital results by air bombardment.[38]

Part of these unrealistic expectations stemmed from the tendency of the army's "great expectations" of the RAF, from whom they requested all manner of support. Collishaw, cognizant of the finite resources he commanded, understood that the "result would probably be that the RAF in Egypt would suffer serious casualties during the early part of the campaign. It is important to realize that our Air Force will have to conduct the campaign on a declining effort and subsequently we ought to husband our air resources from the outset." This meant that air attack had to be reserved for targets of the utmost impor- tance "unless the military situation is such that added risks must be taken."[39]

This series of maneuvers provided a good indication of what to expect in the upcoming conflict. Lieutenant General Wilson was pleased with the atten- tion given to developing closer ties with the RAF and attempts to improve communications between the two services. This confirmed the intent of the Combined Plan. Of greater concern to him were the small numbers and obso- lescent state of the aircraft available and the lack of the modern warplanes in Egypt.[40] Collishaw demonstrated a solid understanding of the strengths and weakness of his command. He knew the types of targets his aircraft could prof- itably attack, understood the types of missions that should be avoided, recog- nized that the closest possible partnership with the army was needed to ensure that intelligence was shared in a timely manner, and sought to provide guidance to the army on the best way to employ the air assets. Overall, Collishaw came away from the exercises convinced that the British Army in Egypt was strong enough to stop and contain any conceivable Italian advance. He believed that these units could accomplish their defensive task without any need for signifi- cant amounts of air support, which left his aircraft free to conduct a counterof- fensive against the Italians upon the outbreak of war.

Soon after the completion of these exercises, the three commanders in chief met in Cairo in mid-November 1939 to review the strategic situation and plan for the defense of Egypt in the event of an Italian attack. Air Chief Marshal Mitchell outlined the implications of the decisions made at the meeting for 202 Group. He told Collishaw, "the primary role of the Royal Air Force strik- ing force operating from Egypt is to be the destruction or neutralization of the Italian air forces, and that their secondary function is to co-operate with the land and sea forces." Mitchell warned that the weak state of the RAF meant that Collishaw needed to conserve his forces until such time as the Italians con- ducted a major air campaign against Egypt. This meant that "bomber units in Egypt will not be required to provide close support to the land forces unless the military situation is so critical that air assistance becomes imperative."[41] The decision to divert aircraft from the primary role of defeating enemy air forces to close support was made at Mitchell's headquarters and not by Collishaw in response to a request from army command. He accepted these orders without question as they reflected RAF policies at the time and reinforced his own expe- rience from the western front and the recent desert-training exercises.

This directive was forwarded to Lieutenant General Wilson's headquar- ters with a covering letter by Air Vice-Marshal Peter Drummond, the senior air staff officer, RAF Middle East, which raised serious concerns for the army regarding the level of close support it could expect from the RAF:

> You may, of course, have already heard from our G.H.Q., M.E., that the chief concern of our bombers will be the destruction or neutralization of the Italian air forces in LIBYA. From this it naturally follows that we shall not be able to provide as much close support for the Army in the Western Desert as has hitherto be contemplated, though naturally if the military situation becomes really acute and air assistance becomes absolutely necessary, we should do our best to provide it.[42]

This letter, with its apparent dismissal of RAF support during land combat, quickly received high-level attention from the army. On 23 November General Wavell wrote a sharply worded reply to Air Chief Marshal Mitchell stating that his understanding of the decisions made at the commanders-in-chief meeting was quite different: "While respecting your opinion, I do not myself entirely agree" with your suggestion that the destruction of the enemy air force was the primary task of the RAF and "did not, I am sure, give approval to it at the conference."[43] Wavell expected the closest cooperation between the air force and the army during any campaign in the Western Desert, not just if the situation turned critical. Mitchell was unapologetic in his reply but offered to convene another meeting of the three services to ensure that everybody was in agreement with the template for future operations.[44] The instructions issued to 202 Group by RAF Headquarters Middle East were subsequently modified in a minor way to allow Collishaw the discretion to respond to requests for air support from the military commander without reference to higher headquarters.[45] This debate was typical of exchanges between the army and the air force over the nature and type of support to be provided to ground forces. Any difficulties of this nature during Operation Compass were avoided by the close, personal working relationship between the officers in the field, especially Collishaw and O'Connor.

While the war raged in Europe, for Collishaw and his men, the first six months of 1940 passed quietly. After a period of high tension following the German invasion of Poland and the start of the war in September 1939, life in the desert returned to a routine of training and boredom. Shortages were rife, but attempts were made to make do with available resources. Air Vice-Marshal Albert C. Maund, a very experienced officer, arrived in Egypt in December 1939 to take over the post of air officer administrative at Mitchell's headquarters. He had joined the Canadian Expeditionary Force as a private in 1914, went overseas with the 8th Canadian Infantry Battalion, and eventually transferred to the Royal Flying Corps as an observer in March 1916. In mid-1917 he was sent to support to the RFC mission in Russia, and by 1919 he was general officer commanding the RAF training mission to Russia; Collishaw's No. 47 Squadron came under his command. In 1924 Maund was a classmate of Collishaw at the RAF Staff College, and they again served together in the headquarters of the Air Defence of Great Britain in 1927 and 1928.[46]

Maund was faced with a major task: to prepare the repair-and-replacement facilities for the increased tempo of wartime operations; the capacity did not exist to deal with the required volume of aircraft-engine repairs. He also took steps to deal with dust, the most serious problem of operating in the desert. Blenheim bombers required their engine filters to be cleaned after five hours of flying time, a job that took nearly three hours. The expedient replacement of the filter took only fifteen minutes, but there were only six spares in all of the Middle East command. Mitchell sent Maund to England in January 1940 to make the case for extra resources to deal with their personnel and equipment issues. Maund was initially told to scale back his establishments due to the great need for the same items in England. Planners in London counted on Italian neutrality to allow the Middle East to be starved of resources in favor of other theaters. The danger of this proposal, however, was soon realized, and Maund learned that he could expect to receive suitable war establishments to meet the needs of Middle East command. The importance of this decision cannot be overemphasized. The disparity of forces meant that Mitchell and Collishaw needed to have every possible aircraft serviceable and ready for operations.[47] To understand the crippling effect of a poor repair-and-maintenance organization, one need look no further than the Italian air force, which abandoned thousands of aircraft in the desert during the early stages of the war due to maintenance issues. The RAF, in contrast, abandoned very few planes during the first German offensive in April–May 1941.[48]

On 13 May 1940 Air Chief Marshal Longmore arrived to take over command of RAF Middle East from Mitchell. He arrived at a time of great change in the strategic situation. Germany had launched its surprise attack on the West three days earlier. In less than a week the Netherlands and half of Belgium was lost, and by 21 May German spearheads had reached the Channel coast, setting in motion the great evacuation at Dunkirk. Italy was not idle during this period. Mussolini had been anticipating war for a number of weeks, and by the time of the German attack, his military was ready. The Italian navy and air force were prepared for operations, and the army had been fully mobilized, including the reinforcement of Libya. The defeat of France in June changed the balance of power in North Africa. The Italians now were free to transfer troops away from French-controlled Tunisia to reinforce Cyrenaica and East Africa.[49]

Longmore was responsible for all British air forces in the Middle East, including the surrounding territories and seas. This encompassed full control of Egypt, the Sudan, Palestine, and Transjordan as well as operational control of Aden, Iraq, and Malta. Longmore was responsible for operations in East Africa (Ethiopia, Eritrea, and Kenya), Cyprus, the Balkans (Greece, Yugoslavia, Bulgaria, and Romania), and over the Persian Gulf and the Mediterranean and Red Seas. This vast territory, some four and a half million square miles, was too much for one man to control, but this was the challenge he faced.[50]

Longmore and Collishaw were both products of the Royal Naval Air Service. Longmore joined the service before the First World War and taught Maj. Hugh Trenchard how to fly in 1912. In 1918 he was appointed senior air staff officer to the commander-in-chief Mediterranean (naval) with responsibility for all RNAS units in the region, including Malta, Italy, Gibraltar, and Egypt. In 1923 Longmore served on Air Marshal Sir John Salmond's staff in Iraq and oversaw operations against the Turks and Kurds, including the Rowanduz expedition, during which Collishaw was the RAF liaison officer. Longmore spent the decade before the Second World War primarily in Great Britain as the commandant at the RAF College and subsequently the Imperial Defence College.[51] Upon taking command in the Mediterranean, he embarked on a visit to his various and far-flung commands. Before the start of hostilities, he visited most of the units under his authority, but his first visit on 27 May was to Collishaw's units in the Western Desert. Longmore started his tour with a visit to Group Captain Brown and 253 Wing at Maaten Bagush and then moved on to Qasaba, where C Flight of No. 208 Army Co-operation Squadron was based. His next stop was Mersa Matruh, the center of the positions held by the Armoured Division and the base of No. 33 Fighter Squadron. The following morning Longmore flew to the frontier to see the advanced landing grounds near the border before returning to inspect No. 45 Bomber Squadron at Fuka and No. 211 Bomber Squadron at Dhaba. Overall, the air chief marshal was content with the quality of the pilots and the competence of the ground crews.[52] He was surprised at the Spartan existence of the air personnel:

> Desert airfields provide few amenities for aircrews in their leisure hours; they were probably more comfortable in the cockpits of their aircraft in the air chasing or bombing Italians, than they were on the ground sitting in sand-blown tents, improvised huts or dugouts. Accommodation was certainly primitive and Collishaw's headquarters at Maaten Bagush consisted of a couple of portable wooden huts and a few tents, in addition to an underground operations room which had been neatly excavated out of the sandstone. . . . Luckily most of these airfields were close to the coast where most excellent bathing was possible.[53]

The conditions at Collishaw's headquarters may have been basic, but the location was important. He was situated beside the headquarters of the Western Desert Force as well as close to the airfields where his squadrons were based. This arrangement facilitated a close working relationship between O'Connor, Collishaw, and their respective staffs during the first months of the war and during the planning stages for Operation Compass. Immediately prior to the commencement of that counteroffensive, O'Connor moved his advanced headquarters into the desert to remain close to his forward divisions. Collishaw's preference was to keep his command center collocated with that of O'Connor, but the communications infrastructure was unreliable at that time in the war and did not allow him to stay in close contact with his airfields if he moved forward.[54] General Wilson recalled that the radios had a "habit of fading out about sundown just when information for deciding the next day's operations was badly needed."[55] A compromise was struck by dispatching Group Capt. "Bingo" Brown along with a signals detachment to accompany O'Connor. Wilson took over command of O'Connor's main headquarters, facilitating communications with the RAF and the Royal Navy.[56]

At the beginning of June, the 7th Armoured Division (as the Armoured Division had been renamed in February 1940) was deployed in a series of defended posts south and east of Mersa Matruh. This offered the best position from which to defend Egypt as there were good rail and road connections back to Alexandria and Cairo. An improved road continued west to Sidi Barrani, but the quality of the track past that to the frontier was poor. The border area was initially defended by the division less one of its armored brigades. After returning from his visit, Longmore decided to concentrate Collishaw's 202 Group in the desert. All leave was cancelled, and RAF units were warned to be ready for operations on forty-eight hours' notice. The imminent collapse of France was set to change the entire situation in Egypt. The loss of the French colonies of Tunisia and Syria gave Italy the freedom to concentrate its forces against Egypt without having to worry about attacks on other fronts in Libya and East Africa.[57]

On the eve of the Italian declaration of war, Longmore outlined RAF objectives in the Middle East once hostilities commenced:

1. Offensive action against enemy air bases with a view to reducing their numerical superiority in aircraft and destroying their repair organization.
2. Offensive action against enemy ports to destroy or damage submarines, shipping and port facilities.
3. Destruction of resources of all sorts in Italian East Africa.

4. Full support of British army operations.
5. Strategic reconnaissance for all the services.[58]

These were the same priorities agreed to by the commanders in chief in late 1939.

The first task of 202 Group was to conduct reconnaissance to keep the British command informed concerning Italian actions, then to make attacks against enemy targets, especially aircraft and airfield infrastructure. Overall direction of the air campaign was vested in Longmore, who established targets for air bombardment, though Collishaw exercised operational control of those missions. To facilitate coordination between the army and Collishaw and to simplify the chain of command, Longmore combined 253 Wing with 202 Group, and Group Captain Brown, freed of his command responsibilities, became the full-time liaison officer between Collishaw and Maj. Gen. Sir Michael O'Moore Creagh, commander of 7th Armoured Division. This close contact between the two services was crucial for effective air operations in support of the ground campaign.[59]

There was a great disparity in the strength of the opposing forces in the Western Desert. On the ground it was estimated that the Italian Tenth Army deployed ten divisions consisting of 215,000 troops, with an additional 200,000 troops in Italian East Africa. Lieutenant General O'Connor commanded fewer than 36,000 men in the Western Desert Force. A qualitative difference between the two forces helped balance some of the disparity in numbers as the Italians were considerably less mechanized than the British.[60] Reinforcements sent to Libya were a "well-intentioned measure," but the Italian high command failed to understand that the quality and quantity of its equipment was more important than "mere numbers." The increased size of the Italian army in North Africa did not improve its combat power, however, and only "swelled the British 'bag' [capture of prisoners]" during Operation Compass.[61]

In the air the Italian 5th Squadra, commanded by Generale Squadra Aerea Felice Porro, was estimated to have some two hundred bombers and two hundred fighters, and reinforcements could rapidly be dispatched from the Italy. An exercise in late 1939 demonstrated that four hundred bombers could be deployed from Italy for long-range strikes on Alexandria on short notice in the event of a crisis.[62] The strength of the RAF in Egypt at the start of June 1940 was sixty-three Gladiators and one Hurricane in three fighter squadrons (Nos. 33, 80, and 112), seventy-two Blenheims in six bomber squadrons (Nos. 11, 45, 55, 113, 211, and 30 [in reserve]), twenty-four Bombays and Valentias, twenty-four Lysanders, and ten Sunderland flying boats. Of this total Collishaw deployed eighty-one aircraft at his forward airfields, most near Mersa Matruh.

The British maintained a considerable advantage in replacement aircraft and spare parts, with the RAF squadrons operating at full strength and maintaining a reserve of 100 percent.[63]

The fall of France greatly complicated the dispatch of reinforcements from England. Fighter aircraft did not have the range to fly directly to the Middle East, and it was slow and dangerous to send a convoy through the Mediterranean. At best, it took two weeks for a convoy to make this voyage, all the time exposed to German U-boats, the Italian fleet, and Axis land-based aircraft operating from France, North Africa, Italy, and Sicily. It was safer to send a convoy around the Horn of Africa, but that journey took even longer. Therefore, the British developed the Takoradi route prior to the war as an overland alternative to the Middle East. Aircraft were shipped to the West African port of Takoradi, where they were assembled and then flown east to Khartoum, then north along the Nile River valley to Egypt. This route was the best alternative to a hazardous voyage through the Mediterranean Sea, but it took a tremendous toll on men and machines. The supply of twin-engine aircraft was somewhat easier to manage as they flew directly from England, stopping only to refuel at Gibraltar and Malta.[64]

From a supply point of view, the Italians had it both better and worse. North Africa's proximity to home meant that replacement aircraft and spare parts could be supplied in a matter of hours. But the maintenance system of the Regia Aeronautica (the Italian Royal Air Force) was far inferior to that of the RAF. At the start of the campaign, Italian squadrons could claim only 60 percent of their aircraft as serviceable, and this number declined substantially following the start of combat operations.[65]

The air war in the desert in 1940–41 was reminiscent of the Great War. Open cockpits, dogfights between biplanes, and poor communications were the norm rather than the exception. In addition, the equipment was largely outdated and obsolescent since North Africa was a secondary theater of war. In 1940 the fighter squadrons of the metropolitan RAF were equipped with sleek new Spitfires and Hurricanes. These high-performance, eight- and twelve-gun aircraft were among the best in the world. Bomber Command was similarly equipped with modern aircraft such as the Wellington, Whitley, and Sterling. Few of these warplanes could be spared for distant operations as they were needed to support the British Expeditionary Force in France and to defend the British Isles against an expected German invasion attempt.[66]

The RAF in Egypt had to make do with what was available, and its frontline fighter was the Gloster Gladiator—the last British biplane fighter. The Gladiator had a top speed of 242 miles per hour (mph) and was armed with four .303-caliber machine guns. It was a sturdy aircraft that performed well in the hands of a familiar pilot. The army-cooperation aircraft operated by the RAF in Egypt was the Westland Lysander. It was intended to work closely with troops to provide reconnaissance, communications, and light attack support. But it was slow and vulnerable, with a cruising speed of less than 200 mph. The Lysander was armed with one .303-caliber machine gun in the rear cockpit and two fixed forward-firing machine guns. After initial losses proved its vulnerability, these planes required a fighter escort to operate in the face of enemy patrols. The primary British bomber in the Middle East was the Bristol Blenheim I. It was one of the fastest twin-engine bombers in the world when it was introduced in late 1936, but it was approaching obsolescence by the start of the war. Nevertheless, it carried a maximum 1,000-pound bomb load over a range of 1,125 miles at a maximum speed of 265 mph and provided yeoman service in the desert. A secondary bomber was the Bristol Bombay, a slow, awkward converted transport. It would have been slaughtered in the skies over Europe, but in the Middle East it was able to operate quite effectively at night.

The obsolescence of the aircraft under Collishaw's command was matched by those of the Italians. The primary fighter of the Regia Aeronautica was the Fiat CR42. This biplane was evenly matched with the Gladiator, though it was slightly more maneuverable and more heavily armed, with two 12.7-mm machine guns. The Savoia-Marchetti SM79 carried out most of the Italian bombing operations. It was one of the fastest aircraft in the theater, with a top speed of 270 mph; had a range of 1,243 miles; and could carry up to 2,200 pounds of bombs.[67]

By May 1940, the RAF in the Western Desert was prepared for war. Longmore and Collishaw controlled an air force that was composed of a small number of obsolescent aircraft at the end of a long supply line with no hope of immediate replacements or reinforcements. The Italians, by comparison, possessed a superior number of aircraft and benefited from a relatively short logistical line to the home country. Relations between the British Army and the RAF were not ideal, but there were indications their different concepts regarding the role of airpower could be overcome. Joint exercises conducted in October–November 1939 highlighted a number of strengths and weaknesses in the provision of air support for ground operations. The RAF after-action reports demonstrated that the air officers came away from the exercises with a solid understanding of what needed to be done when hostilities commenced. Air Marshal Mitchell issued clear operating instructions to 202 Group that set out the RAF's understanding of operations and incorporated the lessons learned during the desert exercises. The destruction of the enemy's air force was the first task, while the provision of support to the army was secondary and only received priority in an emergency. When General Wavell protested that the instructions appeared to minimize the military's need for close air support, Mitchell did not back down. The orders issued to 202 Group were modified to allow Collishaw more discretion to conduct support missions, but the emphasis of its attacks remained on targets beyond the army's battle space. This demonstrated the competing philosophies of the army and the RAF over the proper use of air power during a land campaign. Mitchell believed that Wavell had understood his position as a result of previous conversations, but this was not the case. It was important that Mitchell, and Longmore after him, stood up to army demands for air support and left Collishaw free to conduct his campaign according to the RAF concept of operations. The extensive interservice experience possessed by the senior RAF leadership in the desert played an important role in facilitating the relationship with the army. Air operations in the upcoming battles would be crucial to British success. The working relationship between the army and the RAF established during this period was essential for this to happen.

CHAPTER 3

THE WESTERN DESERT AND THE
START OF THE WAR

By the middle of May 1940, the British knew the Italians were actively pre-paring for war. The combined British and French Mediterranean fleets outnumbered the Regia Marina (Italian Royal Navy), but the balance of land and air forces in Libya and Egypt was tilted toward the Italians. The warning signs prompted the British to place all three services on alert. Major General O'Connor's Western Desert Force was dispatched to the area of Mersa Matruh, with advanced units sent to the Egyptian frontier. Air Chief Marshal Longmore supported this deployment by stationing all but one of his bomber squadrons in the Western Desert.[1] The wait for the declaration of war ended late on the evening of 10 June, when it became apparent that hostilities would soon begin. At 6:30 P.M. Air Commodore Collishaw paraded the 202 Group personnel at Maaten Bagush to inform them that it was believed Italy had declared war. Just before midnight he received orders to "come to immediate readiness for war with Italy, but await (repeat await) further instructions before initiating hostile acts."[2] At midnight it was confirmed that a state of war existed between Italy and Great Britain, and nine minutes later Longmore sent a signal to Collishaw advising: "A state of war with Italy exists. Carry out reconnaissance as arranged. Bomber formations as available should accompany reconnaissance in northern areas. Favourable targets observed, especially concentrations of aircraft."[3] The men of 202 Group were ready to carry the offensive to the Italians, but aircraft were ordered well dispersed in case of enemy attack.[4]

At first light on 11 June, six Blenheims of No. 211 Squadron took off to scout six prearranged areas, but they found no sign of Italian army concen-trations. Later in the day Blenheims of Nos. 45, 55, and 113 Squadrons were sent to attack the harbor at Tobruk.[5] When no visible signs of the enemy could be found, the aircraft diverted to a secondary target—the airfield at El Adem.[6] The first bomber over the target attacked at low level, encountering no flak or defending fighters. Instead, the Italian aircraft were parked neatly in rows, ideal for peacetime convenience but disastrous in time of war; eighteen were confirmed destroyed.[7] Crews claimed that their attack found the Italian airmen lined up on parade astride the main runway. As the bombs began to fall, they ran in all directions to find cover; it was later surmised that the base commander had ordered his troops out so he could read them Mussolini's official announcement of war against England.[8] Fighters scrambled too late to prevent the British attack, but two Blenheims were shot down afterward with the loss of their crews.[9] As late as 12 June air raids on Italian airfields met little resistance and often found aircraft on the ground undispersed and vulnerable. The first small Italian raid was launched thirty-six hours after the start of hostilities, and it took nearly two weeks after the declaration of war for them to mount their first major attack, targeting the port facilities at Alexandria and the RAF maintenance depot at Aboukir. The Gladiators launched in defense were too slow to catch the SM79 bombers, but they disrupted the attack so the bombing was scattered and ineffective.[10]

The high tempo of British operations continued on 12 June, when a joint RAF–Royal Navy operation was directed against Tobruk. The raid was ordered after a reconnaissance flight by No. 113 Squadron reported the harbor full of ships. Air attacks on the port and its airfield were designed to divert attention from a naval sweep down the Libyan coast; planners also hoped that the raids would flush ships out into the path of the Royal Navy. Blenheims from Nos. 45, 113, and 211 Squadrons were impeded by fog and low cloud, however. Some aircraft were unable to find the target, while others were driven off by a strong Italian defensive umbrella of some fifty fighters over the main airfield at Tobruk. One success was achieved when nine Blenheims of No. 113 Squadron bombed the Italian warship *San Giorgio,* setting it on fire. This old 9,000-ton cruiser, employed as a submarine-depot ship, was run aground on a sandbar to prevent it from sinking. The vessel was subsequently used as an antiaircraft-gun platform in the harbor and never sailed again.[11]

With the preliminary phase of the war over, Longmore and Collishaw planned their next move. The dim prospects for receiving replacement pilots and aircraft forced Longmore to adopt a defensive posture. The period from mid-June to the end of July was marked by a slower pace of operations compared to the start of hostilities. Collishaw, however, did his best to achieve the illusion of superiority by keeping the enemy off balance. Described as "Collie's War," he conducted operations on the basis of "hit 'em hard, then hit 'em again. But don't let 'em know where you're going to hit."[12] In general, the RAF attacks were small in scale but wide in scope. Small groups of aircraft struck as many targets as possible. By 22 June, the main El Adem aerodrome outside Tobruk had been attacked ten times by a total of forty-three aircraft. The raids caused limited physical destruction, but the damage to morale was significant. The regular attacks compelled the Italians to mount standing patrols over their military bases, ports, and airfields, while army commanders demanded that an air umbrella cover their troops in the field.[13] This policy had a number of long-reaching consequences. It was terribly wasteful of resources. Aircraft employed in standing patrols could not be used offensively. As well, the wear and tear on the machines and their aircrews was cumulative. Italian serviceability rates, never high, plummeted due to the strain of maintaining these patrols. A good indication of the success of Collishaw's raids can be seen in the period leading up to the Italian offensive in mid-September. At a time when the Regia Aeronautica should have been launching numerous attacks against the British to prepare for the main ground offensive, very few raids were made because of the large number of aircraft devoted to defensive patrols.[14]

Despite the limited success of these Italian strikes, Collishaw remained concerned about future raids. He considered the Gladiator to be wholly inadequate for the task of bomber interception and asked for a flight of Hurricanes to deal with this threat. At a time when there were only four Hurricanes in all of Egypt, Longmore could not fulfil this request, but Collishaw did get one of the modern fighters.[15] At that early stage in the war, the Hurricane outperformed everything else in the North African sky. Collishaw tried to get as much as possible from this single aircraft. He shifted it frequently from one landing ground to another to bluff the Italians into believing there were more of these high-performance fighters available. "Collie's Battleship," as the Hurricane was christened, was used to great effect. The most skilled pilots in the group were tasked to fly it, and they were ordered to be very aggressive in their attacks, primarily to frighten the enemy. Collishaw's order stated: "Success will adversely affect Italian morale as he will be fearful that Hurricane fighters may attack at any moment."[16]

Another innovation by Collishaw addressed the issue of the fast Italian SM79 bombers, which the Gladiators were having trouble catching. He ordered the Blenheims of No. 30 Squadron to be converted to fighters by the addition of four forward-firing .303-caliber machine guns under the nose. This added armament, coupled with the existing machine gun in the wing, made the fast Blenheim capable of catching and killing the bombers. On patrol the Hurricane was always teamed with a pair of Blenheims. As well, a flight of Gladiators was added to protect the Blenheims from the more-maneuverable Italian fighters.[17] This new team achieved its first success on 19 June, when the Hurricane, two Blenheims, and four Gladiators intercepted a formation of twelve Italian fighters (most likely CR42s, though identification was not confirmed). Four Italian aircraft were downed for the loss of one Gladiator. Later in the day the Hurricane, supported by four Blenheim fighters, intercepted another formation of Italian fighters. This time the Hurricane destroyed two CR42s while the Blenheims, despite their relative ungainliness, accounted for another two of the nimble aircraft; a further two CR42s were seriously damaged by the big Blenheims and likely did not make it back to base. These successes induced Longmore to signal Collishaw and congratulate him "on the splendid work of the fighters this morning. The results are most encouraging."[18]

The Blenheim I bombers also devised innovative tactics to harass the Italians. In order to achieve surprise during an evening attack on the airfield at El Adem, three Blenheims of No. 113 Squadron approached the airfield from the sea. While still over water, the pilots put their aircraft into a dive and shut down their engines so they could approach the target area silently. The first the enemy knew of the attack was the sound of explosions on the airfield. This became a standard RAF tactic for attacks in the desert.[19] The success of this approach can be judged by the fact that the Italians quickly adopted it for their own raids. In their hands it was less successful as they pressed their attacks from a too high.[20]

The small but constant attrition caused by the British air raids kept the Italians off balance. Late on the afternoon of 28 June, Blenheims from Nos. 55 and 211 Squadrons attacked El Gubbi airfield outside Tobruk. The nine aircraft approached the target at low level from the northeast at about 5:30 P.M. The raid surprised the defenders, who only managed to fire a few shots at the last aircraft as it departed the area. A few minutes afterward, two aircraft approached the airfield from the west out of the setting sun. Thinking these were the British returning for a second run, Italian gunners were ready. The first aircraft was shot down as it approached, crashing and burning on the edge of the airfield. Unfortunately, this was an Italian SM79 flown by Air Marshal Italo Balbo, governor-general and commander-in-chief of the Italian armed forces in Libya. Balbo was greatly respected by both sides, and his loss was a huge blow to the Italian war effort. Longmore had met the marshal during an official visit to Rome in 1933, and upon hearing the news of Balbo's death, he ordered Collishaw to dispatch an aircraft to drop a note and wreath of condolence: "The British Royal Air Force expresses its sympathy in the death of General Balbo—a great leader and gallant aviator, personally known to me, whom fate has placed on the other side. [signed] Arthur Longmore."[21] Ironically, this plane was fired on as it overflew the funeral, but the antiaircraft gunners were unable to bring it down. Marshal Rodolfo Graziani replaced Balbo.[22]

Collishaw's offensive spirit during this period was not without its costs. The difficulty in obtaining replacements and spares from the United Kingdom meant that pilots, aircraft, parts, and equipment in theater were a finite resource. On 5 July nine Blenheim IVs of No. 113 Squadron "successfully bombed large enemy troop and M.T. [motor-transport] concentration" near Bardia. All the aircraft returned, but Flight Lt. A. M. Bentley was wounded and his observer, Flight Sgt. J. F. Taylor, was killed by ground fire.[23] Longmore was dismayed by this action and sent a message on 8 July to Collishaw: "Whilst fully appreciating the initiative and spirit shown by the squadrons operating under your command in the Western Desert, I must draw your immediate attention to the urgent necessity for conserving resources. Instances are still occurring when Blenheims are being used for low machine gun attack against defended camps and aerodromes. . . . I consider such operations unjustified having regard to our limited resources of which you are well aware."[24]

Collishaw replied that his pilots were acting in contravention of his orders, after which he took steps to prevent any reoccurrence. Of what has been termed a "reprimand" and "sharp criticism" from Longmore, Collishaw recommended that Bentley and a number of other pilots in his squadron be awarded an immediate Distinguished Flying Cross for "valour, courage and devotion to duty in air action with the enemy." This could be viewed as a contemptuous act in the face of criticism the air commodore felt was not warranted, but this type of action was not in his nature. Collishaw recorded the award of these commendations in the 202 Group Operations Record Book the day after the operation and two days before receiving Longmore's telegram.[25]

On 17 July Longmore sent him another cautionary message: "We are rapidly consuming available resources of all types of aircraft in the Command, and must in consequence exercise still greater economy in their employment." This was followed on 13 August by a message directed to the army, stating, "Owing to necessity of conserving R.A.F. resources in Middle East, [Longmore] directs that requests for bombing military targets will not be made to H.Q. 202 Group unless there are clear indications of enemy offensive action."[26] The RAF official history again termed the 17 July message to Collishaw a "rebuke" and mused that his "gay aggressiveness" stemming from his fighter-pilot roots led him to waste his men and aircraft recklessly in meaningless attacks.[27] This interpretation is not supported by an examination of 202 Group records between 5 and 17 July, which reveals that the vast majority of missions flown during this period consisted of reconnaissance flights and attacks against strategic targets such as harbors, airfields, and supply dumps. These raids were consistent with the priorities set out by Longmore at the start of the campaign. One Blenheim was shot down on 13 July while providing air cover to the Royal Navy, two more were lost to antiaircraft fire when attacking Italian airfields in the Tobruk–Gazala area, and two Bombays crashed due to unknown causes in the desert during night missions. Collishaw was conscious of the need to conserve his resources and was careful not to order wasteful missions.

Collishaw understood the problem of overextending resources in combat from his First World War experience. In a two-month span ending in July 1917, Naval Ten lost nineteen pilots during a period of intensive operations in which Collishaw thought the men had been pushed too hard.[28] He put these lessons into practice the following year when he exercised discretion during his time as commander of No. 203 Squadron, and he continued to understand this concept two decades later as demonstrated in his exercise report of November 1939.[29] Most of his interwar career was spent at the end of a long and tenuous supply line in various parts of the empire. He may at one time have been a brash, happy-go-lucky fighter pilot, but those days were long in his past. It is clear that Longmore was concerned that his subordinate might act too aggressively, commenting: "Collishaw's squadrons in the desert had one general complaint, they weren't getting enough work. It was one thing to decide on a policy of conserving resources, it was quite another to get Collishaw and his braves to take kindly to it."[30] But it is equally clear that the operations of 202 Group, and the losses it sustained, were unexceptional and fully in keeping with the directives issued by Middle East command. The documentary record shows that the losses suffered by the group during this period were not caused by reckless attacks on low-priority targets. Context is important, and a superficial reading of Longmore's cables to Collishaw could be interpreted as a response to reckless behavior. The absence of such acts, however, indicates that the cautions were of a preventative nature to remind him of the dangers of such unbridled action as driven by the slow rate of reinforcements, which were not expected to arrive in any significant numbers well into September. Longmore's messages were not reprimands intended to reign in a reckless or careless commander.[31]

Most histories of the air campaign in the Western Desert use this series of cables to question Collishaw's suitability for command and his inability to curb his aggressive tendencies.[32] If the air commodore was truly acting as a renegade and needlessly wasting pilots and aircraft, he would have been quickly removed from command. Yet the opposite happened. In October 1940 Longmore made a point of informing the chief of the Air Staff, Air Chief Marshal Sir Charles Portal: "On no account do I want to release Collishaw who is really doing magnificently in the Western Desert and maintaining a very high morale in the six squadrons there opposed to a vastly superior enemy air force. I cannot risk a change."[33] Longmore's support followed a cable he received from the Directorate of Personnel in London two days earlier that suggested that Collishaw should be sent back to Britain as "tour expired" to make way for Group Capt. J. W. B. Grigson, who was due for promotion to air commodore. Longmore immediately replied, "COLLISHAW doing splendidly with No. 202 Group in Western Desert and is very fit and well. I am very much against moving him from his most responsible post at this critical period in which the Italian offensive may be renewed at any time now. I will make suggestion re. GRIGSON's posting when he is promoted."[34] It is clear that Collishaw enjoyed Longmore's full confidence.

The support of naval operations was an important secondary role for 202 Group. The Royal Navy in the Mediterranean was focused on operations against the Italian navy but also devoted resources to the support of land operations in the Western Desert. These missions would assume greater importance once the British launched their offensive in December 1940, but earlier operations helped keep the Italians off balance. The first major coastal bombardment took place on 21 June. An international task force composed of the British cruisers *Orion* and *Neptune,* the Australian cruiser *Sydney,* and the French battleship *Lorraine,* supported by four destroyers, was ordered to shell the port of Bardia. This would be the last combined Anglo–French naval operation before the French surrender the next day. The targets were coastal batteries, the wireless station, ammunition dumps, and the power and pumping stations.[35]

The Naval Staff in Alexandria approached Longmore's headquarters on 20 June to request air support for the operation. Air Vice-Marshal Peter Drummond, Longmore's senior air staff officer, was initially against the mission as he thought the risk was not worth the return. He was soon convinced otherwise, and late on the afternoon of 20 June, a Blenheim of No. 113 Squadron photographed Tobruk harbor and the airfield at El Adem to provide up-to-date reconnaissance images of the target area. At dawn the next morning Collishaw launched a diversionary attack on Tobruk and provided fighter cover for the ships and naval spotting aircraft. The harbor and the El Adem airfield were bombed by fifteen Blenheims from Nos. 55 and 211 Squadrons; as a result of the air raid, heavy smoke was reported coming from a large ship in the harbor.[36]

Three Gladiators of No. 33 Squadron were sent to provide air cover to the naval spotting aircraft. Upon arriving in the area, the fighters immediately attacked an Italian aircraft found loitering in the vicinity of the fleet. Unfortunately, this turned out to be the Seagull amphibian spotter aircraft launched from HMAS *Sydney.* The pilot of the seaplane, Flight Lt. T. McBride Price, was able to coax his damaged aircraft to a safe landing at Mersa Matruh. The identification error was compounded when the *Lorraine* opened fire on the British fighters and drove them off. The results of the bombardment were judged to be effective, but it was noted that the loss of the spotting aircraft early in the mission had degraded the accuracy of the naval gunfire. The diversionary attacks on Tobruk were successful and prevented Italian air and naval forces from interfering. This joint operation would prove to be a model for future naval expeditions, but there were significant problems in coordination that still needed to be worked out.[37]

A second major naval bombardment was arranged for 17 August. Italian preparations for their upcoming offensive had become clear to the British, and the fleet was ordered to "assist the Army by causing as much damage as possible to the material and morale of the Italian military concentrations."[38] Large numbers of troops had been detected in the vicinity of Fort Capuzzo on the frontier, and numerous ammunition dumps and other supplies were located at Bardia. The bombardment force for this operation was considerably stronger than the previous sortie, consisting of the battleships *Warspite, Ramillies,* and *Malaya;* the heavy cruiser *Kent;* and twelve destroyers, all covered by a strong fighter screen supplied by Nos. 80 and 112 Squadrons and a section of the Fleet Air Arm. The mission was conducted according to plans, and good concentrations were observed to fall in the target areas.[39] Admiral Cunningham, commander-in-chief of the Mediterranean Fleet, recalled that the detailed planning with the RAF had resulted in everything going according to plan. He said that watching the deliberate bombardment was "a satisfactory spectacle and we hoped had good results."[40] Aerial reconnaissance later revealed that Capuzzo and the southern defenses of Bardia had been well hit, but the town itself escaped serious damage.[41]

There was no significant opposition from coastal batteries or the Italian air force during the bombardment, which lasted from 6:58 to 7:20 A.M. The Italian air force made an appearance over the ships during the return voyage to Alexandria. At approximately 9:45 A.M. an Italian Cant Z.501 flying boat was shot down as it shadowed the vessels. Less than an hour later, the first SM79s found the fleet. The initial attacks were driven off by No. 112 Squadron Gladiators. Later attacks managed to penetrate the fighter screen, but the bombing was inaccurate.[42]

The Italian air force suffered heavy losses in their attempt to strike the British warships. Of the twenty-five bomber sorties, three enemy aircraft were confirmed destroyed, and at least eight others were severely damaged but made it back to base. The British suffered no losses. The lessons learned in June were clearly incorporated in the plan for this new operation. Group Captain Brown went to sea aboard *Warspite* alongside Admiral Cunningham to facilitate coordination between the navy and the air force. There was no case of mistaken identity between the naval aircraft, the fleet, and the RAF fighters. Cunningham signaled Longmore afterward that success on the day was due in great measure to the support provided by the RAF.[43]

The Royal Navy also requested aircraft of 202 Group to support purely naval operations. At the end of August, naval reinforcements were dispatched from Gibraltar to Alexandria by way of Malta to make the first complete passage of the Mediterranean since Italy entered the war. This operation was fraught with danger as Italy possessed strong surface and submarine units as well as significant air forces that could menace the warships. On 30 August Admiral Cunningham sortied his fleet, including the battleships *Warspite* and *Malaya* and the aircraft carrier *Eagle,* from Alexandria to meet the reinforcements. Collishaw issued a warning order that same day for his squadrons to be at a "high state of readiness" on the thirty-first. Collishaw's Blenheim squadrons (Nos. 55, 113, and 211) mounted a major effort and flew fifty-five sorties directed at the main Italian landing grounds in Cyrenaica (Timimi, Tobruk, Gazala, Bardia, Derna, and the seaplane base at Derna). The Blenheims were dispatched in pairs throughout the day, and these "fumigation" attacks (that is, to keep the pests down) prevented Italian bombers from interfering with the fleet, which was within easy reach of their aerodromes, and distracted the enemy fighters. Three RAF fighter squadrons (Nos. 33, 80, and 112) also supported the operation.[44]

The RAF and the Royal Navy both considered the air-cover mission a success as no African-based Italian aircraft interfered with the fleet and the British lost only one aircraft, which crash landed due to apparent engine failure. Collishaw conveyed his appreciation to his squadrons at the end of the day: "Excellent results obtained during today's operations. A very important British convoy was protected by your attacks against E.A. [enemy aircraft] attention. THANK YOU."[45] Five days later Collishaw's warplanes supported Cunningham's ships during their return passage from Malta to Alexandria. A similar pattern of "fumigation" operations was mounted by the RAF, and no Italian air attacks from Cyrenaica developed. But these missions on 4 September were more costly for the RAF as two Blenheims were shot down and some of their crews, including Squadron Leader A. R. G. Bax, the commander of No. 211 Squadron, were taken prisoner. The pilot of a third Blenheim was killed during a clash with Italian fighters, but the navigator was able to fly the aircraft back to base.[46]

Interdiction missions were again carried out on 18 September to protect the disabled cruiser *Kent,* which had been torpedoed during a moonlight attack by Italian aircraft as it was taking up position to bombard Bardia. The disabled vessel required a substantial effort by British destroyers to tow it back to Alexandria. The ships were extremely vulnerable to air attacks during this period, so Cunningham requested RAF cover. Collishaw diverted his aircraft from attacks on Italian army positions to concentrate on suppressing the Regia Aeronautica. Blenheims of Nos. 55, 113, and 211 Squadrons were directed to attack landing grounds between Bardia and Tobruk, while fighters from Nos. 30, 80, 112, and 274 Squadrons were sent to provide air cover for the immobilized cruiser. Additional aircraft were dispatched on reconnaissance missions over the Mediterranean to search for a reported enemy submarine that posed a threat to the rescue mission. RAF support helped ensure that no significant Italian attacks against *Kent* developed during the two days it took for the cruiser to reach the safety of Alexandria.[47]

Mussolini, "the most impatient of all Italians," was keen to proceed with the war.[48] Marshal Pietro Badoglio, the Italian chief of the General Staff, urged caution, but Il Duce believed that British leadership in the desert was poor and a "swift Italian drive on Suez" had a good prospect of success. Before his death at the end of June, Air Marshal Balbo had received permission from Mussolini to attack at any time but delayed as he built up his forces.[49]

The hesitations continued when Marshal Graziani assumed command of the Italian military in Libya. He continued preparations for an offensive but, though briefed that the situation was very much in Italy's favor, still did not attack. The greatest threat to Libya came from the French to the west in Tunisia; the British were correctly viewed as presenting a very small offensive threat. The fall of France and the signing of the Franco-Italian armistice on 24 June removed the menace in Tunisia, but it still took the Italians time to reorient their forces to the east to confront the British. Army leadership saw no need for haste as their forces greatly outnumbered the British both in the air and on the ground, and the Regia Marina was numerically superior to the Mediterranean Fleet. The Italian military believed it was just a matter of time until the British were completely thrown out of North Africa. Badoglio even stated that an invasion of Egypt would be "easy and foolproof" now that France was not a threat.[50]

Graziani was in no rush to attack, "deploying all his ingenuity" to convince Rome that such an operation was impractical.[51] Based on assessments by his generals, he argued that time was required to prepare for the offensive, which could not be launched until the end of October at the earliest. Mussolini was not prepared to wait that long and persuaded him that quicker action was necessary. In mid-August Graziani ordered a limited advance on Sidi Barrani rather than the expected march on Alexandria. This proposal was accepted by Mussolini and the marshal's generals and scheduled for mid-September.[52]

Graziani's commitment to the offensive was severely shaken on the night of 31 August, when the RAF "thoroughly and repeatedly" bombed his headquarters in Tobruk.[53] For two and a half hours, the Italian commander was trapped in an underground shelter and endured his first air attack. He considered the experience to be "one of the most dangerous in my life," and as soon as the aircraft left, he relocated his headquarters farther to the rear in Cirene, where deep tombs carved out by the ancient Greeks offered superior protection.[54] Graziani blamed the attacks on espionage and betrayal, but the air raids were launched by 202 Group to screen the passage of Cunningham's fleet.[55]

The British had read the signs pointing to the Italian offensive for weeks. Lieutenant General O'Connor, in consultation with Generals Wavell and Wilson, pulled his units back from the frontier and left only small screening forces to slow an enemy advance. The main British defensive position was organized at Mersa Matruh, the end of the rail line from the Nile. O'Connor planned to stop any Italian invasion on this line and use Matruh as a jumping-off point for his counteroffensive. In response to reports that enemy formations were massing, Collishaw ordered his bomber squadrons, Nos. 55, 113, and 211, to step up their raids. On 9 September enemy airfields, concentrations of transportation, and supply dumps were targeted. The largest attack, composed of twenty-one aircraft, was made on Tobruk's El Adem aerodrome. Collishaw reported:

> When the enemy's concentration for an offensive was apparent in the forward area . . . , vigorous R.A.F. action was taken to retain local air superiority and to prevent the enemy from using Apollonia, Derna, Gazala, Tobruk, Bardia and Sollum as sea bases. Also to hamper the enemy in his use of Benghazi. Successful heavy air attacks were delivered against the enemy's principal air bases at Benina and a number of hangars full with aircraft were destroyed while a large number of aircraft were destroyed on the ground.[56]

The scale of these attacks was never large, but the constant raids over a wide area allowed the RAF to force the Regia Aeronautica to cede the initiative and mount standing fighter patrols over a large region. Collishaw credited this factor with the Italian loss of air superiority and ultimately caused "the final breakdown of the Italian fighter force in Cyrenaica."[57]

The offensive was launched on 13 September, following a spectacular artillery barrage at the Libyan–Egyptian frontier. Graziani moved five divisions into Egypt, sustaining moderately heavy casualties from mines and harassing artillery fire as they pressed along a predictable route. The British held the frontier with weak forces and made way as the Italians advanced. Inexplicably, Graziani halted his offensive at Sidi Barrani, a mere fifty miles from the Libyan border and one hundred miles short of the main British defensive position at Mersa Matruh. The Italians then proceeded to build large fortified camps, which they seemed to intend to use as the jumping-off point for their final assault on Egypt. But the British had no intention of letting the Italians maintain the initiative.[58]

A German history of the campaign calls this limited offensive "one of Italy's most grievous errors in the Second World War."[59] Graziani accomplished little to improve the dispositions of his forces by advancing to Sidi Barrani while greatly complicating his supply situation. The British had systematically destroyed buildings, roads, and water supplies during their retreat, and the Italians had to build fortifications in the empty desert and transport all their supplies over poor roads. The limited advance into Egypt did not disturb the defensive preparations of the British Army, but it did have a significant influence on the conduct of RAF operations. For the British, the move strengthened the defensive posture of the army by relieving O'Connor of the need to garrison the frontier.[60]

The RAF was negatively affected by the loss of its forward airfields. Fighters were restricted by over a hundred miles in the distance they could fly to provide support for bombing raids, and tactical-reconnaissance missions suffered the same loss of range. Collishaw's bombers had made good use of the advanced aerodromes to refuel for distant strikes, meaning Benghazi, the main Italian port in Cyrenaica, was left at the extreme range of his Blenheims. Loss of the airfields also restricted support for naval operations, limiting the ability of the Blenheims to conduct harassing missions and denying ships bombarding Bardia and Sidi Barrani the benefit of fighter cover. Longmore's strategic flexibility also diminished with the inability to transfer Hurricanes between the desert and Malta. Reinforcing Hurricanes could previously make the long overwater journey with the addition of long-range fuel tanks, but this became impossible. These benefits of location subsequently accrued to the Italians and now also reduced warning times for raids on Alexandria.[61]

Air Vice-Marshal Drummond told a gathering of the Royal United Services Institute in London in 1943 that "the 'motif' of our operations in the Middle East would be a battle for aerodromes. Repeatedly throughout the campaign this truth was driven home. Whoever held the airfields on the shores of the Mediterranean could pass his own ships through that sea with reasonable safety, and could forbid the route to the ships of the enemy."[62] Air power could not win the campaign on its own, but without control of the skies, success would be difficult, if not impossible, to achieve.

The continued shortage of aircraft available to Collishaw saw him use unconventional tactics in order to strike at the Italians. Shortly after the offensive began, a member of his command discovered a large stock of old 20-pound antipersonnel bombs in a rear depot. According to Collishaw, "they were quite obsolete and doubtless by all the regulations should have been properly disposed of as being unsafe to handle."[63] The only possible method of employing these bombs was to load them aboard a Bombay, from which they would be fused and deployed individually by the crew. Thus was born the legend of "Bessie the Bombing Bitch."[64]

The first operational use of these bombs was made on the night of 19–20 September 1940, when two Bombays from No. 216 Squadron based at Heliopolis attacked the forward camps at Sidi Barrani. The 202 Group Operations Record Book recorded that the aircraft released more than three hundred "20 lb. bombs in to the area where 1200 M.T. [motor transports] were grouped at BARRANI. Sustained bombing continued for 4 hours. Important physical and moral[e] results bound to accrue from our tactics."[65]

The attack was repeated the next night, when No. 216 Squadron again attacked two Italian defended positions four miles south of Sidi Barrani. The area was observed to contain more than six hundred vehicles, and the attack was timed to correspond with a raid by 7th Armoured Division. The process to drop the bombs was delicate. Each weapon had to be individually fused by a crewman in the Bombay before being passed to another member to toss out the open door of the aircraft. Collishaw estimated that the bombs could be dropped at a rate of about one per minute. The scale and intensity of these attacks never caused substantial damage to the enemy, but it had a significant harassment factor. Collishaw recognized this but thought the morale effect was significant:

> Whether these bombs ever actually hurt anyone on the ground I do not know but we had ample evidence that their use lowered the morale amongst the Italian troops and increased the demands for aerial protection. These raids, despite their near-comedic aspect, called for much fortitude and determination on the part of our crews. Not only did they have to expose themselves to continued anti-aircraft fire for lengthy periods and possible interception by enemy fighters, but there was always the possibility that one of the bombs would explode in the aircraft.[66]

This type of small-scale attack was common for 202 Group in the period following the Italian advance into Egypt. What was lacked in numbers was made up in variety. Raids by small numbers of aircraft were directed at a multitude of Italian targets: harbors, airfields, fortified camps, and the lines of communications. In the period from 13 September to 9 December 1940, Collishaw's aircraft conducted ninety-eight sorties against ports and bases, fifty-two against airfields, and fifty-eight against fortified camps and the lines of communications.[67] A focus on the main supply ports in Cyrenaica compelled the Italians to devote a large proportion of their fighter force to mount standing defensive patrols. This reduced the offensive potential of the Regia Aeronautica so that by October it was largely reduced to sending single aircraft on low-level raids; only three of twenty raids during this period were reported to have caused minimal damage to British targets.[68] The success of the RAF attacks on the Cyrenaican ports, especially Tobruk, forced the Italians to disembark many of their tanks and other armored vehicles at Benghazi and drive them to the front, a distance of nearly 435 miles. This long trek had a significant effect on the mechanical reliability of the Italian armor and contributed to the high rate of breakdowns suffered during the British counteroffensive, which commenced in December.[69]

The strategic situation in the Middle East was a matter of grave concern for the British following the defeat of France and the Italian declaration of war. General Wavell, responsible for a large and vulnerable area that included the Mediterranean Sea, Egypt, the Suez Canal, the Middle East, and East Africa, was desperately short of troops to meet all the demands. He was called back to England to meet with Churchill and the Ministerial Committee on Military Policy in the Middle East in early August to discuss the state of affairs.[70] The exchange resulted in reinforcements, including aircraft, being dispatched to the Middle East. It would take time for this help to arrive, though, as the direct route through the Mediterranean was too risky for large convoys. As a result, most of the troops and equipment were shipped around the Cape of Good Hope, while aircraft were landed at Takoradi in the Gold Coast to be assembled and flown across the continent to Egypt. Three armored regiments along with other reinforcements arrived by the end of September and were ready for action by the middle of October. Aircraft arrived in Egypt at a rate of thirty-six Blenheims, six Wellingtons, and eighteen Hurricanes per month, along with a number of other deliveries, including an additional twenty-four Hurricanes transported by the carrier HMS *Argus* and twelve of thirty-six Hurricanes for the South African Air Force.[71]

In early October Anthony Eden, the secretary of state for war, visited the Middle East to investigate the needs of commanders there. He met with Wavell and Wilson for three hours on the morning of 15 October and was fully briefed on the situation in Egypt.[72] Reinforcements had brought the army up to a strength that would check any further Italian advances toward Alexandria, and expected deliveries in the near future would prepare the army for its counteroffensive. The only caveat was that a successful defense was contingent on the availability of adequate air support. The RAF was having great success in harassing the enemy, but it was doubted that its units had sufficient strength to support the counteroffensive. Wavell was confident that the threat from the Italian army had been contained, but he was worried about the potential of the Italian air force. Intelligence estimated that seven hundred aircraft were deployed in Libya and that this number could be rapidly increased by reinforcements from Italy. Longmore believed that three additional RAF fighter squadrons were needed in the desert to protect the army from air attack, a deficiency that led Wavell to consider postponing the offensive indefinitely. Eden afterward reported to Churchill and Gen. Sir John Dill, the chief of the Imperial General Staff:

> General Wilson's ability to defeat the enemy in any attack that he may make
> in the near future is dependent entirely upon adequate air support. Liaison

between Army and Air Force is excellent and R.A.F. are giving support, for which no praise can be too high, within their existing limited resources. But both C.-in-C. [Wavell] and A.O.C.-in-C. [Longmore] are emphatic that present strength of Air Force in Middle East does not permit of that support being given to the Army in battle which is essential for success. Reinforcement of the R.A.F. is the pressing need of the hour here and will, I am convinced, prove to be the decisive factor.[73]

Eden argued that while steps had been taken to increase the numbers of guns and tanks, it was imperative that the air force be strengthened as well. The Chiefs of Staff Committee agreed with this assessment and quickly directed the Air Ministry to send the reinforcements. This personal intervention by Eden, based on his firsthand knowledge of the situation, was essential in securing the aircraft needed to allow the planned counteroffensive in Egypt to proceed on schedule.[74]

The plan for the air reinforcement of the Middle East was made two days after Eden's telegram. Longmore requested three additional fighter squadrons, and the Air Ministry agreed to send them, but it would take time for these new units to arrive. In the short term Longmore's command was strengthened by replacing obsolescent types with modern aircraft as well as by expanding the establishment of the two heavy- and twelve medium-bomber squadrons from twelve to sixteen aircraft each. To make this happen, the monthly quota of aircraft was raised to forty-eight Blenheims and twenty-four Hurricanes, while twenty-three Wellingtons would be flown out in October. A further step was the allocation of American aircraft (149 Glenn Martin bombers and 227 Mohawk fighters) previously destined for the French air force. Unfortunately, the U.S. bombers would not arrive in sufficient quantities until early 1941, while the American fighters were found to be defective and were relegated to a training role.[75]

In mid-October Longmore took the opportunity to write the newly appointed chief of the Air Staff, Air Chief Marshal Portal, to provide him with a "brief summary of the situation out here."[76] The report filled six-and-a-half pages of foolscap, which gives some indication of the complexity and diversity of his command. Longmore went into considerable detail regarding the state of the defenses in the Western Desert, Egypt, Sudan, Aden, Kenya, Palestine, Malta, and Iraq as well as the situation in Italian East Africa. Overall, he was satisfied with his various commands, though noting some areas of friction. The political situation in Egypt required constant attention. He stated that even though the king of Egypt and his entourage were pro-Italian, the government was supportive of the British effort, yet military support could not be expected in the event of an Italian invasion. Relations with the Royal Navy were difficult.

Admiral Cunningham spent much of his time at sea, which was great for facilitating naval command but made liaison with the other services difficult. Despite the important support provided by 202 Group for naval operations off the North African coast, Cunningham was very critical of the overall amount of support provided by the RAF in the Mediterranean, especially at Malta.[77]

Relations with the army were much better, though Longmore was concerned that Wavell "still hankers" for air units to be placed directly under army operational control. But "it is quite obvious that we cannot afford such luxuries and that what we've got must be used in the common interest, Navy, Army and Air, and not uneconomically locked up for one particular Service."[78] Longmore's chief fear was that Italian air strength in Libya would overwhelm Collishaw's numerically smaller force.

The final page of this summary concerned personnel issues in the Middle East. Longmore was anxious about who would take over his command if he became a casualty. He had requested the appointment of a second in command from the Air Ministry in June and again in August, but nothing had yet happened.[79] A dearth of surplus officers in his command left him few options to replace casualties. His first choice as deputy would be Air Vice-Marshal Sir Ranald Reid, the air officer commanding British forces in Aden. Air Commodore Sir John D'Albiac would then be sent from Palestine to Aden, and Group Capt. J. W. B. Grigson, Collishaw's senior air staff officer at 202 Group, would go to Palestine. As discussed earlier, Longmore took this opportunity to inform Portal that Collishaw was one of the few untouchables in his command.[80]

The period following the Italian declaration of war had the potential to be disastrous for the small British army in Egypt. Marshal Graziani was stronger on the ground and in the air, but his reluctance to attack ceded the advantage to the British. The Royal Navy's Mediterranean Fleet continued to influence matters at sea, while the Regia Marina was hesitant to offer a challenge. In the air the RAF launched an interdiction campaign against enemy ports and airfields in Libya. Though small in scale, this effort took the initiative away from the Italians, who responded by deploying their aircraft in a defensive role that was largely ineffective and wasteful of resources. The use of the air umbrella also came with a significant opportunity cost for the Italians by limiting their ability to conduct offensive air operations of their own. The limited offensive launched by Graziani in September may have complied with Mussolini's orders, but it did nothing to improve his army's tactical position in the Western Desert.

During this period the RAF played a significant role in projecting British strength when the reality was not quite so robust. Royal Navy operations to bombard Italian coastal positions received important air support to prevent interference from the Regia Aeronautica and to facilitate air observation for naval gunfire. Perhaps most importantly, early difficulties in coordination were corrected in later operations by closer liaison between the two services. The aerial-interdiction campaign conducted by 202 Group would be small by the standards established later in the war, but it was effective. Collishaw enjoyed Longmore's full confidence and was considered the only "untouchable" during the reorganization of RAF leadership in the Middle East just before the launch of the British counteroffensive.

Postwar histories have focused on two telegrams sent to Collishaw by Longmore that appeared to reprimand the First World War ace for being too aggressive and wasteful of his scarce resources. This criticism has become one of the key pillars in assessments of Collishaw's command ability. The reality of the situation was quite different. Before the start of the war, Collishaw showed a keen awareness of the finite resources at his command and knew that pilots and aircraft could not be wasted. An examination of operations conducted by 202 Group does not demonstrate a wasteful use of resources. It is true that Collishaw was an aggressive commander in the Western Desert, but this was dictated by the nature of the conflict rather than any inherent bias of his fighter-pilot background. This characterization does Collishaw a great disservice. It is true that he was one of the leading aces during the First World War, but he was not recklessly aggressive in this role. If he had been, it is likely his name would be remembered along with the countless other aerial pioneers who did not survive the war. Staff College and years of command at very senior levels combined with operational experience in various theaters had imbued him with a rational understanding of his responsibilities and the limits of his resources. Collishaw's conduct of the early air campaign reflected the realities of the situation. He adopted offensive tactics to counter a numerically superior enemy but ensured that no exceptional risks were taken; the overall low RAF loss rate during this period confirms the viability of these actions.

CHAPTER 4

OPERATION COMPASS, PART I

THE BATTLE OF THE CAMPS AND BARDIA

Planning for Operation Compass, the first British offensive in the desert, started in the aftermath of the Italian advance in September. General Wavell ordered Lieutenant Generals Wilson and O'Connor to prepare a counteroffensive to be launched once the enemy reached Mersa Matruh. When the Italians stopped short and proceeded to build camps around Sidi Barrani, Wavell recalled: "I began to consider the possibility of an early offensive action. The enemy's defensive arrangements, which I studied daily on a map fixed to the wall facing my desk, seemed to me to be thoroughly faulty. He was spread over a wide front in a series of fortified camps, which were not mutually supporting and separated by wide distances."[1] The British attack would take advantage of this weakness by exploiting one of these gaps to loop around behind the line of camps and attack from the west. In the period leading up to the campaign, O'Connor's forces actively patrolled the gap to prevent the establishment of any defenses in that sector.

The RAF planned to support the offensive with all of its available resources. Longmore ordered Collishaw to use his Hurricanes for low-level attacks on the enemy lines of communications once the attack began and, when in range, also to use Hurricanes for low-level attacks on the Italian airfields. This would keep the Italian fighters in a defensive role and prevent aerial attacks on British troops. Aside from these instructions, Collishaw was left free to work with O'Connor to plan the air portion of the campaign.[2]

Operation Compass was the first major British offensive of the war. It was conceived and planned in a short time period, and little was committed to paper to preserve its secrecy. Lieutenant General O'Connor envisioned a limited counterattack to recover the Egyptian territory lost to the Italians in September. The immediate objectives were the fortified camps south of Sidi Barrani along with the town itself. He had at his disposal only two divisions—4th Indian and 7th Armoured—along with some other assorted units.[3]

This limited five-day operation was divided into three stages. The first phase would see the 4th Indian Division, supported by the 7th Royal Tank Regiment, move through the fifteen-mile-wide Nibeiwa–Rabia gap and sequentially attack the fortified camps at Nibeiwa, Tummar East, and Point 90. This main attack would be supported by 7th Armoured Division, which would prevent interventions from either Buq Buq or Sofafi, while Selby Force, the British garrison from Mersa Matruh, would advance along the coast to fix the Italian garrison in Maktila. In the second phase of the operation, 4th Indian Division would capture Sidi Barrani, while in the final stage 7th Armoured Division would attack either the remaining Italian camps around Sofafi or complete the liberation of Egypt by advancing to Sollum. Air support was to be provided by Collishaw's 202 Group, and elements of the Royal Navy would participate by shelling coastal towns and fortifications held by the Italians.[4]

In the period following the Italian advance into Egypt, RAF attacks were designed to interfere with the enemy's ability to sustain and continue offensive operations. Air raids were made on Bardia, Tobruk, Derna, and Benghazi to make the ports unusable; coastal shipping was interdicted; and Italian infrastructure such as camps, supply depots, and airfields were targeted. The scale of these attacks increased in the days leading up to Compass. The small number of available fighters flew offensive sweeps to prevent Italian air reconnaissance from discovering the approach march as well as to keep the Regia Aeronautica on the defensive. The navy supported the effort by bombarding enemy camps.[5]

The size of Collishaw's command had not changed significantly since the Italian entry into the war, but it had become more powerful. Older, obsolescent aircraft were replaced by newer types that now gave the British a qualitative advantage. In June 1940 Collishaw commanded nine squadrons. On the eve of Operation Compass, his establishment had increased to ten squadrons, according to most accounts, though this included a number of partial units.[6] Some Gloster Gladiators remained, but two squadrons of Hurricanes had been added. The Hurricane I had been one of the victors of the Battle of Britain, but it was well on its way to obsolescence in the skies of Western Europe. In the Western Desert in December 1940, however, it was the fastest, most powerfully armed fighter and had no peer. The strike component of 202 Group had also been upgraded. The Blenheim I was being phased out for the Blenheim IV. This new variant boasted a longer range and greater bombload while increasing crew survivability with cabin armor and more defensive machine guns. The army-support squadrons had started to trade their Lysanders, which made excellent reconnaissance platforms but were too vulnerable to enemy fighters and antiaircraft defenses, for Hurricanes. The biggest change in the offensive power of the RAF was the addition of three heavy-bomber squadrons of Vickers Wellingtons.[7] These squadrons remained under the administration of Longmore but were under the operational control of Collishaw.[8] The range and striking power of the Wellington was significantly

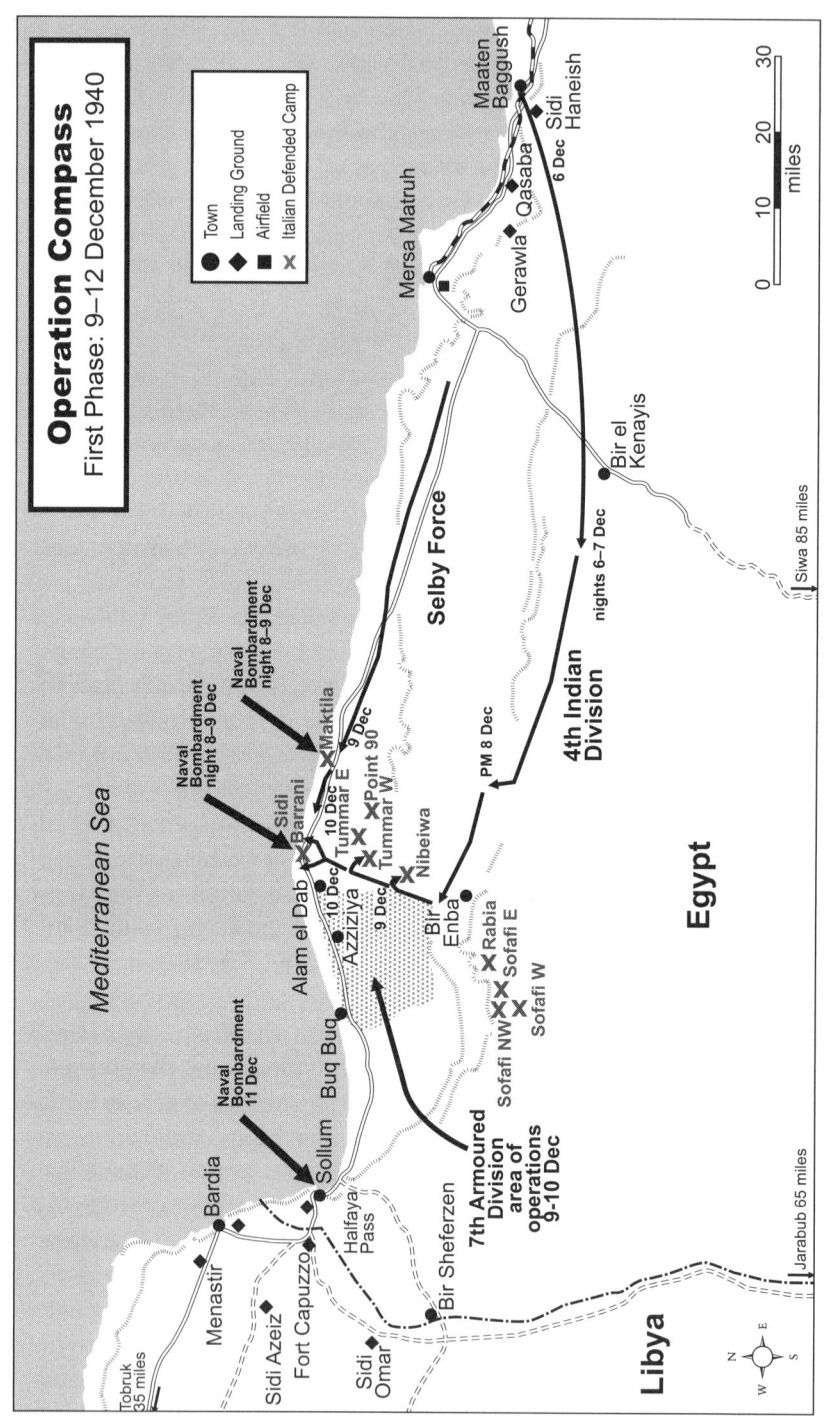

Operation Compass
First Phase: 9–12 December 1940

Legend:
- ● Town
- ◆ Landing Ground
- ■ Airfield
- ✕ Italian Defended Camp

Mediterranean Sea

Naval Bombardment night 8–9 Dec

Naval Bombardment night 8–9 Dec

Naval Bombardment night 8–9 Dec

Naval Bombardment 11 Dec

Maaten Baggush

6 Dec Sidi Haneish

Gerawla Qasaba

Mersa Matruh

Bir el Kenayis

Siwa 85 miles

nights 6–7 Dec

4th Indian Division

PM 8 Dec

Selby Force

Egypt

Maktila

Point 90

9 Dec

Tummar E

Tummar W

10 Dec

Sidi Barrani

Nibeiwa

Alam el Dab

10 Dec

Azziziya

9 Dec

Bir Enba

Rabia

Sofafi E

Sofafi W

Sofafi NW

Buq Buq

Sollum

Halfaya Pass

Bir Sheferzen

7th Armoured Division area of operations 9–10 Dec

Jarabub 65 miles

Bardia

Menastir

Sidi Azeiz

Fort Capuzzo

Sidi Omar

Tobruk 35 miles

Libya

N E S W

miles
0 10 20 30

Operation Compass, First Phase: 9–12 December 1940. Map by Mike Bechthold. Copyright © 2017 by the University of Oklahoma Press.

more than the Blenheim and allowed the British to hit Italian ports and air-fields farther afield.[9]

This qualitative increase in Collishaw's command would be essential once Operation Compass began as the Italians boasted a significantly larger air force that could be rapidly reinforced across the Mediterranean. At the start of the campaign, Collishaw's force stood at 48 fighters and 116 bombers compared to 191 fighters and 140 bombers available to the Italians.[10]

While Operation Compass was the main effort of British forces in the Middle East, it was not the only active front. Air Chief Marshal Longmore's RAF Middle East command conducted operations against the Italians in the Sudan and East Africa, and his squadrons based in Aden and Malta were also engaged. The main diversion from Egypt was Greece. Relations between Italy and Greece deteriorated in the fall of 1940, and on 28 October Mussolini launched a pre-emptive invasion of the neighboring country. Britain pledged to support the Greeks, and the only source of troops and squadrons to provide immediate aid was Egypt. Longmore did his best to balance the competing demands placed on his forces. On 31 October he dispatched No. 30 Squadron (Blenheim fighters and bombers) to Greece, an action applauded by Churchill as a very bold and wise decision, but the transfer was "the thin edge of a substantial wedge."[11] The British chiefs of staff subsequently directed the air chief marshal to send three additional Blenheim squadrons and two Gladiator squadrons; these arrived in Greece by mid-November.[12] Longmore was not pleased with these moves, and he expressed his misgivings to London. The loss of these squadrons was a sig-nificant drain on his resources, but there were larger issues at play. An imme-diate result of these moves was to delay the start of Operation Compass from November to the end of the first week of December. This was not the last time that affairs in Greece would negatively affect the conduct of operations in the Western Desert.[13]

In the week leading up to the campaign, the RAF launched a variety of pre-paratory missions. Despite poor weather, Collishaw continued to send small numbers of aircraft to attack a wide range of Italian targets. The intent was to maintain the initiative and keep enemy fighters on the defensive. Starting on 4 December with an attack on Tobruk's El Adem airfields, the raids increased in scale. The Wellington squadrons based in Egypt had operated primarily in support of the Greek campaign during November, but starting on 7 December, two days before the start of Compass, they were directed against Italian air-fields in Libya. On that same day Wellingtons from No. 148 Squadron based in Malta attacked airfields near Tripoli. The Italians were caught by surprise, and the low-level strikes claimed twenty-nine aircraft destroyed or damaged on the ground. There were no British losses, and only two Wellingtons were damaged by Italian fighters, which scrambled late and chased the bombers over the Mediterranean.[14] The next night, on the eve of the counteroffensive, the airfield raids continued. At dusk twelve Blenheims attacked Benina airfield at Benghazi, then a further twenty-nine Blenheims and Wellingtons based in Egypt repeated the strikes before dawn. The British claimed ten Italian aircraft destroyed on the ground.[15] Longmore believed that these raids "had considerable effect in reducing the scale of the [Italian air] attack at the beginning of the British Offensive."[16]

Collishaw's three fighter squadrons flew patrols over the British concentration areas to prevent interference and discovery by the Italians. The day before the start of the offensive was a vulnerable period for O'Connor's forces as they gathered in the desert. Surprise was essential, and it would only take one Italian reconnaissance aircraft to discover the force. On the night before the attack, British air forces conducted a number of diversionary operations. RAF Blenheims and Fleet Air Arm Swordfish worked with HMS *Terror* and *Aphis* to bombard the Italian camp at Maktila and with HMS *Ladybird* to bombard Sidi Barrani. Collishaw again used his Bombays and their small bombs to attack the Italian camps at Sidi Barrani and Bardia, with the intention of hindering the dispatch of reinforcements. The four older aircraft each carried six hundred 20-pound bombs. As an added security measure, a loud, lumbering Bombay was flown over British lines to drown out the sounds being made by the advancing columns. As a result of these efforts, there were virtually no Italian air attacks prior to the commencement of Compass on 9 December, and the few strikes that did occur caused no significant damage.[17]

One of the more remarkable aspects of Operation Compass was the ability of the Western Desert Force to set up two large, undefended supply points, cross a wide expanse of open desert, and arrive on the doorstep of the Italian camps without detection. The British had taken great care to establish two field-supply points in the desert forty miles west of Mersa Matruh. Only a thin screen of British forces lay between them and the Italians, and their discovery or destruction would have spoiled the counteroffensive. On 6 December the 4th Indian Division departed from Maaten Baggush and halted near Bir Kenayis for thirty-six hours. On the morning on 8 December, the formation crossed sixty miles of desert and arrived at a point about fifteen miles from Nibeiwa before dusk.[18]

Nevertheless, preparations for the offensive were detected by the Italians. Air activity was minimal during the approach march on 7–8 December, and "only one Italian aircraft was seen, at about midday [on the eighth], but nothing occurred to suggest that it had observed anything unusual."[19] The war diary of the 4th Indian Divisional Artillery concurred with this observation, but the after-action report of the Western Desert Force reported, "during the approach march and assembly stages on 7th and 8th December, Italian aircraft were in the air above units and formations, both when halted and on the move, yet the subsequent complete surprise of the enemy suggests that his suspicions were not aroused."[20] This was the important point. The British movements in the desert were observed, but no alarm was raised the enemy.

Italian sources also reveal that their air force had discovered and reported the British presence in the desert. Marshal Graziani received a number of reports of unusual British activity at the beginning of December, but he interpreted these moves as preparations to counter the renewed offensive that he planned. Other sources, including information from captured prisoners, indicated that a British offensive could be expected in the near future. Two factors contributed to the Italian intelligence failure: their inability to make sense of the various intelligence sources, and the disruption of reconnaissance flights by the RAF. While the British did not achieve operational surprise, they were able to maintain tactical surprise. Though some Italian aircraft reported on the preparations, additional reconnaissance flights were prevented from completing their missions, which otherwise might have provided the necessary corroborating evidence of the impending attack.[21]

In contrast, the British received significant intelligence prior to their attack. No. 208 Squadron, the army-cooperation squadron assigned to work with the Western Desert Force, conducted extensive reconnaissance of the Italian camps in the weeks leading up to the commencement of Compass. Air photos showed the position of the camps, the layout of their defenses, and the progression of construction as the Italians improved the quality of their defensive works. These images were invaluable during the planning for the offensive. Lieutenant General O'Connor remarked that due to the short planning period for the operation as well as the need to preserve security, "no continuous close reconnaissance of the objective was possible, [so] information would be restricted to what could be supplied by aerial photography, and specially selected officers' patrols lying out for [a] period of at least 24 hours."[22]

The first objective for the 4th Indian Division was the camp at Nibeiwa. As the base for the Maletti Group, the main Italian armored force, it was the strongest of the defended camps. Lt. Col. A. Anderson, commanding officer of the 2nd Battalion, Queen's Own Cameron Highlanders, the first group of infantry to follow the tanks into Nibeiwa, described the post as

> roughly rectangular in shape, and covered an area of approximately 2,400 by 1,800 yards. The defence perimeter was complete all the way round except for a small gap in the north-west corner, and built up in the form of a wall with sangars. The absence of loose rock probably accounted for the shortage

of "Dragons' Teeth" around the camp. A special type of anti-tank obstacle had been constructed on the eastern and southern faces. Anti-tank minefields were laid all around the camp except in the north-western face. There were no wire obstacles. Machine gun and anti-tank gun emplacements were built in every twenty-five yards of perimeter, about a hundred and fifty in all—twice as many emplacements as any other camp possessed. The centre of the camp was a mass of earthworks with a few tents and about 250 vehicles widely dispersed.[23]

The camp's chief weakness was first discovered in the air photos: a supply route through the mine fields led into the northwest corner. A British patrol confirmed the unmined entrance twenty-four hours before the commencement of Compass. Shortly after sunset on 8 December, the 11th Indian Infantry Brigade, with the 7th Royal Tank Regiment (7th RTR) in support, set out on the final march to capture Nibeiwa camp. As this force advanced, the Italian garrison was distracted by Bombays from No. 216 Squadron, which harassed the camp with small bombs. The ground assault commenced at 5:00 A.M., when an Indian detachment opened fire on the camp from the east. The Italians thought this to be a small-scale raid and were not overly concerned until the seventy-two guns of the 4th Indian Divisional Artillery opened fire at 7:15 A.M. The barrage was timed to cover the main attack from the west by forty-eight Matilda tanks of the 7th RTR.[24]

Nibeiwa had been chosen for the initial strike in part because it harbored the main Italian armored force in Egypt, composed of thirty-five M11/39 medium tanks and thirty-five L3/35 light tanks. The attack out of the mist from the rear completely surprised the Italians, and two-thirds of the medium tanks, which had been deployed outside the camp to protect its vulnerable entrance, were destroyed in ten minutes before they could be fully manned. The camp itself was soon breached by the British tanks and two battalions of infantry. The Matilda, classed a heavy tank in 1940, was slow but boasted 78-mm frontal armor that made it impervious to almost every weapon deployed by the Italians; its 40-mm main gun was able to penetrate any Italian tank. The defenders offered stubborn resistance, but with no ability to stop the British armor, the camp was taken by 10:40 A.M. Its commanding general, Pietro Maletti, was killed and 2,000 troops were captured. The British and Indian forces lost eight officers and forty-eight men as casualties.[25]

Before the capture of Nibeiwa camp was complete, the 5th Indian Infantry Brigade moved to attack Tummar West. Aerial reconnaissance revealed that this camp was built in much the same way as the other, including an unmined entrance in the northwest corner. Consequently, the plan for the assault was a copy of the first attack. By 11:00 A.M., the 4th Indian Divisional Artillery was on the move, though it was bombed from the air while in transit. The 7th RTR lost six tanks in the minefield as it exited Nibeiwa, and mechanical issues with other vehicles meant that the original forty-eight Matildas had been halved, though the remainder were ready to attack Tummar West by 1:00 P.M., following an hour-long preparatory barrage. The Matildas again easily breached the Italian camp, but they found the garrison's resistance significantly stronger than at Nibeiwa. The arrival of two infantry battalions as well as truck drivers from a company of the New Zealand Army Service Corps enabled the capture of the majority of Tummar West by 4:00 P.M.[26]

There was some fear of an Italian counterattack, but the momentum of the advance was maintained by sending six Matildas on to the next camp, Tummar East. Again the unsupported armor forced its way into the Italian post. The tanks were to have been reinforced by Indian infantry (4th Battalion, 6th Rajputana Rifles), but the soldiers were delayed by a counterattack from Tummar East. The Indian infantry, along with a platoon of British Vickers machine guns from the 1st Battalion, Royal Northumberland Regiment, concentrated their fire on the advancing Italians and their supporting tanks, and in ten minutes four hundred of the enemy had been killed or wounded, defeating the counterattack. This delay meant that the capture of Tummar East could not be completed before nightfall, but the tanks and Indian infantry partially secured the position. The remaining Italians surrendered the next morning.[27]

On the second day of the offensive, O'Connor and Maj. Gen. Sir Noel Beresford-Peirse, commander of the 4th Indian Division, continued to pressure the Italians. The 16th British Infantry Brigade was ordered north to cut the coastal road west of Sidi Barrani. Despite opposition in the area of Alam el Dab and a dust storm that reduced visibility and hindered communications, the road was interdicted by 1:30 P.M., effectively isolating the Italian garrison in Sidi Barrani. Brig. Cyril Lomax, commander of the 16th Brigade, quickly organized an attack on the town. The advance commenced at 4:15 P.M., led by two British infantry battalions supported by the divisional artillery and some tanks of the 7th and 4th RTRs. The town was quickly captured, and the Indian Division found "an embarrassing number of prisoners on our hands."[28] Selby Force continued to apply pressure from the east, and by 11 December the remains of 1st and 2nd Libyan Divisions had been encircled and joined the men of 4th Blackshirt Division as prisoners of the British.[29] The number of Italian troops captured was so great that it was difficult to get an accurate count. "About five acres of officers and two hundred acres of other ranks" was the best estimate of prisoners by the headquarters of the 3rd Battalion, Coldstream Guards.[30]

By the end of the second day, the battle was over as the Italians ceased to offer serious resistance. A captured officer was sent into the camp at Point 90 on 10 June to demand the surrender of the garrison. The commanding officer initially agreed with this request but soon changed his mind and refused to capitulate. Beresford-Peirse then ordered an infantry attack, but following an artillery bombardment, his troops found 2,000 Italians formed up as if on parade—it seemed that the commander's "honour had been satisfied" by the show of force.[31] The British prepared to assault the remaining Italian camps of Rabia and Sofafi, but the Cirene Division retreated on the night of 10 December under cover of a sandstorm. O'Connor sent the 7th Armoured Division across the desert to Buq Buq, where it also captured large groups of Italians. By 12 December only a small number of Italians remained in Egypt, guarding the approaches to Libya at Sollum and Sidi Omar. Even these outposts were abandoned in the face of British probes, and by 16 December Bardia marked the Italian frontier in the desert.[32]

The Battle of the Camps, or the Battle of Marmarica as it is known to the Italians, was an overwhelming British success. In an operation largely concluded within seventy-two hours, O'Connor's small force of two divisions had routed a much larger enemy army. As the British official history records: "The Western Desert Force captured no fewer than 38,300 Italian and Libyan prisoners, 237 guns, and 73 light and medium tanks. The total of captured vehicles was never recorded, but more than a thousand were counted. The British casualties were 624 killed, wounded and missing."[33] O'Connor's forces gained the initiative early in the operation, and the off-balance Italians never recovered.

In London Churchill enthusiastically supported a continuation of the offensive into Libya. Writing to Wavell on 17 December, he stated:

> Your first objective now must be to maul the Italian Army and rip them off the African shore. . . . We were very glad to learn your intentions against Bardia and Tobruk, and now to hear of the latest captures of Sollum and Capuzzo.
>
> I feel convinced that it is only after you have made sure that you can get no further that you will relinquish the main hope in favour of the secondary action in the Sudan or Dodecanese . . . , but neither of them ought to detract from the supreme task of inflicting further defeats upon the main Italian army.[34]

This task was problematic due to the competing resources for British forces currently in the Western Desert. On the cusp of the victory at Sidi Barrani, Wavell surprised O'Connor on 11 December by withdrawing the 4th Indian Division, which was sent to the Sudan, and replacing it with the inexperienced 6th Australian Division. Operations also continued in Greece, where it was clear that further diversions of men and material would be needed soon.[35]

With the liberation of Egypt complete and the Italian army in full retreat, O'Connor could have ended Compass and been entirely satisfied with the results, but he saw a greater opportunity. After consulting with his commanders and receiving full support from Wavell and London, he decided to press on into Libya. The objective of phase two of Compass was the capture of the fortified ports of Bardia, Tobruk, and Derna. These ports, needed for the shipment of supplies, were essential for any further advance. Sollum, a small, but useful harbor, was captured on 16 December. But it was soon apparent that the Italians intended to make a stand in Bardia.[36]

For the RAF, the capture of Sidi Barrani meant an opportunity to scale back the tempo of operations. Collishaw's fighters had flown as many as four sorties a day at the start of Compass, an unsustainable rate. RAF casualties in the first week were remarkably low: only four Blenheims and six fighters had been destroyed. Losses on the Italian side were considerably higher. Estimates claimed that British fighters had shot down seventy-four enemy aircraft, and even more were destroyed on the ground. Though RAF combat losses were minimal, the serviceability rate was dropping. The desert was an unforgiving environment, and the forward airfields had limited facilities to overhaul aircraft.[37] The stress of these intensive operations was soon felt on 202 Group. Longmore wrote to Collishaw four days into the operation to caution him: "Our reserves of Gladiators are now practically exhausted. You must consider adjusting your operations according to the fighter situation, relying if necessary on night bombing."[38] Collishaw responded by curtailing close-support missions by his fighters and concentrating on offensive sweeps to disrupt the Italian air force.[39]

The Regia Aeronautica appeared to recover from the initial shock of the British offensive around the middle of December. Heavy bombing attacks were directed at O'Connor's ground forces, and Collishaw's aircraft were frequently called to intervene. On 13–14 December units of the 4th Armoured Brigade were delayed during a night move past Sidi Omar and Bardia to cut the road to Tobruk. As a result the column did not arrive at their first objective, Sidi Asseiz, until after daybreak and were subjected to what Lieutenant General O'Connor referred to as "the worst day's bombing of the campaign." The Italians directed more than twenty separate attacks at the column, but "casualties, in view of the severity of the attack [were] extraordinarily light."[40] Two days later they conducted another large-scale raid directed at British armored units in the Sidi Omar–Azeiz–Bardia area. Formations of SM79s, supported by fighters, supported the retreat of the Italian army; in particular, this air support was directed to help the besieged garrison at Sidi Omar. The British estimated that some fifty-seven bombers supported by thirty-six fighters attacked during the course of the day's fighting. Hurricanes from No. 274 Squadron, with pilots attached from the newly arrived No. 73 Squadron, shot down three intruding bombers. The day proved particularly costly for the Italians, who lost a group commander and two squadron commanders in the ill-fated raids. British losses, in the air and on the ground, were negligible.[41]

British and Indian army records from this period record numerous Italian air attacks during the initial phase of Operation Compass; though they did inflict some casualties and equipment losses, the overall effect of these raids on ground operations was minimal. RAF fighters disrupted many of these attacks by conducting offensive patrols, which damaged and destroyed a significant number of Italian aircraft.[42] On 13 December Collishaw asked for additional Hurricanes for No. 3 Squadron RAAF to "protect forward troops against enemy air attack," but it was not possible to introduce new aircraft in the middle of operations.[43] Though this request was denied, the British continued to account for more enemy aircraft damaged and destroyed than they lost.[44]

The 4th Indian Divisional Artillery reported a strafing attack by three Breda Ba.65 aircraft on the morning of 9 December that killed one gunner and wounded a man from the 31st Field Regiment. The next day a number of CR42s machine gunned positions occupied by the 1st Field Regiment without effect. Shortly afterward, the 31st Field Regiment was again attacked by twelve fighters, resulting in a gun tractor destroyed.[45] The 7th Medium Regiment of the 4th Indian Division was targeted numerous times on 10 December, but each time the Italians were repelled as the troops "replied vigorously" with Bren light machine guns and Bofors cannons. The ability to return fire was "a great morale stimulant to our troops, whatever the damage to the enemy may have been."[46] Like the infantry, the 7th Armoured Division was not greatly bothered by Italian warplanes during Compass. There were numerous reports of air attacks, but no serious damage resulted. The after-action report of the division also highlighted the importance of being able to fight back: "One point was brought out which seems to be worthy of consideration: that there is a definite moral[e] effect in having light A.A. artillery dispersed actually among the troops which they are detailed to protect instead of, for example, out on the flanks."[47] The ability of ground troops to fight back against attacking aircraft, rather than absorb the punishment without recourse, significantly raised the morale of the troops.[48]

Italian bombers scored one notable success in a Christmas Eve raid on Sollum. Following its capture on 16 December, this small port was used by the British to supply their forces and relieve the strain on the overland logistical system. The harbor was an obvious target and was bombed by Italian aircraft and shelled by a long-range gun known as "Bardia Bill." The need to send antiaircraft batteries to Greece left the Western Desert badly shorthanded, and only one battery of four 3.7-inch guns could be spared to defend the port. Collishaw had three fighter squadrons at his disposal, though not enough to maintain a standing patrol over Sollum, and the British lacked any kind of early warning system to provide notice of incoming raids so fighters could scramble for interception. The Italian raid on the twenty-fourth was carried out by three squadrons of SM79 bombers escorted by twenty-two CR42s. Physical damage was minimal as the jetty was struck and one lighter was hit and subsequently beached, but seventeen men were killed and a further thirty wounded in the attack.[49] Overall, minimal damage was caused by the many Italian attempts to stop the flow of supplies at Sollum. The navy reported that the primary consequence of the air attacks and shelling was a delay in landing supplies. There was not much the British could do to diminish the threat of air attack on Sollum other than destroy the Italian air force, but the artillery menace was dealt with on 31 December, when "Bardia Bill" was put out of action by British artillery directed by air observation from No. 208 Squadron.[50]

RAF offensive operations during the first phase of Compass largely blunted any serious attempts by enemy aircraft to stop the advance. The majority of Italian sorties were defensive operations in reaction to Collishaw's moves. They made minimal attacks against the army in the field, and the Italians made no attempt to strike targets farther away, like Alexandria, which had been largely stripped of its defensive fighter squadrons in order to support the offensive.

The British next turned their attention to the reduction of the fortress at Bardia. The Italians had been constructing that town's defenses since 1937, sparing no expense. The port was protected by an eighteen-mile perimeter that featured an antitank ditch, extensive belts of barbed wire, and two lines of prepared defenses. Forward-line posts made of concrete were spaced every 500–750 yards, each protected by its own antitank ditch and barbed wire and featuring one or two antitank guns, two to four machine guns, and deep trenches. The inner defenses were sited to cover the outer line and act as a fallback position. Six large minefields screened the perimeter, with additional mines scattered throughout the belts of barbed wire.[51] Lt. Gen. Annibale Bergonzoli's XXIII Corps mustered elements of five divisions. The general was determined to hold Bardia. Mussolini sent a message to Bergonzoli on 22 December: "I have given you a difficult task, but one suited to your courage and experience as an old and intrepid soldier, the task of defending the fortress of Bardia to the last. I am certain that 'Electric Beard' and his brave soldiers will stand, at whatever cost, faithful to the last." Bergonzoli replied: "I am aware of the honour and I have today repeated to my troops your message—simple and unequivocal. In Bardia we are, and here we stay."[52] He had good reason to express such confidence: Bardia was a natural fortress, its defenses were of considerable strength, and the garrison was strong and well supplied. Bergonzoli was prepared to endure a long siege.

But there was another factor at play in the defense of Bardia. Italian morale was shaken by the unexpected British victory in December, and many of the formations in the garrison had been badly mauled in that fighting. This would prove key to the outcome of the battle as the "tonnage of concrete was not the secret of a tactically sound position. Much would depend on the troops charged with attacking and defending the fortress, and much more on the quality of the plans directing those men."[53]

The British captured plans of the Bardia fortress when they occupied Sidi Barrani. Estimates on 17 December were that the garrison totaled approximately 15,000 to 20,000 men and 100 guns. If commanders had been aware of the true strength of the garrison—over 40,000 men and 400 guns—they might have been more cautious in their approach. To capture this strongly held port, the British deployed two divisions, 6th Australian and 7th Armoured, as well as the 16th British Infantry Brigade and some other assorted infantry, armored, and artillery units. Overall, the attackers numbered some 20,000 troops, 122 guns, and twenty-six tanks—a significantly smaller force than the defending garrison.[54]

O'Connor, aggressive as always, sent the 4th Armoured Brigade forward to cut the Bardia–Tobruk road on the night of 13–14 December. General Wavell, however, was more cautious. On 16 December he sent a telegram to the chief of the Imperial General Staff that outlined three options for Bardia: induce the garrison to surrender, isolate and lay siege, or leave the Tobruk road open and allow the enemy to retreat. Wavell considered surrender unlikely and British forces too weak to attempt the second, even with the low estimate of the garrison, so he proceeded with the third option.[55] The 4th Armoured Brigade was subsequently recalled and sent to capture Sidi Omar on the seventeenth. By the nineteenth it was apparent that the Italians intended to hold Bardia, so O'Connor ordered the Support Group, 7th Armoured Division to advance and close the road to Tobruk. This was accomplished by 20 December, completing the encirclement of the Italian garrison. O'Connor then instructed Maj. Gen. Iven Mackay, the commander of the newly arrived 6th Australian Division, to the capture of the port.[56]

During the pause between the capture of Sidi Barrani and the attack on Bardia, Collishaw was struck by a "miserable bout of the flu that greatly weakened" him.[57] On a visit to the front on 21 December, Longmore discovered the air commodore in his weakened condition and ordered him back to Cairo to convalesce. In the course of his week away from the front, Collishaw was invited by Longmore to spend three days at Luxor, the ancient Egyptian capital of Thebes. They joined a group of other officers, their wives, and Freya Stark, an English explorer and travel writer who was working for the Ministry of Information. Longmore recalled, "we rode donkeys, saw the sights and, as one would expect in such pleasant company, it was altogether a most refreshing interlude in a very strenuous period."[58] It was a welcome—and needed—break from the stress of operations.

Collishaw was temporarily replaced by Air Vice-Marshal Tedder, who had recently arrived in Egypt to serve as Longmore's deputy commander. Tedder used this as an opportunity to gain "an insight into that part of the job which I could never have hoped to acquire any other way."[59] He spent his time visiting units and talking with people, coming away "tremendously impressed by our high morale." Tedder commented on the quality of Collishaw's headquarters staff. Group Captain Grigson, the senior air staff officer, and Wing Commander Charles "Freddy" Guest, who was about to replace him, were both considered assets to the air group. The air vice-marshal remarked that the command was fortunate to have "three first-class liaison officers in the two soldiers and the sailor, who were clearly invaluable in arguing our case" with the army and navy.[60] Tedder was not required to assume much command responsibility during his time with 202 Group as his tenure in charge corresponded with a break in operations. No. 55 Squadron flew one operation between 19 and 28 December, and overall only fifty bomber sorties, largely directed at the main Italian airfields at Gazala, Derna, and Timimi, were flown from 23 to 30 December. This reduced level of operations corresponded with the Christmas holiday, the army's pause before continuing its offensive, and a period of poor weather.[61]

Collishaw returned to his headquarters on New Year's Eve in time to coordinate RAF support for the attack on Bardia.[62] Prior to falling ill, he had directed his bombers to concentrate on the reduction of the port's garrison. The British briefly hoped that a strong demonstration on the ground combined with concerted air attacks would drive the Italians out without a fight, but the enemy intended to hold Bardia. The air program against the port began on 11 December, when Collishaw's Blenheim squadrons attacked in the morning and afternoon. This pattern continued for the next three days without loss until 14 December, when an attack by three squadrons—Nos. 55, 211, and 113—was intercepted by a large formation of CR42s. The Italian biplanes, generally not a significant threat to the Blenheims, surprised the British force due to poor visibility over the target area. The resulting combat cost the British one aircraft shot down, three men killed, and seven aircraft damaged. Subsequent operations were not affected as aircrew losses were light and damaged aircraft replaced with spares. Future daylight raids on Bardia, however, were avoided.[63] On the night of 14–15 December nine Wellingtons struck the port, but the largest attack occurred on the night of 15–16 December, when thirty-six aircraft drawn from six squadrons—five RAF and one Fleet Air Arm—hit the town's main defenses, troop concentrations, and supply dumps. According to No. 55 Squadron's Operations Record Book, this was Bardia's "Night of Hell."[64] Over the next five nights, a further 150 sorties targeted the port. The British also continued to attack Italian airfields at Tobruk, Castel Benito, Benina, and Berka to attrite enemy air units.[65] Italian sources reported that no fewer than forty-four aircraft were destroyed by the raids between 18 and 22 December.[66]

The RAF stepped up its bombing attacks in anticipation of the Australian assault on Bardia on the early morning of 3 January 1941. In the three days preceding the assault, 202 Group flew 100 sorties against targets in and around Bardia. On New Year's Eve twenty-seven Blenheims struck the port. The next night the Wellingtons of Nos. 37, 38, and 70 Squadrons dropped 18,000 pounds of bombs. To ensure accuracy, the Wellingtons used dive-bombing tactics and released their bombs at an altitude of only 2,500 feet. Bombays from No. 216 Squadron and Swordfish from the Fleet Air Arm also attacked that night. The day before the ground assault, forty-four Blenheims carried out "sustained bombing attacks on BARDIA from 06.00 to 16.00 hours, inflicting heavy damage to Italian M.T. [motor-transport] vehicle concentrations and encampments inside the BARDIA defences."[67] The attacks continued into the night, and on the eve of the Australian assault, the Wellingtons and Bombays combined to drop 30,000 pounds of munitions. Thus, more than 80,000 pounds of high explosives fell on the city and its garrison in the days before the battle.[68] The intensity of these raids made an impression on the war diarist of the 16th Australian Infantry Brigade, who recorded, "RAF bombers hailed loads of bombs on Bardia throughout the night . . . , [which gave] our enemy a sleepless, tortured night before the battle."[69] This sustained bombing had a significant effect on the garrison. "The bombing was very terrifying," recalled an Italian doctor, "the Libyan troops were almost completely demoralized and the Italian troops were almost as bad. Half of their food supply had been destroyed by bombs on the port area, and for two days before the surrender certain units had no food. Casualties from the bombing were slight, but the material damage was large."[70] This heavy preparatory bombing leveled the odds of a small assault force successfully attacking a much larger fortified garrison.

An integrated air and naval plan was worked out to support the Australians' attack. The British staff discovered the weakest point in the Italian perimeter 4,000 yards south of the Bardia–Tobruk road. O'Connor's plan was based on "comprehensive air photographs . . . taken of the Bardia defences," supplied by No. 208 Squadron.[71] The 16th Australian Infantry Brigade would breach the line after engineers had cleared the mines. The RAF would deliver "sustained heavy bombing and fighter attacks against the point of entry" and also target enemy positions immediately in front of the advancing troops.[72] While the attack was taking place, Bardia was to be isolated from outside Italian interference. Tobruk would be bombed, and fighters would attack the route between the two ports

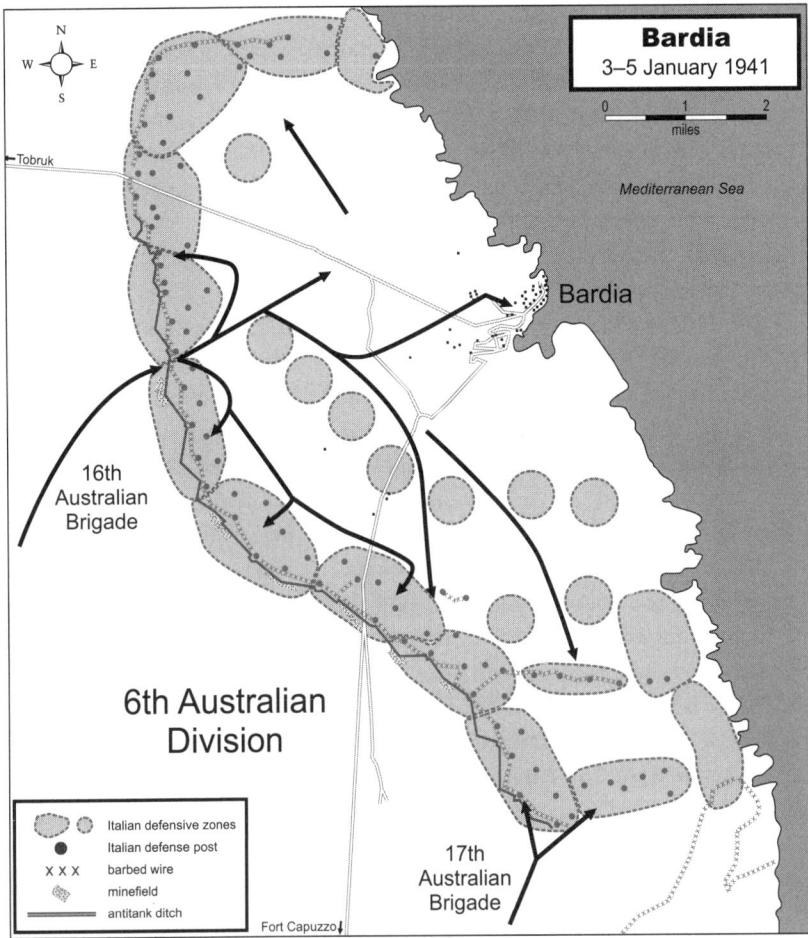

Bardia, 3–5 January 1941. Map by Mike Bechthold. Copyright © 2017 by the University of Oklahoma Press.

to interdict the movement of reinforcements. Counterair operations conducted by Collishaw's bomber squadrons against the principal Italian aerodromes between Derna and the frontier minimized interventions by enemy aircraft. No. 55 Squadron sent out pairs of Blenheims at ten-minute intervals throughout the day to strike enemy airfields.[73] These offensive operations allowed the RAF to take the Regia Aeronautica out of the battle. The air superiority achieved by Collishaw's fighters was noted by the Australians: "We had expected heavy enemy air co-operation with his own troops. Savoia's, Caproni's, CR42's and Macchi's or any other type of Italian aircraft with which we have been familiar, were, as they say, conspicuously absent."[74]

The Royal Navy contributed significant units to support the land battle. The Inshore Squadron, composed of the monitor *Terror* and the Insect-class gunboats *Ladybird, Aphis,* and *Gnat* bombarded the northwest sector of the Bardia perimeter most of the day before the assault and again at dawn on 3 January. This force retired to make way for the battleships *Warspite, Valiant,* and *Barham,* supported by seven destroyers, which pummeled the Italian defenses with 246 rounds of 15-inch shells and more than 500 rounds of 6-inch and 4.5-inch shells for forty-five minutes commencing at 8:10 A.M. The defenders of Bardia "appeared dazed" after being subjected to this heavy fire. After the big ships left the area, the Inshore Squadron returned and continued to shell Italian positions for the rest of the day.[75] The Australians believed the naval bombardment had a significant material and morale effect on the enemy. Craters six yards wide and three yards deep were left in the hard ground by the impact of the 15-inch rounds. A vehicle park hit by the warships looked like a "giant wrecking yard."[76] The Australians encountered weak resistance from the defenders who had been subjected to this devastating naval gunfire.

British commanders feared that the Regia Aeronautica would react to the Bardia assault with a maximum effort. Italian aircraft were grounded early in the morning of 3 January by a sandstorm. When it lifted just before noon, bombers and their fighter escorts flew to attack the naval forces off Bardia, a tactic that offered no relief to the besieged garrison. Just before noon a flight of three or four SM79s, escorted by fourteen fighters, attacked HMS *Terror* as it shelled the port. The Italians were greeted with heavy antiaircraft fire and dropped their bombs without effect. A second formation of five SM79s with no escort approached the monitor at 1:10 P.M. and was intercepted by a single Hurricane from No. 73 Squadron. In the resulting combat, the British pilot shot down three bombers and damaged the other two so severely that they crashed before they could return to base. *Terror* reported a number of other raids, which caused no damage, and at least three bombers were downed by naval gunfire. No effective Italian air raids on the Australians were recorded on 3 January.[77]

The absence of any significant Italian aerial presence led Bardia's defenders to issue a desperate plea for help to "All our aircraft in Libya."[78] This message was intercepted, and the 6th Australian Division's headquarters issued a warning to its units to expect heavy reprisal attacks the next day. The Italians made a number of determined attempts to strike at the attacking troops, but most of the raids were driven off by patrols of British Hurricanes and Australian Gladiators. One exception occurred when a formation of seventeen bombers, escorted by twenty fighters, attacked the Australians. The raid struck near the headquarters of the 16th Australian Infantry Brigade, killing six men and wounding several others.[79]

Australian troops attacked with the benefit of significant support from the RAF and the Royal Navy. General Mackay also used his artillery to offset his numerical inferiority and mask his men as they crossed the open ground of the desert to assault the defenses. The 2/1st Battalion was the first unit to attack at 5:30 A.M., quickly breaching the antitank ditch and barbed-wire barriers in the northwest sector of the Italian perimeter. The other two battalions of the 16th Australian Infantry Brigade, supported by twenty-six Matilda tanks, were then committed to continue the battle. While this was taking place, the 17th Australian Infantry Brigade made a diversionary attack on the southern perimeter and into the teeth of the Italian defenses. Progress in this area was slow and costly. The main assault made good progress and quickly outflanked the Italian infantry and artillery positions northeast of the Bardia–Capuzzo road. The RAF and Royal Navy supported the overall attack by suppressing the defenders in the port and in the area north of the Bardia–Tobruk road. By 5:45 P.M. the next day, the town of Bardia had been captured, and all resistance ended on 5 January, when the strongly held positions of the southern perimeter surrendered. The capture of this well-defended fortress was a substantial accomplishment for the Australians. The battle concluded with the capture of 45,000 Italians troops, 462 guns, 117 light tanks, and twelve medium tanks. The cost for the Australians was a relatively modest 456 casualties.[80]

The RAF engaged a variety of targets during the attack on Bardia. On 3 January Collishaw's Blenheim squadrons (Nos. 39, 45, 55, and 113) repeatedly struck the main Italian landing grounds at Martuba, Gazala, Tobruk, Derna, and Tmimi as well as the seaplane base at Bomba to minimize interference by Italian warplanes. Additionally, Blenheims from No. 55 Squadron bombed enemy troop concentrations south of Bardia to support the Australian advance. The fighter squadrons (Nos. 33, 73, and 274) maintained offensive patrols to screen the battle area, which was essential to allow the army-cooperation aircraft, especially the Lysanders, as well as the Fleet Air Arm aircraft spotting for the naval task force to conduct their missions. No. 208 Squadron flew low over the battlefield to direct the guns of the artillery, while No. 3 Squadron RAAF conducted low-level offensive patrols over the combat area to cover the advance of the infantry.[81]

"Never has so much been surrendered by so many to so few" was how British foreign minister Sir Anthony Eden described the capture of Bardia.[82] The victory is generally portrayed as the remarkable achievement of a green infantry division supported by a small armored force. To read most accounts of Bardia is to understand the battle as an infantry/armor victory.[83] In fact, as described above, the successful assault was the result of a comprehensive joint operation using the combined resources of the army, air force, and navy.

When Wavell thought his attacking force was approximately the same size as the Bardia defenders, he did not intend to attack the fortress. He believed the strength of its garrison was too great and preferred to occupy the port by allowing its defenders to flee. Conventional military wisdom states that an attacking force must outnumber the defenders by a ratio of 3–1 to ensure success, and this ratio should be even higher when attacking a fortified position.[84] Original British estimates of the size of the Bardia garrison were wrong, and the defenders actually outnumbered the attackers by more than 2–1 in manpower and nearly 4–1 in artillery. All things being equal, this was a recipe for disaster for the British unless they possessed some type of force multiplier. This was present in the form of the RAF and the Royal Navy. The RAF isolated the battlefield, neutralized Italian air forces, bombed the garrison, and assisted the land battle with direct support, reconnaissance, and artillery spotting. The Royal Navy used its considerable firepower to neutralize Italian defenses inside the perimeter and acted as bait to dilute those enemy air attacks that did take place. The battle still had to be fought on the ground, and ultimately it was the army that breached the Italian defenses, reduced the garrison, and captured the objective. It can reasonably be concluded that without the support of the air force and the navy, the army's battle for Bardia would have been very different. This does not take away from the impressive achievement of the Australians in their first battle in the Western Desert, but rather it helps explain how such a small force could so quickly and efficiently capture a strongly defended fortress. The successful joint nature of the reduction of Bardia should have become a model for future operations between the three services, but the lessons seem to have been lost almost immediately. It would take considerable time, effort, and cost to again achieve such close cooperation.

The first phases of Operation Compass were a complete and unexpected success. O'Connor and Collishaw were keen to continue the offensive, and Wavell sought approval from Churchill. While the Italians were in full retreat, the continuation of the campaign was not a certainty. The situation in Greece continued to reduce the size of British forces in the Western Desert. Four days after the capture of Bardia, Air Chief Marshal Portal ordered Longmore to reinforce the air contingent in Greece with three fighter and two bomber squadrons; the Gladiators of No. 112 Squadron and the Blenheims of No. 11 Squadron were withdrawn from North Africa immediately. Portal fully understood the effect this would have on operations in the Western Desert, but his view corresponded with that of Churchill, who considered Greece to be a more important theater. O'Connor continued operations toward Tobruk, but there was no certainty on the part of either the air force or the army how long this advance could be sustained as reinforcement of Greece accelerated.[85]

Maj. Raymond Collishaw, commanding officer of No. 203 Squadron, sits in a Sopwith Camel at Izel-le-Hameau aerodrome in France, 12 July 1918. Collishaw was credited with shooting down sixty-one enemy aircraft during the First World War. Courtesy Library and Archives Canada (PA-002788)

HMS *Courageous* off the Portuguese coast in 1931. As a wing commander, Collishaw served aboard the aircraft carrier for three years. Courtesy Canadian Department of National Defence (RE 64-32)

Wing Commander Raymond Collishaw (*left*) on the bridge of HMS *Courageous* during a cruise in the Mediterranean. To his right is Capt. Studholme Brownrigg, the ship's commanding officer. Courtesy Canadian Department of National Defence (PMR 71-755)

Group Capt. Raymond Collishaw (*right*), commanding officer of RAF Station Heliopolis, meets Sir Philip Sassoon, undersecretary of state for air, in 1937. Collishaw described the period before the war in Egypt as "the most pleasant of all those that I spent in uniform." Courtesy Canadian Department of National Defence (RE 64-34)

Air Commodore Raymond Collishaw commanded 202 Group during the early battles against the Italians and Germans in the Western Desert. He recalled that it was a period "when we had to outwit and outfight a numerically superior enemy by a combination of deception, superior tactics, and fighting spirit." Courtesy Canadian Department of National Defence (PMR 71-774)

Air Chief Marshal Sir Arthur Longmore, air officer-commanding in-chief, RAF Middle East. Longmore commanded Collishaw in Iraq in 1923 and again in the Western Desert in 1940–41. Collishaw enjoyed his full confidence and support. When Longmore was asked to replace his subordinate in October 1940, he replied: "On no account do I want to release Collishaw who is really doing magnificently in the Western Desert and maintaining a very high morale in the six squadrons there opposed to a vastly superior enemy air force. I cannot risk a change." Courtesy Canadian Department of National Defence (PMR 71-777)

Gen. Sir Archibald Wavell (*right*), commander-in-chief, Middle East, with Lt. Gen. Richard O'Connor, commander Western Desert Force, during the assault on Bardia, January 1941. Courtesy Canadian Department of National Defence (E1549)

Air Marshal Arthur Tedder, deputy air officer commanding-in-chief, RAF Middle East, visits an RAF fighter squadron during Operation Compass. Tedder later took over from Longmore as the commander of the RAF Middle East, but he did not share his affinity for Collishaw. He considered him a "bull in a china shop" who had the tendency to "go off half-cock," replacing him as soon as he could. Courtesy Canadian Department of National Defence (PMR 71-778)

An aerial reconnaissance image of Benghazi harbor, taken by a 202 Group aircraft early in the war. The large number of transport ships demonstrate the port's importance in supplying the Italian army and air force in Cyrenaica. Courtesy Canadian Department of National Defence (RE 64-37)

Gen. Sir Archibald Wavell, general officer commanding-in-chief, Middle East, (*right*) visits an RAF landing ground in the Western Desert during Operation Compass to confer with Collishaw (*second from right*). Courtesy Canadian Department of National Defence (RE 64-14)

The crew of a Vickers Wellington prepares for a mission over Cyrenaica in 1940. The Wellington was an effective long-range bomber that was primarily employed in attacks against enemy ports and airfields. Courtesy Canadian Department of National Defence (RE 64-66)

Bombs for the Wellington heavy bombers are prepared for use. Courtesy Canadian Department of National Defence (RE 64-15)

RAF Hurricane Mk. I's on a test flight at Ismalia, Egypt, in the summer of 1940. These were the first aircraft reinforcements to join Collishaw's 202 Group following the outbreak of war. They began their journey on a Royal Navy aircraft carrier and were flown off to Malta, where they refueled before flying to the Nile Delta. In 1940 the Hurricane far outperformed any Italian aircraft in the Western Desert, but Collishaw never had enough of them. Courtesy Canadian Department of National Defence (RE 64-13)

An Italian bombing raid in progress on the small port of Sollum at the start of the war. Courtesy Canadian Department of National Defence (PMR 71-769)

A British soldier examines a crashed Italian SM79 trimotor bomber shot down by the RAF over the Western Desert. Courtesy Canadian Department of National Defence (RE 64-46)

The wreck of another SM79 bomber. The Italian air force suffered from low serviceability rates in the Western Desert and was forced to abandon or destroy many aircraft that could not be flown to safety when the British overran their airfields. Courtesy Canadian Department of National Defence (RE 64-42)

The remains of an Italian aircraft shot down by the RAF are examined by British soldiers. Courtesy Canadian Department of National Defence (RE 64-27)

An Italian CR42 biplane fighter sits on a Western Desert airfield captured by the British during Operation Compass. The aircraft was likely destroyed during an RAF raid and abandoned when the Italians retreated. The CR42 was a nimble aircraft that fared well against British Gladiators and Lysanders, but it was overmatched by the Hurricane and too slow to catch most British bombers. Courtesy Canadian Department of National Defence (RE 64-45)

Burnt-out hangars and destroyed aircraft are visible at the Italian aerodrome at Benina after RAF attacks in 1940 ordered by Collishaw. Courtesy Canadian Department of National Defence (RE 64-22)

A flight of Gloster Gladiators from No. 3 Squadron RAAF return to a landing ground near Sollum after a patrol over Bardia, January 1941. Courtesy the Australian War Memorial (SUK 14908)

Collishaw debriefs the officer commanding No. 13 Squadron, an RAF light-bomber unit, following a mission over Cyrenaica. Courtesy Canadian Department of National Defence (AH 280)

The RAF scored a big success two days after the start of the war in the Western Desert when nine Blenheims of No. 113 Squadron bombed the Italian warship *San Giorgio*, setting it on fire. This old 9,000-ton cruiser, employed as a submarine-depot ship, was run aground on a sandbar to prevent it from sinking. The ship was subsequently used as an antiaircraft gun platform in the harbor and never sailed again. Courtesy Canadian Department of National Defence (RE 64-23)

Sunken ships in Benghazi harbor bear evidence of the effective air attacks—British, Italian, and German—on the port. Courtesy Canadian Department of National Defence (19890223-366)

An air raid on Benghazi cratered the road and destroyed a passing truck. Courtesy Canadian Department of National Defence (19890223-369)

An RAF armorer prepares to rearm aircraft on a forward airfield in the Western Desert. Courtesy Canadian Department of National Defence (19890223-298)

The British captured nearly 40,000 Italian soldiers during the first phase of Operation Compass. The number of captured troops was so great that it was difficult to get an accurate count. When asked to report on the number of Italian prisoners, one British officer estimated "about five acres of officers and two hundred acres of other ranks." Courtesy Canadian Department of National Defence (RE 64-17)

Collishaw receives a message from one of his headquarters staff following the capture of Tobruk. Courtesy Canadian Department of National Defence (AH 278)

Collishaw was interviewed by the news media following the capture of Tobruk. One newspaper report stated: "'Colly' looks the man he is. He is big, strongly built, and even when living in a tent swept by desert sand storms he always appears immaculate in a smartly tailored gabardine uniform with four long rows of service ribbons. . . . He seems to have two personalities. In his mess he is the soul of geniality, but when he enters an underground operations room, surrounded by a battery of telephones and planning on great maps his 'sweep' raids, he is crisp, hard-hitting and one might almost say a ruthless commander demanding results and not accepting excuses. He has the vigor and enthusiasm of his youngest pilot and his men idolize him." Courtesy Canadian Department of National Defence (PMR 71-771)

Collishaw, air officer commanding 202 Group, surveys the ruined buildings on the air-field at El Adem, Libya, following its capture on 5 January 1941 during the advance on Tobruk. Courtesy Canadian Department of National Defence (RE 64-40)

After being relieved by Tedder, Collishaw returned to England, where he served for a time at Fighter Command Headquarters before being promoted to air vice-marshal and command of 14 Group in Scotland. His twenty-seven-year air force career ended in July 1943 when he "was retired." He recalled: "Throughout my service career I was able to play some small part in the conduct of two world wars and during the years between the wars my service career was perhaps more varied than that of many others, enabling me to see more action. I commanded seven squadrons, six stations, and four groups." Courtesy Canadian Department of National Defence (PMR 71-775)

CHAPTER 5

OPERATION COMPASS, PART II

TOBRUK AND BEDA FOMM

The defeats in the Western Desert in December and early January 1941 shook the morale of the Italian people and left their king, Victor Emmanuel III, pessimistic about stopping the British advance in North Africa. He advocated a withdrawal from Cyrenaica to prevent the already weak Italian forces from being destroyed, but Mussolini remained resolute that this was a mere setback, and the war would end with a German victory over Britain. He had great confidence that the garrison in Tobruk would halt the British.[1]

While this discussion took place in Rome, General Wavell planned his next attack. He had set his sights on Tobruk even before the conquest of Bardia was complete, and Lieutenant General O'Connor ordered the 7th Armoured Division to continue its westward advance on the morning of 5 January. El Adem, site of the main Italian airfield and repair depot in Cyrenaica, was captured almost without opposition that same day. The British found eighty-seven aircraft abandoned at the airfield, most having sustained bomb or machine-gun damage; the Italians lacked the facilities to return them to service. By 7 January the 19th Australian Infantry Brigade Group had disengaged itself from the fighting at Bardia and began to probe the eastern defenses of Tobruk. This fortress also was surrounded, but logistical concerns delayed an assault for more than two weeks. The field-supply depots at Capuzzo and Sollum were too far back and required additional time to bring forward the daily requirements of the divisions, build reserves for the attack, and prepare stocks for a continued westward advance until the port at Tobruk, once captured, could be made operational.[2]

So far, it was a successful campaign for the RAF, but challenges remained. Collishaw took advantage of the pause following the capture of Bardia to reorganize his forces. The rapid advance from Egypt strained the RAF's supply system as much as that of the army. The move to the outskirts of Tobruk left RAF airfields at least 150 miles from the front, so commencing on 10 January, Collishaw moved his forces forward, and established his headquarters in the old police building near the airfield at Sollum. His bomber and fighter squadrons occupied aerodromes in the Sollum–Bardia area, and his army-support squadrons moved forward to Gambut, halfway between Tobruk and Bardia.[3] The aircrew and ground personnel had worked hard since the start of Compass, with only a brief respite over Christmas. Collishaw took this opportunity to rest his men for the upcoming battles. Between 11 and 18 January, all of the Blenheim squadrons stood down except No. 55 Squadron, which carried out one raid on the barracks and aerodrome at Derna on the sixteenth. The fighter and army-cooperation squadrons remained active, but their operational tempo was significantly reduced. Only the Wellington squadrons kept up their regular nightly attacks on the Italian ports, airfields, and other establishments.[4]

Tobruk was the second major garrison that Marshal Graziani ordered held in the face of the British advance. He had considered evacuating the Bardia garrison to Tobruk but was overruled by Mussolini, who ordered that both ports be held with the aim of delaying and grinding down the enemy until fresh army and air-force units could be deployed from Italy. Tobruk was the more important of the two ports, but its defenses were considerably weaker. Compared to Bardia, its perimeter was twice as long—27.5 miles—but with half the military strength—25,000 troops and 200 guns. This line extended out between 8 and 9 miles in a semicircle from the apex of the port. The forward defenses, not as complete as at Bardia, consisted of a double ring of concrete positions behind a continuous barbed-wire fence. An antitank ditch protected some sections of the perimeter, with mines and booby-traps liberally utilized. The inner defensive line was anchored on the forts at Pilastrino, Solaro, Airente, and Marcucci as well as a number of other smaller defended localities. Significantly, the main aerodrome of El Adem was located outside the defenses; it was already under British control.[5]

The British advance had major repercussions for the Regia Aeronautica besides the loss of El Adem. The airfield at Derna had to be abandoned due to its proximity to the front, leaving the closest Italian airfield to Tobruk 170 miles away at Maraua. This was a great distance for the short-endurance Italian fighters and added to the operational difficulties of an air force hard pressed to keep up with the current tempo of operations.[6]

On the British side, close coordination with the army continued. O'Connor's XIII Corps (as the Western Desert Force was now known) had moved its headquarters forward to Gambut, while the advanced headquarters of British Troops Egypt was established side by side with Collishaw's headquarters to continue close liaison. While the forward deployment eased the distance to the front and facilitated communications with the army, supply continued to be a major problem. Collishaw's squadrons had not been organized as mobile forces and thus lacked the transport, communications, stores, workshops, and

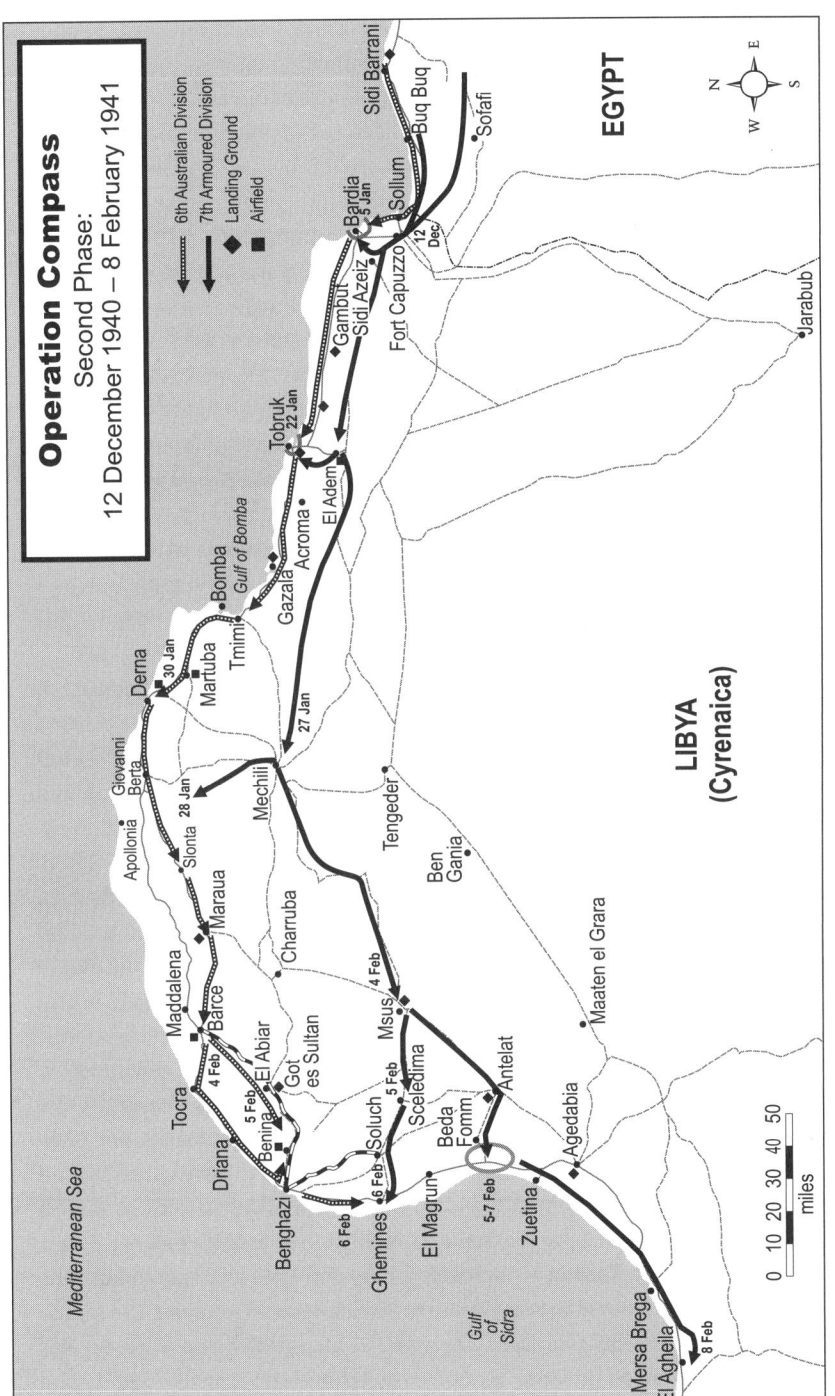

Operation Compass, Second Phase: 12 December 1940–8 February 1941. Map by Mike Bechthold. Copyright © 2017 by the University of Oklahoma Press.

other necessary assets to be truly mobile. But operations continued as the situation demanded due to the perseverance of the men. A major factor supporting this capability during this period was the large stocks of material captured from the Italians. Enemy trucks were crucial to keep the supply lines open, aircraft ran on Italian aviation fuel and dropped Italian bombs, and the men dined on Italian rations.[7]

The RAF worked closely with the army to capture Tobruk. The plan for the ground assault was made based on the comprehensive photo reconnaissance conducted by Collishaw's units. Air attacks during the first week after the investment of Tobruk were limited by a number of factors. Raids on the port were initially suspended on 10 January in anticipation of its early capture; missions resumed when it became clear the Italians intended to fight. The forward movement of RAF units in the first half of the month limited their availability as did the weather, with a series of major sandstorms affecting air operations and particularly the serviceability of the Hurricane squadrons. As well, the diversion of aircraft in support of Greece hindered operations in the Western Desert; from 12 January Collishaw was allotted only six Wellington bombers per night as the rest were devoted to supporting British forces in Greece. On the eve of the Tobruk operation, Longmore had to transfer two additional squadrons from 202 Group to Greece, No. 11 (Blenheims) and No. 112 (Gladiator). Despite these distractions, starting on 19 January, Collishaw directed a third of his available bomber effort against Tobruk while the remainder of the sorties hit the Benghazi airfields, where the main Italian bomber force was based, and Derna, which still functioned as a port and seaplane base.[8]

On 16 January Lieutenant General O'Connor relayed a request to RAF Headquarters Middle East through Collishaw's headquarters for additional Wellingtons to attack Tobruk. Air Chief Marshal Longmore concurred and the next day released ten of the bombers to Collishaw's control. Air attacks occurred for three nights, starting on 19 January, against various targets in and around Tobruk. The port was the main target, but various other defended localities inside the perimeter, including Pilastrino and Sidi Mahmud, the junction where the roads to Bardia, Tobruk, and El Adem met, were also attacked. Over the course of two nights and one day, 202 Group flew approximately one hundred sorties and dropped sixty tons of bombs on the port. On eve of the ground operation, Wellingtons of Nos. 37 and 38 Squadrons attacked various targets between 3:30 and 6:00 A.M. to mask the assembly of the assault force.[9]

The air plan for Tobruk was closely integrated with the army plan. The 16th Australian Infantry Brigade, supported by tanks, was to pierce the Italian defenses in the southeastern edge, where the antitank ditch was shallow. This lead formation was to advance 4,000 yards to overrun the forward Italian artillery positions in this sector. The assault would then be continued by the 19th Australian Infantry Brigade, which was to advance to the junction of the two main roads (Tobruk–Bardia and Tobruk–El Adem). The 2/3rd Battalion of the 16th Australian Brigade commenced this attack at 5:40 A.M. on 21 January.[10]

Lessons learned at Bardia were integrated into the new plan. The biggest change saw the artillery concentrate on counterbattery fire, having seen that infantry supported by tanks were capable of neutralizing the defensive positions but sustained far greater casualties from enemy barrages. The RAF also focused on suppressing the Italian guns. The area around Sidi Mahmud contained a concentration of artillery and a line of thirty-seven dug-in tanks. Collishaw's Blenheim squadrons, Nos. 45, 55, and 113, attacked three areas (Pilastrino, Tobruk harbor, and Sidi Mahmud) until 8:00 A.M., when the 19th Australian Brigade was expected to have reached Sidi Mahmud. At that time air attacks would continue on the first two targets until 2:00 P.M.[11]

During the course of the day, the three Blenheim squadrons made eighty-seven sorties over Tobruk, dropping 85,000 pounds of bombs from heights ranging from 5,000 to 16,000 feet. One Blenheim was shot down, and a second was damaged in these attacks; a third aircraft crashed on takeoff, killing the crew. While this was taking place, the Gladiators of No. 3 Squadron, Royal Australian Air Force, and the Hurricanes of Nos. 73 and 274 Squadrons screened assaults to prevent the intervention of the Italian warplanes and, if time permitted, attacked ground targets of opportunity before returning to base.[12]

The Royal Navy's Inshore Squadron actively bombarded Italian positions in and around the port for two nights prior to the ground assault, and destroyers stood ready at sea to contain a possible breakout by the cruiser San Giorgio, bottled up in the port. On the night before the attack, HMS Terror fired more than a hundred rounds at an area containing a large concentration of Italian troops northwest of Tobruk. The squadron retired to Sollum before dawn of the twenty-first to avoid possible air attack.[13]

By the end of the first day, the Australians had fought through the main defenses and reached the crest of the escarpment overlooking the town. The battle was not yet over, but it was clear that the Italians had been defeated. Late in the day columns of smoke and explosions in Tobruk indicated that the Italians were destroying all they could in anticipation of their capitulation. Australian troops entered the town by midmorning on 22 January, and the last defenders surrendered at 3:45 P.M. The cost of the victory was relatively light for the Australians—49 men killed or mortally wounded and 306 wounded; the British sustained an additional forty-five casualties. The number of Italians killed and wounded is not known, but 27,000 prisoners, 208 field and medium guns, eighty-seven tanks, and more than two hundred vehicles were captured.[14]

In his after-action report Collishaw commented on the close cooperation between the air force and the army. Aircraft bombed targets in advance of the forward troops and provided additional fire support when heavy artillery was unavailable while it deployed closer to the front.[15] General Wavell commented, "Co-operation by Royal Air Force and Royal Naval units was excellent and invaluable."[16] One army report considered the RAF contribution as the number-one factor in the success of the action: "The R.A.F. obtained and maintained complete air superiority, so that our troop concentrations and the land attack were at no time hampered. The air superiority enabled photographs to be taken from a low altitude of all enemy battery positions, strong points and headquarters."[17] Aerial reconnaissance before the assault provided invaluable intelligence to the army regarding Italian defenses and minefields. Warplanes neutralized enemy artillery and directed the counterbattery fire of the Australian and British guns. Fighters and medium bombers flew dozens of sorties at low level in direct support of the troops. The army was confident that the air attacks "undoubtedly had an enormous effect on the morale of the enemy." This assessment was confirmed by Italian sources.[18] Tobruk's port and the town itself were devastated by the time the Australians entered the streets. The cumulative damage, caused largely by months of aerial bombardment, affected the quality of the Italian defense. The destruction of warehouses caused logistical problems for the garrison, including a shortage of food. A total of eighteen ships were found sunk in the harbor, including the cruiser *San Giorgio* and two large transports, the *Marco Polo* and the *Liguria*. As with Bardia, the capture of Tobruk was the result of a coordinated, joint assault.[19]

Following the capture of Tobruk, the steady British advance would soon turn the Italian retreat from Cyrenaica into a rout. Marshal Graziani had lost his last major defensive position, but his forces in Libya had not yet been defeated. Derna on the coast and Mechili some fifty miles inland were held in some strength as the Italians prepared to impose the maximum delay on any British passage through the Jebel Akhdar (Green Mountains). This area, located in the bulge of Cyrenaica roughly north of Bomba, Mechili, and Soluch, was very different from the surrounding deserts. The high ground was a center of Italian colonization due to its fertile soil, temperate climate, and moderate rainfall. The region contained good roads and communications, including a stretch of the Italian–Libya Railways, which ran about sixty-seven miles from Barce to Benghazi and then another thirty-five miles to Soluch. South of the Jebel the harsh desert resumed, and the roads and tracks through the area, on the direct line from Tobruk to Agedabia, ranged from good to terrible.[20]

The Italians considered this region largely impassable and left it weakly defended. Lieutenant General O'Connor believed that the Italian armored brigade, with its two battalions of medium tanks at Mechili, posed the greatest threat. He sent the 4th Armoured Brigade to destroy this force, while the 6th Australian Division advanced along the coast to keep pressure on the defenses backed by Derna. On the night of 26 January, before the British arrived, the Italian armored brigade escaped to the northwest; the 4th British Armoured Brigade pursued this force for the next two days. Hurricanes of Nos. 73 and 274 Squadron maintained offensive patrols over the forward area on 27 January and attacked two convoys of vehicles slowing their progress as they withdrew from Mechili to Slonta. The Italian tanks, however, were able to escape as heavy rains made the already poor roads behind them impassable. This, combined with maintenance issues and a lack of petrol for the British tanks, ended the chase. O'Connor was disappointed by this development but quickly realized a possibility of trapping the remaining Italian forces in Cyrenaica.[21]

After the fall of Tobruk, 202 Group again moved forward. Nos. 73 and 274 Squadrons went to Gazala, while Nos. 208 and 3 RAAF Squadrons moved to Tmimi; Collishaw's headquarters and the Blenheim squadrons relocated to Sidi Mahmoud, just outside of Tobruk. The move brought the squadrons closer to the battle area but brought on serious supply difficulties. The logistical network was hampered by the distance and lack of infrastructure and by aircraft wearing out through long hours of operation and the harshness of the desert environment. The available motor transport was well below the needed quantities. Had it not been for the large number of trucks and great stocks of bombs and petrol captured from the Italians, it may have been impossible for Collishaw to maintain the tempo of operations.[22]

The fragile nature of the RAF was demonstrated twice during this period. During a four-day period just prior to the attack on Tobruk, a fierce sandstorm rendered most of Collishaw's Hurricanes inoperable. This forced the air commodore to mount one-aircraft patrols, a tactic of last resort. On 3 February the limits of the desert aircraft-repair system was revealed when the Hurricane squadrons were pulled from operations due to a shortage of Merlin engines.[23]

As it became clear at the end of the month that the Italians were on the run, the main air effort was redirected at interdicting enemy attempts to escape from Cyrenaica. This focus away from direct support of the army was agreed to by General Wavell and Air Chief Marshal Longmore; the main targets for Collishaw's bombers now would be the Italian landing grounds in the Jebel— Maraua, Derna, Apollonia, Barce, Soluch, and El Magrun.[24] Overall, the air effort was small but was sufficient to drive the Regia Aeronautica from the region and prevent any significant hostile air action as the campaign drew to a close. The absence of any significant air defenses in the region allowed the Blenheims to return to regular daylight attacks, and Italian armor suffered losses on 26 and 27 January as it was attacked by Hurricanes and Blenheims while withdrawing from Mechili.[25]

Derna fell to the Australians on 30 January, but the small port was not bombed during the final assault as it had already been heavily hit. Fighters provided close support to the Australians as they advanced on the town. Starting on 2 February, Collishaw directed all his squadrons to concentrate on interdicting the Italian retreat. All traffic on the routes between Derna and Benghazi was bombed and strafed, with the railway receiving special attention. Enemy columns numbering in excess of three hundred vehicles on the road from Giovanni Berta to Maraua came under low-level attack by Blenheims from Nos. 113, 45, and 55 Squadrons. Hurricanes also harassed the retreating columns. At least fifty trucks and other vehicles were disabled in these attacks, and only intense antiaircraft fire prevented greater losses. Two Blenheims from No. 55 Squadron were lost, and three others were damaged by flak. The bombing and strafing attacks continued the next day.[26]

Prime targets were flatcars carrying Italian tanks found on the rail line near Barce. Wellington heavy bombers contributed to the destruction by attacking that railway station and the airfield at Berka on the night of 3–4 February. More than forty Blenheim sorties flew against road and rail targets in El Faidia, Maraua, and Barce. On 4 February Blenheim attacks were made on Italian convoys withdrawing westward from Barce to Benghazi as well as along the railway. Hurricanes from Nos. 73 and 274 Squadron destroyed at least ten vehicles in another column near Barce. The Benghazi aerodromes at Berka and Benina were successfully attacked by Wellingtons of No. 70 Squadron on the night of 4–5 February, with large fires observed.[27] General Wavell recorded that these attacks were designed to "interfere with the move of enemy tanks to what might become a decisive flank."[28]

Marshal Graziani stated that the constant harassment from the air delayed the overall evacuation and eroded the already fragile morale of his men.[29] These attacks not only affected the combat effectiveness of the Italian troops but also destroyed or damaged many trucks and other vehicles.[30]

By early February Graziani concluded that Cyrenaica was lost and any further delay in pulling back risked losing also the surviving elements of his Tenth Army. On 3 February he handed over command of the remaining Italian forces to Lt. Gen. Giuseppe Tellera and ordered him to establish a new defensive position along the southern shore of the Gulf of Sidra.[31] At the same time, the British contemplated their next move. Generals O'Connor and Wilson planned a fifteen-day pause to allow the supply lines and reinforcements to catch up and to give the men and machines a chance to rest and be repaired. The Italians continued to hold in the Jebel, but there were indications that this was merely a strong rearguard action. The direct route from Mechili to Benghazi was not ideal terrain for tanks and favored defenders. Yet maps indicated another option for Lieutenant General O'Connor: an advance to Msus through the desert to the southwest. From Msus, O'Connor would have the option of conducting a short envelopment of the Italians by continuing west through Soluch to the coast at Ghemines or advancing farther south to Antelat or even Agedabia.[32] This route was not expected to be defended, but the distance and poor quality of the track made it a risky option. British forces in Libya, including Collishaw's squadrons, were badly in need of rest and repair; the long and rapid advance from Egypt to Tobruk had worn out units and created significant logistical difficulties. The general faced two major questions if he chose this perilous plan: "Could the 7th Armoured Division be launched in its mechanically doubtful condition across 150 miles of unreconnoitred desert? If so, could it be maintained?"[33]

O'Connor thought there might still be time to cut off the Italian retreat and was forced to abandon his operational pause. Air reconnaissance first identified the enemy withdrawal on 1 February, and over the next two days, this was confirmed by additional reports indicating large road and rail convoys, well protected by antiaircraft guns, heading west.[34] On the morning of 4 February, the general ordered the 7th Armoured Division to drive from Mechili to Msus. The British were established just east of Msus by daybreak the following morning, and by midafternoon a small force had cut the coastal highway west of Beda Fomm just as the first Italian column reached them. Over the next two days, the 4th Armoured Brigade fought a pitched battle to prevent the breakout of the retreating Italians. It was a near-run struggle, but by the morning of 7 February the battle was won. The usually staid British official history painted a vivid picture of the carnage:

> The battlefield was an astonishing scene of wreckage and confusion—fifteen miles of lorries, guns and tanks in abandoned jumble. Everywhere were herds of prisoners, reckoned at 25,000, amongst them the mortally wounded General Tellera, commander of the 10th Army, his entire staff, and General Bergonzoli, commander of the 23rd Corps, who, having long avoided capture, surrendered at last to the Rifle Brigade. More than 100 medium tanks and well over 100 guns were destroyed or captured. The success of the plan to cut off the 10th Army . . . could not have been more complete; hardly a man or a vehicle escaped.[35]

The RAF contributed significantly to this final victory. On 5 February the Blenheims and Hurricanes of 202 Group made repeated attacks on the railway station at Benghazi to harass the retreat and on the aerodromes at Benina and Agedabia to prevent interference by Italian warplanes. The Italian column trapped on the road between Ghemines and Beda Fomm came under heavy attack as well. Blenheims of Nos. 55 and 113 Squadrons along with Hurricanes of No. 73 Squadron carried out low-level strafing runs against the exposed trucks and other vehicles. Additionally, the Hurricanes provided air cover for the advancing British troops.[36]

Aerial reconnaissance provided to Lieutenant General O'Connor was critical in helping him make his bold decision to cut off the Italian retreat. With no time to scout the way ahead and not wanting to give away British intentions, the only available option for a physical examination of the route across the desert was by low-flying aircraft, which reported that "the 'going' looked possible, though very difficult."[37] On 4 February further reports informed Major General Creagh, commander of the 7th Armoured Division, that the Italian retreat was now desperate and in full swing. Based on this information, Creagh ordered a small force due west to slow down the Italians while the main force headed southwest toward Beda Fomm. Lieutenant General O'Connor credited this timely decision for the scale of the victory.[38] Close air support and reconnaissance for this holding force was provided by a flight of Hurricanes and Gladiators from No. 208 Squadron that was sent forward to Mechili.[39]

The contribution of the RAF to the ultimate victory at Beda Fomm cannot be overestimated. The units of the 7th Armoured Division were free to conduct a dangerous and exposed maneuver without fear of being discovered or attacked by hostile air forces. The same was true for the overextended British logistical system. Any type of concerted attack on the recently captured ports or the vulnerable—and predictable—overland routes may have had serious ramifications for O'Connor's offensive. Following the capture of Tobruk, 202 Group concentrated its resources on attacking the remaining Italian airfields in Cyrenaica. After a few days of these raids, which built upon months of previous attritional attacks, it was clear that the Regia Aeronautica was no longer a factor in the campaign; the RAF had decisively achieved air superiority.

During the final days of the battle, the majority of sorties were directed to interdict the Italian withdrawal. These free-ranging raids sought out targets of opportunity as well as hit the infrastructure in the region—communications hubs such as ports and towns and the railway between Barce and Soluch. These attacks served the dual purpose of delaying the movement of Italian forces as well as preventing any enemy attempt to advance south and interdict the British advance from Mechili. In effect, Collishaw had been assigned the task of securing the long, exposed open right (northern) flank of the British attempt to trap the Italians. This action foreshadowed the role assigned to Maj. Gen. Otto P. Weyland's U.S. XIX Tactical Air Command, which protected the exposed flank of Lt. Gen. George S. Patton's Third Army as it broke out of the Normandy perimeter and raced to trap the opposing German army in August 1944.[40]

The delay imposed on the Italians by these air attacks was crucial to the outcome of the coastal battle that raged in the vicinity of Beda Fomm. For most of the afternoon of 5 February, the British blocking force was vastly outnumbered by the retreating enemy, but the confusion of the situation prevented the Italians from taking advantage of their numerical advantage. Even small delays imposed on the movement of the enemy columns by air attack made a crucial difference in the inability of the Italians to break through the British lines and escape in greater numbers.

By any standard, Operation Compass was a huge success. A British force that never totaled more than two divisions advanced five hundred miles and destroyed an army of fourteen divisions. More than 130,000 prisoners were captured, along with nearly five hundred tanks and more than eight hundred guns. All this came at a cost of only 2,000 British Commonwealth casualties, including 500 fatalities. The Regia Aeronautica in Libya ceased to exist as an effective force. The RAF contributed substantially to this victory. Collishaw's aircraft flew nearly four hundred sorties in support of the offensive during the first week, with the loss of only six aircraft, at a pace of operations for the fighters of as many as four sorties per day. Air superiority was maintained through the period. The Blenheim and Wellington bombers concentrated their attacks on the airfields around Tobruk, while the fighter squadrons flew offensive patrols as far west as the Gulf of Bomba. These flights served the dual purpose of attacking targets of opportunity as well as gathering intelligence on enemy movements. The importance of the control of the air cannot be overstated. O'Connor's ground formations enjoyed the freedom to act without fear of potentially devastating air attacks. The Italians did not have this luxury. Their warplanes were active during this period as the war diaries of British units record frequent attacks, but most of these caused only minor damage.

Collishaw's aircraft significantly interfered with the ability of the Italians to resupply their forces. An active interdiction program against coastal shipping was effective at destroying enemy vessels. Two Fleet Air Arm torpedo-bomber squadrons under the air commodore's command sunk four ships at Gazala and six at Tobruk. The advance to Benghazi revealed the overall success of these raids. Nineteen ships had been sunk or put out of action by air attack at Tobruk. In addition, three disabled or sunken vessels were discovered at Bardia, four at Gazala, one at Derna, and five at Benghazi. This shipping interdiction forced the Italians to rely on trucks to meet their supply needs. As a result, Collishaw reported that hundreds of vehicles were shot up and destroyed by his bombers and fighters as they made the long, exposed trek across the desert.[41]

The close cooperation provided by the RAF was viewed by O'Connor as crucial to the success of Compass:

> The R.A.F. was intimately connected with every phase of the Campaign, and it is mainly owing to its offensive tactics against enemy aerodromes and enemy formations encountered in the Air, that the Army was able to carry out its plan of campaign with so little interference from the enemy Air Force. This was greatly due to the personality and determination of its Commander, Air Commodore Collishaw, to whom this campaign owes much of its success.[42]

O'Connor was quite blunt in this report and did not hesitate to criticize problems and people who came up short during the operation. For instance, he was critical of the command arrangement with Wilson; was very much against the diversion to Greece, which halted a further advance past El Agheila; and was "bitterly disappointed" that he was not permitted to continue the advance to capture Tripoli.[43] He also damned the Royal Navy support with faint praise: "The Navy co-operated as far as it was able, but always its full co-operation was restricted by commitments elsewhere."[44] In this context his praise for Collishaw and the RAF can be seen as genuine and not dictated by the need for service niceties and future cooperation.

O'Connor continued his praise of Collishaw, stating that he was "mainly responsible for making the Campaign possible by his persistently offensive tactics against the enemy Air Forces. Whatever the odds he attacked them both on their aerodromes and in the Air, and literally drove them out of Lybia [sic] and out of the sky." The general lamented that Collishaw "would have been in his element" if Churchill had sanctioned the advance to Tripoli.[45] It is not surprising that O'Connor had a great deal of admiration for Collishaw as they shared a common command style. A recent history of the Western Desert Campaign observed:

> By-the-book operating procedures sat especially badly with O'Connor, who routinely modified or simply ignored Field Service Regulations and set great store in operational initiative and flexibility. He arranged conference discussions to ensure that his intentions were clear to subordinates, after which they were allowed plenty of latitude to perform their individual tasks within the larger scheme while O'Connor maintained control with a combination of succinct and concise orders and contact in person or via liaison officers. His HQ arrangements were optimised for this mode of command.[46]

Change the name and this description works equally well for Collishaw, who also was closely involved with all aspects of the operation of his 202 Group.

Wing Commander J. W. B. Judge, one of his senior staff officers in the Western Desert, had this to say about his commander at the end of Operation Compass:

> I saw the A.O.C. Air Commodore Collishaw walking towards me about 50 yards distant. I had no previous knowledge that he was on his way so it was a pleasant surprise. Studying him as he approached I received an impression which I shall retain for many years. This man, commanding a very inferior force had by personal effort, character and sheer determination, driven the Italian Air Force from Cyrenaica. His task had been to get Benghazi and here he was. It was expressed in his face, walk and manner. As he approached his manner seemed to say "I told you I'd do it" and he had. Many times back at Ma'aten Bagush he had said to me in the Operations Room "We'll fox 'em Judge. We'll fox 'em." In those days I've known him to stay in the Operations Room until nearly 3 A.M. waiting for the night bombers to return in order that he might personally speak to each pilot. Then when they were all home he would turn to me and say "I'm going to bed now Judge, call me at 5.30 A.M."[47]

Echoing Judge's appraisal, Air Vice-Marshal T. W. Elmhirst commented favorably on the command-and-control arrangements of 202 Group, which he discussed in some detail in his report on the lessons of Operation Compass. He noted that while the headquarters staff was of the smallest possible size, it functioned effectively and was able to issue short and concise operational orders to the squadrons in a most satisfactory method.[48]

Elmhirst's report was a comprehensive seventeen-page examination of the lessons learned during air operations in the first desert campaign. His opening comments were a strong confirmation of Collishaw's leadership:

> When in early December the Italian Forces appeared to waver, they were never allowed to get into their stride again. They and their supply posts were hammered consistently both by day and night up to the limits of endurance of Royal Air Force aircraft and crews. The failure of morale and consequent collapse of the Italian Air Force was due to this hammering, coupled with the daily fear that their aerodromes were likely to be surprised and captured by our ground forces.
>
> Throughout the operations every effort was made by those in control to mystify, mislead and surprise the enemy. These efforts were obviously successful in the tactical sphere and also in making the enemy believe that our air forces were much larger than they actually were.[49]

Overall, Elmhirst confirmed the success of operations under Collishaw's management and offered suggestions to improve matters that were out of his control. His balanced appraisal of the campaign highlighted a number of areas that needed to be improved or changed, but he also commented extensively on what worked.

Collishaw was an able and competent commander in the Western Desert. He lead by example and did not ask his staff to do anything that he was not willing to do himself. This command style first emerged in the skies over the western front, where as a flight commander and squadron leader he excelled at introducing new pilots to combat. He would personally lead new pilots on their first operational sorties and ensure that they were carefully shepherded through one of the most dangerous periods of their career. Flight Lt. William Melville "Mel" Alexander, a member of Collishaw's Black Flight in 1917, recalled that the commander would allow an inexperienced pilot to attack a relatively benign enemy two-seater, and while thus occupied, he would slide in behind and shoot down the aircraft. After returning to base, Collishaw would "selflessly slap the newcomer on the back and congratulate them on their first aerial victory."[50] This style served him very well in his various appointments at the squadron and wing level. It may not have been the ideal way to command a group-sized formation, and it certainly was not the "Staff College" model, but it cannot be denied that Collishaw was an effective commander.

General Wavell was not an ardent supporter of an independent RAF and would have preferred to have direct command of the air forces, but nonetheless he was pleased with the support afforded him during the first Western Desert Campaign. He recognized the important role played by the RAF in defeating the Italian air force and the consequent freedom it conferred on the operations of his army, and he was satisfied with the intelligence gathered by reconnaissance flights and the attrition to enemy ground forces caused by aerial bombing. The general concluded his "Despatch on Operations" by noting that the army "owed a special debt" to Collishaw for "his whole-hearted co-operation and for the energy and optimism which were an inspiration to all."[51]

Longmore may have cautioned Collishaw in a move interpreted by some historians as an attempt to "rein him in," but the air chief marshal recognized that his subordinate's aggressive use of the fighter force was the key to the victory:

> With an estimated numerical superiority in fighter aircraft in favour of the Italians amounting to nearly four to one I considered that we were justified in taking substantial risks to neutralise their advantage in numbers by making use of our Hurricanes with their superior performance in low flying attacks on Italian lines of communications immediately in rear of their forward troops. Later in the operations they were also employed for low attacks on Italian fighter aerodromes.
>
> There is little doubt that these methods contributed largely to our success in forcing the Italian fighters on the defensive from the very commencement.

Thus it was that as the operations proceeded, less and less air interference was experienced by Imperial forces operating far forward who suffered very few casualties from air attack.[52]

Longmore concluded his dispatch by asserting that Collishaw "deserves the highest credit for the efficient and effective manner in which he employed his squadrons in full support" of the Western Desert Force.[53]

Longmore's second dispatch on the Western Desert Campaign was no less effusive in its praise of the job done by Collishaw: "He maintained the high standard of resource and initiative which I had grown accustomed to expect from him, and he was an inspiration to all those under his command."[54]

Collishaw's aggressive tactics during the Western Desert Campaign were based on his previous experience. He recalled in his memoirs that "it was proved in France in the Great War that it was essential for an air force to remain on the offensive for successful results, as a long term policy, to be achieved. This experience was borne in mind when conducting the Cyrenaican campaign and the R.A.F. continued on the offensive notwithstanding that it was confronted with a numerically superior enemy."[55]

Collishaw clearly understood the risks facing his command, and he adapted his tactics to match the situation. Early in the campaign his command was outmatched in terms of number and quality of aircraft, thus he primarily employed his fighters on short-range patrols over British lines. As he received larger numbers of Hurricanes, Collishaw tasked them with attacking the fast enemy bombers while leaving the Italian fighters to the Gladiators. This tactic, combined with continuing bombing raids on Italian aerodromes, forced the enemy onto the defensive and granted the British control of the air. As even larger numbers of Hurricanes became available, Collishaw used them on offensive patrols to attack enemy aerodromes and strafe vehicles on the ground. While it was the bomber raids that forced the Italians on the defensive, it was the low-level Hurricane attacks that destroyed the largest number of enemy aircraft.[56] Hurricanes sent to strike targets of opportunity behind the lines, on what would later be classed as "armed reconnaissance" missions in Normandy, also met with great success. Italian doctors interviewed after their capture reported that a large percentage of their casualties during their final retreat were caused by low-level Hurricane strafing.[57] These types of attacks on aerodromes and road convoys would not have been profitable in the early stages of the campaign in the face of a strong Italian air force and a small number of Hurricanes. As conditions changed, however, Collishaw modified his tactics with the desired effect:

The fighters put out to sea from their bases, climbed to their maximum height and re-crossed the coast at their radius of action. The object was for all fighters to scour the main roads so as to shoot up everything moving on the roads with the object of paralyzing the enemy's ground activities. This policy caused the Italian generals to call upon the Italian air force to prevent our fighters from interfering with the lines of communications. The result was that the maximum number of enemy aircraft were kept on patrol over wide stretches of the lines of communications in an attempt to intercept our individual fighters. Our fighters' tactics of crossing the coast at maximum height and then losing altitude at maximum speed to shoot up the M.T. [motor-transport] columns while homeward bound, prevented the enemy from having any important success in interception. The enemy fighters rapidly became unserviceable because of the stress of their activities and as the campaign developed, less enemy fighters were encountered. . . . The Italian fighter units became so involved in trying to thwart our air offensive against his ground forces that he was unable to provide any important fighter force to dispute air superiority over our advancing army.[58]

The risk of this aggressive campaign was high, but as it turned out, the reward was equally high.

The suppression of the Regia Aeronautica benefited the army, but it also granted the RAF a freedom of operations that otherwise would not have been possible. The Lysander, which equipped the army-cooperation squadrons, was hopelessly out of date by 1940. It was slow and lacked maneuverability and as a result had been shot down by the Luftwaffe in large numbers over France in May 1940. The main Italian fighter in the Western Desert, the CR42, though also antiquated, still maintained a significant advantage over the Lysander. In the absence of a hostile air threat, however, these same qualities made the Lysander a very fine army-cooperation aircraft.[59]

Group Capt. L. O. "Bingo" Brown, a South African–born First World War veteran of the Royal Naval Air Service, was Collishaw's primary intermediary with the army during Operation Compass. He attended RAF Staff College in 1929 and served for a considerable period during the 1930s in various army-co-operation postings. He arrived in Egypt just prior to the start of the war and was appointed Collishaw's senior air staff officer.[60] For the British offensive, Brown acted as the air-liaison officer attached to the Western Desert Force and commander of the Army Co-operation Unit, where he forged a very close working relationship with the army. This was an essential component of success in ground-support operations. O'Connor thought highly of Brown: "An Officer of great character and determination, who carried my full confidence and that of his subordinates. . . . I found him excellent to work with, and the excellence of the Units under his command were [sic] greatly due to his inspiring example."[61]

Brown's two army-cooperation squadrons, Nos. 208 and 3 RAAF, were commanded by 202 Group but operationally took their direction from the army corps's headquarters. Planning estimates before Compass assumed that the Lysander would be too vulnerable for tactical-reconnaissance missions. Experiments with the Hurricane found that it was a suitable replacement, but the limited number available would not meet the intelligence needs of the army. Operational necessity during the opening stages of the offensive saw the Lysander used cautiously at first but more aggressively as events progressed. As Group Captain Brown stated, "The inability of the Italians to use their air forces to the best advantage has enabled us to make more use of the Lysanders than was considered possible at the outset of these operations."[62] During the first stage of the campaign up to the capture of Sidi Barrani, the Lysander was not used over the actual area of operations. But at Bardia and Tobruk the aircraft were used to provide continuous tactical reconnaissance over the combat area. With their slow speed and ability to loiter, the Lysanders were able to provide friendly and hostile troop locations as well as detailed intelligence on enemy defenses. They were more adept at this task than the faster Hurricane.[63]

The Hurricane did prove its worth as a reconnaissance aircraft against better-defended Italian positions. Most tactical-reconnaissance flights were conducted at less than 6,000 feet, an altitude that made the aircraft vulnerable to antiaircraft fire. The high speed of the Hurricane, combined with special route planning, allowed a careful study of enemy defenses with the least amount of risk to pilot and aircraft. The need for intelligence, however, exceeded the limited number of planes available to Group Captain Brown. He worked closely with Collishaw and his staff to see that fighters and bombers returning from other missions were routed home over areas of interest to the army. This was not a normal task for these squadrons, but as Brown stated, "It was found that pilots and observers of bomber squadrons became very efficient in reconnaissance work even from the high altitudes in this country."[64] The use of these squadrons worked well enough that the Blenheim squadrons were specifically tasked to conduct reconnaissance as needed.

Not all agreed with this assessment of Collishaw, however. From the time Air Marshal Tedder arrived in Egypt in December 1940, he had expressed misgivings about his subordinate. First impressions are lasting, and the evidence indicated that Tedder formed his opinion of Collishaw during the brief time he took over 202 Group in late December. Tedder recalled in his memoirs that though Collishaw had enjoyed some success early on against the Italians with his "irrepressible 'gay aggressiveness,'" he came away from the experience believing that the air commodore was:

"the village blacksmith in the village cricket match" with the warning that before long we looked like having to compete in a much more serious contest on a wider field than the village green. There is no doubt that Collishaw had his points, but on the other hand he was a "bull in a china shop" with little of the administration without which operations cannot function properly. Moreover, he had a tendency to go off half-cock. To listen to Collishaw while plans were being drawn up for the next advance one would think that the advance would be to Tripoli non-stop![65]

In using this English metaphor, the air marshal ranked Collishaw as a talented amateur unsuccessfully trying to compete at a professional level.

In a letter to Air Chief Marshal Freeman on 11 March 1941, Tedder outlined the reasons for the success of Operation Compass. It was "a first class game of poker, successful bluffing a full house with a couple of pair."[66] He explained how the constant pressure on the Italians led to the breakdown of their morale and their ultimate defeat. Despite this, he complained that

by the time Benghazi fell the whole force, personnel, aircraft and transport, was literally worn right out. To some extent this was inevitable but much quite avoidable wear and tear was due to Collishaw's much advertised "drive"— which consisted to no small extent of bullocking units about at little or no notice, issuing orders for operations and moves without consideration or warning. Despite repeated pressure Collishaw flatly refused to use the quiet periods to give any of his personnel or equipment any rest. We've had to pay a heavy price in withdrawing squadrons for rest and re-equipment when we ought to have been worrying about the Hun.[67]

This damning indictment of Collishaw's leadership is a very different interpretation of the campaign than is found in most other sources and is not supported by the evidence. An examination of the RAF HQ Middle East Operational Record Book for the period shows no indication that Collishaw was warned to change or modify the employment of his squadrons. Such a serious problem would surely have been recorded as were Longmore's earlier cautions in July.[68] The British victory in Operation Compass, both in the air and on the ground, was based on a bold and aggressive offensive against the Italians. All the commanders, including Longmore, Wavell, O'Connor, and Collishaw, were well aware of the risk of pushing men and machines so hard, but it was deemed necessary and acceptable.[69]

A number of pauses occurred during the campaign to deal with maintenance issues, bring forward supplies, and rest the men. One of these periods was the two weeks before the attack on Bardia, when the reduced level of operations corresponded with the Christmas holiday, the army's pause before continuing its offensive, and a stretch of poor weather. This period not only saw a noticeable respite in RAF operations but also partially corresponded with the time Tedder replaced Collishaw, who was on sick leave.[70]

Tedder did not agree with the overall conclusions reached by Elmhirst in his report and condemned it as a "half-baked production [that was] of little real value."[71] In his covering letter to the report, he emphasized that Elmhirst "brings out clearly many of the defects in our organisation for operations of this nature."[72] The air marshal did not comment on any of the positive aspects of the report but chose to highlight the main problems experienced during the campaign: a squadron organization that led to its inherent immobility during operations, the lack of an adequate warning network with observation units and radar, and a shortage of antiaircraft units for airfield defense. The absence of any credit for the job done by Collishaw was indicative of Tedder's opinion of his subordinate and echoed the portrait he painted in the letter to Freeman. It also stands in marked contrast to the opinions of Longmore, Wavell, and O'Connor, who were effusive in their praise for the job done by the air commodore. The rationale behind Tedder's critical reports to London cannot be proven conclusively but may have been an attempt to highlight problems in the Middle East in order to draw significant reinforcements to the theater.

Tedder believed that Collishaw was unable to delegate or use his staff effectively, stating in his memoirs: "I could not help feeling sorry for the Staff at 202 Group. Collishaw did not know how to use them, which left them feeling frustrated and miserable."[73] This opinion was supported by then–Wing Commander Kenneth Cross, who was the commander of 252 Wing and responsible for the air defense of western Egypt. He recalled going forward to Maaten Bagush to meet with Collishaw and being in his office, where they were

> repeatedly interrupted by a succession of corporal clerks bearing signals from all and sundry. Collishaw would read the signals, dictate a reply, sign it and off went the corporal to despatch it. I thought it was a bit odd that none of his staff were consulted, and wondered how they knew what was going on. I heard later that Collishaw had conducted business this way whilst supporting the O'Connor advance earlier in the war . . . and had refused to change now even though the force had more than doubled.[74]

A similar viewpoint was rendered by then–Squadron Leader Frederick Rosier, who considered that Collishaw had "initially done well against the Italians but when the Germans arrived he was soon out of his depth. His efforts to thwart them were amateur in the extreme and he lacked the professionalism needed for the task."[75] Rosier had arrived in the Western Desert following

Operation Battleaxe and served under the air commodore for only a very brief period when there was little activity. Thus, Cross, based on one short meeting and some hearsay, and Rosier, based on a short period of service, dismissed Collishaw's command abilities. It is worth noting that both officers served in senior roles under Tedder in North African and Northwest Europe and thought very highly of the air marshal. It is not surprising that their memoirs, written decades after the war, mirrored Tedder's opinion of Collishaw. Another issue at play was the tendency to dismiss the combat abilities of the Italians. Here we have two officers who successfully fought against the Germans commenting unfavorably about an earlier period in the war when the opponent was considered less competent.[76] These snapshot views by Rosier and Cross are enlightening when placed in the proper context, but their opinions have been used by some historians as a blanket condemnation of Collishaw's command abilities.[77]

The issue of close air support was (and continues to be) one of the most contentious and vexing aspects of air-force operations. During the interwar period and the early stages of the Second World War, the RAF and the British Army maintained differing views on the proper employment of aircraft on the battlefield. This led to inefficiencies and conflict between the two services as they attempted to work out a system acceptable to both sides.[78] Prior to the war the RAF had devoted a large proportion of its resources to the development of strategic bombers, while army-air cooperation received much less attention. RAF prewar doctrine was opposed to exactly the kind of support sought by the army. Group Capt. John Slessor was at the forefront of the development of tactical-air-power doctrine in the interwar years. In 1936 he wrote a book entitled *Air Power and Armies* in which he argued that the air force should not engage in close-support operations except in an emergency. He was very clear on this point: "The first general rule [of any type of warfare] . . . is that *the aeroplane is not a battle-field weapon*—the air striking force is not as a rule best employed in the actual zone in which the armies are in contact."[79] He described how interdiction, the attack of troops and vehicles in the communications zone as they approach the battlefield by road or rail, offered the most practical targets for aircraft.[80] These were lessons that Collishaw had long known to be true. His extensive experience in flying ground-support missions over the western front during the Battle of Amiens and the Hundred Days Offensive of 1918 had taught him that the use of warplanes over the battlefield to attack troop concentrations and artillery positions—the targets of the greatest importance to the army— was difficult and costly. Pilots had trouble finding small, often camouflaged, targets on the battlefield, and attacking those targets brought their aircraft low over the combat zone, where they were dangerously exposed to ground fire. In the Western Desert this task was complicated by the vast, featureless expanse of the terrain, where pilots had trouble identifying friend from foe in the confused space of a battle in progress.

Collishaw's understanding of the issue of close air support was reflected in the conduct of his squadrons during the Western Desert Campaign. Very few sorties were devoted exclusively to close-support missions. On the eve of Operation Compass he issued a memo to his fighter squadrons that outlined his standing orders for low-level attacks. When ordered to strike transport or motorized troops, pilots were to avoid well-defended targets such as the main Italian camps or halted columns with deployed antiaircraft guns that could offer serious resistance. Patrols were to be made at high altitude (20,000 feet), and when dust revealed an enemy column, the pilot was to dive at high speed and attack along the length of the formation before exiting the target area low and at high speed. Under no circumstances were aircraft to maneuver or climb near antiaircraft positions as that would make it an easy target for enemy guns. Collishaw summed up his strategy: "(a) To seriously damage the enemy by casualties to personnel and equipment. (b) To hit him hard at his weakest point. (c) To place E.A. [enemy aircraft] Fighters on the defensive so they will be ordered to be withdrawn to ineffectively chase Hurricanes withdrawing at higher speed."[81] These very sensible orders were at the core of the success experienced by 202 Group in Operation Compass and do not reflect the dangerously aggressive carelessness of a former fighter pilot.

An analysis of the scope of operations carried out by 202 Group shows a campaign plan that first sought to gain and maintain air superiority, then carried out interdiction missions and infrequently devoted sorties to close support. This distinct "priority" of missions would later be honed by the Desert Air Force under Air Vice-Marshal Arthur Coningham and formalized in U.S. War Department Field Manual 100-20, *Command and Employment of Air Power.* This manual, published in July 1943, was based largely on British experience in North Africa in 1942–43 and would provide the basic structure for American (and British) tactical air operations for the remainder of the war.[82]

Group Captain Brown addressed the issue of close-support missions in his after-action report. While the primary task of his squadrons was to support the army by providing reconnaissance and preventing interference by enemy aircraft, a secondary mission was engaging in close support of ground forces when needed. This led to the specialization of his two squadrons. No. 208 Squadron largely acted in the traditional army-cooperation role, providing tactical and artillery reconnaissance to the army. No. 3 Squadron RAAF, in accordance with instructions issued by Longmore's headquarters, was designated to "provide the army some measure of close support either by low flying attacks or by protecting our land forces against enemy low flying attacks."[83] In this role the Australian squadron utilized two flights of Gladiators and a flight of Gloster Gauntlets as specialized dive bombers. Prior to the start of the battle, the Australians were trained in close-support attacks and dive bombing. They worked closely with the army to demonstrate their tactics and to acclimatize the troops to air attack, allowing them the opportunity to train with their antiaircraft weapons.[84] During the first stage of Operation Compass, the Gladiators were used to patrol over the army at medium height to intercept any Italian aircraft that evaded the Hurricanes flying high cover. The Gauntlets initially provided close-air support and later were directed to attack enemy columns retreating from Sofafi to Sollum. The dive bombers were subsequently withdrawn from service before the end of 1940 due to a combination of their age and poor condition and the realization that the "need for low dive bombers was not of sufficient importance to justify persevering with the maintenance and use of the Gauntlets."[85] Fighter aircraft, even older Gladiator biplanes, were more flexible and useful in the types of missions conducted by the RAF. They were not limited to the close-support role of the dive bombers but could engage in air-superiority missions, fly defensive patrols, and conduct tactical reconnaissance as the need arose.

The provision of effective close air support was limited by the ability of the pilots to identify targets on the ground. Not only was this difficult to do when flying over a battlefield, but it was also easy to misidentify what was observed. This occurred during the early battles when RAF aircraft attacked their own ground forces on a number of occasions. For example, British troops chasing the retreating Italians were strafed by Hurricanes as well as bombed by Blenheims near Sofafi on 10 and 11 December 1940. The fluidity of the battle made it difficult for pilots to identify forces accurately by their geographic location alone. Fortunately, no serious damage was caused in the mistaken attacks. Brown attributed the errors to the remoteness of 202 Group headquarters from the battlefield, approximately 110 miles to the rear at Maaten Bagush. Orders for these attacks came from 202 Group without consulting Brown, who had a better grasp of the tactical situation due to his collocation with XIII Corps headquarters. The group captain suggested that any close-support operations in the tactical area requested by Advanced Headquarters of British Troops Egypt (collocated with 202 Group) be controlled from corps headquarters. This request was refused, but aside from one incident at Bardia in early January, there were no further reports of attacks on friendly forces. The problem of identifying troops and controlling aircraft on the battlefield did not go away, but close-support missions by units other than the army-support squadrons were rarely flown for the remainder of the campaign.[86]

Air Chief Marshal Longmore clearly enunciated his views on the value of close air support in a letter to Collishaw on 23 January 1941. He understood that fighters were needed to protect the advance of the army and acknowledged that Collishaw had directed his pilots to avoid unnecessary low-level attacks. Longmore continued: "The fighter's right place is high up; it is I am sure a fallacy to think that the soldiers are such fools as to think that the fighters are not doing their job unless they are seen flying about low down—they have had enough experience to know better. I think you should be pretty curt to any of the chaps who amuse themselves by shooting up ground troops. We cannot afford to waste our fighters on such amusements, except of course on very special occasions such as the S.B. [Sidi Barrani] road."[87] The only other time during the campaign when the Hurricanes again engaged in low-level strikes was toward the end, when the tactical situation dictated such employment. The threat from the Italian air force by that time was low, and an abundance of tempting targets existed as Italian ground forces attempted to flee Cyrenaica. In these circumstances the great risk of low-level operations was justified to slow the exodus and provide time for the army to complete its drive to trap the enemy.

One of the main constraints in Operation Compass was the vast distance covered during the advance. The direct distance from the El Daba area, west of the Nile Delta, where the main RAF bases were located, to El Agheila was nearly seven hundred miles. There was no prewar planning or existing doctrine that contemplated the need to move and supply squadrons over such a distance. The standard squadron establishments were not organized for such rapid relocation, nor were the RAF supply and transport units able to meet the needed requirements over such a distance. Motor transport already had been found wanting during the "Phoney War" in France and completely exposed during the German invasion in May and June 1940. And this was in Northwest Europe, with its relatively short distances and dense network of good roads and railways. Estimates indicated that a single-engine fighter squadron required more than 70 trucks to move its petrol, ammunition, bombs, stores, and personnel. The number of lorries needed to keep such a unit supplied was also significant. A fighter squadron's allotment of 3 million rounds of ammunition, suitable for 104 sorties (or twenty days of operations), alone required approximately 690 trucks to transport it. The lack of vehicles in France in June meant that many RAF squadrons were able to escape only with their serviceable aircraft and personnel—everything else was abandoned and lost.[88]

In France the RAF lacked a modern mobile-repair organization. As a result 174 damaged but repairable Hurricanes were abandoned—34 percent of the force committed to that contest.[89] Two inferences can be drawn from this comparison of North African logistics to the experience of the RAF during the Battle of France. The ability of Collishaw's 202 Group to operate effectively while advancing hundreds of miles across a hostile desert environment was a stunning achievement. His squadrons were not designed, equipped, or staffed for such mobility, yet they made it work. Though the distance and environment took a heavy toll on the men and machines, aircraft continued to fly throughout the campaign, and the RAF maintained the initiative. The second point concerns the criticisms levelled at the Regia Aeronautica for its low serviceability rates and the large number of abandoned aircraft captured by the advancing British formations—losses not drastically different from those suffered by the RAF in France.[90] In many respects it was not the failure of the Italian air force during this campaign that was surprising, but rather the success achieved by the RAF. For this, a great deal of the credit can be given to the leadership and initiative demonstrated by Air Commodore Collishaw.

Operation Compass, the first British offensive of the war, culminated in the expulsion of the Italians from Cyrenaica and was a model of cooperation between the army and the air force. The results far exceeded even the most optimistic forecasts made prior to the campaign.[91] While the Italian military had its problems in North Africa, much of the success should be attributed to the leadership of Lieutenant General O'Connor and Air Commodore Collishaw, who drove their forces hard, though not recklessly, to overcome the challenges of a harsh environment, obsolescent equipment, inferior numbers, vast distances, and severe maintenance and supply issues. What started on 9 December 1940 as a limited five-day offensive to capture a series of Italian camps in Egypt ended with the fall of Benghazi and the complete destruction of the Italian Tenth Army at Beda Fomm less than two months later, sealing an improbable victory.

The role played by Collishaw's 202 Group was crucial to the success of Operation Compass. As a first attempt at harnessing the joint efforts of the land and air forces, it was a model effort. From the outset, Collishaw and O'Connor worked closely together to plan operations. Collishaw even went so far as to collocate his headquarters with that of O'Connor and to advance as necessary. After the initial phase of the operation was over, the chief enemy of the RAF became distance, not the Italians. As British forces advanced across the desert, the air force had to continually move forward to new landing grounds to keep its aircraft within striking distance of the retreating enemy. This was a type of operation for which plans had not been made in the prewar period. Squadrons were previously seen to be largely static organizations not designed for quick advances into unprepared areas. Yet Collishaw realized that war in the desert was a war of mobility, and the air forces must be able to keep up. Ad-hoc solutions were devised during the course of operations that, while not ideal, allowed air support to continue. For instance, the British possessed insufficient motor transport to move equipment, supplies, and personnel forward. The disorganized retreat of the Italians contributed to the British advance, however, through large numbers of abandoned, functioning trucks and vehicles, tons of supplies, and significant stocks of petrol and bombs.[92] The old station basis of organizing squadrons was too cumbersome for the conduct of mobile operations. Instead, it was more efficient to split these units into two parts: an advanced headquarters that operated with the aircraft at a forward landing ground, and a more cumbersome administrative headquarters and repair facilities that remained behind at a rear landing ground.[93]

Tedder, Cross, and Rosier may not have liked or agreed with Collishaw's command style, but it is difficult to argue with his success. Anecdotal evidence suggests that the air commodore did not always make the best use of his staff and on occasion drove them hard, but those qualities reflect an operational pattern dictated by the shortages of the early war years. In contrast to these negative views, both Wing Commander Judge, a staff officer who worked closely with Collishaw in the Western Desert, and Air Vice-Marshal Elmhirst, who wrote a detailed after-action report on Operation Compass, commented favorably upon Collishaw's command arrangements. With such diverging views on his leadership abilities, it may be best to allow his operational record to tell the story. Collishaw's long experience in army-support operations gave him a clear vision of how best to utilize his limited forces to defeat the Italian air force, destroy the morale and capabilities of the Italian army, and support the British army in its advance across Cyrenaica. The first task was to impede the ability of enemy warplanes to resist the advance, which would then permit uncontested attacks on the Italians' logistical network to isolate their troops at the front and impair the movement of supplies and reinforcements to the battlefield. In special circumstances, such as the assaults on Bardia and Tobruk, close-support attacks could be carried out on targets immediately in front of the troops. This pattern of operations worked exceptionally well and was reflected in the positive reports on Collishaw's conduct made by Wavell, Longmore, and O'Connor.

REVERSAL OF FORTUNE

THE RETREAT TO THE FRONTIER

The victory over the Italians, the first successful British campaign of the war, was facilitated by the effective partnership of the army and the RAF. Lieutenant General O'Connor and Air Commodore Collishaw shared a common vision during Operation Compass and worked well together. In March 1941 the king appointed Collishaw and O'Connor, along with General Wavell and Air Chief Marshal Longmore, to the Most Honourable Order of the Bath in recognition of their accomplishments. The text of each man's award noted "the recent successful *combined* operations in the Middle East [italics added]." The word "combined" was missing when Air Marshal Tedder and Air Vice-Marshal Coningham were admitted to the order the following year.[1]

Indeed, relations between the army and air force soured in the year after Compass, tainted especially by events in March, April, and June 1941. The victory over the Italians in Cyrenaica created a strategic dilemma for the British: push their exhausted forces to continue the offensive to Tripoli and expel the Italians from North Africa, or spare the enemy, rest their tired forces, and shift the emphasis to other areas. Intelligence indicated that only one partially formed Italian division and minimal artillery stood in the way of a march through Tripolitania. So long as the Royal Navy prevented enemy reinforcements from landing in Libya, there was nothing to stop a British advance to Tripoli. "No half-hearted measures," O'Connor said, "would be any good; nothing could ensure our success except a wholehearted effort on the part of all three Services, with no other commitments of importance to detract from that effort."[2] Collishaw agreed: "We possessed the momentum and our foe was completely demoralized. Such a decision would have involved risks but it is the responsibility of every military commander to assess all the risks and to decide which are acceptable and which are not. The rewards to be gained were so vast that I felt . . . that a continuance of our offensive involved calculated risks that should have been accepted."[3]

Any further British offensive would have been risky. The tanks and other vehicles of the 7th Armoured Division had been pushed to the limit and, in

General Wavell's opinion, were "mechanically incapable of further action."[4] As such, the entire division was withdrawn to the Egyptian Delta for rest and refit. The squadrons of 202 Group had also been pushed hard too, and Air Chief Marshal Longmore had no substantial reinforcements to replace lost or worn-out aircraft.[5] It was not clear how such an advance across more than six hundred miles of desert could be supplied.[6]

But as weak as the British were, the Italians were in even worse shape. Wavell concluded that they had been "so completely defeated" and had lost nearly all their armor and artillery that there was no serious possibility of a counterattack for a considerable period.[7] Despite this, both he and Longmore were cautious about continuing forward. O'Connor persuaded his superior to seek permission for a continuation of the mission from London, but the text of Wavell's telegram indicated that he did not fully support such a plan. The reply from General Dill, chief of the Imperial General Staff, told Wavell to wait as it was likely that a mission to Greece and/or Turkey would preclude further operations in the Western Desert.[8] Longmore was relieved when other commitments released him of the necessity to advance on Tripoli.[9]

Air Marshal Tedder expressed disappointment in his memoirs that the "Balkan mirage" had closed the door on Tripoli and consequently "opened the door to [Gen. Erwin] Rommel and Cyrenaica," but he made this judgment in hindsight.[10] At the time Tedder was critical of Collishaw's desire to continue the advance as he thought the air commodore had recklessly worn out his units, resulting in their being unfit for further employment until refitted.[11]

In the end, the British advance in Libya did not continue. O'Connor and Collishaw had been right in December 1940 that Operation Compass should be extended into a pursuit to take advantage of the weak Italian position, but their advocacy of a continued advance on Tripoli became moot with the British decision to send substantial reinforcements to Greece. The British were too weak to do both.[12]

The RAF in the Western Desert was reorganized as a result of the changing priorities in the Mediterranean theater. To prepare his "Balkan Reserve," Longmore recalled Collishaw and his 202 Group headquarters along with Nos. 45, 113 (both Blenheims), and 274 (Hurricanes) Squadrons from the Western Desert and reassigned them to the Delta in mid-February; No. 208 Army Co-operation Squadron followed at the end of the month. A new command, Headquarters RAF Cyrenaica, was formed under Group Capt. "Bingo" Brown to control the small number of squadrons remaining in Libya. These included No. 3 Squadron RAAF (Hurricanes) at Benina, No. 73 Squadron (Hurricanes) at Tobruk, No. 55 Squadron (Blenheims) at Maraua, and No. 6 Army Co-operation Squadron at Barce (Lysanders) and Agedabia (Hurricanes). The demands on these units were substantial in February and March as the Luftwaffe began operations in North Africa and the German Afrika Korps deployed to Libya. The two fighter squadrons were hard pressed to defend Benghazi and Tobruk from air attack. The Blenheim squadron was the only bomber unit available in the forward area; it also provided the only long-range aircraft that could conduct reconnaissance in Tripolitania.[13]

After its success at Beda Fomm, the 7th Armoured Division was sent back to Egypt and was replaced by the 2nd Armoured Division. This inexperienced formation was a division in name only, composed of only one under-strength armored brigade after its other brigade and much of its support group left for Greece. The 6th Australian Division had proved itself during Operation Compass without suffering serious losses, and for this reason it was also sent to Greece. Its replacement was the newly formed 9th Australian Division; it would later distinguish itself in Tobruk but was not yet ready for combat. Its two best infantry brigades were detached for Greece and replaced with two partially trained brigades that were short of equipment. In addition, divisional headquarters was understaffed and undertrained, and the formation lacked sufficient artillery, Bren guns, antitank guns, communications equipment, and transport. The gamble to hold Cyrenaica with this weak force was based on the assumption that reinforcements and additional units would be available before the enemy was again ready to attack.[14]

The British success over the Italians in Cyrenaica coincided with a deterioration of the situation in Greece. Italy had invaded the small Mediterranean country on 28 October 1940, but a Greek counterattack two weeks into the invasion reversed most of the Italian gains; by January 1941 the Greeks also occupied a substantial portion of southern Albania. The British had provided limited support, mostly RAF units, during this period, but strengthening Italian forces combined with poor Greek logistics prompted a review of British support. Through January and February, a lively debate raged between London, Cairo, and Athens regarding the size, form, and timing of British support. Churchill was in favor of deploying military units in Greece as was Wavell. The growing evidence of a German buildup in the Balkans soon spurred a British decision. Churchill was keen to avoid another debacle like Norway but supported sending troops and aircraft if success could be achieved at a reasonable cost.[15]

Amid this debate, the British Defence Committee met on 10 February to consider its policy for the Middle East. There were not sufficient forces in the theater to meet all the current challenges, so the options were carefully reviewed. An advance to Tripoli was attractive as it would remove the Italian and German threat to Egypt without requiring a major seaborne invasion as well as provide a base for air operations over the Mediterranean and especially

against Sicily. The occupation of Tripoli, however, would be difficult to supply and defend and would preclude additional commitments to Greece. The
other option was to hold Cyrenaica as a secure flank with minimal strength
to allow an expeditionary force to deploy to Greece.[16] The destruction of the
Italian army and air force in Cyrenaica had removed the immediate threat to
Egypt, and General Wavell estimated that it would take at least two months for
Axis forces to gather sufficient strength to threaten the Western Desert.[17] By
that time, Wavell's position would be substantially strengthened by the arrival
of reinforcements from the United Kingdom, the rehabilitation of forces worn
out during Operation Compass, and the release of formations due to the completion of operations in the Sudan. Churchill decided on the second plan, and
on 7 March Wavell received official confirmation for the Greek deployment;
British troops landed at Piraeus later that day.[18]

Wavell prepared the strongest possible force from his limited resources
in the expectation of a German intervention. The fighting component of
W Force, the unofficial name assigned to the troops embarking for Greece
under the command of Lt. Gen. H. M. Wilson, was composed of the 6th and
7th Australian Divisions, the New Zealand Division, the Polish Brigade Group,
and an armored brigade group drawn from the 2nd Armoured Division. A
large contingent of noncombat troops would accompany them. This left only
two weak and inexperienced formations to hold the line south of Benghazi: the
9th Australian Division and the 2nd Armoured Division. Overall command of
these troops was vested in Cyrenaica Command, led by Lt. Gen. Philip Neame,
which replaced O'Connor's veteran XIII Corps. Neame had been awarded the
Victoria Cross for his actions at Neuve Chapelle in 1915 and had a commend-
able First World War and interwar career, though he lacked recent experience
in the desert. He also was not well served by his headquarters, which was deficient in trained staff and communications equipment, factors that would prove
a serious handicap in the upcoming campaign.[19]

The situation in Libya changed significantly in 1941 with the commitment of German forces to bolster the Italians. On 11 January Hitler dispatched
an expeditionary force under Gen. Erwin Rommel to prevent their complete
defeat. This force comprised the 5th Light Division supported by a Panzer regiment along with 245 aircraft of Fliegerkorps X, which had recently deployed
to Sicily. Rommel's force, known as the Afrika Korps, was later reinforced
by the addition of the 15th Panzer Division.[20] The British had expected the
arrival of the Germans in North Africa since December 1940, and the first
operational Luftwaffe units were identified in mid-January 1941. By mid-February, German air attacks regularly hit Benghazi and Tobruk.[21] Allied intelligence had great difficulty tracking the arrival of German troops in Africa, but

fragmentary evidence indicated a slow buildup. Wavell's best estimate was that an attack would not be forthcoming before mid-April, and it was more likely to occur in May. This evaluation was remarkably close to the timetable envisioned by German and Italian commanders regarding the start of their next offensive. The intelligence estimates, however, could not account for the aggressive nature of Rommel.[22]

Lieutenant General Neame and Group Captain Brown were given the task of defending Cyrenaica against an enemy attack. They were to hold as long as possible but to conserve their forces to prevent a complete defeat. This meant that territory was to be traded for time, even if it meant the loss of Benghazi. Wavell and Neame discussed at great length the various options for the defense of the region. They expected that an enemy attack could be directed at the capture of Benghazi, or a more ambitious trek across the desert to Mechili might be attempted, with the goal of cutting off the British in the Jebel Mountains. Neame prepared plans to meet either situation. The lack of an effective and flexible supply system meant that any movements would be tied to prestocked depots containing essential stores of food, ammunition, water, and most importantly, fuel.[23]

One of Collishaw's final tasks before returning to Egypt was to organize the air defense of Benghazi. The capture of the port in early February corresponded with the arrival of the Luftwaffe in Libya, and as a result the British noted a significant increase in the number of air raids against Benghazi and Tobruk as well as strafing attacks against troop positions, road convoys, and airfields. They had intended to use Benghazi as the main harbor to supply the region, but these plans were reevaluated as a result of Luftwaffe activity. Collishaw ordered that a radar station and an air-observer screen be established along the coast to provide warning of incoming air attacks, but there was not much more that could be done. The majority of army antiaircraft units were now in Greece, and the lone fighter squadron at Benghazi was not strong enough to stop the raids.[24]

The first coastal-supply convoy reached the port on 18 February, though two of its ships were diverted to Tobruk due to the lack of adequate air-defense capabilities at Benghazi. HMS *Terror* accompanied the vessels to provide antiaircraft fire, but the transports were sent to Tobruk after two days without unloading as the local stevedores refused to work due to the threat of air attack. *Terror*, along with the corvette *Salvia* and minesweeper *Fareham*, remained in Benghazi to provide antiaircraft protection for the naval clearance parties working to improve the condition of the harbor. German attacks continued during this period, and on the morning of 22 February a near miss on *Terror* caused severe damage and flooding to the ship. Its captain, Cmdr. Henry John Haynes, reported to Admiral Cunningham, "With no (repeat) no dawn fighter protection as at present, I consider it only a matter of time before the ship receives a direct hit."[25] Radar would have increased the effectiveness of the fighter and antiaircraft defenses by providing warning of approaching raiders and directing fighter patrols to intercept them. The RAF were in the process of setting up a mobile radar unit at Benghazi, but it only arrived on 21 February and was not operational until the twenty-fifth.[26]

The ships were ordered to sail on the night of 22 February for Tobruk, but as they left the harbor two aerial-dropped magnetic mines detonated close to *Terror*, causing additional flooding. The next day a German reconnaissance aircraft discovered the ships off Derna, prompting another air attack. Three Junkers Ju 88s bombed the ships at 6:30 P.M. No direct hits were scored, but three near misses were sufficient to break the back of *Terror*, and the ship was subsequently scuttled early on 26 February.[27] The navy was bitter at the loss of the most important ship of the Inshore Squadron and blamed the RAF: "Thus, through a lack of adequate A.A. defences and particularly fighter protection, at a critical period, we lost a ship which had done more than any other naval unit to start the western advance and keep it going."[28]

The loss of *Terror* was unfortunate but cannot be blamed on the RAF. Contrary to the naval report, a patrol of three Hurricanes was over Benghazi from 6:45 to 9:05 A.M. on the morning of 22 February when *Terror* was first damaged. Squadron Leader A. D. Murray, the commander of No. 73 Squadron, joined two aircraft from No. 3 Squadron RAAF. At 7:30 A.M. he engaged and destroyed a Ju 88; a second German aircraft was observed but not intercepted.[29] The next morning No. 3 Squadron RAAF provided air cover for the ships as they sailed from Benghazi to Tobruk. Three Hurricanes escorted the ships from 6:55 until 9:20 A.M. and were relieved by two additional Hurricanes that remained on station until 11:30 A.M. Unfortunately, no air cover was available in the afternoon when the Luftwaffe attacked.[30] Admiral Cunningham was aware that the Benghazi antiaircraft defenses were still being improved when he ordered the convoy and *Terror* to steam out. The Germans frequently targeted Benghazi during the period 12–22 February, but few of the thirteen raids could be consider heavy.[31] The loss of *Terror* contributed to a worsening of relations between the navy and the air force that would climax during the battle of Crete, when German aircraft sank a large number of British warships.

The navy's decision to abandon Benghazi as a forward supply base "severely handicapped" RAF operations in February and March 1941.[32] All supplies, including important stocks of fuel and bombs, would be delivered to the main airbase in Tobruk and transferred to Benghazi by road. The ongoing shortage of trucks made this final stage of the supply line tenuous. Collishaw reported that "the non availability of supplies of petrol at Benghazi in the early days after it was captured prevented the R.A.F. from further demoralising the enemy's routed troops which were escaping westward of El Agheila in crowded masses on the main road."[33]

The buildup of the German ground forces and their move toward Cyrenaica was detected as early as the end of February by air reconnaissance. Group Captain Brown had myriad tasks to accomplish with his limited air resources, but he dispatched regular sorties by long-range Hurricanes and Blenheims to watch Tripoli and the coastal road leading to El Agheila, the westernmost British position. Tactical-reconnaissance reports relayed to Lieutenant General Neame's headquarters on 21 and 22 February indicted the presence of German troops in the forward area within fifteen miles of El Agheila. Such reports of the eastward movement of Axis forces from Tripoli continued to increase. On 2 March General Wavell signaled the War Office in London a remarkably accurate assessment of German and Italian capabilities in Libya. His intelligence accurately identified the Axis reinforcements being landed in North Africa as well as their limited ability to engage in offensive operations east of El Agheila.[34] It was expected that the Germans would eventually launch a large-scale attack, but "shipping risks, difficulty of communications and the approach of hot weather make it unlikely that such an attack could develop before the end of the summer."[35]

In the same telegram Wavell outlined his defenses in the region, which were based on "two incompletely trained and equipped units"—the 3rd Armoured Brigade and the 9th Australian Division.[36] This report was remarkably accurate regarding the readiness of the enemy, but the threat was discounted by assumptions regarding its likelihood.

Air Chief Marshal Longmore contributed the air-threat assessment to Wavell's telegram, estimating that the Italians and Germans deployed 170 bombers, ninety dive bombers, sixty fighters, eighteen reconnaissance aircraft, and 180 transports to support operations. To counter this force, the British had inadequate antiaircraft defenses and a small RAF contingent of approximately forty-eight aircraft augmented by the periodic support of Wellington bombers from Malta and Cyrenaica.[37] Longmore's chief concern was not the loss of Cyrenaica, which he thought was unlikely, but the effect a growing Luftwaffe presence would have on the ability of British convoys to transit the Mediterranean. In addition, German air raids were increasing against British targets in Libya, and Egypt and the Suez Canal faced a potential threat from Luftwaffe aircraft based in Sicily and southern Italy, which could operate out of the Dodecanese Islands. The RAF did not possess sufficient resources to deal with all these pressures.[38]

In mid-March Group Captain Brown became increasingly worried as the signs of an impending enemy ground attack mounted. Details remained vague, but the westward movement of Italian forces had ceased and reversed as substantial enemy traffic moved east along the southern shore of the Gulf of Sirte. In response to these reports, on 22 March he instructed his forward squadrons to be ready to move at short notice, establishing reserve aerodromes to accommodate this contingency. This order was issued two days before to the first German probe.[39]

Despite the warning signs, Wavell continued to believe that no imminent move was likely against his defenses south of Benghazi. He was aware of the German buildup, but intelligence, especially Ultra, was telling him that an enemy advance was unlikely, but if one occurred, it would be limited in scope.[40] Aerial reconnaissance conducted by Brown's squadrons continued to show the eastward move of enemy forces. On 9 March a concentration of at least 1,600 vehicles was reported between Nofilia and the frontier. Less than a week later No. 55 Squadron Blenheims indicated the presence of 1,300 vehicles, including medium tanks, dispersed along the shore of the Gulf of Sirte; reports of large numbers of vehicles continued to be made almost daily.[41] The mounting evidence of Axis intentions did nothing to prompt Wavell or Neame to adjust their defensive preparations.

General Rommel was keen to exploit what he interpreted as a major weakness in British defenses and appealed to Berlin for permission to launch an attack on 24 March to recover Cyrenaica and possibly advance to the Suez Canal.[42] This request was refused as being overambitious. Instead, Rommel was reluctantly permitted to conduct a minor offensive against El Agheila, which would be allowed to develop into a larger advance to Benghazi and Tobruk if conditions proved favorable. He was not to launch this attack until after the arrival of 15th Panzer Division in May.[43] Despite these orders, Rommel directed his 3rd Reconnaissance Battalion to attack El Agheila based on intercepted British radio messages indicating that the position was weakly held. His instincts proved correct, and the probe on 24 March caused the British garrison to retreat, leaving the fort and its valuable water supply in German hands.[44] Group Captain Brown immediately increased the number of reconnaissance flights made by No. 55 Squadron along the Libyan coast west of El Agheila, which detected a substantial enemy buildup underway. On 25 and 26 March more than a thousand vehicles were at Ras Lanuf moving east, and on the morning of 27 March a convoy of one hundred vehicles was detected just twenty miles west of El Agheila. RAF reports also indicated a buildup of enemy aircraft on airfields in the region.[45] This substantial increase in enemy forces posed an immediate threat to British defenses in the region.

General Wavell still ignored the warnings. His director of military intelligence, Brig. John Shearer, produced an estimate on 24 March predicting that one German armored division and one Italian motorized division would be able to launch a counteroffensive against Cyrenaica by 16 April, with additional divisions ready by 14 and 24 May.[46] Churchill, concerned about the German attack, cabled Wavell on 26 March: "It is their habit to push on whenever they are not resisted. I presume you are only waiting for the tortoise to stick his head out far enough before chopping it off. It seems extremely important to give them an early taste of our quality."[47] The general, however, was still convinced that there was no imminent threat to Cyrenaica and believed that available intelligence indicated no imminent threat of a significant Axis attack at El Agheila. He understood that he was taking a significant risk by leaving Cyrenaica weakly defended, but he had little choice given his other commitments.[48]

The cost of the decision to support Greece became apparent on 31 March, when Rommel launched a major attack against the main British position at Mersa Brega. A cautious probe of the defenses was repelled in the morning, but a vigorous attack in the afternoon forced a British withdrawal. German and Italian forces advanced along the coast to Benghazi, from Msus to Mechili, and farther south along the desert track from Maaten el Grara to Tobruk. What followed was a rapid two-week advance by Rommel that took advantage of weakness, confusion, and hesitation in the British command and ended with the British pushed almost completely out of Cyrenaica. One of the few bright spots was Rommel's failure to capture Tobruk.[49]

Wavell later claimed that his available intelligence was "meagre" and he was "working almost entirely in the dark as to the possibility of German formations being sent to Libya." He even stated that the available evidence indicated that no German troops had yet arrived.[50] The evidence does not support this line of reasoning. Wavell knew of the German buildup as early as 2 March, as indicated in his cable to Churchill. The decision that confirmed the commitment of troops to Greece on 7 March was made with the full knowledge that a significant German deployment to Libya was underway. Evidence, primarily from aerial reconnaissance but also from small engagements on the ground, clearly showed that Germans were not content to remain in Tripoli but were quickly advancing eastward. British signals intelligence provided another layer of information for Wavell regarding Axis capabilities and intentions.[51] The general was largely correct in his estimations of the expected timing of a German offensive, and the mid-April–early May timetable was substantiated by Axis logistical preparations and directives issued to Rommel by the German high command. What Wavell could not know was that Rommel would disobey his orders and attack earlier than authorized. This, however, does not absolve the

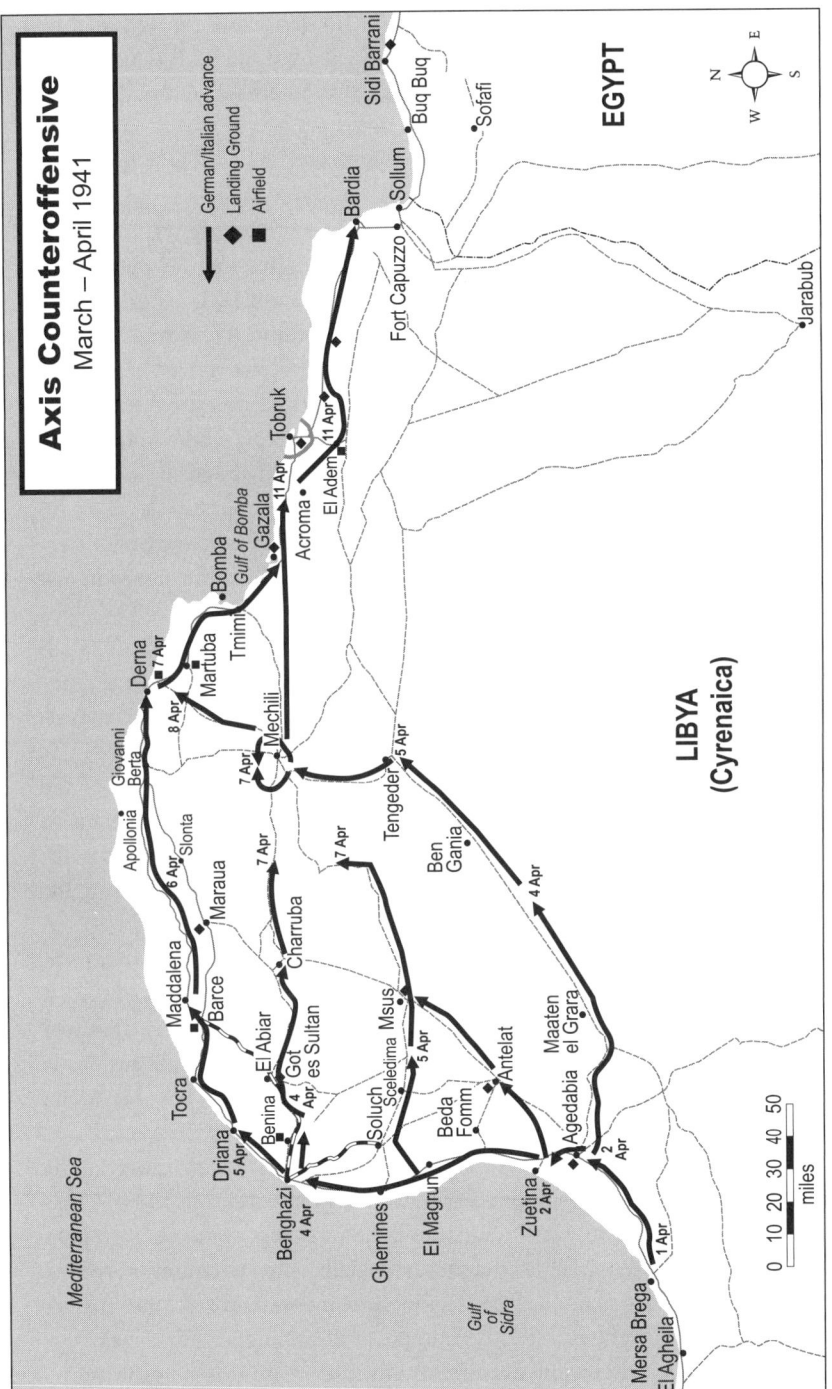

Axis Counteroffensive, March–April 1941. Map by Mike Bechthold. Copyright © 2017 by the University of Oklahoma Press.

British commander of his neglect to provide a stouter defense in Cyrenaica.[52] Wavell attempted to shift the blame for the debacle onto the RAF, which in his estimation did not provide him with the intelligence necessary to make better decisions during this period.

The experience of the 2nd Armoured Division from 31 March to 8 April was disastrous. The plans prepared by Neame and Wavell for a fighting withdrawal designed to buy time to establish a new line of defense were upset by the enemy's rapid advance, the lack of essential supplies such as petrol, and confusion regarding the situation, which was compounded by inexperience. By the morning of 8 April, the remaining elements of the 2nd Armoured Division and the 3rd Indian Motor Brigade were trapped and destroyed by Italian and German forces, while the fortress of Tobruk was surrounded three days later. Rommel's spearheads took Bardia and pushed into Egypt, where Sollum and the important Halfaya Pass were captured by 13 April. Though these frontier positions were recovered two days later, a renewed German attack on 25–26 April forced the British to retire to the general area of Buq Buq and Sofafi.[53]

All the gains made by O'Connor at the start of the year were erased in just over two weeks. The British retained only the port of Tobruk, defended by a garrison of approximately 24,000 combat troops anchored by the 9th Australian Division. Rommel was determined to eliminate this threat to his lines of communications and launched a number of poorly planned attacks on the fortress, each defeated in turn. The British maintained their hold on Tobruk.[54]

The RAF experience during the retreat was less chaotic than that of the army. Group Captain Brown was disturbed by the state of British defensive preparations as early as mid-March and made extensive plans for the rapid withdrawal of his air units if it became necessary. As a result of this planning, the small number of available squadrons was able to render excellent support given the circumstances. On most days No. 55 Squadron employed its Blenheims to provide strategic reconnaissance, while the Hurricanes and Lysanders of No. 6 Squadron conducted tactical reconnaissance. Following the pattern that had worked so well during Operation Compass, the Blenheim squadrons made numerous attacks on enemy aerodromes, joined by Wellingtons based in Malta and Egypt when available.[55]

The majority of the RAF's sorties during the first week of April covered the withdrawal of the army and conducted attacks on enemy columns to slow their pursuit. No. 3 RAAF and No. 73 Squadrons flew regular offensive patrols to prevent Luftwaffe and Italian interference, especially when to columns reached bottlenecks in the mountainous Jebel region. Brown observed that "the enemy's knowledge that our fighters were operating over our vulnerable areas was sufficient to deter him from using his aircraft in those areas. This is borne out by the fact that whenever our fighters were engaged in protecting the Australian Division withdrawing to the BARCE area, our Armoured Division, withdrawing on MECHILI, was attacked in the open country south of the hills."[56]

Enemy columns were frequent targets during this period in an attempt to slow their advance. On 31 March No. 55 Squadron sent five Blenheim bombers, escorted by two Blenheim fighters, to strike a concentration of enemy trucks and tanks in the area of Mersa Brega and Agheila. The bombers attacked from medium altitude, and the fighters made a low-level strafing pass. On 2 April another attack in the same area resulted in a big column of black smoke after five Blenheims bombed a concentration of vehicles. That afternoon seven Blenheims bombed and strafed a convoy near Agedabia and damaged at least twenty vehicles. On 7 April the arrival of a second Blenheim squadron, No. 45, heralded an increase in the tempo of air attacks. The fighting was costly, especially for the fighter squadrons: by 6 April No. 3 Squadron RAAF and the attached flight of No. 73 Squadron had been reduced to only three flyable aircraft. The squadrons were rested that day, but following operations the next day, only one or two fighters were available for action.[57]

Air Marshal Tedder promised more aircraft, so the Hurricane squadrons were committed to the ground battle even with the enhanced risk. A severe sandstorm limited operations on 9 April, but the next day the two Blenheim squadrons were joined by the Hurricanes of No. 73 Squadron in attacking enemy motor columns. One Hurricane was lost to ground fire, but the combined attacks inflicted heavy casualties on the enemy, the RAF claiming the destruction of more than eighty-five vehicles. For the next three days, the Blenheim and Hurricane squadrons continued to operate at a high tempo in an attempt to slow the enemy advance. Good to excellent results were claimed each day, but there was a cost for these operations. On 12 April two Hurricanes were lost to ground fire and one pilot killed, while the next day two Blenheims were lost during attacks against enemy transport south of Tobruk.[58] Overall RAF losses during the retreat, from 31 March to 14 April, were costly but not crippling: twelve Hurricanes, two Blenheims, and one Wellington.[59]

Despite the chaos of the retreat, the army and the air force were able to operate jointly during the battle. Group Captain Brown stated that army requests to attack enemy columns were regularly carried out. When the plight of the 2nd Armoured Division and 3rd Indian Motor Brigade at Mechili became known, the RAF concentrated on providing them air support. On 7 April the RAF were notified that a breakout would be attempted. Blenheims from Nos. 45 and 55 Squadrons attacked enemy columns in the vicinity of Msus and Mechili, while No. 3 Squadron RAAF provided air cover as well as low-level attacks. When the breakout did not occur that day, the squadrons prepared to mount a major effort on 8 April to again support the trapped units, but this proved impossible as a major dust storm grounded most aircraft.[60] Lost in the encirclement at Mechili were some 2,700 prisoners along with Maj. Gen. Michael Gambier-Parry, commander of the 2nd Armoured Division; Brig. Edward Vaughan, commander of the 3rd Indian Motor Brigade; and most of their headquarters establishments.[61]

General Wavell asserted that the overall effectiveness of the Luftwaffe and the Regia Aeronautica during this battle was low. His report made numerous references to the damage and dislocation caused by their air attacks and maintained that the enemy achieved air superiority during the fighting. Though there were numerous low-level and dive-bombing attacks on British troops during the retreat, little serious damage was caused. These raids were of a "tip and run" nature rather than a sustained interdiction campaign. The enemy made no concerted attempt to neutralize the RAF. British aerodromes were only attacked once with any success on 5 April, when eight German Me 110 twin-engine fighters made a strafing attack on the Derna landing ground and damaged four Blenheims, a Hurricane, and a Lysander; these aircraft were subsequently destroyed by the RAF to prevent their capture when the airfield was abandoned. The Blenheim squadrons were very active in support of the British retreat but were not intercepted a single time by enemy fighters during their many strikes on enemy ports, airfields, and battlefield targets. Most of the aircraft lost fell to ground fire rather than air-to-air combat.[62]

The one outstanding success achieved by the Luftwaffe was the destruction of a British petrol convoy on 5 April. The 3rd Armoured Brigade was desperately in need of fuel as it attempted to escape the region, and a convoy containing 8,000 gallons of petrol from divisional headquarters at El Abiar attempted to resupply the brigade. On its way south the column joined with a second convoy heading north that was evacuating supplies from Msus, including an additional 8,000 gallons of petrol. At 1:00 P.M. this combined group was bombed and machine gunned by eighteen Me 110s and Ju 88s for over thirty-five minutes. All twenty-one vehicles were destroyed, and the loss of this valuable fuel sealed the fate of the brigade. The success of this raid was not repeated.[63]

Brown recognized on 5 April that Luftwaffe attacks were concentrating on the 3rd Armoured Brigade in the Mechili area and were not interfering with the withdrawal of the 9th Australian Division. He took advantage of this by sending the Hurricanes of No. 3 RAAF and No. 6 Squadrons farther south, where they intercepted a number of attacks by German Ju 87 Stuka dive bombers. In one instance two Hurricanes from No. 73 Squadron and three from No. 3 Squadron RAAF claimed five Stukas destroyed and two damaged. Later in the afternoon nine Hurricanes from the two squadrons intercepted an attack by a dozen

Stukas, resulting in nine additional claims. The cost was two Hurricanes lost and one Australian pilot killed. After the war it was revealed that the Germans lost only eight dive bombers that day, not fourteen, but this was an unsustainable rate of attrition.[64] As the Germans had discovered during the Battle of Britain, unescorted Stukas could not operate in the presence of enemy fighters.

A week into the German offensive, Longmore ordered Collishaw to take command of RAF forces responsible for the defense of Egypt. The first week of April had not been good for the British, and Longmore later recalled that on 6 April, "the whole outlook was depressing."[65] In addition to Rommel's offensive, the British faced a number of other serious threats in the Mediterranean. On 6 April the Germans commenced their invasion of Greece and Yugoslavia and within days had captured Thrace and Macedonia.[66] Earlier that month a long-simmering dissatisfaction with the British mandate in Iraq led to a coup d'état on the first, conducted with Nazi support. Within two weeks the new Iraqi government had sent troops to besiege the RAF base at Habbaniya, and fighting erupted in early May when the British moved to break the siege. The conflict subsequently widened in June and July to include the Vichy France mandate of Syria as Germany attempted to support the Iraqi coup by moving forces through that region. The British feared the Germans would use Syria as a jumping-off point for an attack against Egypt. As a result Wavell and Longmore were forced to commit scarce ground and air forces to deal with these emerging threats.[67] The air chief marshal also had to contend with an ongoing campaign in Italian East Africa.[68] It is no coincidence that in the middle of these crises, Longmore turned to his most trusted commander to deal with the main threat to Egypt.

RAF Cyrenaica had been created primarily as a caretaker force to hold the front west of Benghazi. The rapid Axis advance had eliminated that mission, and it was necessary to return to the original task of the RAF in the Western Desert: the defense of Egypt. Longmore's confidence in Collishaw was confirmed by ordering the air commodore to reconstitute his old command.[69] On 8 April he proceeded to Mersa Matruh to establish the advanced headquarters of 204 Group. Within a week, Collishaw's unit, which absorbed the now-dissolved RAF Cyrenaica, was operational. This new organization was to prepare an "Air Striking Force" ready to operate at short notice against enemy air and mobile ground forces. The underlying intent of Collishaw's new orders was to ensure the enemy advance stopped at the Egyptian border, but the directive clearly established that this was not a defensive mission.[70]

For the RAF, operations prior to the first major German attack to capture Tobruk on 14 April were primarily of a defensive nature designed to cover the withdrawal of the British and Australian troops. Once the situation stabilized,

Collishaw launched an offensive against enemy aerodromes, ports and shipping, and lines of communications.[71] He stated that these "intensive air operations" against the enemy's "faulty L. of C. [line of communication] from Tripoli to Sollum would retard his advance."[72] The air commodore realized that any Axis advance beyond the Egyptian frontier would require a significant buildup of supplies, which could be slowed or prevented by interdicting vehicles on the axis of El Agheila–Benghazi–Tobruk–Bardia. Bombers and fighters immediately focused on this vulnerable line. Orders went out to make low-level attacks against only thin-skinned vehicles, especially ten-ton fuel trucks, that were on the move. This would keep the risks associated with such attacks to a minimum since armored fighting vehicles were difficult to destroy and halted convoys deployed substantial antiaircraft defenses. Collishaw directed his aircraft to interdict the entire length of the German supply line. The Blenheims, with the greatest radius of action, attacked the route between El Agheila and Benghazi. Long-range Hurricanes refueled at Tobruk and concentrated on the sector between Benghazi and Tobruk, while short-range Hurricanes patrolled closer to the frontier.[73]

From 8 April, the number of sorties devoted to these interdiction missions steadily increased as did the claims of destroyed enemy columns. Sorties by small groups of bombers and fighters in the beginning days increased to multisquadron missions that caused significant damage to Axis port and airfield facilities. Daylight attacks by the Blenheim and Hurricane squadrons were complemented by heavy night raids by Wellingtons from Egypt and Malta.[74] The Afrika Korps had overextended its advance to the frontier, and supply problems limited future operations. The logistical situation was manageable through April, but by early May the situation was so severe that Rommel, a commander who expected his subordinates to deal with such issues, was forced to write to the army high command on 10 May about it: "Because of concentrated pressure on ships and ports, with present protective measures arrival of supplies by ship cannot be guaranteed."[75]

The RAF offensive also forced the enemy air forces to adopt a largely defensive posture. German air attacks on Tobruk continued, but everywhere else the Luftwaffe and Regia Aeronautica flew defensive patrols to protect shipping, port facilities, and aerodromes. This tactic was largely futile and a wasteful use of air resources. RAF reports showed that very few of their offensive missions were intercepted and even fewer aircraft damaged or destroyed by aerial combat. British losses during this period were low, the majority suffered as a result of ground fire or mechanical issues.[76]

The overall effectiveness of the Axis air forces during the advance was less than expected, especially considering that they faced an opponent that was straining under the burden of a retreat. The German and the Italian air forces achieved some success, but there were many missed opportunities. It is clear that the Luftwaffe was as surprised by Rommel's offensive as were the British.[77] British aviators accomplished all that could be asked of them. Reconnaissance gathered intelligence for the army, air cover prevented most interference by the enemy warplanes, and airstrikes hit a variety of targets, both in the battle area and beyond, helping the army extricate its forces and prevent a total collapse. The decision to hold Tobruk was the deciding factor in avoiding a catastrophic disaster for the British. Actions by the 2nd Armoured Division supported by the RAF gained the 9th Australian Division sufficient time to retreat behind the Tobruk defenses and prepare for a siege. Rommel's inability to capture the port greatly hindered his future operations. Containing the British at Tobruk consumed a major portion of his combat power and, combined with the threat to his lines of communications, prevented a deeper incursion into Egypt.

One of the major outcomes of the retreat from Cyrenaica was a breakdown in relations between the RAF and the army. During the period of success, Collishaw and O'Connor worked closely to meet the needs of both services. Unfortunately, the realignment of forces necessary to support operations in Greece dismantled this successful team. O'Connor and Collishaw were reassigned, the 7th Armoured and 6th Australian Divisions were reallocated, and new forces arrived in the desert. All the senior army commanders were new. The only senior officer remaining was Group Captain Brown, who was given command of the newly formed RAF Cyrenaica. During the dark days of Rommel's offensive, when confusion and a lack of knowledge dominated events, relations between the two services deteriorated, especially at the higher levels. Lieutenant General Neame blamed the defeat on the weakness of his command, deficiencies in the signals infrastructure, and a lack of air reconnaissance and air support. He lamented the weak air forces supporting his command that provided minimal reconnaissance and air support while he had to face one hundred German fighters and one hundred German bombers and dive bombers.[78] The 9th Australian Division's report echoed these sentiments: "Air support too, was quite inadequate for the purpose. We were unable both to obtain information of enemy movements or to prevent aircraft flying low over our own area because of our shortage in planes and anti-aircraft guns. 6 Squadron R.A.F., operating from AGEDABIA, was under orders 9th Aust Div, but it was greatly understrength."[79] This was a very different tone compared to the harmonious relations of Operation Compass and the gratitude for RAF support expressed in the after-action reports of Wavell and O'Connor.

A key sign of this friction was contained in General Wavell's report detailing the actions of the 2nd Armoured Division. He attempted to make sense of the confusion that engulfed that division at the start of April. One of its major conclusions was that on 3 April, "a day of mischances, misunderstandings and counter-orders," an air report indicated that an enemy column was approaching Msus, a key supply point for the division.[80] The 3rd Armoured Brigade was redeployed to Msus but arrived after the troops guarding the dump had withdrawn and destroyed the fuel cache. Combined with mechanical breakdowns and enemy action, the loss of this petrol halted the brigade by the fifth. Wavell blamed this situation on the false air report.[81]

The British commander was also critical of a second air report made on the evening of 5 April that indicated an enemy column was on the move north from Msus. This information caused Lieutenant General Neame to issue an order for a general withdrawal, though this was subsequently countermanded when a second report stated that there was no enemy approaching. Wavell attributed the erroneous information to partially trained pilots and an ineffective system of relaying air-to-ground signals from reconnaissance aircraft. At the end of his report, the general listed the eight main factors that contributed to the disaster; three of his points directly blamed the failure of the RAF while all but one of the remaining reasons was exacerbated by those shortcomings. Thus, in large measure Wavell was blaming the RAF for the retreat.[82]

As might be expected, this angered RAF leadership. Wavell had "warmly praised" the tactical-reconnaissance reports provided by No. 6 Squadron in the immediate aftermath of the disaster, but his views on the overall RAF support changed after further reflection.[83] The general submitted his report directly to the British cabinet without consulting Air Chief Marshal Longmore, Air Marshal Tedder, Group Captain Brown, Brig. A. F. Harding, or the Brigadier General Staff of Cyrenaica Command.[84] Air Chief Marshal Portal, the chief of the Air Staff, sought clarification from Tedder, who had recently taken over from Longmore as the air officer commanding-in-chief Middle East two days after the report was released. Portal wanted to understand the facts behind Wavell's assertions, but he was most concerned about the future ramifications to army–air force relations. Churchill, in his role as minister of defense, wrote a scathing note appended to the start of the report making it clear that he placed the blame for defeat on the poor state of preparedness and general weakness of British forces in Cyrenaica. Though he did not blame the RAF for the failure, he accepted Wavell's criticisms and stated that there was "an imperative need for every armoured formation to have attached to it, and working with it, aircraft whose pilots and observers have been for some time in intimate association with the armoured unit, and who have the military knowledge and experience necessary to enable them to report as correctly as possible, in all the difficulties of war, what they see."[85] The implementation of this recommendation had serious implications regarding the future autonomy of the RAF.[86]

"Bingo" Brown, who had been promoted air commodore and was air officer commanding RAF in Palestine and Trans-Jordan, wrote two reports in response to Wavell's comments. The first addressed the questions posed to Tedder by Portal and was openly critical of the army's performance. The second report, written in conjunction with Brigadier Harding, covered many of the same points but adopted a more balanced approach to rebuffing Wavell's remarks.[87] The reports examined in great detail the circumstances surrounding the "false air report" made on 3 April that, according to Wavell, led to such confusion among British forces. Brown and Harding confirmed that at 2:00 P.M. a tactical-reconnaissance flight was made from Msus by Flight Lt. H. G. Fletcher, one of the senior pilots in No. 6 Squadron. He discovered "a column consisting of a few armoured cars and between 50 and 60 large Italian lorries filled with troops" only five miles south of the town. After the column opened fire on his aircraft, Fletcher strafed the vehicles and returned to Msus.[88]

The Harding and Brown report demonstrated that the timing of the flight made it impossible for this information to have been responsible for the change in orders given to the 3rd Armoured Brigade, which occurred shortly after 2:00 P.M. To report his discovery, Fletcher flew to the aerodrome at Barce, a distance of over sixty miles, where he gave his findings to the air-intelligence liaison officer. This army officer then dispatched a courier to convey the information to command headquarters, where it was transmitted to the 2nd Armoured Division's headquarters. If the system was working perfectly, the message would not have arrived before the 3rd Armoured Brigade's orders were changed, and given the chaotic state of communications at that time, it was well-nigh impossible.

Capt. A. H. P. Hore-Ruthven was the British liaison officer with the Free French detachment guarding the fuel cache at Msus. He talked with Fletcher before the pilot departed at 2:00 P.M. The flight lieutenant promised to return and share the details of his reconnaissance mission, but at 2:30 P.M. Hore-Ruthven saw Fletcher's Lysander fly over Msus, not landing there. The captain thus was not privy to Fletcher's discovery of the enemy convoy, but the fact that the aircraft did not land influenced his decision to blow the dump based on his own assessment of the situation.[89] Regarding the false air report of 5 April, Harding and Brown point out that there was no report made of enemy troops advancing north from Msus but that another report was made at the same time of enemy troops advancing east in the vicinity of Churruba. A withdrawal based on this information was ordered but then cancelled when army reports indicated that the column was British. Events the next day proved that the forces in question were in fact German, and the withdrawal was again ordered. Harding and Brown countered Wavell's contention that there was a shortage of air reconnaissance by demonstrating that all requests for tactical and strategic reconnaissance made by the 2nd Armoured Division were met during the battle.[90]

While the jointly authored report is relatively neutral in tone, Brown's private report to Tedder argued more forcefully that it was army confusion and poor decision making that caused the difficulties. On the night of 2 February, the 2nd Armoured Division's headquarters, which was collocated with the forward flight of No. 6 Squadron at Antelat, had retreated. The airmen awoke the next morning to discover themselves alone without any support or friendly forces between themselves and the enemy.[91] The disorder and confusion during the army's retreat was again shown by the decision to ignore RAF reports on 5 April that detailed the advance of a large enemy column eastward along the El Abia–Mechili road. Based on this information, Brown ordered his headquarters and Nos. 3 RAAF and 6 Squadrons to move from Maraua to Derna. Neame's headquarters also issued orders for a general withdrawal. Later that night Brigadier Harding telephoned Brown to tell him his pilots had misidentified a column of British forces and ordered him to return his squadrons to Maraua, where the division headquarters would remain. Brown interrogated his pilots, who were convinced the column was German. The next day it was discovered this column was in fact German, and a general retirement was once again ordered. Brown stated that this incident "directly" resulted in the capture of Generals O'Connor and Neame along with Brigadier John Combe. Wavell had summoned O'Connor to the front on 2 April to deal with the crisis caused by Rommel's advance. His intention was to replace Neame, but after consultations it was agreed that while Neame would remain in command, O'Connor would stay and act in an advisory role. On the evening of 6 April, the staff car carrying the generals made a wrong turn while returning to their headquarters and ran into a German patrol; they were captured.[92]

Brown described the process for the conveyance of intelligence gathered by RAF pilots. Upon landing, pilots were interviewed by an air-intelligence liaison officer, who gathered the information to report to army headquarters. This army officer was responsible for the interpretation of any information provided by the pilots. Brown stated that "one elementary principle laid down regarding air reconnaissance is that the pilot only reports what he sees and that it is for the army to interpret the information in the light of their knowledge. . . . The point, therefore, is that any confusion arising out of air reports is the responsibility of the Army and that the reports were not incorrect."[93]

According to Brown, the 2nd Armoured Division ceased to be an efficient fighting force soon after the start of the German attack. This resulted in the breakdown of communications and the absence of accurate intelligence upon which to base plans for the duration of the battle. His squadrons met all the demands made for reconnaissance, and any problems with that intelligence were not the result of "false reports," but rather the failure of the army to "interpret the information received and to arrive at a correct appreciation of the situation."[94] Brown provided Portal with the evidence he required to prove that Wavell was wrong in his criticisms of the RAF. The general subsequently withdrew his accusations and dispatched a telegram to London that stated: "Regret A.O.C.-in-C. not consulted. False deductions may have been made from air reports but please withdraw suggestion that false air reports were rendered by R.A.F. and that there was a lack of TAC.R. [tactical reconnaissance] in latter stages."[95]

The two months following the destruction of the Italian Tenth Army at Beda Fomm marked a reversal of fortune for the British in Cyrenaica. A fleeting opportunity existed to complete the expulsion of Axis forces from Libya, but this risky option, supported by Collishaw and O'Connor, was rejected. British army units and RAF squadrons were in a poor state of preparedness after the demands of the previous campaign, no substantial new units or reserves were available, and the great distance from El Agheila to Tripoli was a logistical nightmare. Ultimately, the decision not to proceed was made by the commitment of forces to other theaters in the Middle East, primarily Greece. Cyrenaica, as the gateway to Egypt, was held by a weak screening force justified by intelligence estimates that showed the Italians to be a defeated force and German reinforcements not yet ready for offensive operations.

No one was able to predict Rommel's aggressive nature as he recklessly drove his forces forward without a secure logistical base. The weakened state of the British, however, allowed this bold move to succeed, and by mid-April the Axis forces had advanced across the bulge of Cyrenaica all the way to the Egyptian border, with only the fortress of Tobruk resisting their assault. The loss of territory was costly for the British, but overall the retreat had been conducted with more control than the Italian reverse, thus the forfeiture of men and equipment was minimal. The German advance was largely meaningless because there had been no "victory of annihilation"—Rommel's small force "had overrun a vast wasteland, but it hadn't destroyed anything."[96] Egypt and the Suez Canal were still safe from Axis predations, and the possession of Tobruk threatened the supply lines of any further enemy advance.

Early in the withdrawal Longmore brought Collishaw forward to take over command of the RAF response. The reversal in Libya was serious for Longmore, but he also had to contend with active campaigns in Greece and Italian East Africa along with a developing situation in Iraq. He needed a trusted commander to oversee the defense of Egypt and did not hesitate to recall Collishaw for this task.

The lost territory was a setback, but more troubling was the breakdown in relations between the army and the air force. The month of April had not been kind to the British in the Mediterranean. On 6 April, a week after the launch of the Libyan offensive, the Germans attacked in Greece and quickly routed W Force. By 21 April, General Wilson was compelled to order the evacuation of Commonwealth forces to Crete and Egypt. The small number of RAF squadrons sent to Greece could do little to prevent the catastrophe, but in the eyes of many soldiers, who were subjected to seemingly constant Luftwaffe attacks, the air force earned the sobriquets "Royal Absent Force" or "Rare As Fairies."[97] Army postmortems on this campaign were quick to blame the lack of air support for its failure. Wilson went so far as to claim that events in Greece demonstrated "the need for an Army Air Force."[98]

The setbacks in Greece combined with the loss of Cyrenaica exposed a rift between the army and the RAF. The chaos of these retreats led ground commanders to blame the air force for a lack of support. Wavell, who should have known better, took this issue all the way to the British cabinet. Though he was ultimately proven wrong and censured by Churchill, the damage to the previously good army-air relations had been done. The close working relationship of XIII Corps and 202 Group developed by O'Connor and Collishaw during Operation Compass was replaced by a climate of distrust that would be further exposed by upcoming operations in Tobruk, Crete, and the Western Desert.

The Siege of Tobruk, Operation Brevity, and Crete

"Disaster seemed to follow on disaster" was Collishaw's summation of the situation in mid-April when he returned to the Western Desert to command 204 Group.[1] The British loss of Cyrenaica was followed by the evacuation of Greece in late April. The Australian defenders of Tobruk repulsed a number of Axis assaults, but the German and Italian air forces continued to bomb the garrison on a daily basis, and a renewed attack was imminent. The size of 204 Group at the time was relatively small and comprised only four heavy-bomber, three medium-bomber, and two fighter squadrons. Despite this, Collishaw used his meagre forces to its fullest extent to interfere with enemy plans. As the RAF staff history noted, "A remarkable feature of the last half of April was the high scale of effort maintained by this comparatively small force working under the difficulties imposed by the Axis advance, the chief of which was the great distance of the air bases from the target area."[2]

The air offensive launched by Collishaw targeted enemy ports, airfields, and the lines of communications. The port of Benghazi was a prime target, but Tripoli was also struck repeatedly by Wellingtons operating out of Malta. A number of large Italian ships were sunk by these attacks, and the port capacity at Benghazi was seriously diminished.[3] The low-level raids on the aerodromes in Libya were effective at distracting the Luftwaffe and Regia Aeronautica. Though Tobruk remained a regular target for enemy air attack, few other offensive air missions were carried out by the enemy during this period. Regular RAF strikes also focused on enemy motor convoys traveling between Benghazi and the frontier.[4]

The strength of 204 Group grew slowly during this period. Collishaw recalled that "one cheering note was the arrival of new squadrons, including two from South Africa."[5] Replacement aircraft and aircrew also became available and were posted to the operational squadrons. Less glamorous than fighters and bombers, though just as valuable, were the noncombat echelons. Collishaw, concerned that another retreat might be necessary but also remembering the lessons of Operation Compass (when his squadrons traveled great distances during the advance), ensured that his units had all the necessary motor transport to facilitate such a move. He also improved the capability of the salvage-and-repair organization in his group.[6] Overall these improvements allowed the squadrons to "face the enemy in the air with some degree of confidence."[7]

Rommel's offensive halted at the Egyptian border in mid-April due to logistical difficulties. The British decision to hold Tobruk created an operational dilemma for the German commander. The port was not central to his main ambition to drive the British from Egypt and capture the Suez Canal, but it sat astride his main supply line and thus could not be ignored. Rommel was determined to capture the port but did not accord its 24,000 defenders much respect. Starting on 12 April, he launched a series of impromptu attacks on the Tobruk perimeter that made limited gains at the cost of high casualties.[8] The men of the 9th Australian Division, supported by the remaining tanks of the 2nd Armoured Division and the RAF, were determined to repel any attack. After the destruction of the German Machine-Gun Battalion 8 on the morning of 14 April and abortive attacks by the Italians on 16–17 April, Rommel ordered his forces to dig in as he prepared a new plan.[9] The failure to capture the port left the enemy "surprised, disappointed, widely dispersed, and in difficulties with the stony ground."[10] Rommel's impetuosity served him well at the start of his offensive, but at Tobruk it "seriously weakened" his overextended forces.[11] The general was widely criticized by his superiors, his junior officers, and his Italian allies for not taking the time to prepare a proper attack on the fortress. It would take him nearly two weeks to prepare his next major attempt to dislodge the Australians.[12]

For the army, Lieutenant General Neame's Cyrenaica Command ceased operations in Tobruk on 13 April, and Maj. Gen. Leslie Morshead, commander of the 9th Australian Division, assumed command of the besieged forces. Neame's old headquarters was subsequently re-formed the next day at Maaten Bagush as the Western Desert Force under the command of Maj. Gen. Noel Beresford-Peirse, who had previously led the 4th Indian Division during the opening stage of Operation Compass. The common feature of these changes was the reintroduction of experienced commanders. Both Neame and Major General Gambier-Parry, commander of the 2nd Armoured Division, were criticized for their lack of desert experience, and the loss of Lieutenant General O'Connor was acutely felt. As for the RAF, Brown had considerable experience and had performed as well as could be expected, but Collishaw was highly respected by Longmore and considered a better choice to reestablish the air dominance the British had previously enjoyed.

The repulse of the initial attacks on Tobruk led to a period of relative quiet for Morshead's men as they worked hard to improve their defenses, but there was no respite for the RAF. The Luftwaffe did not have sufficient forces to be strong everywhere in the Mediterranean, but the importance of Tobruk led to a major commitment of its air assets. The Germans dive bombed the harbor, airfield, and defensive positions while the RAF did its best to contest the skies. These air raids were generally large-scale affairs designed to overwhelm the defenders. For example, on 19 April a force of twenty Ju 88 twin-engine bombers escorted by five fighters attacked; three days later thirteen Hurricanes scrambled to intercept a force of fifty Ju 87s escorted by thirty Me 110s, twelve Me 109s, and twelve Italian Fiat G.50s; and a raid of the same scale was again made on 23 April.[13] Despite this large commitment by the Luftwaffe, Rommel was unhappy with his air support. RAF bomber attacks plagued his ground forces, and British fighters appeared to operate without opposition. The problem was deemed serious enough that the first Me 109 units arrived in North Africa in mid-April in response to the uneven contest at Tobruk. These reinforcements sufficiently increased the pressure on RAF units that they were soon forced to withdraw from Cyrenaica.[14]

Two British squadrons, Nos. 6 and 73, were based at El Gubbi airfield inside the Tobruk perimeter, but it soon became clear that the challenges of operations there were too demanding. By 21 April the pilots of No. 73 Squadron were exhausted, and only five serviceable aircraft remained. Two days later the squadron lost three aircraft shot down and three others damaged in crash landings or strafed on the ground. As early as 14 April Collishaw advised Tedder that the squadrons needed to be withdrawn as the situation was too dangerous. The army, however, argued that it was essential that aircraft be retained in Tobruk to fly air-defense and reconnaissance missions. Tedder supported the army and ordered that a minimum of ten Hurricanes be kept in Tobruk. This would not be the last time that the air marshal acceded to the demands of the army over the objections of his subordinate. On 23 April Collishaw again appealed to Tedder for permission to withdraw the Hurricanes from Tobruk; he understood the importance of air cover for the port, but the small number of aircraft available could only fight a losing battle unless significantly reinforced. He was finally given permission on 24 April to evacuate No. 73 Squadron to Sidi Hanesh, near Mersa Matruh.[15] Henceforth, air cover over the port would be provided by fighters based near Mersa Matruh and refueled at Sidi Barrani. This decision conceded air superiority over Tobruk to the Luftwaffe, but there was no other option. Air operations within a besieged perimeter was untenable for the RAF.

Not surprisingly, Major General Morshead was incensed. The RAF liaison section in Tobruk cabled 204 Group on 25 April to report "GOC here

[Morshead] considers present fighter policy precludes adequate measures for defence of TOBRUCH [*sic*] as it is impossible to carry out Lysander air shoots without escort thus rendering our artillery vulnerable to enemy counter battery action. Considers policy also hampers return of our raiding parties and will lower morale of troops."[16] Morshead appealed directly to Major General Beresford-Peirse: "I view with gravest concern change in air policy resulting in withdrawal of fighters to BAGUSH area. This must give enemy aircraft considerably greater freedom to operate against troops and port and will affect morale more quickly than anything else. Most strongly urge that despite risks at least one squadron be stationed here."[17] Beresford-Peirse sympathized with Morshead's concerns but supported Collishaw's action. He pointed out that the RAF had lost twenty-seven of thirty-two aircraft based in Tobruk, and only eleven Hurricanes remained in the Western Desert for all types of missions—tactical reconnaissance, naval escort, and fighter cover. He assured Morshead that this decision was not taken lightly, but "until fighter strength increase your 'drome cannot be maintained. . . . I know it is deplorable from your point of view—but it is hard necessity."[18] Tobruk continued to suffer from frequent air raids until mid-May, when Luftwaffe units were reassigned for the Crete operation.

Despite the withdrawal from Tobruk, the RAF continued to provide a high level of support. Hurricanes from Nos. 73 and 274 Squadrons flew regular patrols over the besieged port, intercepting enemy air raids and inflicting a heavy toll on enemy motor transport through low-level machine-gun attacks. Blenheims of Nos. 45 and 55 Squadrons interdicted enemy transport around Tobruk and struck enemy airfields.[19] These raids significantly impeded German operations against Tobruk. On 13 and 14 April the medium bombers maintained a high tempo of operations against Axis forces preparing to attack the fortress. Low-level attacks with small bombs took a heavy toll on the enemy. Contrary to the view of Morshead, the Afrika Korps war diary recorded on 14 April: "During the entire period since the encirclement of Tobruk, the British had complete air superiority and daily attacked the investing forces with successive waves of bombers. . . . The Commander, 10th Air Corps gave the Commander Afrika Corps a verbal undertaking to provide fighter aircraft at an early date."[20]

The British hoped that these offensive operations would help check enemy air attacks on Tobruk. Morshead, however, continued to be dissatisfied with the air support provided as he found that the request system was not sufficiently responsive to attack targets of opportunity. It took too long to transmit requests, fighters and bombers were not available on call, and support could only be provided if aircraft were available.[21]

On 30 April Rommel was ready to make another attempt to capture Tobruk, ordering his two German divisions, the 5th Light and 15th Panzer, to break into the Australian line west of Ras el Medauar. The Italian Ariete and Brescia Divisions would then expand the breach as the Germans renewed their attack on the port. In advance of the attack an additional group of dive bombers were transferred from Sicily to North Africa to compensate for the Afrika Korps's lack of artillery. The preparatory bombardment was largely concentrated in the eastern portion of the bridgehead to take attention away from the actual point of the assault. Stuka attacks were similarly directed at the area in front of the demonstration being made by the 5th Light Division to the southwest as well as targeting the main road junctions at Sidi Mahmud and the roads leading into Tobruk. The German assault was launched at 8:00 P.M. and quickly breached the outer defensive line, but the advance was halted by stubborn Australian resistance and an undetected minefield. Major General Morshead deployed his reserves to contain the breach and requested RAF support for first light on 1 May. Hurricanes from Nos. 73 and 274 Squadrons flew standing patrols over the enemy penetration and encountered large numbers of enemy fighters and dive bombers. The British aircraft disrupted the intended attacks and shot down three Me 109s and one Stuka at the cost of one Hurricane lost and two damaged. By 4 May the battle concluded as Rommel realized no further gains were possible. The small area captured (three miles wide by two miles deep) came at a high cost for Axis forces, which suffered 1,200 German and 500 Italian casualties. The Australians incurred nearly 800 casualties to hold their line.[22]

The failure of this attempt at Tobruk led British intelligence to conclude that the possibility of further offensive operations directed against Egypt in the near future was minimal. This pause was essential to allow the regeneration of British combat power in the desert. General Wavell was desperately short of tanks and possessed only two weak units, one in Tobruk and the other near Mersa Matruh, compared to an estimated 150 enemy tanks. The RAF was also greatly weakened by operational losses in March and April. At the start of May, 204 Group possessed only forty serviceable aircraft, well below half-strength, but in less than two weeks Collishaw's squadrons were at near full strength. Given the circumstances, Air Chief Marshal Longmore ordered his area commander to return to the policy of interdiction missions that had proven effective at the start of the war. Enemy lines of communication would be attacked in an effort to delay or prevent a renewed Axis offensive.[23]

General Wavell retained his command after the loss of Libya, unlike the senior air commander. Longmore had performed a masterful juggling act during his time in the Middle East by matching his meagre resources to many competing demands. Churchill and Portal, however, began to lose confidence in him in early 1941 as differences over strategy and questions over the supply of aircraft led them to doubt his suitability for command.[24] When Air Marshal Tedder was sent to the Middle East in late 1940 to become Longmore's deputy commander, Air Chief Marshal Sir Wilfrid Freeman, the vice chief of the Air Staff, asked him to "tell Longmore that we fully appreciate all his difficulties, but we are becoming tired of moan, moan, moan."[25] Tedder dutifully informed Longmore that his messages were causing "irritation and antagonism." For a while his cables to London were more temperate, but on 30 April the air chief marshal sent yet another sharp demand for aircraft, including new types such as the Hawker Typhoon, Bristol Beaufighter, Westland Whirlwind, Avro Manchester, and Short Stirling. This raised the ire of Churchill, who had long believed that the number of aircraft available to operational squadrons was far too low when compared to the number dispatched to the Middle East.[26] Freeman was a supporter of Longmore, but this latest request revealed "a fundamental failure to understand the vital contribution that salvage and repair could make to keeping the squadrons supplied . . . , [and] asking for unproven new aircraft with all the problems of maintenance and spares at the end of such a tenuous supply line, was inane."[27] The next day Longmore was recalled to London for consultations and would not return to the Middle East. Tedder immediately became the acting air commander-in-chief and was confirmed in the position on 1 June.[28] This development would have significant implications for Collishaw as Longmore had been his stalwart supporter, fighting to keep him as his commander in the Western Desert; Tedder had consistently criticized Collishaw in personal letters sent to Freeman between January and June 1941 and would seek to replace the air commodore as soon as possible.[29]

May 1941 began as a period of relative quiet for the RAF in North Africa. The Wellington squadrons based near the canal continued nightly attacks against the Cyrenaican ports, especially Benghazi, while the Blenheim and Hurricane squadrons made occasional raids on the Axis supply lines and airfields between the Egyptian frontier and Tripoli. Typical for this period were the operations that took place on 5 May: Eight Blenheims from No. 14 Squadron, operating in pairs, bombed and machine gunned enemy motor-transport convoys near Gambut, Bir Chleta, and Capuzzo, destroying and damaging a number of vehicles. No. 39 Squadron conducted strategic reconnaissance of Benghazi, Giarabub, and Derna, while Nos. 6 and 274 Squadrons made tactical-reconnaissance flights over Acroma and Capuzzo. That night ten Wellingtons bombed the port at Benghazi along with the airfields at Berka, Benina, Derna, Gazala, and Bardia. One Maryland from No. 39 Squadron was lost to a German fighter near Acroma.[30]

Low-level Hurricane attacks were very effective at interdicting the movement of Axis convoys. A large fighter sweep on 17 May saw Hurricanes of Nos.

73, 274, and 1 SAAF Squadrons interdict the Tobruk–Bardia–Capuzzo area. "The Hurricanes destroyed nineteen vehicles and severely damaged a number of others. They also shot up several staff cars and motor-cyclists on the road and destroyed a petrol dump on BU AMUD landing ground. The enemy's M.T. movements were considerably disorganized by these operations."[31] Collishaw appreciated that any further advance by Rommel into Egypt would require the transportation of a vast stock of supplies to the frontier. It would be considerably easier to destroy these soft targets rather than repel an invasion. The road convoys, especially the petrol and troop-carrying lorries, were very susceptible to machine-gun attacks. Collishaw ordered that only moving convoys be attacked as they were least likely to be protected by antiaircraft guns, which could only be deployed when the vehicles halted. The normal tactic was for

> two Hurricanes to leave the base [Mersa Matruh] at brief intervals, refuel at Barrani, and then proceed at maximum height out to sea, crossing the coast in the neighbourhood of GAZALA and having located M.T. vehicles by the dust cloud, to descend at high speed and shoot up the convoy. Our aircraft then proceeded homeward along the main roads, keeping low and attacking all vehicles as they came to them. When the ammunition became low our aircraft put out to sea.[32]

Collishaw was correct in his estimation that the most profitable targets for his aircraft were the enemy lines of communication. Rommel was notorious for ignoring his logistics, and his advance in April took place despite his tenuous supply line. Between 8 February and 1 May, the Germans transported 33,549 men, 11,330 vehicles, and 36,332 tons of supplies and equipment across the Mediterranean Sea to Tripoli, but twelve of the twenty-nine ships involved in this passage were sunk and another five put out of action indefinitely. This amounted to the loss of 59 percent of the total shipping tonnage available. The 932-mile road trek from Tripoli to Tobruk was equally vulnerable as the Germans possessed enough trucks to move normal supplies to the front but lacked the capacity to transport reinforcements and the large quantity of ammunition necessary for a renewed offensive.[33] As early as 20 April Gen. Stefan Fröhlich, commander of Fliegerführer Afrika, the main Luftwaffe command in North Africa, signaled Gen. Otto Hoffmann von Waldau, chief of the Operations Branch of the General Staff of the Luftwaffe, to express concern over the air situation. He declared that the British enjoyed air superiority and the supply lines and airfields were vulnerable and highly susceptible to attack. He also lamented the lack of antiaircraft guns available in the theater as well as the fact that many of the batteries possessed by Rommel were unavailable for air defense as they were committed to an antitank role.[34] This last point is interesting. The German 88-mm Gun was a very effective weapon in either the antiaircraft or antitank role, but due to operational demands, it could often not be employed in both roles at the same time.

Benghazi was a prime target for the British interdiction campaign. The long overland route from Tripoli, combined with a shortage of trucks, forced the enemy to use Benghazi harbor and the other smaller ports to shorten the road distance. Axis attacks on the port during the first months of 1941 were never able to close Benghazi to Allied shipping, but they forced the British to make alternate arrangements. Collishaw hoped for a similar outcome by directing his Wellington squadrons to make regular nightly attacks, augmented by occasional daylight raids by his Blenheims. The last two weeks of April saw twelve separate raids (forty-four sorties) made on Benghazi. Intelligence reports indicated the port's capacity had been sufficiently reduced that the enemy could not rely on it to supply his continued advance. This pattern continued in May, though commitments to Greece and Crete meant that Wellington operations in the Western Desert were largely confined to these attacks. A total of twenty-four raids (forty-five sorties) during the month continued to cause considerable damage to the port and limit its usefulness to the enemy. The Luftwaffe in North Africa signaled on 9 May to confirm the success of this campaign: "Supply position of D.A.K. (Africa Corps) very serious owing to continued and successful pressure by British fleet and Air Force on communications via Benghazi and Tripoli."[35] Prior to being diverted to Crete, Collishaw's Blenheim squadrons contributed to the interdiction campaign by regularly attacking Axis airfields in Cyrenaica as well as targeting columns of motor transport.[36]

The effectiveness of this denial campaign, combined with the Royal Navy's success in interdicting enemy supply ships, was offset by an increasing German use of air transport to augment the supplies delivered to Rommel. In February and March a daily average of twenty to twenty-five transport flights crossed the Mediterranean, but in April this had more than doubled, some days in excess of one hundred aerial-supply sorties. These transports were targeted by 204 Group fighters and bombers whenever their presence in Cyrenaica was detected, and RAF records mention numerous successful attacks in April, May, and June.[37]

The continued RAF attacks kept the German and Italian air forces largely on the defensive. The Luftwaffe in North Africa had many tasks, and most of its fighters were devoted to protecting the air bridge to Libya as well as providing air cover for their ports and airfields. The small number of offensive sorties made by the Luftwaffe were directed at Tobruk and British naval forces attempting to resupply the garrison, with a small number of largely ineffective raids on Alexandria and the Suez Canal. As in the past, the Italians devoted the vast majority of their aircraft to maintaining standing air patrols over their ports and airfields as well as along the main roads. As a result of this defensive posture, attacks on British airfields and troop positions were rare beyond the Tobruk perimeter. An indication of the effectiveness of British attacks was the Axis decision to place armored vehicles every five miles along the main road between Tobruk and Capuzzo as well as along the Trigh Capuzzo between El Adem and Sidi Aziez. These pickets did not destroy many British aircraft, but they achieved their purpose:

> The flak fire from a single A.F.V. may be expected to have little effect against a fast low flying aircraft, but the stationing of these vehicles five miles apart severely handicapped our operations and our tactics, because our aircraft had previously enjoyed freedom from flak while flying homeward at ground level along the roads in search of further prey. Each A.F.V., opening fire successively as our aircraft flew low along the road, had the effect of disconcerting our low-flying attacks, and to that degree was effective.[38]

Pilots were warned not to engage these armored vehicles as previous experience had shown that such attacks were ineffective and costly. It was much better to attack soft-sided motor transport, especially the ten-ton fuel bowsers, which were largely undefended and easily destroyed. The enemy also countered the British attacks by limiting road travel to the hours of darkness and halting during the day, with vehicles widely dispersed to limit their exposure. This tactic minimized losses to air attack but imposed its own delays on resupply efforts. British casualties in these low-level attacks was remarkably low, and very few aircraft were lost with one notable exception. On 21 May the RAF attacked large concentrations of enemy vehicles in the Capuzzo area. Hurricanes of Nos. 73, 274, and 1 SAAF Squadrons made strikes along the main road, destroying numerous vehicles including two petrol or ammunition lorries, which burned furiously. One Hurricane from No. 73 Squadron was lost when attacked by six Me 109s; the British claimed one enemy fighter shot down in flames. Later in the morning, seven Blenheims from No. 14 Squadron went out individually to continue the attacks on a large convoy estimated at 350 vehicles. The first two aircraft bombed successfully, claiming a number of vehicles destroyed, but the remainder were pounced by enemy fighters. Over a span of ten minutes, the five trailing aircraft were shot down by Me 109s, and all fifteen crewmembers were killed.[39]

In late April Generalleutnant Friedrich Paulus, assistant chief of staff for operations on the Army General Staff, was sent to North Africa to report on Rommel. Gen. Franz Halder, chief of the General Staff, was concerned that a crisis had developed at the Egyptian frontier near Sollum, where the British were preparing an offensive. Following the failure of the 30 April attacks on

Tobruk, Paulus ordered Rommel to adopt a defensive posture and to seek permission before again launching any offensive operations. His report to Halder stated, "The crux of the problem in North Africa is not Tobruk or Sollum, but the organization of supplies. . . . By overstepping his orders Rommel has brought about a situation for which our present supply capabilities are insufficient."[40] Within two days of its transmission, Paulus's full report was being read in London and Cairo thanks to Ultra. German supply problems were confirmed in this cable, which also revealed that the 15th Panzer Division was being sent to Libya but had not yet arrived. This intelligence "directly influenced" Wavell's decision to launch a minor offensive, Operation Brevity, to take advantage of the situation in mid-May.[41]

Brig. William "Strafer" Gott, the commander of the Support Group, 7th Armoured Division, was ordered to strike a rapid blow across the frontier to capture the Halfaya Pass, Sollum, and Capuzzo and then exploit toward Tobruk. The plan was for three parallel forces to advance: the 7th Armoured Brigade Group on the desert flank to Sidi Azeiz, the 22nd Guards Brigade Group in the center to clear the top of the Halfaya Pass and then advance to Capuzzo and beyond, and the third group to advance along the coast and occupy the bottom of the pass and then exploit to Sollum.[42]

During the planning for Brevity, a disagreement emerged between the army and the RAF over the proper employment of aircraft. Due to the relative weakness of his attacking forces, Brigadier Gott urged Major General Beresford-Peirse to demand complete RAF support. He requested that bomber and fighter attacks "should be conducted directly against the A.F.V.s. [armored fighting vehicles] of the enemy, the intention being that the R.A.F. should act as artillery with the object of putting enemy A.F.V.s out of action."[43] Gott displayed his complete ignorance of British air capabilities by requesting that the warplanes perform their least effective mission: attacking targets they would have difficulty finding, hitting, and destroying, all of which would come at a high cost to the attacking aircraft. Collishaw realized this problem and sensibly replied that the Italian air force had dropped thousands of bombs on the 7th Armoured Division but caused little damage. Rather, the RAF would be better employed attacking "the thin-skinned vehicles in the rear of the A.F.V.s, on the ground that the A.F.V.s. cannot fight without petrol and ammunition, and the paralyzing of the L. of C. [line of communications] would automatically bring about the breakdown of the fighting services."[44] Beresford-Peirse agreed to this plan with the stipulation that the air force would intervene directly on the battlefield if the army encountered serious resistance.[45]

The RAF plan for Operation Brevity was cleverly designed to isolate the battlefield and prevent the movement of enemy reinforcements and supplies.

Prior to the campaign, air attacks occurred on enemy concentrations in the Tobruk area as well as low-flying strikes on the lines of communications from El Agheila to Benghazi and Tobruk. Once the battle commenced, low-level fighter and bomber attacks were concentrated in the area immediately behind the battlefront, essentially between Sollum and Tobruk, to disrupt the movement of enemy reinforcements and supplies. The intensity of attacks meant that no fighters could be diverted to provide air cover during the action. Continual reconnaissance was carried out in the Tobruk area to discover the movement of any significant enemy forces toward the frontier. In that event Collishaw was prepared to concentrate his strikes on those targets, but no movement of that nature developed.[46]

The operation was launched on the morning of 15 May and surprised the German and Italian frontier defenders. The 7th Armoured Brigade Group pushed aside weak screening forces to advance to Sidi Aziez, while the Guards Brigade Group captured the top of Halfaya Pass before proceeding to Bir er Regima, three miles south of Bardia, before retiring to Fort Capuzzo. The coastal group met stubborn resistance at the bottom of the pass, but this was overcome, and by evening the force was established in Sollum. The attack, though it had been expected by the Germans, caused a crisis for them as it was feared this was a major operation to relieve Tobruk. By 8:00 A.M. forward German units were demanding the strongest possible support from the Luftwaffe, but the weak air response that developed was defeated by small offensive patrols from Nos. 73 and 274 Squadrons, which Collishaw had tasked to defend the advancing troops.[47]

RAF operations during the first day successfully prevented the intervention of the Luftwaffe. The only significant attempt, by seventeen Ju 87s escorted by ten Me 109s, was intercepted before it could attack. At noon eight Blenheims from No. 14 Squadron, newly deployed to the Western Desert, along with eight Blenheims from Nos. 45 and 55 Squadrons bombed and machine gunned Italian troops holding up the advance of the coastal group in the Halfaya-Sollum area. Later in the afternoon Hurricanes made numerous low-level attacks along the Bardia–Tobruk road and destroyed a number of enemy vehicles, including a petrol or ammunition lorry, which burned fiercely.[48]

A local counterattack on the first afternoon by the 2nd Battalion, 5th Panzer Regiment recaptured Capuzzo and forced the British back to Musaid, where both sides remained uneasy during the night of 15–16 May. The local German commander, Col. Maximilian von Herff, prepared to withdraw, but Rommel sent forward an additional armored battalion and ordered a counterattack in the morning. Brigadier Gott felt his forces at Musaid were too exposed and ordered them to withdraw to the Halfaya Pass early on the morning of 16

May. The German reinforcements arrived in the area of Sidi Azeiz by 3:00 A.M. and Fort Capuzzo by 8:00 A.M., but both columns were immobilized for most of the day due to a lack of fuel.[49]

Collishaw's aircraft were busy on the second day as they mounted a major effect to interdict and isolate the battlefield. Hurricanes of Nos. 73, 274, and 1 SAAF Squadrons along with Blenheims of Nos. 45 and 55 Squadrons conducted low-level attacks from the Bardia-Sollum area to as far west as the Barce–Derna road, where a large convoy of more than one hundred vehicles was attacked by fighters and bombers. The entry in the 204 Group Operations Record Book for the day noted that these attacks destroyed or damaged more than a hundred vehicles and motorcycles, including at least three fuel convoys with the confirmed destruction of nine petrol lorries. Heavy attacks by Wellingtons on Axis airfields in Cyrenaica on the night of 15–16 May contributed to the absence of the Luftwaffe over the battlefield on the second day; enemy fighters did not appear over Capuzzo in strength until late in the day and caused no problems for the army, though three British aircraft engaged in strafing missions were shot down. Though the RAF was not able to stop the flow of reinforcements to the front, their destruction of enemy petrol lorries helped stall the German counterattack during a period when British forces were at their most vulnerable.[50]

Operation Brevity concluded on 17 May as British forces withdrew to new positions anchored on Halfaya Pass and Bir el Khireigat, retreating in good order as the German advance was unable to bring them to battle. The Germans subsequently established a new defensive line at Sidi Omar–Sidi Suleiman–Sollum. Though ground combat was finished, the RAF continued to pound the enemy as it reinforced its frontier garrisons. Low-level strikes were made in the area between Tobruk and Sollum, with nineteen vehicles set on fire on 17 May. The next afternoon a large enemy column estimated at one hundred vehicles and seventy-five tanks was discovered advancing from Capuzzo toward Sidi Suleiman and Halfaya. A call for air support was quickly answered, and twenty-eight Blenheims and Marylands from Nos. 14, 24 SAAF, 45, and 55 Squadrons were dispatched to attack the enemy force. Initial contact between the Germans and British drove the 7th Armoured Brigade and 7th Support Group from the pass, but repeated attacks by the medium bombers destroyed a number of German vehicles and caused the abandonment of at least three tanks. As a result of the RAF invention, the enemy column retired, leaving the pass in British hands.[51]

The British official history considered Brevity to be a "failure" since the ultimate goal of relieving Tobruk was not achieved, but the immediate post-mortems on the operation were not as negative.[52] Churchill cabled General

Wavell immediately after its conclusion and expressed his satisfaction with the outcome: "Without using Tiger cubs you have taken offensive, have advanced 30 miles, have captured Halfaya and Sollum, have taken 500 German prisoners and inflicted heavy losses in men and A.F.V.s upon the enemy. For these, 20 'I' tanks and 1,000 or 1,500 casualties do not seem to be all too heavy."[53] The Germans considered the action a setback. Rommel felt the loss of Halfaya was the key to the outcome.[54]

The loss of the pass forced the Germans to stage a major attack with strong support from the Luftwaffe on 27–28 May to recapture the important position. They were also forced to commit much stronger forces to garrison the frontier than had previously been the case.[55]

Overall, though Operation Brevity did not achieve its stated goal of relieving the besieged port, the RAF contribution was a success. Its interventions alone could not clear a path to Tobruk, but it prevented a much poorer outcome. No effective enemy air attacks on British forces developed during the action due to the air cover and interdiction missions flown by the RAF. These strikes successfully disrupted the Axis ability to refuel and resupply its armored forces, and air reconnaissance kept a close watch on the battlefield. Collishaw was prepared to destroy any large enemy forces that attempted to move from the Tobruk area to the battlefront. The Germans suffered serious fuel shortages on the second day of the battle. The resulting immobilization of German units at a point when an aggressive thrust may have destroyed the Guards Brigade Group was crucial. This unit was left in an exposed position as it was mauled and cut off from the 7th Armoured Brigade, which had been ordered to hold its position at Sidi Azeiz in order to protect the flank of the Guards Brigade. Finally, a German attack on 18 May that forced a British withdrawal was turned back by quick and aggressive action by Collishaw's medium-bomber squadrons following the abandonment of Halfaya Pass. This air action forced the enemy to retreat, and the British were able to hold the pass. RAF actions in Brevity cannot be considered decisive, but the air support materially affected the outcome of the operation and prevented a defeat from becoming a rout or worse.

The situation in the Mediterranean did not improve for the British after the conclusion of Operation Brevity as the German airborne invasion of Crete commenced on 20 May. The Luftwaffe heavily bombed the island in the week leading up to the invasion, and on the morning of 20 May, Ju 52 transports conveyed a large force of paratroopers to commence the attack.[56] The British and Commonwealth garrison was a motley force comprised largely of Australian and New Zealand troops who had been evacuated from Greece. The paratroopers suffered heavy casualties as the defenders fought hard to hold their positions; the outcome of the battle was in doubt until 26 May when the Commonwealth troops were forced to concede defeat and evacuate. British aircraft provided only limited support to the Cretan defenders. The small force of fighters and bombers stationed on the island were quickly overwhelmed by the Luftwaffe attacks and the subsequent loss of their airfields.[57]

The loss of the Cretan airfields ceded the Germans air superiority over the island; subsequent RAF operations were launched from bases in Egypt. Some British aircraft had the range to make the long roundtrip over the water, but their loiter time was minimal. "Hit and run" raids were conducted, but it was impossible to maintain any type of effective air cover over the island. Air Marshal Tedder recognized the challenge posed by the distance: "The bulk of our operations had necessarily to be based on Africa, near the operational limit of the Blenheims and Marylands, and outside the range of Hurricanes and Tomahawks. All this meant diverting practically the whole of our effort from the Western Desert to Crete, but I felt this was unavoidable at so critical a juncture."[58] The recent loss of Cyrenaica materially affected this operation. The roundtrip distance from the main RAF bases in the Western Desert at Mersa Matruh to the center of Crete was approximately 620 miles; the distance from the lost bases at Derna and Martuba was some 155 miles shorter.[59]

Tedder ordered Collishaw to do everything he could to support Crete. The air commodore halted most missions in the Western Desert and commenced distant operations with his Blenheims and Hurricanes. The confused situation early in the invasion restricted the ability of the RAF to attack targets with confidence, but by 23 May there was a clear delineation between enemy and friendly troops, and air attacks concentrated on the airfield at Maleme, which was being used as the main landing ground for German transports. Low-level strafing attacks by Blenheim fighters and long-range Hurricanes were most effective, but success was also achieved by Blenheims dropping small bombs and spikes.[60] A slow but steady attrition was suffered by the RAF during these attacks. One Blenheim and a Hurricane were shot down over Crete on 23 May; two Hurricanes were lost at sea the next day; and the following three days saw the loss of twenty-three aircraft. By the conclusion of the campaign, forty-seven RAF aircraft had been destroyed, including thirty from 204 Group. The losses were particularly crippling to the Blenheim squadrons: Nos. 45 and 55 Squadrons were so decimated that they were withdrawn from operations to regenerate, making them unavailable for the upcoming Operation Battleaxe.[61]

The RAF did not change the outcome of the fighting on Crete, but it did cause significant problems for the Germans. By 26 July, British air attacks had taken a heavy toll on German aircraft at Maleme. Luftwaffe general Alexander Löhr, commander of XI Air Corps, was deeply concerned that his aircraft would be unable to deliver the necessary quantity of troops and supplies to

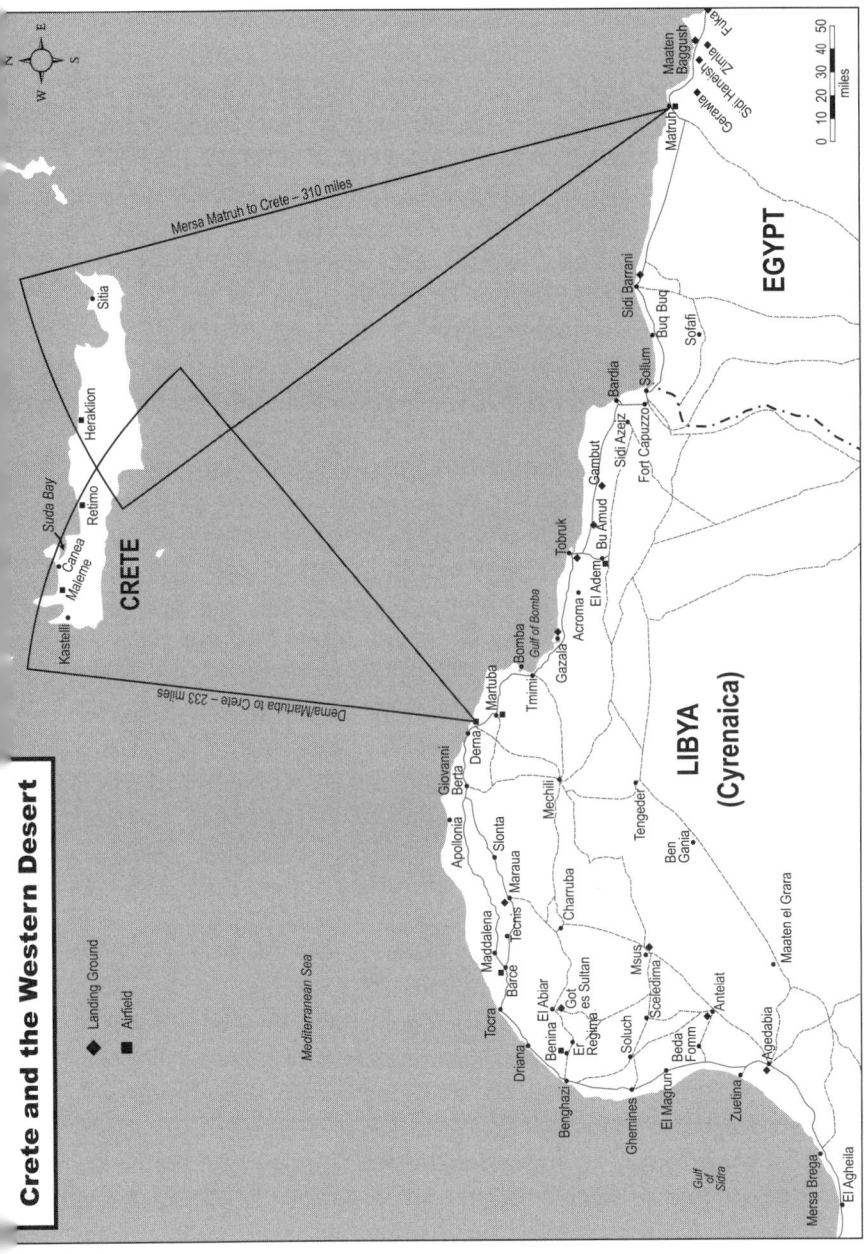

sustain the operation. He ordered a renewed attack near Heraklion to capture the airfield there and remove the threat of British aircraft using it to refuel and rearm. Partially in response to the effectiveness of the air attacks, a German request for Italian assistance was initiated; Mussolini was pleased to come to the aid of his ally, and two days later an Italian brigade landed on the eastern part of the island. The RAF threat was finally neutralized as the campaign drew to a close when the German VIII Air Corps sent additional fighters to provide cover.[62] Though the British suffered heavy losses in the battle, the German XI Air Corps was crippled: 150 aircraft were destroyed, 165 heavily damaged, and only 185 remained operational. These losses were caused by a combination of British air attack, antiaircraft defenses, artillery barrages, and accidents. It is not possible to attribute definitive numbers to any one source, but German accounts acknowledged that British air attacks were very effective.[63]

After a week of desperate fighting with heavy casualties on both sides, the British again found themselves conducting a seaborne withdrawal. Much went wrong during the contest for Crete, but one unifying factor was the army's dissatisfaction with its air support. "I deeply regret failure to hold Crete and fully realize grave effect loss of it will have on other problems in Middle East," began General Wavell's cable to London on 27 May. His second paragraph blamed the defeat on the enemy's "overwhelming air superiority," with the unstated criticism that the RAF was not able to match this air effort.[64] Sir Miles Lampson, the British ambassador to Egypt, communicated these misgivings to London, where they reached the chief of the Air Staff. Portal subsequently cabled Air Marshal Tedder and suggested that he needed to do a better job of communicating the reasons for the problems with the army and other officials in the region.[65] Tedder replied that he would do this, but a week later he cabled Air Chief Marshal Freeman: "There is, as I expected, a first class hate working up in the Army against the Royal Air Force for having 'let them down' in Greece and Crete. Wavell is very worried about it and is doing his best to stamp on it. But I am not sure that even now the real reasons for the lack of air support are appreciated in higher places in the Army here."[66] Wavell may have given this assurance to the air marshal, but it did not prevent him from criticizing RAF support in the Western Desert (as noted in chapter 6) and at Crete. Tedder and Collishaw countered this criticism by linking the inability of the RAF to provide a better fighter defense over Crete to the loss of local air bases. "This was primarily," stated Tedder, "a battle for aerodromes."[67]

Collishaw directly blamed the army for this problem: "The R.A.F. was unable to obtain air superiority over the area of operations in Crete because our Army was unable to safeguard the aerodromes against attack by German forces operating on the ground."[68] In a paper written after the war, he expounded on the problems of the Crete campaign, maintaining that the inability of the army to protect the landing grounds condemned the mission to failure. The loss of the airfields severely curtailed RAF operations over Crete due to the distance from bases in Egypt. Short-range Hurricanes could not be utilized, and even long-range fighters had a limited endurance over the island. Collishaw identified five lessons from this operation:

a. There is NO substitute for Air protection against an airborne invasion.
b. An Island loses its insular immensity when air superiority is lost.
c. The Army by itself is not equipped to withstand an air invasion.
d. Expect air invasions to develop upon aerodromes.
e. The Navy can do nothing to interfere with an air invasion of an island.[69]

Tedder blamed the failure on a number of factors including the distance of the island from bases in Egypt, the lack of sufficient numbers of aircraft due to conflicting commitments (support of Crete operation, air cover for Royal Navy vessels in the Mediterranean, and continuing operations in the Western Desert and Syria), and poor coordination between the three services.[70] He suggested that the turning point in the battle was the loss of the airfields on Crete, which ceded the advantage to the Germans, who were then able to reinforce the island by air. He thought the RAF put up a good fight, though "on far too small a scale to be really effective."[71]

In his Crete postmortem Tedder singled out Collishaw for special criticism. On 29 May he cabled Air Chief Marshal Freeman to share his views on the outcome of the operation. He thought that the RAF put up a "magnificent show" over Crete and caused heavy losses to the Luftwaffe, but the overall effort was too small to be really effective. Tedder worried that the heavy losses in aircraft and aircrew had seriously weakened the RAF in the Western Desert, especially the Blenheim squadrons, which he called a "broken remnant." In the next sentence the air marshal shifted the responsibility for the losses onto Collishaw: "I feel I am to blame in not having kept a tighter rein on Collishaw but it is not easy to control detailed operations up here."[72] It is not clear what he expected the air commodore to do differently. Tedder ordered Collishaw to devote the majority of his aircraft to support Crete, and that is exactly what he did.[73] The aircraft made a minor contribution to the battle, but the long range and overwhelming odds ensured high losses among them. Tedder had to know this. During the period 23–30 May, virtually all of Collishaw's aircraft were devoted to Crete. A small number of reconnaissance and air-superiority missions were carried out over the Western Desert, but no offensive attacks were made; a single aircraft, a Lysander supporting the army, was lost. Even after the conclusion of operations over Crete, Collishaw's aircraft covered the Royal Navy during the first days of June, and it was not until about a week before Operation Battleaxe that offensive missions over the Western Desert resumed.[74] The only serious losses suffered by 204 Group during this period occurred over Crete. Tedder's primary motivation for the negative comments was to build a case for the removal of Collishaw.

May 1941 marked a pivotal transitional month for British forces in the Mediterranean theater. The success of Operation Compass was reversed when the German counterattack in April reclaimed Cyrenaica and renewed the threat to Egypt and the Suez Canal. Greece and Crete were also lost to German assaults, and the only positive factor was the escape of substantial numbers of troops, albeit without their equipment, vehicles, or tanks. Perhaps the biggest casualty during these setbacks was the damage done to the relationship between the army and the RAF. Unlike the relationship between the two services in England and during the Battle of France in 1940, when acrimony and distrust were common, the men under the command of Wavell and Longmore had worked out an effective partnership. Unfortunately, this harmony was broken in Cyrenaica during the German offensive, where Wavell blamed the RAF for contributing to the defeat by not providing the necessary aerial reconnaissance, and in Greece and Crete, where the army and Royal Navy thought that the lack of air cover had affected the outcome of those battles. Tedder's letters to London in late May and early June related numerous incidents demonstrating the strained relationship between the RAF and the other services. Wavell and Cunningham both expressed their dissatisfaction to Tedder, and Capt. Louis Mountbatten, the future chief of combined operations, argued forcefully with him about the lack of RAF air support for the Royal Navy that contributed to the loss of his destroyer, HMS *Kelly*. The fallout over the perceived lack of RAF support over Greece and Crete resonated for months. New Zealand prime minister Peter Fraser, told that his forces received scant air support in Greece and Crete, appealed directly to Churchill in October and sought assurances that his country's forces would not again be committed to battle without adequate air cover.[75]

Another setback during the month was the inability of Operation Brevity to relieve the besieged garrison at Tobruk. The army was checked in its assault by German and Italian forces that garrisoned the frontier in greater numbers than had been expected. The army had counted on the RAF to augment its limited strength during the campaign by destroying enemy tanks and other vehicles on the battlefield. Generals Gott and Beresford-Pierse were disappointed when Collishaw told them that this was not possible. The air commodore then proceeded to successfully fight the kind of air battle for which the RAF was designed: sealing off the battlefield and limiting the movement of enemy reserves, reinforcements, and supplies as well as interfering with enemy air operations. Though the battle was too short for the full effect of these measures to be felt, German freedom of movement on and behind the battlefield was significantly diminished, and air action made a difference at a number of key points during the combat. Air operations during Brevity should have served as the pattern for future battles, but Wavell and his army commanders did not appreciate the lessons displayed. This breakdown in relations between the two services would play a major role during Operation Battleaxe, the next major action to be fought in the Western Desert.

For Collishaw, May was a busy month as he was responsible for a number of disparate tasks. He continued to prevent the German advance toward Egypt, supported distant operations against Crete, defended the isolated port of Tobruk, and participated in a renewed British attack to relieve that garrison. These multiple operations were conducted with exhausted units, limited resources, and in a cautious manner to prevent unnecessary—and irreplaceable—losses. Overall, the operations of 204 Group during this period have to be considered a success. The interdiction missions against targets in Libya were a success and continued to frustrate the logistical situation of the Afrika Korps, allowing Tobruk to continue to hold out. Operations against Crete were conducted at the Hurricanes' extreme range, which meant that their time over the island was at a premium, but RAF air operations caused heavy losses to the Luftwaffe and the consequent commitment of additional assets. The severe loss in aircraft helped turn the German capture of Crete into a Pyrrhic victory. Much of the RAF success during this period can be attributed to Collishaw's veteran leadership.

Tedder, however, was not impressed by his subordinate's actions during this period. As early as 4 January 1941, after taking over 202 Group for a brief period when Collishaw was sick, Tedder considered sacking him. He wrote to his wife, Rosalinde, that "Collishaw no doubt has his points but he is an awful bull in a china shop, has no conception whatever of the administration without which operations cannot function and goes off half-cock in an appalling way."[76] Tedder was also consistently critical about Collishaw in his regular letters to Air Chief Marshal Freeman, on 11 March criticizing his "much advertised 'drive'" and blaming it for causing much "quite avoidable wear and tear" on his units.[77] At the end of May the air marshal lamented that he had not been able to "keep a tighter rein on Collishaw," which had resulted in a "very serious" weakening of the strength of the Blenheim squadrons.[78] Overall, Tedder considered him too aggressive and lacking the necessary administrative skill for higher command.

CHAPTER 8

OPERATION BATTLEAXE

Operation Battleaxe was a crucial turning point in the development of British tactical-air-power doctrine, and its outcome would exert a powerful influence on the future course of army-air relations. The attack was designed as a three-phase operation with the goal of relieving the besieged garrison at Tobruk by destroying all enemy forces along the frontier. The plan was essentially a replay of Operation Brevity in which brigades would replace battalions and divisions would replace brigades. The first phase anticipated that the 7th Armoured and 4th Indian Divisions would recapture Halfaya Pass, Sollum, and Fort Capuzzo by destroying Axis forces in the sector. The second phase would see British forces exploit to Tobruk and relieve the trapped garrison, while the final phase envisioned a farther westward advance of some sixty to seventy miles to provide security for the approaches to Tobruk.[1] The British chiefs of staff expected this operation to alter the balance of power in the Middle East, and Churchill placed great hopes on its success. German forces in North Africa were being maintained by tenuous sea lines across the Mediterranean via Sicily and the west coast of Greece to Tripoli. Due to the range limitations of British aircraft, secure air bases between Sollum and Derna were required to allow the RAF to interdict this Axis shipping.[2]

These strategic imperatives led the British to commit all their available strength, both ground and air, to ensure the success of Battleaxe. Churchill strongly supported the concept of Battleaxe and was prepared to accept great risks. As he told General Wavell, "Now . . . is the time to fight a decisive battle in Libya and go on day after day facing all necessary losses until you have beaten the life out of General Rommel's army."[3] He directed Wavell to concentrate on destroying enemy units; securing territory was of secondary importance. This attritional battle, combined with the naval and air interdiction of the long and tenuous Axis supply line, would lead to British ascendancy in the Western Desert.[4]

The importance placed on the success of Battleaxe was echoed by Air Marshal Portal, chief of the Air Staff, who told Air Marshal Tedder:

The outcome of this battle must be of supreme and possibly decisive strategic importance to the Middle East and the whole war. Its political effect will
be profound and worldwide. The importance of seizing and maintaining the
initiative cannot be overrated. . . . Every nerve must be strained and no effort
ought to be spared to bring the maximum possible force to bear on the enemy.
. . . I urge you to throw in everything you can at the outset, regardless of the
future, and I will do my best to make good your losses.[5]

Tedder maximized the number of aircraft available for Battleaxe, augmenting
Collishaw's 204 Group with additional squadrons from East Africa and by reas-
signing pilots and aircraft from squadrons re-forming in Egypt following the
tough campaigns in Greece and Crete. At the outset of the battle, Collishaw
would have five fighter, three medium-bomber, and two army-support/recon-
naissance squadrons available.[6] This gave the RAF a rough parity with the Axis
air forces, with an approximate strength of 203 serviceable aircraft compared to
101 German and 114 Italian warplanes.[7] In actuality, the RAF for the first time
enjoyed a substantial advantage in the air as the majority of the Italian aircraft
were deployed to the rear (Derna–Benghazi–Tripoli line) and would not participate in the battle. The Luftwaffe possessed an additional 157 aircraft in Crete
and Greece, but these did not reach the battle area until the second or third day
of the battle.[8]

Churchill demonstrated his commitment to Battleaxe by authorizing the
reinforcement of forces in the Middle East. The British were dangerously weak
in tank strength at home, but Wavell was seriously inferior to the Germans in
tank strength in North Africa, which needed to be rectified before Battleaxe.
Churchill was prepared to accept the risks of sending a convoy on the direct
route to Egypt, even if it meant losing half the tanks. The "Tiger" convoy, as it
was called, soon transited the Mediterranean Sea. A significant naval commitment, including Force H (one aircraft carrier, two battleships, four cruisers, and
eleven destroyers) and the entire Mediterranean Fleet (one aircraft carrier, three
battleships, three cruisers, and all available destroyers) were provided to ensure
safe passage. One of the five fast cargo ships was lost during the voyage when
it hit a mine and sank, taking with it fifty-seven tanks and ten Hurricanes. The
rest of the convoy arrived in Egypt on 12 May with its precious cargo of eighty-
two cruiser, 135 "I," and twenty-one light tanks as well as forty-three Hurricanes.
These would reinforce the RAF and allow the 7th Armoured Division, commanded by Major General Creagh, to be rebuilt in time for the operation.[9]

Despite these preparations there were significant misgivings. Wavell wrote
to Sir John Dill, chief of the Imperial General Staff, expressing his doubts regarding the prospects of success. He lacked confidence that his forces could rout
the Germans the same way they had the Italians. As well, he listed problems

with reconnaissance by armored cars and the suitability of British infantry and cruiser tanks against German armor and antitank guns.[10] Wavell was under pressure from London to launch Battleaxe at the earliest possible date, but he was forced to delay the start of the operation by two weeks, principally because time was needed to integrate the new tanks into the 7th Armoured Division. This formation had to be virtually reconstituted following its losses earlier in the year, its men needed to be trained on the newly arrived tanks, and a variety of maintenance tasks were required to get the vehicles ready for battle. Another complication was the need to devise tactics to allow infantry and cruiser tanks, with their vastly different speeds, to be employed in the same formation.[11]

Wavell recognized the risks inherent in the Battleaxe plan. He assessed that its first stage, consolidation of the area around Sollum–Capuzzo, could be successfully accomplished with the available forces, but this result would be in doubt if the Germans reinforced their forward troops with some of the forces opposite Tobruk.[12] German reinforcement of the frontier area could be prevented in two ways. One was by the Tobruk garrison attacking out of their perimeter. This would represent a significant threat to Axis forces in the area that would prevent their redeployment. Wavell, however, dismissed this option as he feared compromising the defense of the Tobruk should Battleaxe fail.[13] The second option was to use the RAF to strike the enemy lines of communications. This tactic had worked effectively the previous month during Brevity, but Wavell undermined this possibility by allowing his deputy, Lieutenant General Beresford-Peirse, commander of the Western Desert Force, to demand a continuous fighter umbrella over the army. This commitment to a defensive role negated the RAF's offensive contribution during the battle.

RAF operations during the first week of June were characterized by daylight fighter patrols to protect British ships resupplying Tobruk and nightly Wellington attacks on Benghazi harbor and the Cyrenaican airfields. The Blenheim squadrons, decimated and exhausted by the Crete operation, were mostly out of combat during this period, contributing occasional reconnaissance sorties. The task of convoy escort was a significant commitment for the Hurricane squadrons, but the survival of the Tobruk garrison depended on the regular delivery of supplies. The Luftwaffe had some success interdicting these convoys; the number of antishipping strikes increased significantly as German aircraft were reassigned after Crete, but no ships were lost when fighter cover was provided. The RAF commitment to support Battleaxe limited the availability of fighters for naval support and forced Admiral Cunningham to adjust his operations. Air cover would still be provided when available, but after 7 June only destroyers were used to transport supplies as they were fast and could defend themselves.[14]

A week before the launch of Battleaxe, the operational pattern of 204 Group changed as it prepared for the offensive. Initially, RAF attacks occurred on the distant German lines of communication, then two days before the battle the focus switched to attacks on the lines of communication in the forward areas.[15] On 9 June Hurricanes from Nos. 73 and 274 Squadrons and Blenheims from No. 14 Squadron made a series of low-level strafing attacks on airfields at Tobruk, Bardia, Derna, and Gazala. The following day Blenheims from No. 113 Squadron discovered a hundred-vehicle convoy traveling east on the road between Barce and Derna. Repeated attacks on the column, believed to be transporting petrol from Benghazi to the forward area, destroyed twenty-eight large trucks towing trailers, mostly tankers. On 11 June Blenheims from No. 113 Squadron machine gunned eighteen aircraft at Berka airfield while Marylands from No. 24 SAAF Squadron destroyed eighteen large vehicles on the road between Gazala and the frontier. No offensive operations were carried out on 12 June, but the medium-bomber squadrons attacked vehicle convoys and airfields throughout Cyrenaica over the following two days. The fighter squadrons were withdrawn from offensive operations to provide convoy cover on 11, 12, and 13 June. The day before the launch of Battleaxe, Hurricanes made a series of dawn raids led by No. 24 Squadron Marylands. A successful attack was made by No. 1 SAAF and 73 Squadrons on the Gazala airdromes, where eleven enemy aircraft were reported destroyed. A similar raid against the Derna landing ground failed when the Hurricanes of No. 274 Squadron lost their Maryland pathfinder and returned to base without making an attack. Later in the day additional Hurricane sweeps between Gazala and Capuzzo reported the destruction of nineteen vehicles. Additionally, an attack by a cannon-armed Hurricane on an enemy armored column near the frontier destroyed four vehicles and disabled three light tanks. On 14 June Collishaw's fighter squadrons commenced air cover for the Western Desert Force. This defensive umbrella would be the primary task of the fighters for the next three days.[16]

By this point in the war, the RAF was well aware that the use of an air umbrella was an unprofitable use of resources. Collishaw's success during the early part of the war was derived from an aggressive, offensive use of his limited aircraft. His constant sorties against enemy airfields, port facilities, and lines of communications during Operation Compass forced the Italians to mount standing air patrols in an effort to counter the attacks. The ineffectiveness of these defensive patrols was recognized by Collishaw after the first British offensive:

The failure of the Italian air force to strike at our aircraft on their aerodromes while the R.A.F. continued their sustained attacks on the Italian aerodromes brought about the destruction of the Italian air force at Cyrenaica. Our attacks

on the enemy's bases, lines of communication and his aerodromes forces
the Italian air force on the defensive and the policy of maintaining standing
fighter patrols over many bases wore out the fighter units. . . . The [army] generals also contributed to the failure of the Italian air force by insisting on having fighter patrols flying over roads to prevent our air force from attacking the
M.T. [motor-transport] columns.[17]

A British Army report written about the same time observed that RAF air cover
during Operation Compass was relatively ineffective, and though some Italian
air raids were intercepted, the air umbrella was insufficient to stop all, or even
a majority, of strikes. The medium-level Italian bombing attacks caused some
disruption in the movement of British units, but casualties were light. Ignoring
the evidence, the report concluded that though ineffective, air cover was still
needed to protect ground forces.[18]

This army belief in the efficacy of standing air patrols was incorporated
into the Battleaxe plan. Beresford-Peirse insisted that RAF fighters provide an
umbrella during the approach march to the battlefield and during the operation itself. This request was not surprising given the outcome of the campaigns in Greece and Crete, where the army had been subjected to constant
and heavy Luftwaffe air attacks. Lt. Gen. Henry Wilson partially blamed the
defeat in Greece on the inability of the RAF to provide the support requested
by the army, while General Wavell had been very critical of the air force's role
during the disastrous retreat through Cyrenaica in April. Collishaw, however,
was very much against this plan and preferred to use his fighters in an offensive
manner; the outcome of Operation Brevity supported his assessment.[19] During
initial planning meetings for Battleaxe, both Wavell and Beresford-Peirse
expressed concern over expected German air attacks. Tedder, with Collishaw's
agreement, was able to pacify them with the promise that the available fighters
"should be able to secure and maintain reasonable air superiority."[20] This agreement allowed Collishaw to devote a small portion of his fighter force to the air
umbrella while sending the majority on offensive missions.

There were, however, larger issues involved that moved the issue of air support for Battleaxe from the operational to the political level. The army perception of being abandoned by the RAF in Greece and Crete was a major issue for
Tedder in late May and early June based on his communications with Portal. At
the height of the battle of Crete, he started a telegram to Portal stating, "Small
scale of effective air support we are able to give to defence of CRETE has been
and is my main concern."[21] Subsequent communications with the chief of the
Air Staff make it clear that though it was a difficult mission for Collishaw's
squadrons, all possible efforts were being made to support the army in Crete.[22]
It was on 27 May that Tedder signaled the first warning that the RAF would be

blamed for the loss of Crete.[23] The next day Portal signaled back to him to confirm these suspicions and warn that the issue had grown to the point where the British ambassador to Egypt, Sir Miles Lampson, and the New Zealand prime minister, Peter Fraser, were "expressing serious concern at what is regarded as our neglect or failure to provide adequate air forces for Mideast resulting in Army having to fight in Greece and Crete without adequate air support."[24] Tedder confirmed this situation in a letter to Freeman on 3 June, stating that there was a "first class hate working up in the Army" for the RAF for allegedly not providing adequate air support in Greece and Crete.[25]

On 11 June Portal intervened in the planning for Battleaxe due to his concern about the ramifications of this recent criticism. He told Tedder:

> Political circles here will be on the lookout for any failure on the part of the R.A.F. to afford close repeat close support to troops in forthcoming operations. Suggestion is being made that we shall pay too much attention to shooting up lines of communication and aerodromes in rear and not enough to dealing with anti-tank guns, tanks and artillery that may be firing on our troops . . . it is essential that you and Collishaw at your respective levels should obtain before hand complete agreement of Army to your tactical plans. . . . If their requirements appear to you unsound and if persuasion fails to move them you should do your best to act as they require and register your disagreement to them and to me before the action starts.[26]

These instructions left Tedder with no flexibility but to accept the army's demands for the upcoming battle.[27] For better or worse, Battleaxe would be fought according to army principles for air support.

Tedder did not object to Portal's cable but immediately thanked him for the warning. Though the air marshal did "not see any immediate danger [or] disagreement here" over the plan for Battleaxe, he recognized that "if there is any failure [it is] quite clear that any opportunity of making R.A.F. scapegoat will be seized." Beresford-Peirse had requested attacks on the enemy lines of communications prior to the operation but expected close fighter protection once the campaign commenced. Tedder observed that interdiction during the past two months "have contributed very considerably to restricting enemy action." This did not prevent Beresford-Peirse from complaining about the level of RAF support, though Tedder dismissed this: "Having been given the jam and cream Army now complain they do not always have both." Despite these complaints, Tedder reported that Beresford-Peirse and Collishaw "appear to work well together."[28]

Based on Portal's directive and the continued insistence of Beresford-Peirse that the fighter force be used to protect the army during its approach march and combat, Tedder ordered Collishaw to devote the majority of his fighters to maintaining a dawn-to-dusk air umbrella. As a result, Collishaw deployed his fighters in a defensive role during the key phase of Battleaxe. There is no record of Tedder overtly registering his disagreement with this plan before the battle, and afterward he stated that the policy was justified in the short term, though he recognized that its continuation over a longer term would cause fighter strength to be "gradually frittered away."[29]

Collishaw faithfully carried out his orders, but the plan went completely against his concept of the proper use of air power in support of the army. In his after-action report on Battleaxe, the air commodore stated that he "desired to employ his fighters offensively, either to operate in force over the enemy's advanced aerodromes, or to 'shoot up' the thin-skinned vehicles comprising the second Echelon—petrol ammunition supply vehicles immediately behind the armoured fighting vehicles. The G.O.C. Western Desert Force, however, insisted on our fighter force being used to carry out 'umbrella' tactics to cover our troops."[30] Collishaw discovered over the western front in the First World War that the air umbrella was an ineffective use of assets. While at RAF Staff College in 1924, he wrote of the problem of maintaining standing air patrols, which "permitted the enemy to assemble superior force (moral and physical) to maintain a war of attrition. History teaches us the folly of the attempt to be strong everywhere."[31] This point was reinforced during his time as the head of operations and intelligence at the headquarters of Air Defence of Great Britain, where he served for two years in the late 1920s. Though the increasing speed of bombers challenged the ability of the existing network of coast watchers and antiaircraft guns to react in time to stop an attack, the idea of using standing patrols of fighters was discarded as "this plan would soon wear out the defence."[32] His after-action report on Operation Compass, written before Battleaxe, contained numerous mentions of how the Italian use of the air umbrella contributed significantly to its defeat. The problem was caused by generals who insisted on "having fighter patrols flying over roads to prevent our air force from attacking the M.T. columns."[33] This caused the enemy to become so focused on "trying to thwart our air offensive . . . that he was unable to provide any important fighter force to dispute air superiority over our advancing army."[34]

Tedder also understood that attacks on the enemy lines of communications were more effective in supporting the army than maintaining a continuous defensive fighter umbrella, but his freedom to act was limited by a number of factors. The recent failures in the Western Desert, Greece, and Crete left the army deeply disappointed with the air support it had received. The navy too was unhappy with its RAF support. These complaints were frequently repeated in Cairo and London in the weeks preceding Battleaxe and had poisoned the relationship between the three services. Portal was acutely aware of these grievances and, in an attempt to prevent a further breakdown, ordered Tedder to accede to army air-support demands. As Tedder recalled in his memoirs, "Portal saw to it that I understood the R.A.F. to be fighting a battle, not only in the Desert, but in London."[35] Though Churchill placed great hopes in the success of the offensive, Portal understood that any failure would be blamed on the RAF. Thus, he directed Tedder to do his best to convince the army of the proper employment of air power but, failing that, to carry out the support as requested by the army. The evidence suggests that Portal and Tedder understood that the RAF must do everything possible to avoid being blamed for the failure of Battleaxe. Such a circumstance would set back the development of future air operations. Conversely, a battlefield defeat while following the army's directions would be regrettable but might have positive long-term ramifications for convincing the army—and London—of the validity of RAF methods.[36]

As a result of these political dimensions, RAF operations prior to and during the first two days of Battleaxe were a significant departure from the successful template employed by Collishaw up to this point in the war. In fact, they more closely followed the tactics that doomed the Regia Aeronautica during Compass. Beresford-Peirse and the army were pleased to be receiving the support they requested, but the problems in this approach soon became apparent.

Wavell believed that the plan for Operation Brevity was solid, but it had failed because he underestimated the enemy. Consequently, Operation Battleaxe was a larger version of the previous plan and differed only slightly in its concept of operations. Two full divisions were employed, with the 7th Armoured Division benefiting from the recent influx of new tanks. The only major change was the manner in which the RAF was to be employed. All things were not equal, however, and Rommel redeployed his forces based on the Brevity experience. In particular, the earlier British attack revealed the Axis forces in the frontier to be dangerously weak, so Halfaya Pass and Points 206 and 208 were fortified. These three positions, along with Sidi Azeiz, were equipped for all-round defense and formed the outer perimeter. A second line based on strongpoints at Fort Capuzzo, Musaid, and Sollum were held by Italian troops. The armored regiment of 15th Panzer Division was held in reserve along the main road between Capuzzo and Bardia. Maj. Gen. Walter Neumann-Silkow, commander of the 15th Panzer Division as well as of the Sollum front, planned to use the first line of strongpoints to slow the British advance while the second line's antitank guns and artillery destroyed the British armor. The armored regiment would then be committed to the battle in a major counterattack to annihilate the weakened attackers. These German preparations were completed just before the commencement of the British offensive.[37]

Battleaxe opened on the morning of 15 June with mixed results. The only British success of the day was the capture of the Fort Capuzzo–Bir Wau area by the 4th Armoured Brigade. A two-pronged attack by the 4th Indian Division on the Halfaya Pass was stalled by the strong resistance of its Axis defenders along with a timely armored counterattack along the top of the escarpment. The attempt of the 7th Armoured Brigade to capture the main Hafid Ridge–Point 208 position was defeated late in the afternoon by hidden antitank guns. Beresford-Peirse was not overly concerned about these developments and made plans for a new set-piece attack on Halfaya to be made the next day: while the 4th Armoured Brigade attacked Hafid Ridge, the 7th Armoured Brigade would "attack and smash" the German attempt to outflank the British positions from the west.[38] He was confident that after a short operational pause, 7th Armoured Division, supported by the 22nd Guards Brigade, would continue the advance to Tobruk after masking Bardia. The Tobruk garrison was ordered to prepare its "main offensive when and if 7th Armoured Division comes within striking distance."[39] There was good reason for British optimism. Large numbers of German guns had been captured and destroyed, the 8th Panzer Regiment had been severely mauled, the defended locality at Point 206 had been eliminated, the mobile reserve of infantry and antitank guns at Capuzzo had been scattered, and Halfaya Pass was isolated.[40]

Early on the morning of 16 June, the 2nd Support Group captured Musaid by a silent bayonet charge and soon after occupied Sollum Barracks. A series of three major counterattacks by the 8th Panzer Regiment at Capuzzo with as many as eighty tanks were defeated with heavy losses, but these actions prevented the 4th Armoured Brigade from striking at Hafid Ridge. The 7th Armoured Brigade fought a series of running battles with the reinforced German 5th Light Division as it attempted to outflank the British in the direction of Sidi Omar. The enemy garrison at Halfaya Pass was attacked twice on 16 June, at 7:30 A.M. and again twelve hours later, but the 11th Indian Infantry Brigade was unable to secure the position.[41] Wavell's assessment of the battle at the end of the second day was still positive: "General impression [is] heavy fighting and close run battle. Position appears not repeat not unsatisfactory but obviously losses are considerable and there will have to be a pause and reinforcements before second stage can be attempted."[42]

Any optimism in a successful outcome to the battle disappeared on the morning of 17 June as the German counterattacks could not be checked. Strong thrusts at Capuzzo prevented the tactical withdrawal of the 4th Armoured Brigade, which had been ordered the previous night. By 8:00 A.M. the situation

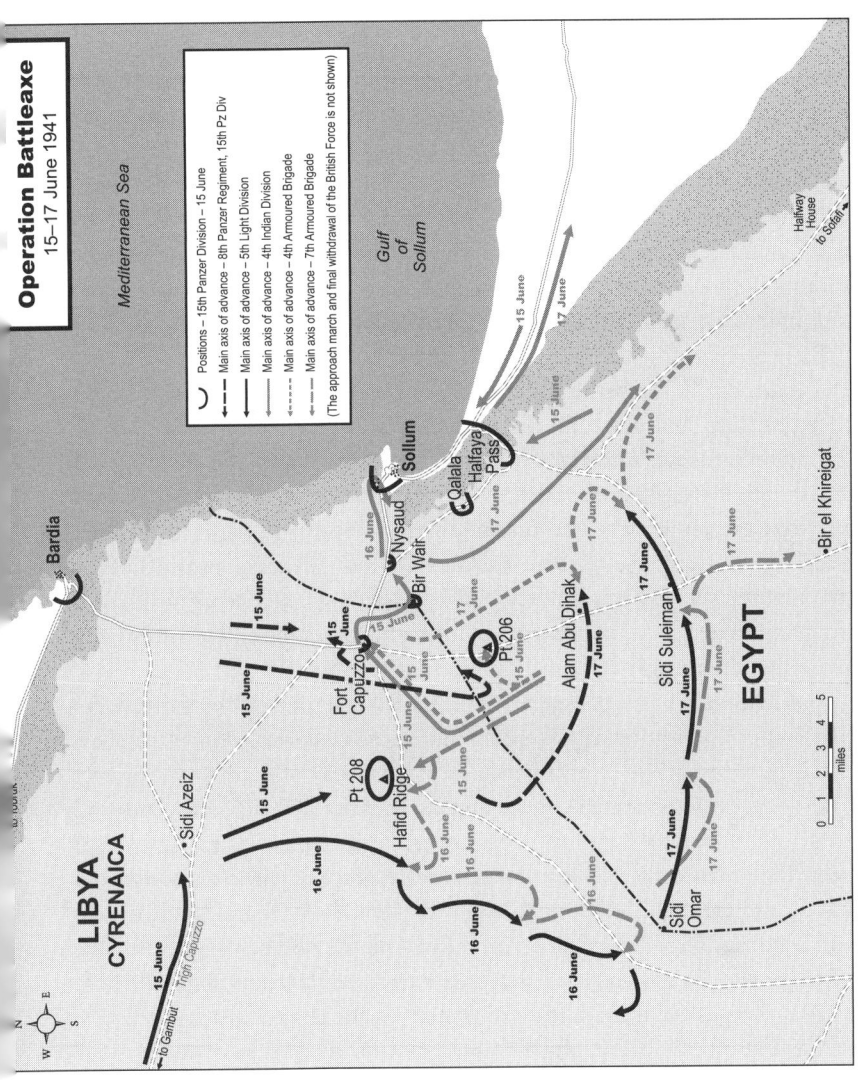

Operation Battleaxe, 15–17 June 1941. Map by Mike Bechthold. Copyright © 2017 by the University of Oklahoma Press.

became serious when it was reported that the lead enemy armored column had pushed aside attempts by the 7th Armoured Brigade to slow its progress and was at Sidi Suleiman heading for Halfaya Pass. General Wavell realized that a critical point in the battle had been reached and flew to the front with Beresford-Peirse to meet with the divisional commanders. Before he could make a decision, Wavell learned that Maj. Gen. Frank Messervy, commander of the 4th Indian Division, had ordered the withdrawal of the 22nd Guards Brigade, fearing it would be trapped and destroyed. Wavell soon confirmed Messervy's decision and ended Battleaxe by ordering the general disengagement of British forces. The 4th Indian Division and 22nd Guards Brigade began their retreat along the escarpment around midmorning, and intervention by the 4th and 7th Armoured Brigades allowed the formations to successfully withdraw. Before nightfall all British troops had escaped the encircling German forces and were established along a Buq Buq–Sofafi–Habata line.[43]

Early on morning of 18 June, Wavell cabled London, "Regret to report failure of Battleaxe."[44] The battle ended in a draw as both sides maintained their earlier positions, but given the failure to break through to Tobruk and the resulting severe losses in tanks, the action cannot be considered anything but a British defeat. The Western Desert Force suffered 969 casualties, while Axis losses were greater at 1,277 total casualties.[45] More telling in the British failure was the loss of twenty-seven cruisers and sixty-four "I" tanks, nearly half the armor that started the battle. In excess of sixty German tanks were knocked out during Battleaxe, but Axis possession of the battlefield at the end of the fighting allowed them to recover and repair most of those losses.[46]

The RAF effectively performed its assigned role during the early stages of the battle. Continuing with the air umbrella started on 14 June, Collishaw committed the majority of his fighters on the first day of Battleaxe to protect the advancing troops from enemy air attacks. Six squadrons of Hurricanes and Tomahawks mounted standing patrols over the battlefield from dawn until sunset. The provision of such comprehensive coverage required the designated squadrons to dispatch three aircraft every forty minutes. Separate patrols were maintained at 9,000, 13,000, and 18,000 feet, and the number of aircraft were doubled during the four-hour periods after daybreak and before sunset.[47] These patrols accomplished their mission of protecting the attacking troops, but the cost was high: three enemy fighters were shot down, but the RAF lost four Hurricanes destroyed and two others heavily damaged.[48]

Offensive missions flown by 204 Group were limited by this defensive commitment as well as the small number of Blenheims available. At dawn on 15 June, eight Hurricanes of No. 274 Squadron attacked two enemy motor-transport columns between Capuzzo and Gazala and claimed fifteen vehicles destroyed. Two missions later that morning by flights of six and ten Hurricanes strafed twenty-five vehicles; unfortunately, four Hurricanes were lost in the low-level attacks. At the special request of the army, a cannon-armed Hurricane made a successful low-level attack on enemy gun positions at Halfaya, but it too was shot down. Only four Blenheims from No. 113 Squadron were active on 15 June, attacking enemy motor columns near Benghazi. Reconnaissance flights by No. 39 Squadron revealed three large enemy columns advancing westward toward Capuzzo along the main road from Tobruk, but no attacks were made. A Hurricane from No. 6 Squadron was lost during a tactical-reconnaissance mission, bringing RAF losses to ten aircraft on the first day of the operation.[49]

The next day Collishaw continued to provide the air umbrella but reorganized the tasking so his fighters patrolled in greater strength to meet the large formations of attacking enemy aircraft. This comprise left more holes in the air cover, which the enemy exploited. At least ten Ju 88s, thirty Stukas, and eleven Me 110s attacked British positions in the Capuzzo–Halfaya and Gasr el Arid sectors without interception. Italian bombers and fighters were also active, striking at British troops at Sidi Suleiman, Sidi Omar, and Gasr el Arid. Army sources confirmed these attacks, but the absence of any specific mention of casualties indicates that they were generally ineffective.[50] Remarkably, the RAF carried out no offensive operations on 16 June. Collishaw's fighters were completely committed to the umbrella, and his medium bombers were not employed due to the lack of escorts.[51]

Reports on the progress of Battleaxe were closely followed by Churchill, Dill, and Portal. Wavell and Tedder sent brief but regular updates, and both received direction from London as the operation unfolded. The cables from Egypt on the first two days revealed cautious optimism. The anticipated destruction of enemy forces had not yet occurred while heavy casualties had been sustained. Overall success was still expected, but there were also indications that failure was a possibility. A three-page note on the progress of Battleaxe sent to General Dill on 16 June revealed that resistance in the frontier area remained fierce and air reconnaissance reported enemy forces concentrating for a possible counterattack. No mention was made of RAF operations, especially offensive missions, other than to state that the command was "most active in support of the [ground] operations."[52]

The absence of any reports on RAF offensive operations prompted Portal to send a query/directive to Tedder early on the morning of 17 June:

It appears your fighters are mainly being used on defensive patrols throughout the day in small numbers over our forward troops. Protection afforded to Army by this method appears successful though our fighters are out-numbered and combats are inconclusive whenever the enemy puts up a sweep in force. Do not of course know from here that better results could be obtained and equal freedom given to our troops if Blenheims escorted by strong fighter formations make daylight attacks on known enemy concentrations. Moreover situation at Halfaya as reported yesterday appeared to us to give ideal opportunity for intensive bombing of enemy positions by Blenheims. If successful this would undoubtedly force enemy to employ fighters on defensive patrols and so enable our fighters to engage with superiority.[53]

Although in London, Portal understood that the misallocation of air resources had prevented the RAF from contributing to the destruction of the enemy. By the end of the second day of operations, he realized that the air cover demanded by the army was not materially contributing to the battle and a change in focus was necessary.

Dill, concurrent with Portal's message to Tedder on 17 June, issued a similar directive to General Wavell: "Urge most strongly that Tedder should use his superiority (a) to bomb Germans surrounded at Halfaya as our troops were bombed in Crete and (b) smash up any concentrations which enemy may make in the desert. All this you may be doing but I have no information of part being played by our bombers."[54] It appears the army was slowly realizing that warplanes could accomplish more than provide protection from enemy air attacks.

Tedder reacted quickly to Portal's message by issuing a directive to 204 Group that marked a complete reversal of his earlier orders: "MOST IMMEDIATE. . . . Concentrate on ground strafing regardless of possible presence of German fighters. Do not waste fighters protecting Army against possible enemy air attacks."[55] Tedder cabled the Air Ministry late on 17 June to respond to Portal's query regarding the employment of the RAF in the battle: "Discussed this with Collishaw last night. . . . Army had specifically request Umbrella. Agree that escorted bombers would ultimately force enemy to defensive patrols. . . . This morning in view of information re enemy fighter weakness I instructed Collishaw that Umbrella now appeared relatively unnecessary and he should concentrate effort against land movements."[56]

On the third day of the battle, Collishaw was finally free to conduct the offensive operations he desired. Comprehensive air-umbrella coverage ended by noon as the morning flights returned to base and were not replaced. For the remainder of the day, the warplanes conducted offensive operations. An unprecedented total of 193 fighter and bomber sorties were devoted to close-air-support missions in the Sidi Omar–Sollum area. Blenheims of Nos. 14 and 113 Squadrons and Marylands of No. 24 SAAF Squadron made numerous bombing and machine-gun attacks on large numbers of enemy armored fighting vehicles and motor transport. Many of these attacks were directed at units of the

German 5th Light Division that were attempting a flanking maneuver to trap British forces at Sidi Suleiman and Halfaya. The low-level bombing and strafing attacks claimed the destruction of dozens of vehicles, and Beresford-Peirse believed that the RAF "played an important part in bringing this enemy column to a halt."[57] In addition, all seven fighter squadrons along with the bomber squadrons were directed to conduct offensive patrols against enemy vehicles on the roads from Gazala to Capuzzo and Sidi Omar. Collishaw reported that "it was subsequently confirmed that the enemy motorized units suffered heavy casualties during the attacks, particularly from the four forward guns of the Maryland aircraft."[58]

Enemy attacks continued on British Army targets in the absence of the air umbrella, though these strikes were mostly ineffective. Small patrols of Hurricanes from Nos. 33 and 229 Squadrons caused Axis aircraft to jettison their bombs on three occasions and intercepted a raid by thirty-five Ju 87s on the retreating British forces near Abu Fayres, claiming the destruction of ten Stukas. Enemy sources record the loss of only one dive bomber, but regardless, the British patrol severely disrupted the German attack.[59] The Luftwaffe achieved one notable success on 17 June when seventeen Stukas bombed the 8th Field Regiment, 4th Indian Division, causing one hundred casualties. This successful attack was unfortunate, but it was also lucky; the unit was surprised just as it was getting into action. As a result the unit's vehicles were bunched up, the troops were not vigilant to the possibility of air attack, no antiaircraft guns were deployed, and the men had not yet had a chance to dig in and were above ground in the open with no available cover.[60] These unusual circumstances, however, did not stop army commanders from blaming the RAF for the absence of air cover.[61]

The high tempo of ground-support missions continued after the Western Desert Force had withdrawn from the battlefield and assumed a defensive posture. On the night of 17–18 June, two Wellingtons of No. 70 Squadron, supported by Fleet Air Arm Swordfish, attacked enemy motor transport near Bardia and reported large fires. Six heavy bombers struck at the port of Benghazi, while others targeted the airdromes at Derna and Gazala. The following morning Blenheims and Marylands attacked enemy concentrations in the frontier area, while Hurricanes and Tomahawks conducted successful and wide-ranging low-level raids in the afternoon.

These missions came with a cost. While no bombers were lost, nine Hurricanes were shot down. Four aircraft from No. 1 SAAF Squadron, escorting a Blenheim mission, were shot down by German fighters; three Hurricanes were shot down either by ground fire or enemy fighters while conducting low-level strafing missions; and two others were lost engaging enemy dive bombers.

Four Tomahawks of the newly arrived No. 250 Squadron were lost on 18 June when they were pounced on by Me 109s while returning from a strafing mission.[62] The full effect of these attacks on the enemy is not known, but a recent German history reported that "German movements during the entire operation were seriously hampered by the Royal Air Force, which mounted very successful attacks against German rear communications and supply-columns."[63] Considering that such strikes were minimal on 14 and 15 June and nonexistent on 16 June, this comment must largely refer to the attacks carried out on 17 and 18 June. An earlier commitment of air power to interdicting Axis movements may not have affected the outcome of Battleaxe due to Rommel's strengthening of the frontier defenses in the aftermath of Brevity, but it is worth considering that significant German reserves were rushed from Tobruk to the frontier on 15 and 16 June, a distance of seventy-five miles by road. A small number of RAF attacks on the afternoon on 17 June had "disorganized and delayed transport" along the Trigh Capuzzo.[64] During Brevity and again during the closing phase of Battleaxe, airstrikes had slowed and blunted the pace of enemy operations. The influence of nearly 200 daily interdiction sorties from the outset of the campaign can only be surmised.

The failure of Battleaxe was a major setback for British ambitions in North Africa and led to serious recrimination as the commanders tried to understand what went wrong. In a telegram sent to London on 18 June, General Wavell ascribed three factors for the failure of the operation: The Germans possessed greater tank strength than expected; they were prepared for the attack and immediately counterattacked; and the 7th Armoured Division did not have sufficient time to train and integrate its new tanks into an effective and battle-ready formation.[65] Noticeably absent was any blame attributed to the RAF.

Wavell had great confidence in his armored force and had crafted Battleaxe to bring about a "big tank battle" in the frontier. He expected the movement of German reinforcements from Tobruk once the battle began and even welcomed this development as it would give the 7th Armoured Division the opportunity for a decisive victory and allow the relief of Tobruk.[66] This might explain the general's failure to use the RAF to interdict this movement on 15 June. Yet by the end of the first day, Wavell's telegrams to London indicated that he knew the armored thrust had failed and his plan should have been reconsidered.[67] Instead, German reinforcements were allowed to move to the frontier on 16 June uncontested as the RAF continued its defensive combat patrols.

The Germans took advantage of poor British signals discipline before and during Battleaxe. Intercepted radio broadcasts had alerted Rommel to the imminent launch of the operation, and he responded by placing his units on alert. During the course of the battle, further signals intelligence allowed him to understand British intentions, and the general redeployed his forces to halt the British advance.[68] These countermoves proved to be the decisive element of the battle.

Wavell addressed the role of air power at the end of his report: "Our air forces protected our troops effectively from enemy bombing except on certain occasions when their protection had been temporarily withdrawn. . . . We never had sufficient superiority to afford entire protection to our troops or to stop enemy's movements. We are not organized or trained for the type of close support the enemy employs and cannot expect it."[69] Wavell believed the RAF could not concurrently provide air cover and conduct interdiction strikes. This was a fair criticism, though unfair in that the army received exactly the form of support they had requested. The accusation brought storms of protest from the air force, and Tedder cabled London to express his displeasure. He pointed out the "utter inaccuracy" of the general's statements and stated that "further argument in the face of such apparent inability to understand principles of air warfare appeared valueless." Tedder believed that Wavell's discussion of air power in his signal was "naive and meaningless."[70]

This disagreement illustrates the large gulf that existed between the army and the air force in their attempts to create an effective system of close air support. At the heart of the debate was the question of who should control the air resource. Army commanders believed they best knew their needs and that responsibility for air assignments should lie with them. Conversely, the RAF argued that air power was capable of much more than simply acting in intimate support of ground forces, and as such they should be able to act independently. In Battleaxe Tedder provided the army with what they requested: large-scale air cover of the army by fighters and small-scale attacks on the lines of communications by bombers. This allocation of resources meant that the RAF was not available to interdict the movement of German reinforcements to the front during the crucial first forty-eight hours of the battle, which may have cost the British victory.

Both the army and air force reported insignificant German air attacks on the battlefield. The majority of German fighters were retained to provide defense to rear areas in the face of RAF attacks. The few air raids launched by the Germans were ineffective. These attacks caused consternation among the ground troops targeted, but little damage resulted. RAF bombers proved effective at hitting enemy targets during the course of the battle, but they were not able to stop the flow of enemy units to the front. British tanks had a range of only forty miles, and after covering half that distance, they would have to refuel to ensure a sufficient combat reserves. German tanks operated under a similar constraint. The destruction of the supply vehicles and fuel trucks would have quickly rendered them unable to conduct operations. It was the timely arrival of German reinforcements on the battlefield that turned the tide of the campaign. Any delay or weakening of those reinforcements would have had a significant effect on British fortunes.[71]

In his after-action report Tedder defended his use of the air umbrella during the first two days of the operation. He argued that the air cover had been effective in protecting the army, and "with 2 possible exceptions in the extreme forward area[,] enemy attempts [to] attack troops were intercepted and bombs dropped unaimed." He explained that to maintain the umbrella required the use of relatively weak patrols, which meant higher casualties when the small number of defenders met large groups of enemy aircraft. Tedder did not address the opportunity lost by considering what the squadrons might have contributed if they had been released earlier from their air-cover responsibilities. RAF casualties were very high—thirty-six aircraft lost during the battle; an even larger number of warplanes were damaged but eventually returned to service. All but three of these aircraft were Hurricanes and Tomahawks, representing nearly 40 percent of the initial serviceable strength of the fighter squadrons. A major factor in the losses was a general lack of experience among the pilots. Four squadrons had recently been transferred to the desert, and though these pilots had considerable experience in East Africa, this was the first time they fought an enemy with modern, first-class aircraft. Experienced pilots were also lacking in the other squadrons due to recent losses in Greece and Crete. Many had not been through the operational-training unit, squadron-level training was deficient, and there was no time to train with the land forces.[72]

Another problem exposed during Battleaxe was the lack of close cooperation between the army and air force. The two services worked together to form the initial plan for the operation, but limited provisions were made to sustain this teamwork in combat. Beresford-Peirse and Collishaw worked well together, but they did not have the time to form the same close relationship enjoyed by the air commodore and Lieutenant General O'Connor. Army after-action reports were universal in their criticism of the problems experienced in interservice cooperation. Beresford-Peirse lamented the 112 miles of separation between his headquarters at Sidi Barrani and Collishaw's 204 Group headquarters at Maaten Bagush. The major general considered the issue of RAF cooperation to be the main point of interest for the Western Desert Force:

> Lack of comn [communications] and the fact that all aircraft operated from LGs [landing grounds] east of MATRUH, fighters refuelling at SIDI BAR-RANI, made close support and quick response to calls for fighter protection

impossible. . . . I regard the provision of ways and means for closer co-operation with the RAF, and the development of a satisfactory system for the use of
aircraft in close support of ground troops as the most important and urgent
problems we have to face at the moment.[73]

This letter demonstrated the army's continued treatment of the RAF as an
adjunct similar to the artillery and did not appreciate the wider influence that
air power could have on the conduct of a battle.

Major General Creagh, commander of the 7th Armoured Division, was
also disappointed with the support provided by the RAF: "There is no doubt
that the whole problem of air co-operation has yet to be solved. . . . [The RAF]
never really got into the ground picture [because] they operated too far back."
He recommended that a senior RAF officer needed to be collocated at divisional headquarters in an armored car with a radio link so he could advise the
rear air headquarters of the situation at the front.[74] This point was reiterated
by Major General Messervy. He pointed out that German armored operations
presented tempting targets due to the large number of petrol, ammunition,
and repair-and-recovery vehicles that followed close behind the spearheads.
"Bombers quickly 'whistled up' to deal with such targets might have a decisive
effect in any battle in which enemy tanks are engaged in considerable numbers.
I would go so far as to say, that, especially in the Western Desert, no formation
can be tactically complete till close air support with the necessary communications to ensure its rapid intervention is provided."[75]

These were valid criticisms and suggestions, but the main point of the
problem of distance was intractable at this stage of the war. Without depend-
able communications links and secure airfields close to the front line, ground
and air commanders had no choice other than to be at their respective headquarters. These coordination problems would be largely solved as the war progressed.[76] Creagh and Messervy raised the problem of the RAF's inability to
react quickly to army requests for support, yet it must be noted that "this criticism could hardly have sprung from actual operational experience since the
Army have failed to make requests for air support."[77]

The army paid minimal attention to the issue of interservice cooperation
when planning Operation Battleaxe. Brigadier Harding issued his directive on
RAF cooperation three days before the operation, and it contained only a brief
reference to joint operations. The two-page memo was primarily concerned
with tactical, artillery, and strategic reconnaissance, while the issue of communications between the two services was limited to the mention of a two-star
cartridge flare to be fired as a challenge signal. Also revealing was the consideration given to fighter protection: "Emergency calls for fighter protection will

be signalled to 204 Gp RAF through WQU sets with formations. These methods will only be used in *really* serious emergencies [emphasis in original]."[78] There was no plan for coordinating impromptu air attacks during the course of the battle. The directive's annex detailed the specific air tasks required by the army. The first two columns provided specific descriptions of the army's tactical- and strategic-reconnaissance requirements, the third column concerned fighter protection, and the fourth and fifth columns provided a terse overview of ground strafing and bombing targets. The emphasis in order and detail of the mission annex indicated that ground commanders were least concerned with the offensive potential of the RAF.[79] Generals Beresford-Peirse, Creagh, and Messervy were right to point out the poor air–ground coordination in their after-action reports, but the lack of prior planning for this cooperation was largely the result of the army dictating to the RAF the form its support should take without asking the air force how best it could contribute to the success of the campaign.

The problem of poor interservice communications was particularly acute on 17 June, when the RAF was called to slow the advance of the enemy columns to allow the Western Desert Force to escape the closing trap. Tedder recognized the problem and did not hesitate to blame the army.[80] RAF calls during the battle for ground formations to display their recognition panels went unacknowledged, and army headquarters did not provide regular position updates or bomb-line information to the air force. This made it difficult for pilots to provide close support due to the risk of hitting friendly forces. Collishaw reported, "great care had to be exercised at this stage in the operations because the Army Headquarters in the Field was unacquainted with the dispositions and locations of the 7th Armoured Division and they could not therefore tell us whether our air reconnaissance was reporting the movements of friend or foe."[81] The best the RAF could do in this situation was to assume that all traffic moving southeast was friendly, while that moving northeast was enemy; if in doubt, attacks were not carried out. Fortunately, this was an effective, if inelegant, solution, and only one minor case of friendly fire resulted.

Tedder also faulted the army for not making better use of the Bomber Striking Force, which maintained aircraft on call to meet army demands: "No doubt that opportunities of giving support were lost owing to absence of accurate information."[82] He knew of only one instance during the campaign when close air support was requested—when the cannon-armed Hurricane attacked enemy gun positions at Halfaya. There were also problems with the transmission of information and interpretation of reports. Reconnaissance made by the RAF discovered the advancing German columns, but this information was not acted upon promptly. On the afternoon of 17 June, air reconnaissance observed a large, slow-moving column making its way down Halfaya Pass toward Sollum. Army reports indicated that this might be a missing column from the 7th Armoured Division that had captured the pass in a bid to escape along the coast. Army headquarters could not confirm the identity of this force, so no attacks were made. It was subsequently discovered to be an enemy column, which proceeded to attack the 4th Indian Division in the Buq Buq area.[83] Tedder believed that there was "no black art in close support" but that a lack of training and communications breakdowns due to inferior equipment were the main reasons for the difficulties.[84]

Operation Battleaxe marked the nadir of army-air relations in the Middle East. The attack was hastily carried out in response to the demands of Churchill and the chiefs of staff. On paper, the British were ready for the attack, with a large, well-rested force that possessed a number of advantages over the enemy. But the strength was largely illusory. The 7th Armoured Division, recently reequipped with large numbers of new, untried tanks, was not yet ready to be committed to battle. Its men did not have the necessary training on the unfamiliar machines. The division even lacked a plan to coordinate the movements of the infantry and cruiser tanks with their different top speeds. Cooperation between the infantry and armor required time to refine.

The RAF was in a similar situation. Its numerical strength in the Western Desert was high, but its severe losses over Greece and Crete introduced many untried replacement pilots, and the new squadrons transferred to the theater had not yet completed the necessary training. The British plan was unoriginal and erroneously assumed that enemy defenses on the frontier remained unimproved in the aftermath of Brevity. German and Italian fortifications along the frontier actually were significantly reorganized and strengthened to deal with any new British attack. Perhaps the deciding factor in the land battle was the ability of the enemy to react quicker to the developing situation than the British. There were a number of points where the British threatened to rout the defenders, but on each occasion Rommel and his commanders rapidly deployed reserves to deal with the crisis.

The one major advantage the British Army held during this operation was the support of the RAF, which had demonstrated its ability to severely dislocate the enemy on and behind the battlefield. Yet rather than exploit this proven offensive potential, the army demanded that the RAF adopt the tactics of the Italian air force, which had been decisively defeated during Operation Compass. This insistence on a defensive air umbrella over its troops is somewhat understandable given its recent experience in Greece and Crete, where frequent Luftwaffe attacks had caused considerable anxiety and some dislocation, if not much damage.

The main difference between Compass and Battleaxe was the inability of the RAF and the army to agree on a common plan. General Wavell consistently demonstrated a poor grasp of air matters, but during the first campaign, he was willing to defer to Lieutenant General O'Connor, who had a much better understanding of RAF capabilities than did Major General Beresford-Peirse. During Compass, Air Chief Marshal Longmore directed and supported Air Commodore Collishaw's concept of operations, which proved so successful. This was not the case during Battleaxe, when overarching political considerations forced Air Marshal Tedder to endorse the army's demands for the defensive employment of the RAF. Collishaw recognized this was a missed opportunity, but Tedder, informed by Air Chief Marshal Portal, understood that the RAF could not afford to be seen as the cause for the failure of this operation. By acceding to the army request, the RAF avoided blame for conducting an independent campaign that left the ground forces exposed and unsupported.

This misemployment of the air force was a major factor in the outcome of Battleaxe. German reinforcements advanced to the frontier rapidly and largely uncontested during the first two days of the campaign, when they prevented a British breakthrough and contained the attack. Rommel then launched a series of counterattacks that drove the British back as he committed additional forces to the battle. It was only the timely intervention of the RAF during this final phase of Battleaxe that prevented the retreat from turning into a rout. Heavy air attacks on German columns on 17 June slowed their pursuit and allowed British units the time needed to conduct an orderly withdrawal.

It is worth considering how the outcome of Battleaxe may have differed if Collishaw had been allowed to use his fighters and bombers to interdict enemy supply routes during the first two days. There may have been a slight increase in the number of enemy air attacks on British ground forces, but more Luftwaffe and Regia Aeronautica sorties would have been drawn into defensive tasks in response to the RAF offensive. During Brevity, RAF attacks destroyed enemy logistical capability to the point that by the second morning, numerous Axis units were immobile and out of the battle due to a lack of fuel. The stronger attack of Battleaxe forced Rommel to deploy larger forces from the Tobruk area to stop the offensive. An effective interdiction campaign by a much stronger 204 Group on 15 and 16 June would have seriously complicated the Axis ability to oppose the campaign successfully.

The failure of Operation Battleaxe was devastating for the British Army and Churchill, but it proved a minor setback in the general war effort. Of more lasting importance was the campaign's consequences in shaping relations between the army and the RAF over the future form of tactical air support. Prior to the battle, Churchill had cautiously endorsed the army view; his position changed considerably in the weeks after the defeat in the desert. He solicited Portal's views on Tedder's report. The chief of the Air Staff conceded that while the umbrella may have been "efficacious," it was not needed, and it would have been much better to employ Collishaw's squadrons offensively:

> A defensive policy is bad for marale [*sic*], expensive in casualties and give[s] the enemy freedom of action which he has to forego when thrown on the defensive. The adoption of [the] offensive mean[s], however, that the troops must put up with some apparently unopposed bombing which they must deal with as best they can with their own weapons, and must *not* demand protection whenever this happens. The side which gives way to the cry of the troops and ships for protection will probably lose air superiority, forces being equal [emphasis in original].[85]

Churchill considered this note of such significant importance that he ordered it brought before the Chiefs of Staff Committee and printed for the Defence Committee. These ideas, largely based on the experience of the RAF in the Western Desert under Collishaw's command, would guide the prime minister's reassessment of tactical air support.

CHAPTER 9

AFTER BATTLEAXE

Operation Battleaxe lasted only three days, but its repercussions would be felt much longer. Winston Churchill had placed great hopes in this offensive. He accepted significant risks in dispatching his precious "Tiger cubs" to Egypt, but he judged this an acceptable gamble for the opportunity to relieve Tobruk, destroy Rommel's Afrika Korps, and push the enemy back beyond Benghazi. For him, the failure of Battleaxe was a "most bitter blow," and upon learning of the defeat, he wandered "disconsolately for some hours."[1] Jock Colville, one of Churchill's private secretaries, recalled that the prime minister was "gravely disappointed by the failure of Battleaxe," considering it a "major defeat."[2] On another level, Battleaxe illustrated the large gulf that existed between the army and the air force in their attempts to create an effective system of tactical air support. At the heart of the debate was the question of who should control the air resource. The interservice problems encountered during this operation would see a renewal of the debate at the highest levels of government and the military and result in the establishment of a new paradigm for army-air cooperation.

The consequences of the failure of Battleaxe were not long in coming. On 21 June General Wavell was relieved by Churchill, who never had full confidence in him: "I have come to the conclusion that public interest will best be served by appointment of General [Claude] Auchinleck to relieve you in command of armies of Middle East."[3] Though dismissed from the Middle East, Wavell essentially traded commands with Auchinleck, who was the commander-in-chief in India. Wavell is remembered as a "soldier's soldier" and "one of the great commanders in military history."[4] This may be true, but during the early battles in the Western Desert, he benefited enormously from some very capable subordinates but consistently struggled to understand the role and potential of air power on the modern battlefield.

The other change during this period was the replacement of Air Commodore Collishaw. Air Marshal Tedder believed that despite Collishaw's accomplishments while leading 202 and 204 Groups, he was the wrong man for the job and was in over his head. He shared these impressions with Wilfrid

Freeman in a scrawled, handwritten postscript to a typewritten letter sent three weeks after the conclusion of Battleaxe: "I am rather worried about the command situation in the W. Desert. Collishaw has had enough (5 years out here) and in any case I don't think he is the right man to tackle the Hun and the Army."[5] Two days later Tedder cabled Air Chief Marshal Portal about the same issue and stated that while in the past Collishaw "had done some fine work," he was now "played out," that the "present and future problem is quite beyond him." Tedder proposed to relieve him immediately and replace him with "a first class man with drive and judgement," qualities he believed Collishaw did not possess.[6]

The air marshal wrote Collishaw on 10 July informing him that he was to be sent back to England:

> Now that the Battleaxe phase is over I am proposing to give you the relief that you have so well earned. It may be that they will send out a permanent successor from home but in the meantime I am getting [Air Commodore Leonard] Slatter down from the Soudan [sic] to take over for you. What I am hoping, and I think the people at home will agree, is to let you go back to the U.K. by the first really comfortable ship we can find. I do feel that if anyone earned a standeasy you have and so far as it is within my power I am determined that you get it.[7]

Collishaw's time in the Western Desert was finished, but the pattern and success of his air campaigns would provide a template for future army-air operations.

An examination of the development of Allied tactical-air-support doctrine during the Second World War shows that many of the underlying principles regarding its use were developed and codified based on the experiences of Collishaw's command. The failure of Battleaxe led the army and the air force to debate the future form of air support. There were three parallel, though related, debates during this period. The first two, shaped by the army's Home Forces and by the RAF's Army Cooperation Command, took place in England and dated back to the interwar period. The third stream was based on the experiences of the two services in the Middle East. All three "compartments" eventually arrived at similar "common sense" conclusions:

i. Intimate relations between the two Services at key points, i.e. at top Command level (e.g. Tedder and Auchinleck), at important field headquarters (significantly missing in BATTLEAXE) and at the very front of battle. . . .

ii. An independent signals network—vitally important, so that there should be no competition for signals priorities and the minimum of hierarchical delay.

iii. Recognition that at certain times and in certain circumstances Army cooperation would be the function, not of "special" aircraft designed and allocated for the purpose, but of *the whole available air power,* using all its types: bombers, reconnaissance, transport, special duties [emphasis in original].[8]

These points were fundamental to the smooth provision of tactical air support, but what was missing was a common understanding of the form that support would take. The need to resolve the future form of air support reached a crisis point in the aftermath of Battleaxe as the army attempted to gain direct control of air assets to support its operations.

In the interwar period RAF thinking on the issue was led by John Slessor, Collishaw's classmate at RAF Staff College. Slessor commanded No. 4 (Army Co-operation) Squadron for three years after graduating from Andover in 1925 and developed an interest in air–ground cooperation. After spending three years at the Plans Branch of the Air Ministry's Directorate of Operations and Intelligence, Slessor was sent as an instructor to the Army Staff College in Camberley. His role there was to instruct officers in the roles and capabilities of air power, especially tactical cooperation. After leaving Camberley for a posting in India, which included operational flying in Waziristan, Slessor compiled his staff-college lectures into an exposition on tactical air operations called *Air Power and Armies* (1936).[9] Described as, "the best treatise of airpower theory written in English before World War II," this book offered a thoroughly modern appreciation of the potential of air–ground operations.[10] Slessor analyzed Great War operations in considerable detail, especially the role of air power during the Battle of Amiens in August 1918. He argued that the RAF emerged from the war as "the best led, best trained, and most efficient air force in the world," but planning future operations based on that experience must be tempered with the expectation that "sealed-pattern, trench-warfare, infantry and artillery battle on the 1914–18 model will never be seen again."[11] Slessor believed that any future conflict would be marked by maneuver and that air power would have a central role to play, principally in defeating the enemy air force and interdicting the lines of communications and supply. Though achieving air superiority was the RAF's first objective, others roles, such as strategic attacks, interdiction at the theater (operational) level, and tactical cooperation with ground forces would also be carried out. Slessor understood that the ability of the service to carry out these missions in parallel rather than sequentially distinguished air operations from those of the army and navy.[12]

Slessor's "masterful volume served as a transition between the RAF of the post–World War I era and the RAF of the pre–World War II era."[13] He foreshadowed the development of air-ground doctrine that took place during the latter war. His ideas reflected the evolution of army–air force relations as they would exist by 1945. Unfortunately, this interservice partnership at the start of the war was characterized by internecine fighting and parochial, inward-looking opinions on relations between the two services. It would take years of active operations to work out a method of cooperation acceptable to both services.[14]

The relationship between the RAF and the British Army at the start of the Second World War was strained at best. During the interwar period, the army and Royal Navy viewed the air force as an "aberration" and wanted ownership of the dismantled pieces.[15] Chief of the Air Staff Trenchard fought hard to prevent this from happening by advocating an offensive, or strategic, role for the RAF. The ability to take the war to the enemy through strategic bombing gave the air force a role equivalent to the other two services. But this theory could not be tested in a period of peace, meaning that "air control" was the prime mission of the RAF between the wars.[16]

A study of army–air force relations during this period concluded: "There is unlikely to be a more extreme example than that afforded by the relations between the British Army and Air Force in the interwar years. . . . There was hardly an area of contact between the two departments throughout this period where there was not, at best, friction, or, at worst, open hostility."[17] The two services did work together on the issue of air support in the 1920s and 1930s, but their divergent paths meant that little was accomplished. There were fundamental disagreements over the form of the air-support organization. The army believed that air-support tactics were sufficiently different from other air operations that a separate army-air organization and training system was required. It also feared that without its own organic air support, the RAF would focus its attacks on targets away from the battlefield and not provide the necessary close cover. For these reasons the army demanded that RAF squadrons form an integral component of ground formations. The RAF endorsed a very different concept of air power that was based largely on Slessor's ideas. In addition, little progress was made in the development of communications systems, which were crucial to the effective provision of air support.[18]

As a result, the British fought the Battle of France in 1940 without an effective air-support system. The initial army deployment saw a single corps of two divisions form the British Expeditionary Force. It was joined by the RAF's Advanced Air Striking Force and the Air Component of the Field Force. The

Striking Force attacked strategic targets with its ten squadrons of Fairey Battles. The Air Component, composed of four squadrons each of fighters, bombers, and army-cooperation/reconnaissance aircraft, provided direct support to the ground forces and was under the operational control of Gen. John Gort, commander-in-chief of the Expeditionary Force. Army complaints and the Air Staff's desire to streamline the command-and-control arrangements led to the creation of a single air command under Air Marshal Arthur Barratt known as British Air Forces in France. Barratt attempted to collocate his headquarters with the army, but Gort believed this to be unnecessary.[19]

The Battle of France was a monumental defeat for the British, and only the successful evacuation from Dunkirk prevented a complete German victory. The effect of the experience on army-air relations was almost as devastating. Poor coordination between the two services confirmed for the army the need to have its own air contingent under its command. This would require fighters that could be tasked for air-umbrella missions as well as light and dive bombers to provide close air support against targets "of vital tactical importance."[20] The RAF, however, also saw France as a confirmation of its doctrine. The main problem encountered by the air force was its numerical inferiority, which did not allow it to conduct a campaign of its own design. Effective air support was contingent on air superiority, and there were never enough fighter squadrons in France to achieve this. The Air Ministry believed that more aircraft, better mobility, and improved communications were the only defects in the existing system.[21]

The poor state of the British air-support system in 1940 demanded refinement. The RAF and army each remained convinced of the correctness of its approach, and neither side was willing to compromise. Various initiatives in the United Kingdom attempted to improve the situation. Sir Anthony Eden, the secretary of state for war, moved the process forward in mid-September 1940 when he observed: "Progress in this vitally important matter is now the secondary responsibility of a number of officials. It should surely be the primary responsibility of highly placed officers of the Army and the R.A.F. working in co-operation."[22] As a result, the RAF formed the Army Co-operation Command in November, which was "responsible for implementing the policy decided upon by the Air Ministry and the War Office for the development of all forms of Air Support for the Army." The command was responsible for training and fostering a commonality in the approach of the two services to air support.[23]

The future direction of air support received attention at the highest levels of the British government in the first half of 1941. In March Churchill told his cabinet that it was the Royal Navy and especially the RAF that would win the war, and the army had no role to play in the defeat of the enemy.[24] This ignited an extended debate over the summer and fall of 1941 regarding the number and type of aircraft to be devoted to army-support operations. Air Chief Marshal Portal preferred to focus RAF development on the strategic-bombing program and assign a small number of aircraft to the army. Conversely, General Dill, chief of the Imperial General Staff, wanted 109 army-support squadrons and various other attack and transport aircraft dedicated to work with ground forces. In total, this demand worked out to nearly four thousand aircraft, more than the existing RAF frontline strength.[25] This acrimonious strategic debate focused exclusively on the allocation of resources and did not consider the employment of army-support squadrons at the operational or tactical levels.

Work was also underway on the development of air support at the tactical level. In September and October 1940 the Air Staff authorized a series of joint army-air signals trials to experiment with improvements to battlefield communications between the two services. Group Capt. A. H. Wann and Lt. Col. J. D. Woodall devised a networked system of communications links that would allow the army and air force to converse more effectively in the field.[26]

At the start of May 1941, Slessor wrote a note for the vice chief of the Air Staff on the question of RAF support for the army in an attempt to set out the future direction of policy on the matter. He stated, "there has been far too much of a tendence [sic] in all these battles for the Army to turn around and ask the Air Force to do what it should be doing itself."[27] The role of the air force was not to destroy enemy tanks but to make it impossible for them to fight due to a lack of fuel and ammunition. He countered the army contention that the German successes in Poland, the Low Countries, and France were due to close support provided by the Luftwaffe was inaccurate—its main accomplishment was to isolate the battlefield and dislocate the lines of communications. Luftwaffe success against battlefield targets occurred because it had first accomplished the other tasks.[28] Slessor used the example of the Luftwaffe air campaigns to prove his points, but he could just as easily have used Collishaw's conduct in Operation Compass as his example.

The creation of Army Co-operation Command and the Wann-Woodall experiments were positive developments that would aid the process of developing an effective British air-support system. The procedures were being worked out, and the army and the air force were slowly coming to understand the needs of the other service. But a crucial feature was still lacking—success in battle. This would come from operations in the Middle East.

Churchill was the prime figure in sorting out army–air force relations, and Operation Battleaxe was the trigger for his intervention. His view on the relationship between the two services, which had previously favored the army, began to change. He was not pleased with the failure of Battleaxe, and on 20

June he was "ruminating deeply" about the fate of Tobruk and how to resume the offensive in the Western Desert.[29] He wrote to Gen. Hastings Ismay, his chief military advisor, to request written proposals for the "more intimate association of the Army and the co-operating Air Force squadrons."[30]

Churchill sought a solution to one of the main problems evident during the failed operation. Both Tedder and Auchinleck identified difficulties in the provision of air support during the fighting. For the army, the main issue was the defense of its troops, but for the air force it was a question of "opportunity cost"—aircraft could be used for the close protection of the army, but Collishaw had shown that distant attacks on enemy bases, airfields, ports, and lines of communications were more effective and had the additional benefit of forcing the enemy to adopt a defensive posture and limit its offensive missions.[31] Such a use of air power would achieve the operational goal sought by the army, but it would not provide the comforting sight of aircraft overhead so desired by many ground commanders. Tedder ordered Collishaw to provide an air umbrella during Battleaxe in response to army demands backed by urging from London, especially Portal, to get along with the army. After the operation Tedder realized the problems with this approach, and though he stated that the use of the umbrella was appropriate given the circumstances, it was a tactic that should be avoided in the future.[32]

Churchill placed primary blame for the failure of Battleaxe on General Wavell. He told South African prime minister Jan Smuts that though the British had superiority in tanks and aircraft, the enemy were able to move their tanks from Tobruk unmolested as the Tobruk garrison did nothing to prevent it. Churchill did not directly indict Wavell in the letter, but his observation that "the battle was hard and even and might easily have turned our way" indicated that he thought his commander had handled his forces poorly.[33]

Churchill also considered Tedder culpable for the defeat. In writing to Auchinleck on 19 July to try to better understand the problems of the battle, Churchill remarked that "the Air Force was used as a mere series of small umbrellas" over the troops, and "its large superiority was frittered away in passive defence by standing patrols, instead of being used in offensive strategic combination with the Army." He continued that this situation "no doubt arose from the earnest desire of the Air Force to protect the Army," but that did not change the outcome of the fighting.[34]

The War Office in London drew different lessons from Battleaxe, which it used to shape the air-support debate. Following Wavell's dismissal, Dill wrote to Auchinleck on 26 June with "a few words on the situation and perhaps of advice."[35] He outlined the dissatisfaction of the War Office over the issue of air cooperation—"Nowhere [sic] is it good"—and observed that the RAF has "no complete understanding of what is required of them from the purely Army point of view."[36] Dill then left little doubt regarding army expectations of Tedder and the RAF in the Middle East: "his main mission in life is to support the Army to the *n*th degree in any operation it has to undertake and to support it in the manner most acceptable to the Army Commander concerned."[37]

Churchill received personal reports from two outside observers on the RAF–army relationship in the Middle East. Averell Harriman was U.S. president Franklin D. Roosevelt's special envoy, but he also enjoyed a special relationship with Churchill and reported directly to the British prime minister. He arrived in Egypt immediately after the completion of Operation Battleaxe and interviewed the senior commanders involved—Wavell, Auchinleck, Tedder, and Cunningham as well as Beresford-Peirse and Collishaw. His main conclusion was that there was a "dangerous lack of military cooperation" between the three services.[38] Admiral Cunningham observed that the navy was not notified about the operation, and it could have provided significant naval gunfire at Halfaya, which might have made a difference in capturing and holding the important pass.[39] Beresford-Peirse bitterly complained that the air force had not supported the advance of his troops, while Collishaw countered that the army's requests for air support were unreasonable given the existing state of the communications network. Harriman told Churchill that the theater required a unified military command but passed along Tedder's caution: "Neither the Army nor the Navy understands the use of the air. If [either one were] given control, the Air Force would be wasted."[40] In his final report submitted to Churchill and the British War Cabinet on 16 July, Harriman declared, "Unified command is essential and in my mind cannot be attained to an effective degree unless one man is charge with responsibility for the defense of the Middle East."[41]

Oliver Lyttelton, the newly appointed minister of state in the Middle East, was sent to Cairo by Churchill to relieve Auchinleck of the burden of nonoperational matters. After arriving on 5 July, he met with the commanders in chief. His report to Churchill on 26 July echoed the findings of Harriman. Lyttelton commented favorably on the state of the RAF in Egypt but noted the poor coordination between the three services. He also suggested that a unified command was necessary for the success of future operations.[42]

Auchinleck's first cable to London after taking command in the Middle East reflected the War Office view of the nature of the relationship between the army and the RAF. He considered that armored reinforcements were the "first essential" for a new offensive into Libya, but the "second essential," echoing Dill's view, was the need for a large and well-trained air component that would be "*at disposal [of the] Army for all its needs* including fighters medium bombers tactical reconnaissance and close support on the battlefield. This is *non-existent* at present [emphasis added]."[43] His "third essential" was that the Royal Navy must provide "close support of Army and in harrying enemy sea communications," and the RAF must be at the "disposal of the Navy" for these operations.[44]

Auchinleck proposed an army-centric command structure in the Middle East whereby the RAF and Royal Navy would assume subservient roles to the land campaign. He demanded the air component be placed under army command, taking its direction from ground commanders, and that it along with the navy should design their operations almost exclusively in support of ground operations.

The Air Ministry was not pleased with Auchinleck's letter. Group Capt. Ronald Ivelaw-Chapman, deputy director of Plans (Operations) wrote, "We cannot agree that the formation of what will, in effect, be three separate air forces is either possible or desirable in the Middle East."[45] This plan for the "rigid and uneconomical employment of the Air Force" led Air Chief Marshal Portal to immediately raise his objections with Churchill.[46]

The prime minister's reply to Auchinleck's telegram of 4 July bore the influence of Portal, Tedder, and Harriman. He made it clear that he expected a coequal role for the air force. The RAF would fully support the land campaign, but this did not mean that air resources would be under army control:

> I feel that for all major operational purposes your plans must govern the employment of the whole Air Force through the Middle East, bearing in mind of course that the Air Force has its own dominant strategic role to play, and must not be frittered away in providing small umbrellas for the Army, as it seems to have been in the Sollum battle (Battleaxe). In your telegram you speak of aircraft supporting the Army and aircraft supporting the Navy and aircraft employed on independent strategic tasks. The question is, what are the proportions? These will have to be arranged from time to time by the Commanders-in-Chief in consultation. But nothing in these arrangements should mar the integrity of the Air Force contribution to any major scheme you have in hand. One cannot help feeling that in the Sollum fight our air superiority was wasted.[47]

Auchinleck accepted Churchill's mild rebuke and modified his view on air support. He replied that, in consultation with Tedder, he agreed that the "RAF cannot be subordinated exclusively to implement army plans."[48]

To ensure that there was no misunderstanding regarding his orders, Churchill summoned Auchinleck to London for a talk in late July. Tedder, not invited by the prime minister, decided he needed to go too as it was "vital that [discussions of land strategy] should not be divorced from the parallel problems of air strategy in the Middle East."[49] Over the course of two days, Auchinleck and Tedder met with senior officials in London and dined with Churchill at his country estate.⁵⁰

The crux of the Auchinleck–Tedder visit to London was their attendance at the War Cabinet Defence Committee meeting on 1 August. The situation in the Western Desert dominated the discussion, and Churchill remarked that the next three months offered a great opportunity to press the enemy, possibly to the point of forcing an Axis evacuation of North Africa. His intent was to impress upon Auchinleck the importance of the earliest possible commencement of the next major offensive in the Western Desert, to be known as Crusader. He believed that sufficient forces were already in place for such an offensive, and it should be launched right away. On 22 June the Germans had launched Operation Barbarossa, their invasion of the Soviet Union, and experienced great success in its early days. Churchill calculated that an offensive in the desert would benefit from German distraction. He also feared that British inactivity at this crucial point would not be respected by a new ally in the Soviets "bearing the full brunt" of the German attack.⁵¹

Auchinleck agreed that there was a need for an immediate offensive, but he was holding out for reinforcements, especially tanks, and would not commit to an attack before November. He also pointed out that Battleaxe had failed because the army had not yet been ready to attack. Churchill countered that the war effort could never proceed by waiting until preparations were complete, and he was willing to authorize "exceptional measures" to allow the offensive to proceed earlier.⁵²

The final issue discussed at the meeting concerned the air situation in the Middle East. The prime minister was not pleased that with 50,000 airmen, 2,000 aircraft, and 1,500 pilots, Tedder was only able to marshal 450 aircraft for battle. The air marshal replied that many of the difficulties had to do with the great distances involved as well as the lack of suitable repair and maintenance sections in Egypt. He then detailed the efforts being undertaken to improve the ability of the RAF to "provide the Army with the opportunity which they wanted for an offensive."⁵³ These developments included the formation of an army-cooperation wing, a joint training program with the army, and improvements to the communications establishment between the two services. Churchill concluded the meeting by again stressing the "vital importance" of intensifying the air and naval campaign against the enemy lines of communications. He then stated that "during the next day or two he would set down the general conclusions which had emerged from the discussions which had been held in the last two or three days."⁵⁴

The meetings were productive for Churchill, who came away with a better appreciation of his Middle East commander, even though he was unable to persuade him to move up the attack date.[55] Auchinleck was exhausted by the meetings but was also satisfied with the outcome.[56] Tedder felt that he had successfully set forth the RAF Middle East view to Churchill and the other senior officers in London. An additional benefit was the opportunity to get to know Auchinleck as "the trip had done a great deal to bring us together."[57]

During the summer, Churchill "brooded" on the necessary steps to obtain success in Operation Crusader, and his meetings with Auchinleck and Tedder ultimately prompted him to write a directive that would address the major problems he saw in the Middle East.[58] He considered the positions presented to him by Portal, Dill, Auchinleck, and Tedder and also took into account the independent information he received from Harriman and Lyttelton, among others, in an attempt to mitigate future arguments over the direction of air support in the Middle East. While aboard HMS *Prince of Wales* en route to Placentia Bay, Newfoundland, for the Atlantic Conference in early August, he composed a statement "in light of all the reports which I had studied of the spring fighting [Battleaxe]."[59]

Churchill's missive began with the words "Renown awaits the Commander who first in this war" and defined the roles and relationship of the army and the RAF in the upcoming campaign.[60] Jock Colville recalled that the prime minister added this opening to denote "masterly documents" that he used to "direct the conduct and strategy of the war."[61] The first draft was shown to Generals Dill and Brooke, who suggested a few minor changes that did not affect its main principles, and it was then sent to Auchinleck and Tedder in late August or early September.[62] This seminal directive confirmed the independence of the RAF in the Middle East, put to rest any consideration that it was a junior partner, and effectively settled the pattern for future army-air cooperation.

The memo was entitled "A Note by the Minister of Defence" and began with a discussion of the importance of antitank guns, which, he argued, could stop an attack by heavy armor if used properly. Churchill recognized the threat of German tank attacks but urged that guns should be "fought to the muzzle"; even if overrun their sacrifice was of the "highest honour," and the destruction of tanks repaid the loss of any antitank guns.[63] He considered antiaircraft guns essential for the close air defense of ground forces. To ensure sufficient protection and relieve the RAF of the need to provide an air umbrella, Churchill sent an additional 250 Bofors antiaircraft guns to the Middle East so Auchinleck's columns could defend themselves from enemy air attack. This meant:

> Nevermore must the ground troops expect, as a matter of course, to be protected against the air by aircraft. If this can be done it must only be as a happy make-weight and a place of good luck. Above all, the idea of keeping standing

patrols of aircraft over moving columns should be abandoned. It is unsound to "distribute" aircraft in this way, and no air superiority will stand any larger application of such mischievous practice.[64]

Churchill further explained that the RAF would be required to provide the army commander with "all possible aid irrespective of other targets" when a battle was planned. The army and the air force would then work together to decide on targets for air attack before and during the fighting. Rather than provide an air umbrella to protect the army, the RAF's primary responsibility was to attack "all assembly or refuelling points or marching columns of the enemy . . . by bombers during daylight with strong fighter protection, thus bringing about air conflicts not only of the highest importance in themselves but directly contributing to the general result."[65]

These instructions fundamentally changed the dynamic of army-air cooperation in the Middle East and set out the parameters that would guide air support in future battles. Churchill provided "executive guidance for the air support arrangements that would be used in Operation Crusader [and] he also established an authoritative definition of the general precepts of the 'combined operation,' which the Army and the RAF adhered to throughout the rest of the war."[66] The problems of Battleaxe were addressed: the air force would no longer provide air cover, and the two services would work closely toward a jointly developed and executed battle plan.

Churchill's directive on the issue of army-air cooperation marked an almost complete reversal of the position he had held prior to Operation Battleaxe. A month before that campaign, the issue of air cooperation with the army was discussed a meeting at 10 Downing Street in London attended by Churchill, Dill, Portal, Lord Beaverbrook, and others. During the meeting, General Brooke admitted that he "became a bit heated and attacked the Air Ministry strongly, as regards recent attitude towards Army Co-operation. PM [Churchill] backed me up strongly and meeting was a great success!"[67] Churchill continued his support of the army position on 10 June 1941 during a parliamentary debate on the Battle of Crete when RAF support for the army was discussed. When pressed on the issue, he stated that it was desirable that every division should have the chance to train with the RAF and have a "close and precise relationship with a particular number of aircraft that it knows and that it can call up at will and need."[68] He further stated that those warplanes should be under the command of the army "for the purposes of everything that is a tactical operation."[69]

Battleaxe was the catalyst for Churchill to redefine the relationship between the army and the air force, but he did not give the RAF carte blanche to act in its own self-interest. At the same time Auchinleck was making his first declarations on air support in the Middle East, Wavell released his report on the 2nd Armoured Division during the retreat in Cyrenaica, which was soon followed by the rebuttal report by Brig. A. F. Harding and Air Commodore L. O. Brown.[70] Churchill accepted Wavell's report but made a number of comments, including the observation that the commander of an armored division must have a small number of aircraft at his disposal for the purpose of reconnaissance.[71] Portal was not pleased with the criticism of the RAF in Wavell's report and made his objections known. The prime minister agreed that the air force was not to blame for the defeat, but he used the opportunity to tell Portal that "the lack of effective and intimate contact between the air and the ground forces calls for drastic reform. The needs of the Army should be met in a helpful spirit by the Air Ministry."[72] A week later he sent Portal another letter, which observed that the RAF had been "most hard and unhelpful both to the Army and the Navy in meeting their special requirements," and he expected that "the Army's grievances and complaints will be met."[73] Churchill understood that successful joint operations required willing and helpful partners.

Relations between the RAF and the army continued to be adversarial during the planning for Operation Crusader, but an agreement was eventually achieved along the lines outlined by Churchill. On 3 October during one planning meeting, Lt. Gen. Alan Cunningham, commander of the Eighth Army, argued strenuously that his corps commanders "would feel lonely and unsupported unless they had a fighter and bomber squadron at their own personal beck and call."[74] Tedder was not moved by this appeal and countered that "to divide up our forces into penny packets would be to fritter away out strength without leaving his [Cunningham's] forces any effective support."[75] The air marshal described the subsequent debate as a "good, friendly but gloves off discussion" that was eventually settled when Auchinleck stated that he had given the issue a lot of thought and was "quite convinced" that the RAF position was the correct option.[76] Churchill's directive was not specifically mentioned in the accounts of the meeting, but his ideas ultimately underscored Auchinleck's acquiescence to the RAF plan.[77]

Churchill's pronouncements on air support were a direct response to events in the Middle East. His first major statement was prompted by Auchinleck's War Office–influenced attempt to establish the army as the senior partner, with the air force under its command and control. His second statement, the "Renown awaits the Commander who first in this war" message, was made in anticipation of the forthcoming Crusader offensive and the need to ensure a smooth working relationship between the two services. The evolution of Churchill's thinking on the question of air support was a refinement of the example set in the Western Desert by Collishaw as the only successful air–ground battlefield partnership employed up to that point in the war. Tedder, through Portal, was the main conduit to the prime minister for these ideas. During a planning meeting for Operation Crusader, Tedder confirmed this point when he advocated an offensive role for the RAF in the upcoming battles based on the RAF's prior experience: "in each of the last two operations in the Western Desert [Brevity and Battleaxe], in which air action on both occasions was successful and had very considerable effect, action was taken as a result of direct air reconnaissance and on the initiative of the A.O.C. [Collishaw] after squadrons had been standing by for hours 'at call' without any call having come from the Army."[78] Tedder referred to Collishaw's use of offensive air power during these campaigns, not the air umbrella that he ordered him to carry out during the first two days of Battleaxe.

As the strategic-level exchanges were taking place in London, work was proceeding in the Western Desert to improve the tactical level of cooperation between No. 253 Army Co-operation Wing of 204 Group and Eighth Army. The first training maneuver, Western Desert Exercise No. 3, was planned and executed under Collishaw and took place on 11–12 July 1941. It examined the offensive and defensive use of aircraft with the aim of determining the most suitable targets for air attack as well as how to find, engage, and destroy those targets. A key feature of this and successive trials was determining the best methods for the two services to communicate in battle as well as recognition exercises to determine the most suitable method for ground forces to identify themselves to aircraft.[79] By early September sufficient experience had been gained to call a conference in Cairo to determine the future direction of joint army-air operations in the Middle East. This meeting resulted in the publication of "The Middle East (Army and RAF) Directive on Direct Air Support," jointly issue by GHQ Middle East Forces and HQ RAF Middle East, on 30 September 1941. One historian has argued that "in the course of the development of army air co-operation it was perhaps the most important directive issued during the war."[80]

The publication of this directive marked the beginning of the creation of the system of air support that would carry to Allies to victory. The historical record has largely credited Tedder and Coningham for its development. As one historian stated, "Tedder was the thinker who conceived the new air-support system but Air Vice-Marshal Coningham (AOC WDAF) was the practitioner who made it work."[81] Another observed that Churchill's pronouncements were "widely publicised and vigorously enforced by Coningham with Tedder's wholehearted support."[82] Tedder recalled in his memoirs, "I was heartily glad when the perennial controversy about the economical use of air power was clarified by a directive from the Prime Minister early in September." He then quoted verbatim Churchill's words, starting with "Never more must the ground troops expect, as a matter of course, to be protected against the air by aircraft" and concluded by relating, "I found it most satisfying to be supported in this authoritative way by a ruling which recognized that we could not be so prodigal of our resources as to scatter them in driblets here and there, and which recognized also that apart from the essential aid which the air alone could render to the Army and Navy, there had emerged a new dimension in the Middle East struggle, air warfare in its own right."[83] For a variety of reasons, Tedder had endorsed the use of the air umbrella during Battleaxe, but his operational-level concept of air operations reflected the campaign plan successfully employed by Collishaw prior to Battleaxe.

This may be the commonly accepted version of events, but it would be more accurate to credit Tedder and Coningham with the refinement rather than creation of the Allied system of air support. Coningham took over command of the Western Desert Air Force at a point when serious study and trials were already being devoted to improving the methods of tactical air support. Experiments were begun under Collishaw's direction to devise better methods of communications and establish air-support controls to facilitate closer liaison between the army and air force and allow a more responsive deployment of aircraft to meet army needs along with improvements to the logistics of providing support. Coningham's tenure in the desert also corresponded to a period when greater resources were available, especially greater numbers of modern fighters and bombers.

This system was improved and refined starting with Operation Crusader (November 1941–January 1942) and culminating a year later with Operation Lightfoot, the Second Battle of El Alamein (October–November 1942). Operation Torch, the invasion of North Africa launched in November 1942, did not benefit from the lessons learned in the Western Desert, and there were major problems in army-air relations from the start. Gen. Dwight Eisenhower, the overall commander, reorganized his air command in early January 1943, drawing on the British experience in the Western Desert. Following further refinements to the command structure after the Casablanca Conference, the Allies arrived at the mature air-support system that would carry them through to the end of the war. On 16 February 1943 a meeting of senior Allied commanders convened in Tripoli to discuss the lessons learned during the Libyan campaign. The highlight of this meeting were presentations by Gen. Bernard Montgomery, then commander of Eighth Army, and Air Vice-Marshal Coningham, then commander of the Northwest African Tactical Air Force. Montgomery unveiled a pamphlet he wrote called "Some Notes on High Command in War," which Tedder called the "gospel according the

Montgomery."[84] Churchill recalled that during his visit to Tripoli at the beginning of February, he "chanced to show" Montgomery a copy of his "Renown awaits" directive. Seeing it for the first time, the general remarked, "It is as true now as it was when it was written." Within two weeks Montgomery had written his own pamphlet on air power, which shared many traits with Churchill's missive.[85]

In his pamphlet Montgomery set out his beliefs about air power. "Any officer who aspires to hold high command in war must understand clearly certain principles regarding the use of air power." Flexibility was its greatest asset and allowed it to be applied as a "battle-winning factor of the first importance." Radical for an army officer, Montgomery argued that centralized control of the resource was essential as "nothing could be more fatal to successful results than to dissipate the air resource into small packets placed under the control of army formation commanders, with each packet working on its own plan. The soldier must not expect, or wish, to exercise direct command over air striking forces." He concluded with the warning that the ground and air forces must "work together at the same HQ in complete harmony, and with complete mutual understanding and confidence."[86]

Coningham made a presentation after Montgomery and revealed the principles that would become the foundation of British and American tactical air power for the remainder of the war.[87] Indeed, these principles still hold true today. He stated:

> The Soldier commands the land forces, the Airman commands the air forces; both commanders work together and operate their respective forces in accordance with a combined Army–Air plan, the whole operations [sic] being directed by the Army Commander. . . . An Army has one battle to fight, the land battle. The Air has two. It has first of all to beat the enemy air, so that it may go into the land battle against the enemy land forces with the maximum possible hitting power.[88]

He concluded his talk by stating, "no soldier is competent to operate the Air, just as no Airman is competent to operate the Army."[89]

The tenets of the tactical air system outlined by Montgomery and Coningham at the Tripoli meeting would guide Allied tactical air operations through the end of the war. The successful partnership of Eighth Army and the Western Desert Air Force and their defeat of Rommel finally convinced senior army officers that a centralized air-support system under air force command was the best practice. This doctrine was at the core of the successful tactical air operations conducted in Sicily, Italy, and Northwest Europe by both British and American tactical air forces.[90]

Important changes were made to the British air-support system in the period between Operations Battleaxe and Crusader. The failure of the offensive to relieve Tobruk in June 1941 was caused in part by a misallocation of air resources during the first campaign. Generals Wavell and Beresford-Peirse had requested continuous air cover over their forces, and Air Marshal Tedder agreed to this allocation. Collishaw understood at the time that this was a misuse of his potent offensive weapon, but he was overruled by Tedder, who complied with army requests made in the wake of defeats in Cyrenaica, Greece, and Crete. The army's perception of these battles was that the Luftwaffe had very effectively carried out attacks on British troops, and the RAF, or "Royal Absent Force," had been busy on other less important tasks that left the ground forces exposed.

To his credit, Churchill studied the issue of air support and understood that it needed to be resolved to ensure British success in the war. Before Battleaxe he had endorsed the army view of air support, but the failure of the operation exposed problems with that model. His "Renown awaits" directive clearly and succinctly enunciated the concept of air support executed in the Western Desert by Collishaw while it explicitly proscribed the air umbrella requested by the army and employed in Operation Battleaxe. During Operation Compass, Collishaw had devoted all the aircraft at his disposal to the support of the ground offensive. Bombers and fighters worked together to attack aerodromes, ports, and transportation hubs that would delay and distract the dispatch of enemy reinforcements, both air and ground, to the front and allow the army to concentrate on defeating the enemy in the zone of contact without interference. A similar plan was executed during Brevity as well as during the closing stages of Battleaxe. These latter operations showed the promise of positive results, but their short duration did not allow the full effect of air power to be felt before the end of combat. Much work remained to be done on the technical and tactical details of the air-support system, though a start had been made toward that process before Collishaw left. Yet the broad theoretical foundations of army-air operations employed by Collishaw had been tested and proven during the battles of 1940–41 and would now be further refined to form the basis of Allied tactical air doctrine employed for the rest of the war.

CHAPTER 10

CONCLUSION

A t the start of 1941 the RAF and the British Army in Egypt remained far apart in their conception of air support. The Middle East Combined Plan of 1939 created early harmony between the two services, but this trust and coordination eroded as failures mounted after the initial success of Operation Compass. The army was dissatisfied with the cooperation it had received from the air force in France and considered that the only way forward was to have an air force of its own, or at least one under its command. Relations between the two services were further damaged by the defeats in Greece and Crete, the retreat through Cyrenaica, and the failure of Operations Brevity and Battleaxe. Air Marshal Arthur Tedder was aware of the troubled history between the two services, so for Battleaxe he acquiesced to the army's demand to mount a continuous defensive air umbrella over its forces. The operation ended in a failure that was deeply disappointing for Prime Minister Winston Churchill, who had placed much hope in the effort to relieve the Australian division besieged in Tobruk. Though there were many problems with Battleaxe, Churchill identified the continuing army and air force bickering as the most pressing need, making a series of pronouncements in the late summer and fall of 1941 that set the basis for future cooperation between the RAF and the army.

For all the problems between the two services during the first two years of the war, the relationship in the Middle East was remarkably smooth during the first battles in the Western Desert. Air Commodore Raymond Collishaw and Lt. Gen. Richard O'Connor formed a close partnership that facilitated a successful campaign against the Italians, ending with the capture of Benghazi and the destruction of the Tenth Army in February 1941. As the commander of 202 Group, Collishaw was left by Air Chief Marshal Arthur Longmore to run the campaign as he thought best, and he fought a model air campaign that embodied all the tenets of successful tactical air operations. As Collishaw recalled after the war, they had to "outwit and outfight a numerically superior enemy by a combination of deception, superior tactics and fighting spirit."[1] He understood that before anything else he needed to achieve and maintain air superiority over the battlefield. Once that was accomplished, his aircraft could strike the logistical lifeline of the enemy—bases, ports, airfields, and the lines of communications. Only when necessary were aircraft used in battlefield attacks. He also understood from past experience, and from what his attacks did to the Italians, that the defensive use of fighters was unprofitable.

Despite his successful tenure as the senior RAF operational commander in the Western Desert, Collishaw has been largely forgotten by historians, or when remembered, the importance of his role is minimized. A good example is contained in an official Air Ministry publication: "The experience of the first six months of the war in the desert could not easily be applied to the future, as it was not likely that the air superiority which had been maintained by the Royal Air Force owing to the comparative lack of enterprise of the much larger Italian Air Force, would persist."[2] In other words, the British victory had more to do with Italian failings than RAF ability. Operation Compass was portrayed as a second-class victory over the Italians instead of the more vaunted Germans. Mussolini's soldiers and airmen were mediocre, poorly equipped, and more apt to run away rather than fight. In this narrative the real war in the desert did not start until the Germans arrived.

In fact, Compass was a magnificent accomplishment at a point in the war where the British desperately needed a victory. The outnumbered forces of Lieutenant General O'Connor achieved a near miracle by routing the enemy in Cyrenaica at a remarkably small cost, while Collishaw's small air force similarly defeated a numerically superior opponent against the odds.

Collishaw's role in these early victories is thus undervalued. Even the otherwise excellent RAF narrative on the early war in the Western Desert advocated this perception in explaining the reasons for the failure of Operation Battleaxe: "It should be borne in mind that this was the first pitched battle fought against the Germans in the desert, and that the contrast between their fighting powers and those of the Italians was considerable."[3]

This view of events ignores the crucial contribution made to the process and development of tactical-air-support doctrine by Air Commodore Collishaw. The decisive point was the intervention of Churchill following the failure of Battleaxe. He chose to endorse the operational-level campaign concept that had been developed and proven in battle by the air commodore as the basis for future army-air cooperation. By the summer of 1941, Collishaw was the sole senior advocate of this system in the Western Desert. During Operation Compass, he had been ably supported in his mission by Air Chief Marshal Longmore and Lieutenant General O'Connor, who fully sanctioned the offensive use of air power. As a result Collishaw was free to use his aircraft to obtain air superiority over the battlefield and then punish the enemy with wide-ranging attacks on his ports, airfields, and lines of communications.

The result was the catastrophic defeat of the Italians in Cyrenaica despite their numerical and often qualitative superiority. By May–June 1941, however, Longmore and O'Connor were gone, and Collishaw received his directions from Air Marshal Tedder, who at this point in the war was forced to conduct an air campaign defined by political necessity rather than sound RAF principles. Tedder's endorsement of the army view of air power during Operation Battleaxe meant that Collishaw's fighter and bomber squadrons could not make a meaningful contribution to the offensive. By the third day of the campaign, operational necessity replaced political need, and Tedder, with a little prodding from Air Chief Marshal Sir Charles Portal, released Collishaw to conduct the offensive campaign he desired. Though the battle was already lost, the large-scale RAF attacks conducted in its closing stages played a major role in helping the Western Desert Force successfully extricate itself from the battlefield without crippling losses. Tedder subsequently adopted the methods proven by Collishaw as his own and successfully conveyed them to Portal and ultimately Churchill in London.

There are a number of reasons why Collishaw's role has been overlooked and forgotten. One of the main factors was the British tendency to view the Italians as a less capable foe than the Germans, which discounts the importance of any victories over them. A second but potentially more important reason was the animosity with which Tedder viewed Collishaw. Tedder "contemptuously dismissed" Collishaw in his autobiography and considered him "'a bull-headed unimaginative cuss' who busied himself too much with routine duties and was unduly optimistic about what could be done with a handful of men and aircraft."[4] Yet Operation Compass succeeded because Collishaw *was* able to do quite a lot with a small handful of men and aircraft. The origins of Tedder's negative opinion are not known, but from his arrival in the desert he consistently criticized Collishaw. It seems that he formed his opinion of the air commodore long before they worked together in the Western Desert.

Part of the problem may have been a personality clash between the quiet, reserved Tedder and the loud, boisterous Collishaw. Tedder possessed a serious demeanor and was a moderate drinker who liked to create "Cambridge-like oases of comfort and gossip, neatly decorated and comfortably furnished, for himself and men of similar taste." He also preferred "quiet chat, serious music and solitary walks."[5] In contrast, Collishaw possessed a large, gregarious fighter-pilot personality. He enjoyed his drink, and the officers' mess was a favorite destination. A *New York Times* article observed:

"Colly" looks the man he is. He is big, strongly built, and even when living in a tent swept by desert sand storms he always appears immaculate in a smartly tailored gabardine uniform with four long rows of service ribbons. . . . He seems to have two personalities. In his mess he is the soul of geniality, but when he enters an underground operations room, surrounded by a battery of telephones and planning on great maps his "sweep" raids, he is crisp, hard-hitting and one might almost say a ruthless commander demanding results and not accepting excuses. He has the vigor and enthusiasm of his youngest pilot and his men idolize him.[6]

Collishaw recalled that the Naval Ten mess was "a lively spot after dinner each night," which occasionally resulted in hangovers that lasted into the next morning's dawn patrol, during which "the onrush of fresh, cold air into our open cockpits had a remarkable sobering-up effect."[7] Dennis Conroy, a pilot who served under Collishaw in Egypt, remembered:

> There were many stories circulating around camp about Collie's ability to absorb alcoholic beverages. . . . After dinner in the Officers' Mess he would stand drinking and talking with a group of young officers until they collapsed one by one leaving him still standing, unruffled and alone round midnight or later. . . . The lads [had trouble] trying to keep up with a man who had done his drinking training in a naval fighter squadron and on vodka when he was posted to Russia at the end of the war.[8]

Collishaw, however, was not one to boast of his accomplishments. Frank Woolley, an officer who served with him in the Sudan, stated, "Although R.C. [Raymond Collishaw] had few equals as a fighter pilot, he was reluctant to be drawn into discussion on air combat tactics."[9] Woolley also recalled that Collishaw's "boyish enthusiasm was infectious and unlimited, yet he could be as obstinate as a mule and exasperating beyond bearing."[10] These habits and traits may have put him at odds with Tedder, a commander with a more restrained personality.

Tedder did not trust or respect Collishaw and wanted him gone. This was not possible so long as Longmore was in command, but Tedder dismissed the air commodore soon after he took over. Though Operation Battleaxe did not fail due to any misconduct by Collishaw, the air marshal used the opportunity to remove him.

The political nature of the RAF also worked against Collishaw. It appears that he had no patron or champion in London, whereas Tedder benefited from a very close personal relationship with Air Chief Marshals Wilfrid Freeman and Portal, among others, which saved his career on more than one occasion. Tedder maintained an extensive professional and personal correspondence with the two officers during the war, and he never hesitated to share this opinions. In particular, he was very candid with Freeman about Collishaw. Tedder was one of the rising stars of the RAF, and Collishaw's personal conflicts with him limited his own wartime career. In the postwar period Tedder continued to recount, most notably in his memoirs, what he saw as Collishaw's weaknesses and failures, and this viewpoint has colored almost all subsequent considerations of his wartime career.[11]

What has been lost in this story is that Collishaw successfully implemented and proved in battle the operational underpinnings of the system of tactical air support employed by the Allies in the Second World War, which had not yet been accomplished. The Battle of France in 1940 was marked by great disharmony between the two services as were operations in Norway and Greece. A promising start to better coordination between the army and the air force had been made in the United Kingdom but had not yet passed the test of battle. The failure of Battleaxe led the army and RAF in the Middle East to work out improved methods for cooperation on the battlefield. This took the form of joint exercises and a conference that produced a joint army-air document on direct air support that would have a major influence on future operations. This was the beginning of a process to design the tools needed to make air support work at the tactical level. Yet none of this could take place until the form of air support at the operational level was decided. This was Collishaw's contribution.

It ultimately took the intervention of Churchill to promulgate the nature of the relationship between the RAF and the army at the operational level. His statements to Gen. Claude Auchinleck in the late summer and early fall of 1941 set the parameters for future cooperation between the two services. The prime minister put to rest the notion that the army should control the RAF and established the principle that the two services were coequal but interdependent. Churchill also made it clear that at certain times, such as during a major offensive, the RAF was to do everything possible to assist the army in fulfilling its mission. This was the pattern of operations utilized by Collishaw during the opening stages of the war in the Western Desert and especially during Operation Compass. It differed significantly from any other British operations up to that point in the war.

The line connecting this pattern of operations from Collishaw to Churchill was not straight. There were no direct communications between the two men, but the ideas embodied in Churchill's pronouncement bear the clear hallmarks of Collishaw's methods, which were different than anything being employed by the RAF at that point in the war. After the failure of Battleaxe, Tedder advocated these ideas in London, where they ultimately reached the prime minister through Portal and were used as the basis for his directives on army air support. Collishaw's role in developing and successfully implementing these ideas during the early battles in the Western Desert cannot be overlooked.

Collishaw benefited substantially from the knowledge gained during his long career in the RAF. For the battles of 1940–41, he drew heavily upon his experiences in the First World War, having amassed considerable ground-attack experience over the western front and learned the types of targets that were profitable for aerial bombing and strafing and those that were fleeting, hard to find, and dangerous to aircraft. He understood that air power had to be concentrated to be effective, and defensive standing air patrols were too weak to prevent attacks by an enemy who could marshal his strength and overwhelm a select part of the front. The need to conserve scarce resources and avoid cost and unnecessary operations was also learned in 1917–18. Collishaw recorded these lessons as early as 1924, when he attended RAF Staff College, an experience that provided him with the necessary training for high command.[12] The importance of these Great War lessons were confirmed by his successor, Air Marshal Arthur Coningham, in a 1946 address to the Royal United Services Institute in London, during which he declared, "I stress this period of 1914–18 because the principles there thrashed out have remained constant, only their degree and their application changing in accordance with the technical advance of aircraft, weapons, modern aids and the method of control."[13]

Collishaw's First World War experience was reinforced by his numerous interwar postings, when he was involved in operations in South Russia, Mesopotamia, Palestine, and the Sudan. During this period, he worked closely with the other services, in 1923 with the army in Kurdistan, and from 1929 to 1931 with the Royal Navy aboard the aircraft carrier HMS *Courageous*. These experiences, combined with his great familiarity with Egypt and the Western Desert, where he had been posted since 1936, left him uniquely qualified to command 202 Group at the start of hostilities with Italy.

This does not mean that Collishaw was an ideal commander. Anecdotal evidence indicates that he had a tendency to micromanage the administration of his unit, a charge leveled by Tedder and corroborated by others. This style worked effectively through Operations Compass and Battleaxe, when 202/204 Group was a small organization. Tedder argued that the growing size of the RAF in the Western Desert required a commander who was better able to delegate. His ultimate choice was Air Marshal Coningham, who he subsequently had to support by appointing a deputy to handle the administrative/logistical side of the Western Desert Air Force. Without question Collishaw would have needed to adapt to the changing circumstances of a larger command, but considering his demonstrated growth as a commander during a long career combined with his Staff College training and the right support personnel, there is nothing in his record or professional conduct to indicate that he could not have excelled at this next level.

None of the supposed faults identified by Tedder prevented Collishaw from being an extremely effective commander. His combat record in the Second World War was virtually unblemished. He conducted an extremely successful air campaign against the Italians, starting with their entry into the war in June 1940 and concluding with their decisive defeat in February 1941. Air Marshal Sir Roderic Hill commented after the war that the effect of air support conducted during a period when that support was overwhelming was not the real test. Rather, "the really interesting times are when the machine you have is put to the test," and you have to meet the situation with "careful planning and the clever use of bluff."[14] This was certainly the situation faced by Collishaw in the Western Desert.

Collishaw was posted out of the desert to the Nile Delta before the initial stage of the German offensive in March–April 1941 and was not involved in the first attempts to stop Rommel. Once he returned to combat he conducted an offensive campaign that contributed to Axis logistical difficulties in Libya. Tedder once suggested that Collishaw was a "village blacksmith slogger" who was not fit to "tackle the Hun," but the evidence shows he held his own against the Germans.[15] Crete was a terrible defeat for the British, but the limited number of long-range Hurricanes and Blenheims Collishaw was able to dispatch to the island were effective and caused significant problems for the German invaders. Similarly, although Operation Brevity was a failure for the army, 204 Group successfully accomplished their mission during the short duration of the fighting. Operation Battleaxe was also a sharp setback for the British, but when Collishaw was finally released to conduct the air battle he envisioned, he directed his aircraft in offensive strikes that slowed the forward movement of Rommel's armored columns. These air attacks allowed Maj. Gen. Noel Beresford-Peirse the time he needed to successfully extract his forces from the battlefield and prevent their decisive encirclement and defeat. The total destruction of British ground forces during Battleaxe may have opened the way to Egypt and the Suez Canal for Rommel and decisively altered the balance of power in the Middle East. If Collishaw is to be judged, it should be for what he accomplished in battle, not for traits that may or may not have prevented him from success in the future at higher levels of command and responsibility.

The air commodore made a number of important contributions to the development of tactical air doctrine during his time commanding 202 and 204 Groups. He attempted to facilitate coordination between fighter and bomber squadrons as well as to improve their ability to work with the army. He improved communications and attempted to limit the threat of friendly fire incidents by establishing effective bomb lines that could be identified from the air. The U.S. Field Manual FM 100-20, *Command and Employment of Air Power,* published in July 1943 benefited substantially from British experience in the Western Desert, and it enshrined the ranking of tactical-air-support missions. The first priority was to establish air superiority, the second was interdiction sorties that would be conducted to prevent or limit the movement of enemy troops and supplies to and within the battle area, and the third priority or phase of operations was the support of the army on the battlefield. This last mission was the most expensive and least profitable form of air support and would only take place at critical times.[16] FM 100-20 was considered by the U.S. Army to be a "declaration of independence" by the U.S. Army Air Forces and was essentially the template for American and British tactical air operations from the Normandy invasion to the end of the war.[17]

The pattern of operations outlined in the U.S. manual was established by Collishaw in 1940 during Operation Compass. He first used his air resources in an offensive manner to establish air superiority. Once that task was accomplished, a wide range of interdiction missions followed that targeted enemy ports, airfields, and lines of communications. These raids caused severe disruptions to enemy operations and aided the maintenance of air superiority by destroying and distracting the enemy air force and preventing it from launching offensive missions of its own. Close-air-support missions against targets on the battlefield were only attempted in special circumstances such as major operations when air superiority had already been achieved. This was the case during the opening stages of Operation Compass, at Bardia and Tobruk in January 1941, during Operation Brevity, and on the third day of Operation Battleaxe.

Collishaw recognized the importance of a close relationship with the army, especially with the army commander. This was achieved with Lieutenant Generals O'Connor and "Jumbo" Wilson, who Collishaw worked with over many months, but not with Beresford-Peirse. With the latter, the air commodore did not have time to develop an effective relationship and dissuade him of his army-centric view of air power. Also, it should not be forgotten that Collishaw was able to wage an effective and successful campaign against the Axis powers despite having meagre and often second-rate equipment at his disposal during Western Desert campaign.

After Collishaw was dismissed by Tedder, he returned to England to serve as the duty air commodore at HQ Fighter Command from August 1941 until March of the following year. On 21 March 1942 he was promoted to air vice-marshal and given command of 14 Group in Scotland. This unit was responsible for the air defense of Scotland as well as protection of the Royal Navy base at Scapa Flow. By this point in the war, the Luftwaffe seldom "made an appearance," and the group was used as a resting ground for fighter squadrons worn out over continental Europe.[18] The appointment to command this group based away from the action was indicative of Collishaw's diminished importance to the RAF.

On 15 July 1943, 14 Group was disbanded, and Collishaw left the military with the rank of air vice-marshal after twenty-seven years in uniform with the RNAS and RAF. The timing of his retirement is puzzling; though not fifty years old, he was leaving the service in the middle of a major war. His memoirs offered no illumination on the issue other than to say "I was retired," which indicates his departure from the RAF was not a willing one.[19] It is conceivable that health issues, which kept him in hospital for nearly two months earlier in the year, played a role in his retirement.[20] The other possibility is that the RAF had no further use for him, but this seems odd for an experienced senior officer in the prime of his career and still able to make a meaningful contribution.[21] But such an act would not be unique in the RAF as Air Chief Marshal Sir Hugh Dowding, the victor of the Battle of Britain, was forced to retire soon after the conclusion of that contest.[22] Dowding's situation was different than Collishaw's, though, in that he was eleven years older and had been scheduled to retire before the start of the war, but the date kept getting postponed. There were political factors at play, however, that ultimately lead to his retirement at what was arguably the peak of his career.

Whatever the reason for his retirement, Collishaw remained in the United Kingdom for the duration of the war and served as a regional air liaison officer with the civil-defense organization. He returned to Canada at the war's end to join his family and, following in his father's footsteps, started a very successful second career in the mining industry.[23] In his later years he became interested in the history of his conflicts and spent a considerable amount of time and effort creating lists of First World War pilots, tracking aces and their kills, and attempting to solve mysteries such as establishing the identity of the pilots who shot down German aces such as Manfred von Richthofen and Karl Allmenröder. He carried out an extensive correspondence with fellow pilots and other historians of the Great War. He also maintained a long-running dialogue with Ronald Dodds, a civilian historian who worked for the office of the Royal Canadian Air Force (RCAF) air historian. Dodds had been tasked to help draft the First World War volume of the RCAF's operational history and started to correspond with Collishaw in this capacity. Over the years they developed a relationship that culminated in Dodds helping Collishaw write his memoirs, which were published in 1973.[24] Notwithstanding his health problems in 1943, Collishaw lived a long and productive life; he died in West Vancouver, British Columbia, on 29 September 1976.

At the end of his memoirs, Collishaw compared himself to Sir Arthur Conan Doyle, the acclaimed author who brought Sherlock Holmes to life.

Conan Doyle always felt that his painstakingly researched historical novels were the pinnacle of his writing career but that he was destined to be known for the adventures of his fictional detective. In much the same way, Collishaw recalled that he was most proud of his time in the Western Desert, but "if I am known at all to my fellow Canadians and others it is through more carefree days, when as a young fighter pilot . . . I had the good fortune to shoot down a number of the enemy without in turn being killed."[25]

Raymond Collishaw made a significant contribution to the development of Allied tactical-air-power doctrine in the Second World War that has gone largely unrecognized in the literature. His ideas on the role of the RAF in the land battle were developed during more than two decades in the air force and were based on extensive personal experience in France, South Russia, Mesopotamia, and the Middle East. Although his ideas were not unique, he was the first RAF commander to successfully conduct a campaign using air power to gain air superiority, interdict the enemy's lines of communications, and support the army on the battlefield. These same ideas would later be endorsed by Churchill and enshrined as the pillars of Allied air-support doctrine. Collishaw should be recognized for his role in their development and operational proofing. He was proud of his achievements in the desert, but the memory of his accomplishments has been tarnished by the view that it was a victory over a lesser enemy and by the ruminations of a commander who considered him the wrong person to fight the Germans. These views should not be allowed to detract from an appreciation of Collishaw's successful and important career in the Western Desert.

Notes

Abbreviations

ADM	Admiralty Records
AHB	RAF Air Historical Branch
AIR	RAF Records
Armd Div	Armoured Division
AVIA	Ministry of Aviation Records
CAB	Cabinet Records
CAS	Chief of the Air Staff
CB	Companion of the Order of Bath
C-in-C	Commander-in-Chief
Comd	Commander
COS	Chiefs of Staff
CWM	Canadian War Museum
D.P.	Director of Personnel
DEFE	Records of the Ministry of Defence (U.K.)
DFC	Distinguished Flying Cross
DHH	Directorate of History and Heritage
DSC	Distinguished Service Cross
DSO	Distinguished Service Order
FM	Field Manual
HQ RAF ME	RAF Headquarters Middle East
Ind Div	Indian Division
LAC	Library and Archives Canada
MG	manuscript group
NAA	National Archives of Australia
Op Sum	Operational Summary
ORB	Operations Record Book
PREM	Prime Minister's Office Records
SAAF	South African Air Force
TNA	The National Archives, United Kingdom
WD	War Diary
WO	War Office Records

Note on Conventions

1. Playfair et al., *Mediterranean and Middle East*, 1:261; Schreiber, Stegemann, and Vogel, *Germany and the Second World War*, 646.

Chapter 1

1. Collishaw, *Air Command*, 255. Collishaw made similar statements in an earlier unpublished manuscript and multipart magazine profile. See Raymond Collishaw, "Memories of a Canadian Airman," n.d., Raymond Collishaw Biography File, DHH, Canadian National Defence Headquarters, 42. This account was later serialized in the Royal Canadian Air Force's monthly magazine, *The Roundel*, and formed the core of his autobiography, *Air Command*. See Collishaw, "Memories of a Canadian Airman"; and Collishaw, *Air Command*, 166–67.

2. The two best academic works on the Allied tactical air forces in Northwest Europe are Gooderson, *Air Power at the Battlefront*, and Hughes, *Overlord*. See also Cooling, *Case Studies in the Development of Close Air Support*.

3. Hall, *Strategy for Victory*, chaps. 3–4.

4. Telegram, Prime Minister to C-in-C, ME, 6 July 1941, quoted in "Army-Air Co-operation," TNA CAB 101/136, 25.

5. Winston S. Churchill, "A Note by the Minister of Defence," 7 Oct. 1941, TNA AIR 8/983.

6. Vincent Orange relates that Churchill's pronouncement was based on arguments made by Air Marshal Arthur Tedder, commander-in-chief, RAF Middle East Command, relayed to him by Air Chief Marshal Charles Portal, chief of the Air Staff. Orange, *Churchill and His Airmen*, 176.

7. For details on Coningham's refinements of the air-support organization, see Orange, "Getting Together," 1–44.

8. For a full discussion of the North African Campaign and its role as the genesis of Allied tactical-air-support doctrine, see Bechthold, "Question of Success"; Gladman, *Intelligence and Anglo-American Air Support*, introduction.

9. Orange, *Churchill and His Airmen*, 176.

10. "Penny packets" was an air force term for dispatching small numbers of aircraft on a wide variety of missions, usually in support of the army, rather than concentrate on larger objectives. Orange, *Tedder*, 210. For other usage, see Buckley, *Air Power in the Age of Total War*, 149; and Slessor, *Central Blue*, 284, 421.

11. The body of scholarship by David Ian Hall, especially *Strategy for Victory*, examines the differences between the army and the RAF concepts on air support and air operations and who should control air assets. See Hall, *Strategy for Victory*, 4–7, 23–25, 28–29, 32–34, 46–47, 61–67.

12. For the basic details of Collishaw's First World War career, especially his air-to-air combat, see Bashow, "Four Gallant Airmen"; and Bashow, *Knights of the Air*.

13. Raymond Collishaw, DSO, DSC, TNA ADM 273/8/147.

14. Maj. B. C. Bell, "Raymond Collishaw, D.S.O., D.S.C., D.F.C.," *Reveille* 10, no. 4 (1 Dec. 1936), 22, clipping in Raymond Collishaw Fonds, LAC, MG 30-E280, vol. 1.

15. Westrop, *History of No. 10 Squadron Royal Naval Air Service*, 24.

16. Ibid., 24–25; P. S. Sadler, "Bell, Bertram Charles (1893–1941)," *Australian Dictionary of Biography*, National Centre of Biography, Australian National University, http://adb.anu.edu.au/biography/bell-bertram-charles-5190/text8727, accessed 15 Apr. 2013.

17. Collishaw, *Air Command*, 33–70; Raymond Collishaw, "Notes on Experiences," n.d., [ca. 1940], CWM 19770669-025, 2–6.

18. Collishaw, *Air Command*, 165. Collishaw's flying logs for this period show that 51 of 168 missions were low-level attack missions. It is likely that a significant number of additional sorties were also ground-support missions that cannot be specifically identified from the logs. See Raymond Collishaw, "Pilot's Flying Log Book No. 1, 1915–1918," and "Pilot's Flying Log Book No. 2, 1918–1926," CWM 19770669-019.

19. On 1 April 1918 the Royal Flying Corps and RNAS joined to form the Royal Air Force. RFC squadrons retained their old numbers, while naval squadrons received a new 200-series designation. Thus, Collishaw's No. 3 Squadron RNAS became No. 203 Squadron RAF. Collishaw, *Air Command*, 166–67; Wise, *Canadian Airmen and the First World War*, 549–50; J. C. Nerney, "The Western Front—Air Operations, May–November 1918," n.d., TNA AIR 1/677/21/3/1887, 230–67.

20. Collishaw, *Air Command*, 152–53. John Slessor, considered the foremost theoretician on close air support in Britain between the wars, came to the same conclusion in the mid-1930s. He argued that the air force should not engage in close-support operations except in an emergency. See Slessor, *Air Power and Armies*, 90.

21. Collishaw, *Air Command*, 153.

22. Gen. Erich Ludendorff, the chief of the German General Staff, recorded in his memoirs, "August 8th was the black day of the German Army in the history of this war." Quoted in Nicholson, *Canadian Expeditionary Force*, 407.

23. Slessor, *Air Power and Armies*, 148–99.

24. "Royal Air Force Operations Summary for 1st Brigade, 4 PM—7th August to 4 PM—8th August 1918," Raymond Collishaw Fonds, LAC, MG 30-E280, R2492-0-5-E, vol. 9.

25. Collishaw, "Pilot's Flying Log Book No. 1."

26. Collishaw, *Air Command*, 165.

27. Gen. Sir Henry Rawlinson, "Memorandum to V Brigade RAF," 16 Aug. 1918, quoted in Nerney, "Western Front—Air Operations, May–November 1918," 152.

28. WD, 5th Canadian Infantry Battalion, 8 Aug. 1918, LAC RG 9, Ser. III-D-3, vol. 4916, reel T-10709.

29. Jones, *War in the Air*, 6:445–46. To put these numbers in perspective, during the Second World War, RAF Bomber Command considered that loss rates above 5 percent were unsustainable, even in the short term.

30. A. Montgomery, *Story of the Fourth Army in the Battles of the Hundred Days*, 50.

31. No. 203 Squadron Record Book, Aug. 1918, Raymond Collishaw Fonds, LAC, MG 30-E280, R2492-0-5-E, vol. 9.

32. Collishaw, "Notes on Experiences," 18.

33. Collishaw, "Pilot's Flying Log Book No. 1," and "Pilot's Flying Log Book No. 2."

34. Collishaw, "Notes on Experiences," 19. This account is particularly noteworthy because it was written before the Western Desert Campaign of 1940–41.

35. A full account of the British intervention in Russia may be found in Ullman, *Anglo-Soviet Relations*. Details of the Canadian role may be found in Wise, *Canadian Airmen and the First World War*, App. A; MacLaren, *Canadians in Russia*; and Swettenham, *Allied Intervention in Russia*.

36. Raymond Collishaw, "A Review of the Counter-Revolution in South Russia in the period 1917–1918 [sic]," n.d., CWM 19770669-019, 2. Contrary to the title, Collishaw's report examines the period 1919–20. For the background to this period, see J. Smith, *Gone to Russia to Fight*, 15–48; and Wise, *Canadian Airmen and the First World War*, 623–27.

37. Raymond Collishaw to R. V. Dodds, 11 June 1964, Raymond Collishaw Fonds, LAC, MG 30-E280, R2492-0-5-E, vol. 9; Collishaw, "Review of the Counter-Revolution in South Russia," 2. Collishaw noted that most of the airmen selected were British, while the pilots were principally Canadian.

38. Wise, *Canadian Airmen and the First World War*, 627. The RAF contingent in South Russia contained a very high proportion of Canadian pilots. In addition to Collishaw, No. 47 Squadron contained no fewer than fifty-three Canadian pilots.

39. Smith, *Gone to Russia to Fight*, 194–95.

40. Collishaw, *Air Command*, 212.

41. Ibid. In terms of page count, Collishaw only devotes more space to his First World War career. His nine months in Russia are covered in twenty-three pages. By comparison, his three years each in Iraq and aboard HMS *Courageous* rate nine and three pages respectively, while his years in Egypt and the Western Desert, the part of his career of which he was most proud, is told in fifteen pages.

42. Quoted in Omissi, *Air Power and Colonial Control*, 25.

43. For a full discussion of the implications of the Cairo Conference, see ibid., chap. 2; and Malcolm Smith, *British Air Strategy between the Wars* (Oxford: Oxford University Press, 1984), 22–24.

44. Group Capt. Arthur M. Longmore, "Some Notes on RAF Co-Operation during Operations in Kurdistan, March to June 1923," n.d. [but written shortly after completion of the operation], TNA AIR 5/292, 1, 4.

45. Ibid., 7.

46. Ibid., 7–8.

47. English, "RAF Staff College and the Evolution of British Strategic Bombing Policy," 410.

48. Ibid., 411.

49. Collishaw, "Notes on Experiences," 38.

50. Collishaw used the term "enthusiast" to describe himself and others who maintained a similar "big picture" view on the future role of air power. See ibid., 34.

51. For Collishaw's discussion of his time at Air Defence of Great Britain, see ibid., 41–42. See also Collier, *Defence of the United Kingdom*, 16–17; Air Marshal Sir Hugh Trenchard, "Address at Cambridge University," Apr. 1925, quoted in Andrew Boyle, *Trenchard* (London: Collins, 1962), 520; and Powers, *Strategy without Slide-Rule*, 190.

52. Collishaw, *Air Command*, 229.

53. Don Baker quoted in Sturtivant, *British Naval Aviation*, 14.

54. For details on the Fleet Air Arm, see Philpott, *Royal Air Force*, 2:246–49; and S.W. Roskill, *War at Sea*, 29–31.

55. Collishaw, "Notes on Experiences," 43.

56. Collishaw, *Air Command*, 229.

57. Sturtivant, *British Naval Aviation*, 14–15; Omissi, "Technology and Repression," 47–50.

58. "Schedule of Flying carried out in Palestine by 'Courageous' Flights," 7 Sept. 1929, enclosure to Capt. Studholme Brownrigg, commanding officer of *Courageous*, "Report of Proceedings during Emergency in Palestine 1929," 7 Sept. 1929, TNA AIR 5/1243; Wing Commander Raymond Collishaw, "Report on Air Operations by Aircraft from H.M.S. 'Courageous' operating from Gaza, Palestine," 5 Oct. 1929, ibid.

59. Omissi, "Technology and Repression," 47–50.
60. Air Vice-Marshal H. C. T. Dowding, "Report on Operations," 22 Nov. 1929, TNA AIR 5/1243.
61. Collishaw, "Report on Air Operations by Aircraft from H.M.S. 'Courageous' operating from Gaza."
62. Capt. Studholme Brownrigg, "Report on 'Courageous' Air Operations in Palestine," 5 Oct. 1929. TNA AIR 5/1243.
63. Collishaw, "Report on Air Operations by Aircraft from H.M.S. 'Courageous' operating from Gaza," 4.
64. Ibid.; Brownrigg, "Report on 'Courageous' Air Operations in Palestine."
65. Gooch, *Mussolini and His Generals*, chap. 5.
66. Collishaw, "Notes on Experiences," 48.
67. ORB, Middle East Command, Air Staff, HQ Unit, vol. 1: Aug. 1935–Dec. 1941, TNA AIR 24/1051.
68. Air Chief Marshal Sir Robert Brooke-Popham, "Notes on the Emergency in the Near East, September 1935 to June 1936," 15 July 1936, TNA AIR 23/810, 5.
69. Ibid., 8–9.
70. Gooch, *Mussolini and His Generals*, 343–45; Gibbs, *Grand Strategy*, chap. 6.
71. ORB, Middle East Command, Air Staff, HQ Unit, vol. 1: Aug. 1935–Dec. 1941, TNA AIR 24/1051; ORB, Headquarters, No. 5 Wing, 1935–36, TNA AIR 26/19; Collishaw, "Notes on Experiences," 49; Morewood, *British Defense of Egypt*, 123–24, 145–46.
72. Collishaw, *Air Command*, 233.
73. See Raymond Collishaw Fonds, LAC, MG 30-E280, R2492-0-5-E; Air Vice-Marshal Raymond Collishaw Fonds, CWM; Raymond Collishaw Biography File, DHH, National Defence Headquarters, Ottawa, Canada.
74. Dodds did not leave any personal papers, but his extensive personal correspondence with Collishaw may be found in Collishaw's papers at Library and Archives Canada as well as those at the Directorate of History and Heritage, both in Ottawa. These two sources are the prime repositories of the Collishaw–Dodd correspondence, though some additional material can be found in the Canadian War Museum archives as well as in The Beatrice Hitchens Memorial Collection of Aviation History, Western Archives, Western University, London, Ontario. Details of Dodds's career in the Office of the Air Historian may be found in Halliday, "Air Historian—Part II."
75. William Bishop's memoirs were particularly embellished but were not unique. Bishop, *Winged Warfare*. For more details, see Bashow, "A Note on Sources," in *Knights of the Air*, 188–89.
76. Collishaw, *Air Command*. A second edition of the book was published in 2008 by CEF Books under a different title: Raymond Collishaw, CB, DSO, DSC, DFC (with Ronald Dodds), *The Black Flight: The Memoir of Air Vice-Marshal Raymond Collishaw* (Ottawa: CEF Books, 2008).
77. Collishaw, "Notes on Experiences."
78. Collishaw, *Air Command*, 234.
79. *Times Literary Supplement*, no. 3745, 14 Dec. 1973, 1549.
80. Collishaw, *Air Command*, 245.
81. Longmore, *From Sea to Sky*, 245.
82. Ibid., 260.

83. For Tedder's assessment of Collishaw, see Tedder, *With Prejudice*, 55. For examples of Tedder's influence in subsequent appraisals of Collishaw, see Owen, *Desert Air Force*, 60; Shores, Massimello, and Guest, *Mediterranean Air War*, 128–29; and Terraine, *Right of the Line*, 311.

84. Orange, *Tedder*, 126.

85. Tedder, *With Prejudice*, 55.

86. Ibid.

87. Regarding Tedder's correspondence, see especially his letters to Air Chief Marshal Sir Wilfrid Freeman in TNA AIR 20/2792, to Portal in TNA AIR 23/1395, and to his wife as cited in Orange, *Tedder*, 126–27.

88. Playfair et al., *Mediterranean and Middle East*, vols. 1, 2.

89. The first volume of Richards, *Royal Air Force*, references the Western Desert Campaign in 1940–41. In total the study comprises three volumes authored by Denis Richards and Hilary St. G. Saunders.

90. AHB, *The Middle East Campaigns*, vol. 1, *Operations in Libya and the Western Desert, September 1939 to June 1941*, TNA AIR 41/44.

91. Hall, *Strategy for Victory*.

92. Gladman, *Intelligence and Anglo-American Air Support*.

93. Ibid., 2, 18.

94. Guedalla, *Middle East;* Elton, "Guedalla, Philip (1889–1944)," *Oxford Dictionary of National Biography* (Oxford: Oxford University Press, 2004), online ed., Jan. 2008, http://www.oxforddnb.com/view/article/33595, accessed 19 July 2011.

95. Owen, *Desert Air Force;* Owen, *Tedder*.

96. Bickers, *Desert Air War*.

97. Christopher Shores's most important book for the purposes of this study is Shores, Massimello, and Guest, *Mediterranean Air War*. But also useful are his other books, Shores and Ring, *Fighters over the Desert;* Shores, Cull, and Malizia, *Air War for Yugoslavia, Greece, and Crete;* and Shores, *Dust Clouds in the Middle East*.

Chapter 2

1. Morewood, *British Defense of Egypt*, 1–2.

2. Owen, *Desert Air Force*, 16–18.

3. Morewood, *British Defense of Egypt*, 3, 86–97, 101–2.

4. Kelly, *Lost Oasis*, 124; Morewood, *British Defense of Egypt*, 50–52. There were two other existing tracks through the desert leading to Cairo, but they were not suitable for large mechanized formations.

5. Air Chief Marshal Sir Robert Brooke-Popham, "Notes on the Emergency in the Near East, September 1935 to June 1936," 15 July 1936, 8, TNA AIR 23/810.

6. Morewood, *British Defense of Egypt*, 66; Playfair et al., *Mediterranean and Middle East*, 1:262.

7. Group Capt. Wilfred McClaughry, "Truforce General Report," Mar. 1936, TNA AIR 23/777.

8. AHB, *The Middle East Campaigns*, vol. 1, *Operations in Libya and the Western Desert, September 1939 to June 1941*, TNA AIR 41/44, 2.

9. Playfair et al., *Mediterranean and Middle East*, 1:11–12; AHB, *Middle East Campaigns*, 1:3; Owen, *Desert Air Force*, 21–22; Morewood, *British Defense of Egypt*, 98–111.

10. "Conclusions of a Meeting of the Cabinet," Cabinet 30 (37), 14 July 1937, TNA CAB 23/89, 10.

11. Playfair et al., *Mediterranean and Middle East*, 1:11–12; AHB, *Middle East Campaigns*, 1:3; Owen, *Desert Air Force*, 21–22; Morewood, *British Defense of Egypt*, 107.

12. Playfair et al., *Mediterranean and Middle East*, 1:11–12; AHB, *Middle East Campaigns*, 1:3; Owen, *Desert Air Force*, 21–22; Morewood, *British Defense of Egypt*, 98–111.

13. Hall, *Strategy for Victory*, 69.

14. According to the British official history, there were 250,000 Italian and Libyan troops supported by 313 aircraft in Libya, and 350,000 Italian and native troops supported by 325 aircraft in Italian East Africa. In between, the British deployed 36,000 men in Egypt and 27,500 in Palestine supported by 205 aircraft, along with 19,000 men in Sudan, Somaliland, and Kenya supported by 163 aircraft. See Playfair et al., *Mediterranean and Middle East*, 1:93–96.

15. For a full discussion of the Combined Plan, see AHB, *Middle East Campaigns*, 1:3–7; and Hall, *Strategy for Victory*, 68–72.

16. Collishaw, *Air Command*, 234.

17. Quoted in Owen, *Desert Air Force*, 22–23.

18. The Mobile Division, later known as the Armoured Division, ultimately became the 7th Armoured Division.

19. Egypt Group Standing Operational Instructions, Apr. 1939, TNA AIR 23/6813, 2.

20. Ibid., 3.

21. Ibid.

22. ORB, RAF Middle East, Air Staff, HQ Unit, Sept. 1939, TNA AIR 24/1066, app. 2.

23. For details of conditions in England, see Gladman, *Intelligence and Anglo-American Air Support*, chap. 1 (esp. 33–34); and Hall, *Strategy for Victory*, chap. 2.

24. Winton, *To Change an Army*, chap. 6; Gladman, *Intelligence and Anglo-American Air Support*, 34.

25. Gladman, *Intelligence and Anglo-American Air Support*, chap. 1. See also Woolven, "Mitchell, Sir William Gore Sutherland," accessed 11 Feb. 2013; Lee, "Longmore, Sir Arthur Murray," accessed 11 Feb. 2013. Detailed descriptions of postings and commands held by senior RAF commanders (air commodore and above) can be found at Air of Authority—A History of RAF Organisation, http://www.rafweb.org.

26. Playfair et al., *Mediterranean and Middle East*, 1:31–32; Fergusson and Brown, "Wavell, Archibald Percival, first Earl Wavell," accessed 12 Jan. 2013. For more details on Wavell, see Connell, *Wavell*; Raugh, *Wavell in the Middle East*; and Ian Beckett, "Wavell," in Keegan, *Churchill's Generals*, 70–88.

27. This reference was made shortly after the successful completion of Operation Compass. Winston Churchill, Speech to the Nation, quoted in *Glasgow Herald*, 10 Feb. 1941, 5–6. For more on Wilson, see J. W. Hackett, "Wilson, Henry Maitland, first Baron Wilson," accessed 12 Jan. 2013; Wilson, *Eight Years Overseas*; and Michael Dewar, "Wilson," in Keegan, *Churchill's Generals*, 166–82.

28. For more on O'Connor, see Carver, "O'Connor, Sir Richard Nugent," accessed 12 Jan. 2013; Baynes, *Forgotten Victor*; Forty, *First Victory*; and Barrie Pitt, "O'Connor," in Keegan, *Churchill's Generals*, 183–99.

29. Simpson, *Life of Admiral of the Fleet Andrew Cunningham*, 42.

30. Cunningham, *Sailor's Odyssey*, 203.

31. Playfair et al., *Mediterranean and Middle East*, 1:32–33.

32. Air Commodore Raymond Collishaw, "Command Exercises, Matruh—1939," 12 Oct. 1939; and Wing Commander E. B. Addison, "Egypt Command Exercises—1939,"

Report on Air Aspect of Exercise No. 3: 3rd–4th November 1939," 23 Nov. 1939, in app. 3A to ORB, 202 Group, Aug. 1939–Nov. 1940, TNA AIR 25/803.

33. Air Commodore Raymond Collishaw, "Egypt Command Exercise, 1939," 6 Nov. 1939, 3, in ibid.

34. The use of satellite or auxiliary airfields allowed aircraft to be spread out over a larger area, making them more difficult to locate and destroy by enemy air raids. Ibid., 6.

35. Ibid., 8.

36. ORB, RAF Middle East, Air Staff, HQ Unit, Jan.–Feb. 1941, TNA AIR 24/1072.

37. Collishaw, "Egypt Command Exercise, 1939," 11–12.

38. Ibid., 11.

39. Ibid., 13–14.

40. Wilson, *Eight Years Overseas*, 35.

41. Air Chief Marshal W. G. S. Mitchell to Air Commodore R. Collishaw, 16 Nov. 1939, TNA WO 201/335.

42. Air Vice-Marshal Peter Drummond to Brig. A. R. Selby, 18 Nov. 1939, ibid.

43. Gen. A. P. Wavell to Air Chief Marshal W. G. S. Mitchell, 23 Nov. 1939, ibid.

44. Air Chief Marshal W. G. S. Mitchell to Gen. A. P. Wavell, 27 Nov. 1939, ibid.

45. Royal Air Force Middle East Operational Plan, HQ RAF ME, 14 Sept. 1940, ibid., 7.

46. Details of Maund's career may be found in "Air Vice-Marshal A. C. Maund," Air of Authority—A History of RAF Organisation, http://www.rafweb.org/Biographies/ Maund.htm, accessed 1 June 2013.

47. AHB, *Middle East Campaigns*, 1:15–16.

48. For details of Italian aircraft abandoned during their retreat from Libya in 1941, see Air Commodore Raymond Collishaw, "Brief Report on Royal Air Force Operations in the Western Desert from the Outbreak of War with Italy—the Capture of Cyrenaica to the Time of the Enemy Counter Offensive," 19 Apr. 1941, TNA AIR 23/6475; and AHB, *Middle East Campaigns*, 1:92. MacGregor Knox observed that a "crippling" weakness of the Italian air force was its basing and logistical arrangements, which led to the abandonment of large numbers of repairable aircraft and large stocks of fuel and supplies during their retreat in 1940–41. See Knox, *Hitler's Italian Allies*, 140–41. For details on the small number of British aircraft abandoned during Rommel's first offensive in April 1941, see Group Capt. L. O. Brown, "Report on Operations Carried out by the R.A.F. Cyrenaica during Enemy Advance," 22 Apr. 1941, TNA AIR 23/6486.

49. Playfair et al., *Mediterranean and Middle East*, 1:88. Knox confirmed this state of readiness but noted that while Mussolini was keen to join the war, other voices, including Count Galeazzo Ciano, the Italian minister of foreign affairs, and Gens. Rodolfo Graziani, Pietro Badoglio, and Italo Balbo, urged caution. Knox, *Mussolini Unleashed*, 98–100.

50. AHB, *Middle East Campaigns*, 1:25; Shores, Massimello, and Guest, *Mediterranean Air War*, 11–13.

51. Longmore, *From Sea to Sky;* Lee, "Longmore, Sir Arthur Murray," accessed 23 Aug. 2012; "Air Chief Marshal Sir Arthur Longmore," Air of Authority—A History of RAF Organization, http://www.rafweb.org/Biographies/Longmore.htm, accessed 23 Aug. 2012.

52. ORB, RAF Middle East, Air Staff, HQ Unit, June–Nov. 1940, TNA AIR 24/1051; AHB, *Middle East Campaigns*, 1:26–27.

53. Longmore, *From Sea to Sky*, 226.

54. Collishaw, "Brief Report on Royal Air Force Operations in the Western Desert," 1.

55. Wilson, *Eight Years Overseas*, 49.

56. "Report on Operations in Libya by Lt. General R. N. O'Connor, from September 1940 to April 1941 (written when Prisoner-of-war in Italy)," n.d., TNA WO 106/2148, 3, 6.

57. Playfair et al., *Mediterranean and Middle East*, 1:97; AHB, *Middle East Campaigns*, 1:24, 27–28; Wavell, "Operations in the Middle East from August, 1939, to November, 1940."

58. "R.A.F. M.E. Operation Instruction No. 5," 7 June 1940, in ORB, RAF Middle East, Air Staff, HQ Unit, June–Nov. 1940.

59. Ibid.; ORB, 253 Wing, Aug. 1939–Aug. 1945, Appendices, TNA AIR 26/351.

60. AHB, *Middle East Campaigns*, 1:28–29; Wavell, "Operations in the Middle East from August, 1939, to November, 1940."

61. Knox, *Mussolini Unleashed*, 99.

62. AHB, *Middle East Campaigns*, 1:18–19.

63. Ibid., 28–29; Wavell, "Operations in the Middle East from August, 1939, to November, 1940."

64. AHB, *Middle East Campaigns*, 1:38–39; Richards, *Royal Air Force*, 247–48.

65. AHB, *Middle East Campaigns*, 1:28–29; Bickers, *Desert Air War*, 17–18; Richards, *Royal Air Force*, 247–48.

66. AHB, *Middle East Campaigns*, 1:29; Richards, *Royal Air Force*, 241.

67. AHB, *Middle East Campaigns*, 1:29–30; Richards, *Royal Air Force*, 269; Bickers, *Desert Air War*, 19–20. Details on aircraft range, performance, and armament are taken from Angelucci and Matricardi, *World War II Airplanes*.

Chapter 3

1. Playfair et al., *Mediterranean and Middle East*, vol. 1, chaps. 5–6.

2. Owen, *Desert Air Force*, 30.

3. Bickers, *Desert Air War*, 21.

4. ORB, 202 Group, June 1940, TNA AIR 25/801.

5. Ibid.

6. Collishaw's orders were explicit that civilian casualties must be avoided: "It is the policy of His Majesty's Government to confine air bombardment to military objectives only, which must be identifiable as such, and which it is possible to bomb with reasonable chance of confining damage to them." The order went on to state that while all steps would be taken to avoid civilian casualties, enemy action might force a departure from this policy. Egypt Group Standing Operational Instructions, Apr. 1939, TNA AIR 23/6813, 3.

7. Italian losses on 11 June are derived from an account by Generale di Squadra Aerea G. Santoro as quoted in Playfair et al., *Mediterranean and Middle East*, 1:112.

8. Collishaw, *Air Command*, 241; Bickers, *Desert Air War*, 22; Owen, *Desert Air Force*, 31.

9. Shores, Massimello, and Guest, *Mediterranean Air War*, 23.

10. Collishaw, *Air Command*, 242.

11. ORB, 202 Group, June 1940. See also Shores, Massimello, and Guest, *Mediterranean Air War*, 24; and Playfair et al., *Mediterranean and Middle East*, 1:112–13.

12. Guedalla, *Middle East*, 85.
13. ORB, 202 Group, June 1940; AHB, *The Middle East Campaigns*, vol. 1, *Operations in Libya and the Western Desert, September 1939 to June 1941*, TNA AIR 41/44, 37–39.
14. ORB, 202 Group, June–July 1940; ORB, RAF Middle East, Air Staff, HQ Unit, June–Nov. 1940, TNA AIR 24/1051; Playfair et al., *Mediterranean and Middle East*, 1:113–18; Owen, *Desert Air Force*, 33; Bickers, *Desert Air War*, 36.
15. ORB, 202 Group, June–July 1940; ORB, RAF Middle East, Air Staff, HQ Unit, June–Nov. 1940. The other three Hurricanes were assigned to No. 80 Squadron, tasked with defending the Suez Canal zone. Shores, Massimello, and Guest, *Mediterranean Air War*, 13; Bickers, *Desert Air War*, 25–26.
16. Air Commodore Raymond Collishaw, "Memorandum on the Tactical Employment of Hurricane Aircraft," in ORB, 202 Group, June–July 1940.
17. AHB, *Middle East Campaigns*, 1:37–38.
18. ORB, RAF Middle East, Air Staff, HQ Unit, June–Nov. 1940. For more on the employment of the Blenheim fighters, see Shores, Massimello, and Guest, *Mediterranean Air War*, 16; and Bickers, *Desert Air War*, 25–26.
19. ORB, 202 Group, June–July 1940; Bickers, *Desert Air War*, 25.
20. Bickers, *Desert Air War*, 29.
21. Segrè, *Italo Balbo*, 402.
22. For the best account of Balbo's death, see ibid., chap. 18. Collishaw reported on 1 July: "To A.O.C.-in-C. Your letter despatched satisfactorily." ORB, 202 Group, June–July 1940. For details on Longmore's visit with Balbo in Rome and his great respect for the man, see Longmore, *From Sea to Sky*, 154–58. Other aspects may be found in Playfair et al., *Mediterranean and Middle East*, 1:113, 207; and Richards, *Royal Air Force*, 243.
23. ORB, 202 Group, June–July 1940.
24. ORB, RAF Middle East, Air Staff, HQ Unit, June–Nov. 1940.
25. Hall, *Strategy for Victory*, 73; AHB, *Middle East Campaigns*, 1:44; ORB, 202 Group, June–July 1940.
26. ORB, RAF Middle East, Air Staff, HQ Unit, June–Nov. 1940.
27. Richards, *Royal Air Force*, 246–47.
28. Between late April and the end of July 1917, Naval Ten lost twelve pilots killed, four to serious injuries, and three as prisoners of war. For details on this period, see Collishaw, *Air Command*, 90, 117; Raymond Collishaw, "Notes on Experiences," n.d. [ca. 1940], CWM 19770669-025, 8; and "Appendix E—Casualties, Crashes and Incidents," Westrop, *History of No. 10 Squadron Royal Naval Air Service*, 176–77.
29. Air Commodore Raymond Collishaw, "Command Exercises, Matruh—1939," 12 Oct. 1939, app. 3A to ORB, 202 Group, Aug. 1939–Nov. 1940, TNA AIR 25/803.
30. Longmore, *From Sea to Sky*, 226.
31. AHB, *Middle East Campaigns*, 1:11.
32. For example, see ibid., 44–45; Hall, *Strategy for Victory*, 73; Richards, *Royal Air Force*, 246–47; and Bickers, *Desert Air War*, 34–35.
33. Air Marshal Sir Arthur Longmore to Air Marshal Sir Charles Portal, 14 Oct. 1940, TNA AIR 23/1337, 5.
34. Message A.484, personal for D.P. from A.O.C.-in-C, 14 Oct. 1940, sent in response to Message X.739, Personal for C-in-C from D.P., 13 Oct. 1940, ibid.
35. AHB, *Middle East Campaigns*, 1:40–41; Titterton, *Royal Navy and the Mediterranean*, 1:27.

36. ORB, RAF Middle East, Air Staff, HQ Unit, June–Nov. 1940; ORB, 202 Group, June–July 1940.

37. ORB, RAF Middle East, Air Staff, HQ Unit, June–Nov. 1940; ORB, 202 Group, June–July 1940; AHB, *Middle East Campaigns*, 1:40–41; Titterton, *Royal Navy and the Mediterranean*, 1:27; Shores, Massimello, and Guest, *Mediterranean Air War*, 29.

38. "Operation 'M.B.2,'" Office of Commander-in-Chief, Mediterranean Station, HMS *Warspite*, 14 Aug. 1940, TNA ADM 199/446.

39. ORB, 202 Group, June–July 1940; "Operation M.B.2—Narrative. Bombardment of Italian Forward Positions on the Libyan Coast on 17th August, 1940," 12 Oct. 1940, TNA ADM 199/446.

40. Cunningham, *Sailor's Odyssey*, 271.

41. ORB, 202 Group, June–July 1940.

42. Ibid.; "Operation M.B.2—Narrative."

43. "Operation M.B.2—Narrative"; Titterton, *Royal Navy and the Mediterranean*, 1:61, 63–64; AHB, *Middle East Campaigns*, 1:55; Shores, Massimello, and Guest, *Mediterranean Air War*, 47–48.

44. ORB, RAF HQ Middle East, Air Staff, HQ Unit, Aug.–Sept. 1940, Appendices, TNA AIR 24/1068; ORB, 202 Group, Aug. 1939–Nov. 1940. For an overview of the naval convoy, see Cunningham, *Sailor's Odyssey*, 271–73; and Playfair et al., *Mediterranean and Middle East*, 1:201–204.

45. ORB, 202 Group, Aug. 1939–Nov. 1940.

46. Ibid.; ORB, RAF Middle East, Air Staff, HQ Unit, Aug.–Sept. 1940, Appendices.

47. ORB, 202 Group, Aug. 1939–Nov. 1940; AHB, *Middle East Campaigns*, 1:60; Cunningham, *Sailor's Odyssey*, 274; Playfair et al., *Mediterranean and Middle East*, 1:211–12.

48. Knox, *Mussolini Unleashed*, 87. Knox used this quotation as the title for chapter 3 in his book.

49. Ibid., 122–23. See also Gooch, *Mussolini and His Generals*, 516–18.

50. Quoted in Knox, *Mussolini Unleashed*, 137. See also Ministero della Difesa, *In Africa Settentrionale*, 94–96; Ciano, *Diaries*, 268–73; and Knox, *Mussolini Unleashed*, chaps. 3–4.

51. Knox, *Mussolini Unleashed*, 150. See also Ministero della Difesa, *In Africa Settentrionale*, 102–103; and Ciano, *Diaries*, 285–86, 290–91.

52. Knox, *Mussolini Unleashed*, 160–63; Gerhard Schreiber, "Political and Military Developments in the Mediterranean Area, 1939–1940," in Schreiber, Stegemann, and Vogel, *Germany and the Second World War*, 246–59, 266–77; Playfair et al., *Mediterranean and Middle East*, 1:207–209.

53. Knox, *Mussolini Unleashed*, 163.

54. Rudolfo Graziani Diary, 31 Aug. 1940, quoted ibid., 163.

55. ORB, 202 Group, Aug. 1939–Nov. 1940.

56. Air Commodore Raymond Collishaw, "Brief Report on Royal Air Force Operations in the Western Desert from the Outbreak of War with Italy—the Capture of Cyrenaica to the Time of the Enemy Counter Offensive," 19 Apr. 1941, TNA AIR 23/6475, 2.

57. Ibid.

58. ORB, 202 Group, Aug.–Sept. 1940, TNA AIR 25/801; Knox, *Mussolini Unleashed*, 164.

59. Schreiber, "Political and Military Developments in the Mediterranean Area," 277. The authors do admit, however, that this assessment was made based on 20/20 hindsight and knowledge of the outcome of the British counteroffensive from December 1940 to February 1941.

60. Ministero della Difesa, *In Africa Settentrionale*, 132–43; Playfair et al., *Mediterranean and Middle East*, 1:212.

61. Collishaw, "Brief Report on Royal Air Force Operations in the Western Desert," 2–3; AHB, *Middle East Campaigns*, 1:63–64; Playfair et al., *Mediterranean and Middle East*, 1:212.

62. Drummond, "Air Campaign in Libya and Tripolitania," 250–51.

63. Collishaw, *Air Command*, 244.

64. The October 1966 issue of *Stag*, a men's adventure magazine, contained an article titled "'Bessie the Bombing Bitch': Zaniest Air Raid of WWII." Authors Martin Caidin and Lino Morris told a sensationalized account of this raid. Many details are wrong, including the date (stated as the night of 10 June, when the Italians declared war), the aircraft (a Vickers Valentia rather than a Bristol Bombay), and the weapon (hand grenades). But the other details, including the target of the attack, are correct. The initial erroneous telling of this episode appears to date to an article in the June 1963 issue of the *RAF Flying Review* by Keith Hine titled "Bessie's Night Out." This article also gets the above details wrong and even has Collishaw piloting the Valentia on the first British attack of the war against the Italians. It makes for great reading, even if it only contains a kernel of truth.

65. ORB, 202 Group, Sept. 1940.

66. Collishaw, *Air Command*, 244.

67. AHB, *Middle East Campaigns*, 1:73.

68. Ibid., 69.

69. The first stage of the eastward movement from Benghazi to Barce, a distance of about sixty-eight miles, made use of a local railroad. Collishaw, "Brief Report on Royal Air Force Operations in the Western Desert," 3.

70. Playfair et al., *Mediterranean and Middle East*, 1:186.

71. Ibid., 185–90, 197–201; AHB, *Middle East Campaigns*, 1:50.

72. Eden had met with Wavell and Longmore the previous day.

73. Secretary of State for C.I.G.S. and P.S. to S. of S. for Prime Minister, 15 Oct. 1940, Annex to COS (40) 837, 16 Oct. 1940, TNA CAB 80/20.

74. Ibid.; AHB, *Middle East Campaigns*, 1:68; Playfair et al., *Mediterranean and Middle East*, 1:250–52.

75. Secretary of State for C.I.G.S. and P.S. to S. of S. for Prime Minister, 15 Oct. 1940, Annex to COS (40) 837, 16 Oct. 1940; AHB, *Middle East Campaigns*, 1:68; Playfair et al., *Mediterranean and Middle East*, 1:250–52. See also "Air Reinforcements in the Middle East, Note by Air Staff," 17 Oct. 1940, COS (40) 838, TNA CAB 80/20.

76. Air Marshal Sir Arthur Longmore to Air Marshal Sir Charles Portal, 14 Oct. 1940, TNA AIR 23/1337, 1. Portal officially took up the post of chief of the Air Staff on 25 October 1940. His predecessor, Air Chief Marshal Sir Cyril Newall, left the position on 2 October 1940, and two days later Portal, the air officer commanding-in-chief, Bomber Command, was notified that he was to be the next chief of Air Staff. See Richards, "Portal, Charles Frederick Algernon," accessed 16 Sept. 2012.

77. Longmore to Portal, 14 Oct. 1940, 3–4. See also Cunningham, *Sailor's Odyssey*, 267–68, 316–17.

78. Longmore to Portal, 14 Oct. 1940, 4.
79. Air Vice-Marshal O. T. Boyd was appointed to be deputy air officer commanding-in-chief, Headquarters RAF Middle East on 8 November 1940. But when he flew out from England to take up the post, his aircraft mistakenly landed in Sicily rather than Malta, and Boyd was taken prisoner. Air Vice-Marshal Tedder was subsequently appointed to the post on 29 November and arrived in Cairo on 10 December. See Longmore, *From Sea to Sky*, 225; Richards, *Royal Air Force*, 269–70; AHB, *Middle East Campaigns*, 1:81; and Tedder, *With Prejudice*, chap. 1.
80. Longmore to Portal, 14 Oct. 1940, 5.

Chapter 4

1. A. P. Wavell, "Operations in Western Desert October to December 1940 (Notes on Genesis and Working Out of 'COMPASS' Plan)," 15 Dec. 1940, TNA WO 201/2691, 3.
2. Ibid., 6; Longmore, *From Sea to Sky*, 245; AHB, *The Middle East Campaigns*, vol. 1, *Operations in Libya and the Western Desert, September 1939 to June 1941*, TNA AIR 41/44, 75.
3. "Report on Operations in Libya by Lt. General R. N. O'Connor, from September 1940 to April 1941 (written when Prisoner-of-war in Italy)," n.d., TNA WO 106/2148.
4. Ibid.; Wilson, *Eight Years Overseas*, 46–48; Playfair et al., *Mediterranean and Middle East*, 1:260–62.
5. Air Commodore Raymond Collishaw, "Brief Report on Royal Air Force Operations in the Western Desert from the Outbreak of War with Italy—the Capture of Cyrenaica to the Time of the Enemy Counter Offensive," 19 Apr. 1941, TNA AIR 23/6475, 3–4; AHB, *Middle East Campaigns*, 1:75–76; Playfair et al., *Mediterranean and Middle East*, 1:260–62.
6. June 1940: Nos. 30, 45, 55, 113, and 211 (Blenheim I); No. 70 (Valentia); No. 216 (Valentia and Bombay); No. 208 (Lysander); and No. 33 (Gladiator) Squadrons.
   December 1940: No. 45 (Blenheim I), Nos. 55 and 113 (Blenheim IV), Nos. 33 and 274 (Hurricane I), No. 208 (Lysander and Hurricane I), and No. 3 Royal Australian Air Force (RAAF) Squadrons (Gladiator & Gauntlet) were the only full units and were joined by elements of No. 112 (Gladiator), Nos. 11 and 39 (Blenheim I and IV), and No. 6 (Lysander) Squadrons.
7. The Wellington was considered a heavy bomber early in the war, but the advent of the Avro Lancaster and Handley Page Halifax led to its reclassification as a medium bomber. Two useful sources on aircraft performance are Angelucci and Matricardi, *World War II Airplanes*, and Guedalla, *Middle East*, 223–34. Guedalla's work contains a useful appendix, "Aircraft Who's Who," which gives details of aircraft speed, range, armament, etc. Other discussions of the relative merits of the warplanes employed in the Middle East may be found in most histories, but the following sources are recommended: AHB, *Middle East Campaigns*, 1:28–29; Terraine, *Right of the Line*, 303–4; and Owen, *Desert Air Force*, 27, 34–35.
8. Air Chief Marshal Arthur M. Longmore, "Despatch on Middle East Air Operations, 13 May 1940 to 31 December 1940," 1 Feb. 1941, TNA AIR 23/808, 15.
9. The Wellington IC had more than twice the range and four-and-a-half times the bombload of the Blenheim I (2,550 miles and 4,500 lbs. compared to 1,125 miles and 1,000 lbs.). Guedalla, *Middle East*, 227, 229.
10. These are the numbers quoted in Playfair et al., *Mediterranean and Middle East*, 1:262; and Collishaw, *Air Command*, 244. The British estimated before the operation

that the Italians had 250 fighters and 250 bombers available to them. AHB, *Middle East Campaigns*, 1:76.

11. AHB, *Middle East Campaigns*, 1:70.

12. This directive included No. 30 Squadron. The other units were Nos. 84 and 211 (Blenheim) and No. 80 (Gladiator) Squadrons.

13. Longmore, "Despatch on Middle East Air Operations, 13 May 1940 to 31 December 1940." See also AHB, *Middle East Campaigns*, 1:69–71; and Playfair et al., *Mediterranean and Middle East*, vol. 1, chap. 12.

14. AHB, *Middle East Campaigns*, 1:74–75; Shores, Massimello, and Guest, *Mediterranean Air War*, 491. British claims were very close to the actual number of aircraft reported damaged or destroyed by the Italians during the attack.

15. Shores, Massimello, and Guest, *Mediterranean Air War*, 86.

16. AHB, *Middle East Campaigns*, 1:75 (quotation). See also Longmore's account in *From Sea to Sky*, 245.

17. Collishaw, "Brief Report on Royal Air Force Operations in the Western Desert," 4; AHB, *Middle East Campaigns*, 1:77; Collishaw, *Air Command*, 245; Playfair et al., *Mediterranean and Middle East*, 1:266, 272; Richards, *Royal Air Force*, 270–71.

18. Playfair et al., *Mediterranean and Middle East*, 1:262.

19. Ibid., 267. This comment was likely derived from an observation by O'Connor made in the report he wrote while a prisoner of war. See "Report on Operations in Libya by Lt. General R. N. O'Connor," 6.

20. "Report of the Lessons of the Operation in the Western Desert December, 1940," 31 Dec. 1940, TNA WO 201/352, 4; "Report of Capture by 4th Indian Division of Enemy Positions at Nibeiwa, the Tumars, etc., South of Sidi Barrani, Culminating in the Capture of Sidi Barrani Itself, 9, 10, 11 December 1940," n.d. [ca. Jan. 1941], app. B to "War Diary of 4th Indian Divisional Artillery Covering Period 7 Nov 40 to 14 Dec 40," TNA WO 201/352, 3.

21. Italian sources included aerial-reconnaissance reports as well as prisoner-of-war interrogations and limited signals intelligence. Ministero della Difesa, *La Prima Offensiva Britannica*, 102. These details are confirmed by Hinsley, *British Intelligence in the Second World War*, 375; and Playfair et al., *Mediterranean and Middle East*, 1:273–75.

22. "Report on Operations in Libya by Lt. General R. N. O'Connor," 3. The appendices to the ORB, No. 208 Squadron, for November and December 1940 contain thousands of images of the Italian camps. See TNA AIR 27/1249–52.

23. G. Stephens, *Fourth Indian Division*, 16.

24. Collishaw, "Brief Report on Royal Air Force Operations in the Western Desert," 4; "Report of Capture by 4th Indian Division of Enemy Positions at Nibeiwa, the Tumars, etc.," 6–8.

25. "Report of Capture by 4th Indian Division of Enemy Positions at Nibeiwa, the Tumars, etc.," 6–8; Playfair et al., *Mediterranean and Middle East*, 1:266–68; Ian W. Walker, *Iron Hulls, Iron Hearts: Mussolini's Elite Armoured Divisions in North Africa* (Marlborough, Wiltshire: Crowood, 2003), 62; AHB, *Middle East Campaigns*, 1:78.

26. "Report of Capture by 4th Indian Division of Enemy Positions at Nibeiwa, the Tumars, etc.," 9–10; Playfair et al., *Mediterranean and Middle East*, 1:267–69; Wavell, "Operations in the Western Desert from December 7th, 1940, to February 7th, 1941," 3263–64.

27. "Report of Capture by 4th Indian Division of Enemy Positions at Nibeiwa, the Tumars, etc.," 9–10; Playfair et al., *Mediterranean and Middle East*, 1:267–69; Wavell, "Operations in the Western Desert from December 7th, 1940, to February 7th, 1941," 3263–64.

28. "Report of Capture by 4th Indian Division of Enemy Positions at Nibeiwa, the Tumars, etc.," 15.

29. Ibid., 13–15; Playfair et al., *Mediterranean and Middle East*, 1:270.

30. Cited in Churchill, *Second World War: Their Finest Hour*, 610–11.

31. Stephens, *Fourth Indian Division*, 23; "Report of Capture by 4th Indian Division of Enemy Positions at Nibeiwa, the Tumars, etc.," 15.

32. Playfair et al., *Mediterranean and Middle East*, 1:270–71.

33. Ibid., 273.

34. Quoted in Connell, *Wavell*, 298–99.

35. "Report on Operations in Libya by Lt. General R. N. O'Connor," 8–9.

36. Ibid., 10.

37. Even taking the notorious unreliability of pilots' claims into account, it is clear that there was a large discrepancy in the fortunes of the British and Italian air forces by this point in the campaign. See Collishaw, "Brief Report on Royal Air Force Operations in the Western Desert," 4; and Playfair et al., *Mediterranean and Middle East*, 1:272.

38. ORB, RAF Middle East, Air Staff, HQ Unit, Dec. 1940, TNA AIR 24/1051.

39. Collishaw, "Brief Report on Royal Air Force Operations in the Western Desert," 2; ORB, RAF Middle East, Air Staff, HQ Unit, Dec. 1940.

40. "Report on Operations in Libya by Lt. General R. N. O'Connor," 11.

41. AHB, *Middle East Campaigns*, 1:81; Shores, Massimello, and Guest, *Mediterranean Air War*, 96–97; Gustavsson and Slongo, *Desert Prelude: "Operation Compass."*

42. Shores, Massimello, and Guest, *Mediterranean Air War*, 86–102; Gustavsson and Slongo, *Desert Prelude: "Operation Compass,"* 72–78.

43. ORB, RAF Middle East, Air Staff, HQ Unit, 13 Dec. 1940, TNA AIR 24/1051.

44. This accounting is based on the recent examination of British and Italian records conducted by Christopher Shores and his team as well as a new study that provides a very detailed examination of air operations during Operation Compass based on British and Italian documentary evidence. See Shores, Massimello, and Guest, *Mediterranean Air War;* and Gustavsson and Slongo, *Desert Prelude: "Operation Compass."*

45. "Report of Capture by 4th Indian Division of Enemy Positions at Nibeiwa, the Tumars, etc.," 5, 7.

46. Ibid., 14.

47. "Report of the Lessons of the Operation in the Western Desert December, 1940," 31 Dec. 1940, TNA WO 201/352, 22.

48. The phenomenon of men breaking down under constant air attack was a problem during the siege of Tobruk, but those most susceptible to battle exhaustion were those with no ability to fight back. For example, very low levels of battle exhaustion were experienced by the antiaircraft crews at Tobruk. For a more detailed discussion, see Cooper and Sinclair, "War Neuroses in Tobruk"; and 9th Australian Division, "Report on Operations in Cyrenaica, March–October 1941, including the

Defence of Tobruch," n.d., TNA WO 201/353. There is also a discussion of this issue in Fennell, *Combat and Morale in the North African Campaign*, 62–63.

49. The casualties were primarily sustained by two Cypriot pioneer companies and a New Zealand motor-transport company. RAF Middle East Op Sum 198, "Period 24 hours ending 1800 hours 25th December, 1940," TNA AIR 23/1071; RAF Middle East Op Sum 199, "Period 24 hours ending 1800 hours 26th December, 1940," ibid.; Playfair et al., *Mediterranean and Middle East*, 1:280; Buckingham, *Tobruk*, 92; Gustavsson and Slongo, *Desert Prelude: "Operation Compass,"* 95–96.

50. "Artillery Reconnaissance at Bardia, 23 Dec 1940 to 8 Jan 1941," annex to Group Capt. L. O. Brown, "Report on Army Co-Operation Carried Out in Connection with the Land Operations in the Western Desert and Libya," 31 Jan. 1941, TNA WO 201/348.

51. "Summary of the Battle of Bardia," [ca. 1945], TNA CAB 106/833; Long, *To Benghazi*, 147–48.; Playfair et al., *Mediterranean and Middle East*, 1:282; Stockings, *Bardia*, 109–15.

52. "Summary of the Battle of Bardia," 11–12. This was also quoted in Long, *To Benghazi*, 201. Bergonzoli was nicknamed "Barba Electrica" (Electric Whiskers, or Beard) due to his "spiky white beard parted down the middle." Stockings, *Bardia*, 63–64.

53. Stockings, *Bardia*, 114–15.

54. The strength estimate for the Bardia garrison comes from a situation map dated 17 December. This estimate was increased to 24,100 men and 130 guns on 24 December but was then revised downward again on 26 December to 17,215 men. See "Operation 'COMPASS': Situation and Operational Reports," TNA WO 106/2136.

55. Telegram, Personal for C.I.G.S. from General Wavell, 16 Dec. 1940, "Operation 'COMPASS': Situation and Operational Reports"

56. "Report on Operations in Libya by Lt. General R. N. O'Connor," 11; Wavell, "Operations in the Western Desert from December 7th, 1940, to February 7th, 1941," 3265; *Lessons of Cyrenaica Campaign, December 1940–February 1941*, Middle East Training Pamphlet 10, n.d., copy in author's possession (also found in TNA WO 201/2586), 18.

57. Collishaw, *Air Command*, 247.

58. Longmore, *From Sea to Sky*, 247.

59. Tedder, *With Prejudice*, 44.

60. Ibid., 45–46, 55.

61. ORB, No. 55 Squadron, Dec. 1940, TNA AIR 27/516; AHB, *Middle East Campaigns*, 1:82.

62. Tedder, *With Prejudice*, 55.

63. Shores, Massimello, and Guest, *Mediterranean Air War*, 94–95; Gustavsson and Slongo, *Desert Prelude: "Operation Compass,"* 60; Playfair et al., *Mediterranean and Middle East*, 1:13; AHB, *Middle East Campaigns*, 1:80. This incident would bring Squadron Leader Tony Dudgeon, the commanding officer of the Blenheim squadron that was shot to pieces, to severely criticize Collishaw's command abilities.

64. ORB, No. 55 Squadron, Dec. 1940.

65. Details of these attacks may be found in the daily operational summaries in ORB—Appendixes, RAF HQ Middle East, TNA AIR 24/1071.

66. Giuseppe Santoro, *L'aeronautica italiana nella IIa Guerra mondiale* (Rome: Danesi, 1950), 397, quoted in Playfair et al., *Mediterranean and Middle East*, 1:278; AHB, *Middle East Campaigns*, 1:79–81.

67. HQ RAF Middle East Op Sum 207, "Period 24 hours ending 1800 hours 3rd January 1941," ORB—Appendices, RAF HQ Middle East, TNA AIR 24/1071.

68. Air Chief Marshal Arthur M. Longmore, "Despatch on Air Operations in the Middle East from January 1st, 1941 to May 3rd, 1941," 1 Nov. 1941, 2nd supplement to *London Gazette*, 17 Sept. 1946, 4674 (also in TNA AIR 23/809); AHB, *Middle East Campaigns*, 1:83; Gustavsson and Slongo, *Desert Prelude: "Operation Compass,"* 106–16; Playfair et al., *Mediterranean and Middle East*, 1:284.

69. WD, 16th Australian Infantry Brigade, 2 Jan. 1941, Australian War Memorial 52, 8/2/16.

70. Quoted in Owen, *Desert Air Force*, 37.

71. Collishaw, "Brief Report on Royal Air Force Operations in the Western Desert," 4b.

72. AHB, *Middle East Campaigns*, 1:83.

73. Collishaw, "Brief Report on Royal Air Force Operations in the Western Desert," 4b; ORB, No. 55 Squadron, Dec. 1940; AHB, *Middle East Campaigns*, 1:83.

74. WD, 16th Australian Infantry Brigade, 3 Jan. 1941.

75. Titterton, *Royal Navy and the Mediterranean*, 2:57–58.

76. Stockings, *Bardia*, 358–59.

77. HQ RAF Middle East Op Sum 208, "Period 24 hours ending 1800 hours 4th January 1941," in ORB—Appendices, RAF HQ Middle East, TNA AIR 24/1071; Shores, Massimello, and Guest, *Mediterranean Air War*, 104–106; Gustavsson and Slongo, *Desert Prelude: "Operation Compass,"* 112–17.

78. WD, 16th Australian Infantry Brigade, 3–4 Jan. 1941.

79. Shores, Massimello, and Guest, *Mediterranean Air War*, 106–7.

80. Wavell, "Operations in the Western Desert from December 7th, 1940, to February 7th, 1941," 3265; *Lessons of Cyrenaica Campaign*, 17–20; Long, *To Benghazi*, chaps. 7–8; Playfair et al., *Mediterranean and Middle East*, 1:282–87.

81. HQ RAF ME Op Sum 207, "Period 24 hours ending 1800 hours 3rd January 1941"; HQ RAF ME Op Sum 208, "Period 24 hours ending 1800 hours 4th January 1941"; Collishaw, "Brief Report on Royal Air Force Operations in the Western Desert," 4b; Longmore, "Despatch on Air Operations in the Middle East from January 1st, 1941 to May 3rd, 1941," 4674.

82. Telegram, Foreign Minister to Prime Minister, 6 Jan. 1941, quoted in Churchill, *Second World War: The Grand Alliance*, 14. Churchill's original quote about the Battle of Britain was, "Never in the field of human conflict was so much owed by so many to so few." See Richards, *Royal Air Force*, 196.

83. Conventional accounts of this battle abound. The British and Australian official histories concentrate on the ground battle, though Playfair does describe RAF operations leading up to the ground assault. Even the official RAF history does not provide a detailed description of the battle. The capture of Bardia does not rate a mention in the Royal Navy official history, though there is better coverage of naval operations in volume 2 of the Naval Staff history. See Playfair et al., *Mediterranean and Middle East*, 1:282–87; Long, *To Benghazi*, chaps. 7–8; Richards, *Royal Air Force*, 272–73; and Titterton, *Royal Navy and the Mediterranean*, 2:56–58. Craig Stockings provides the most comprehensive account of the battle and recognizes the importance of the RAF and Royal Navy contribution to this battle. See Stockings, *Bardia*, chap. 18.

84. For a full discussion of the 3–1 ratio, see Mearsheimer, "Assessing the Conventional Balance."

85. Playfair et al., *Mediterranean and Middle East*, 1:286–88; Connell, *Wavell*, 303–7; AHB, *Middle East Campaigns*, 1:84–85.

Chapter 5

1. Ciano, *Diaries*, 333–34, 336.
2. Wavell, "Operations in the Western Desert from December 7th, 1940, to February 7th, 1941," 3265; Playfair et al., *Mediterranean and Middle East*, 1:287–90; Bernd Stegemann, "The Italo-German Conduct of the War in the Mediterranean and North Africa," in Schreiber, Stegemann, and Vogel, *Germany and the Second World War*, 650–51.
3. AHB, *Middle East Campaigns*, vol. 1, *Operations in Libya and the Western Desert, September 1939 to June 1941*, TNA AIR 41/44, 85–86.
4. Details of operations carried out during this period may be found in the daily operational summaries in ORB—Appendices, RAF HQ Middle East, TNA AIR 24/1071.
5. *Lessons of Cyrenaica Campaign, December 1940–February 1941*, Middle East Training Pamphlet 10, n.d., copy in author's possession (also found in TNA WO 201/2586), 20–21; AHB, *Middle East Campaigns*, vol. 1; Playfair et al., *Mediterranean and Middle East*, 1:281, 287–88.
6. Knox, *Hitler's Italian Allies*, 138–41.
7. "Report on Operations in Libya by Lt. General R. N. O'Connor, from September 1940 to April 1941 (written when Prisoner-of-war in Italy)," n.d., TNA WO 106/2148, 16; AHB, *Middle East Campaigns*, 1:85–87; Playfair et al., *Mediterranean and Middle East*, 1:288–90.
8. The effects of the sandstorms were so serious that Collishaw was forced to fly single-fighter patrols. This resulted in a question from RAF HQ Middle East to which Collishaw replied, "four days sand storms had rendered majority of Hurricanes under [my] command unserviceable." ORB, RAF Middle East, Air Staff, HQ Unit, Jan. 1941, TNA AIR 24/1051. See also AHB, *Middle East Campaigns*, 1:86–87; and Playfair et al., *Mediterranean and Middle East*, 1:290–91.
9. ORB, RAF Middle East, Air Staff, HQ Unit, Jan. 1941; *Lessons of Cyrenaica Campaign*, 20–21, app. E; Air Chief Marshal Arthur M. Longmore, "Despatch on Air Operations in the Middle East from January 1st, 1941 to May 3rd, 1941," 1 Nov. 1941, 2nd supplement to *London Gazette*, 17 Sept. 1946, 4674 (also in TNA AIR 23/809); AHB, *Middle East Campaigns*, 1:87.
10. Long, *To Benghazi*, chap. 9.
11. *Lessons of Cyrenaica Campaign*, 21–22, app. F; AHB, *Middle East Campaigns*, 1:87–88.
12. Details of these attacks may be found in the daily operational summaries in ORB—Appendices, RAF HQ Middle East; Longmore, "Despatch on Air Operations in the Middle East from January 1st, 1941 to May 3rd, 1941"; AHB, *Middle East Campaigns*, 1:87–88.
13. Titterton, *Royal Navy and the Mediterranean*, 2:58–59; *Lessons of Cyrenaica Campaign*, 20–21, app. F.
14. Wavell, "Operations in the Western Desert from December 7th, 1940, to February 7th, 1941"; AHB, *Middle East Campaigns*, 1:87–88; Long, *To Benghazi*, chap. 9; Playfair et al., *Mediterranean and Middle East*, 1:291–93.

15. Air Commodore Raymond Collishaw, "Brief Report on Royal Air Force Operations in the Western Desert from the Outbreak of War with Italy—the Capture of Cyrenaica to the Time of the Enemy Counter Offensive," 19 Apr. 1941, TNA AIR 23/6475, 5.

16. Wavell, "Operations in the Western Desert from December 7th, 1940, to February 7th, 1941," 3266.

17. This paragraph is the first point listed under the heading "Factors of Success." "Summary of the Battle of Tobruk," [ca. 1945], TNA CAB 106/834, 1.

18. Ibid., 8. The effect of the heavy bombing on the Tobruk garrison is confirmed by the Italian official history. See Ministero della Difesa, *La Prima Offensiva Britannica*, 291, 306.

19. Longmore, "Despatch on Air Operations in the Middle East from January 1st, 1941 to May 3rd, 1941," 4674; Long, *To Benghazi*, 238.

20. Wavell, "Operations in the Western Desert from December 7th, 1940, to February 7th, 1941," 3267; Playfair et al., *Mediterranean and Middle East*, 1:351–53. For information on the Italian Libya Railway, see Stefano Maggi, "Le Ferrovie Nell'Africa Italiana: Aspetti Economici, Sociali e Strategici," in *Il problema ferroviario dell'Africa*, ed. R. Astuto (Milano: ISPI, 1943), 1–25.

21. HQ RAF ME Op Sum 232, "Period 24 hours ending 1800 hours 28th January 1941," in ORB—Appendices, RAF HQ Middle East; Wavell, "Operations in the Western Desert from December 7th, 1940, to February 7th, 1941," 3267; Playfair et al., *Mediterranean and Middle East*, 1:351–53.

22. Collishaw, "Brief Report on Royal Air Force Operations in the Western Desert," 5–6. O'Connor's headquarters was located at Bomba at this time.

23. ORB, RAF Middle East, Air Staff, HQ Unit, Jan. 1941; Playfair et al., *Mediterranean and Middle East*, 1:357. There were no replacement Merlin engines or spare parts available in Egypt, and thirty-two engines awaited overhaul in the depots. This measure removed the Hurricanes from one day of the battle, 4 February. The next day all flying operations were suspended due to a sandstorm, and on the sixth the campaign had ended. Full details contained in AVM Longmore to AC Collishaw, 4 Feb. 1941, TNA AIR 23/1391.

24. Wavell, "Operations in the Western Desert from December 7th, 1940, to February 7th, 1941," 3267; Longmore, "Despatch on Air Operations in the Middle East from January 1st, 1941 to May 3rd, 1941," 4675.

25. Details of these attacks may be found in the daily operational summaries in ORB—Appendices, RAF HQ Middle East.

26. Ibid.; Collishaw, "Brief Report on Royal Air Force Operations in the Western Desert," 6.

27. Details of these attacks may be found in the daily operational summaries in ORB—Appendices, RAF HQ Middle East; Collishaw, "Brief Report on Royal Air Force Operations in the Western Desert," 6; Wavell, "Operations in the Western Desert from December 7th, 1940, to February 7th, 1941," 3267; Longmore, "Despatch on Air Operations in the Middle East from January 1st, 1941 to May 3rd, 1941," 4675; RAF Middle East Weekly Intelligence Summary 33, Feb. 1941, TNA AIR 23/6769.

28. Wavell, "Operations in the Western Desert from December 7th, 1940, to February 7th, 1941," 3267.

29. Graziani, *Africa Settentrionale*, 223.

30. Ministero della Difesa, *La Prima Offensiva Britannica*, 349.
31. Buckingham, *Tobruk*, 123.
32. Wavell, "Operations in the Western Desert from December 7th, 1940, to February 7th, 1941," 3267; Wilson, *Eight Years Overseas*, 58–60; Playfair et al., *Mediterranean and Middle East*, 1:355–56.
33. Playfair et al., *Mediterranean and Middle East*, 1:356.
34. AHB, *Middle East Campaigns*, 1:90.
35. Playfair et al., *Mediterranean and Middle East*, 1:361.
36. Details of these attacks may be found in the daily operational summaries in ORB—Appendices, RAF HQ Middle East.
37. Playfair et al., *Mediterranean and Middle East*, 1:357.
38. "Report on Operations in Libya by Lt. General R. N. O'Connor," 24–26.
39. Playfair et al., *Mediterranean and Middle East*, 1:357–58.
40. For a full discussion of this period, see David Spires, *Air Power for Patton's Army: The XIX Tactical Air Command in the Second World War* (Washington, D.C.: Air Force History and Museums Program, 2002).
41. Collishaw, "Brief Report on Royal Air Force Operations in the Western Desert," 3.
42. "Report on Operations in Libya by Lt. General R. N. O'Connor," 30.
43. Ibid. For his comments on Wilson, see ibid., 31. For his comments on Greece, see ibid., 29. For his comments on the advance to Tripoli, see ibid., 27–29.
44. Ibid., 30.
45. Ibid., 33.
46. Buckingham, *Tobruk*, 90.
47. Judge, "Airfield Creation for the Western Desert Campaign," accessed 10 Mar. 2013. Judge was an Australian who served with the RAF in the Middle East for almost his entire career. He wrote this account of his wartime experiences in the 1940s, and it was subsequently posted online by his son in 2009.
48. Air Vice-Marshal T. W. Elmhirst, "Report on Lessons Learnt during Air Operations in the Western Desert, August 1940–February 1941," 17 Mar. 1941, TNA AVIA 15/2376, 1–3.
49. Ibid., 1.
50. Quoted in Bashow, "Four Gallant Airmen," 170.
51. Wavell, "Operations in the Western Desert from December 7th, 1940, to February 7th, 1941," 3269.
52. See Air Chief Marshal Arthur M. Longmore, "Despatch on Middle East Air Operations, 13 May 1940 to 31 December 1940," 1 Feb. 1941, TNA AIR 23/808, 16.
53. See ibid.
54. Longmore, "Despatch on Air Operations in the Middle East from January 1st, 1941 to May 3rd, 1941," 4678.
55. Collishaw, "Brief Report on Royal Air Force Operations in the Western Desert," 12.
56. Elmhirst, "Report on Lessons Learnt during Air Operations in the Western Desert," 10.
57. Ibid., 5.
58. Collishaw, "Brief Report on Royal Air Force Operations in the Western Desert," 12–13.
59. Group Capt. L. O. Brown, "Report on Army Co-Operation Carried Out in Connection with the Land Operations in the Western Desert and Libya," 31 Jan. 1941, TNA WO 201/348, 3.

60. For details of Brown's career, see "Air Vice-Marshal Sir Leslie Brown," Air of Authority—A History of RAF Organisation, http://www.rafweb.org/Biographies/Brown_L.htm, accessed 5 June 2013.

61. "Report on Operations in Libya by Lt. General R. N. O'Connor," 32.

62. Brown, "Report on Army Co-Operation," 3.

63. Ibid.

64. Ibid., 3–5.

65. Tedder, *With Prejudice*, 55.

66. Air Marshal A. W. Tedder to Air Chief Marshal Sir W. R. Freeman, 11 Mar. 1941, TNA AIR 20/2792.

67. Ibid.

68. ORB, RAF Middle East, Air Staff, HQ Unit, July 1940–Feb. 1941, TNA AIR 24/1051; ORB, RAF Middle East, Air Staff, HQ Unit, Appendixes, June–July 1940, ibid., 24/1067; ORB, RAF Middle East, Air Staff, HQ Unit, Appendixes, Dec. 1940, ibid., 24/1071; ORB, RAF Middle East, Air Staff, HQ Unit, Appendixes, Jan.–Feb. 1941, ibid.

69. Longmore, "Despatch on Air Operations in the Middle East from January 1st, 1941 to May 3rd, 1941," 4673–75; Collishaw, "Brief Report on Royal Air Force Operations in the Western Desert."

70. The operational pause began before Collishaw departed on sick leave. ORB, No. 55 Squadron, Dec. 1940, TNA AIR 27/516; AHB, *Middle East Campaigns*, 1:82.

71. Comment from "Extract of Letter from Air Vice-Marshal Tedder to D.O.," 25 Mar. 1941, Air Ministry File CS 8981, TNA AIR 20/5466.

72. Cover letter, Air Marshal A. W. Tedder, 24 Mar. 1941, in Elmhirst, "Report on Lessons Learnt during Air Operations in the Western Desert," 10.

73. Tedder, *With Prejudice*, 55

74. Cross, *Straight and Level*, 147–48.

75. Rosier and Rosier, *Be Bold*, 70–71.

76. These comments were based on minimal personal experience backed up by gossip and were committed to paper many decades after the war.

77. These observations were used, along with Tedder's impressions, as evidence of Collishaw's apparent failings. See Shores, Massimello, and Guest, *Mediterranean Air War*, 94, 128–29.

78. It should be noted that the Middle East Combined Plan of 1939 ensured that better relations existed between the army and air force than was in the case in Britain.

79. Slessor, *Air Power and Armies*, 90.

80. Ibid., 90–98.

81. "Signal to No. 33 Squadron from HQ 202 Group," 6 Dec. 1940, reproduced as app. 22 to AHB, *Middle East Campaigns*, vol. 1.

82. For a full discussion of the development of British and American air support in North Africa and Normandy, see Bechthold, "Question of Success"; and Bechthold, "'Development of an Unbeatable Combination.'"

83. Brown, "Report on Army Co-Operation," 1.

84. The squadron was fully trained in army-cooperation work and possessed a flight of Lysanders, but these aircraft remained in the Alexandria area to train reinforcement pilots. By the end of December, both the Lysanders and Gauntlets had been withdrawn from the squadron and replaced with Gladiators. In January 1941 the unit began to reequip with Hurricanes following the capture of Tobruk. Ibid., 6–7.

85. Ibid., 6.
86. Ibid., 7–8.
87. AVM Longmore to AC Collishaw, 23 Jan. 1941, TNA AIR 23/1391.
88. Higham, *Unflinching Zeal*, 133.
89. Ibid., 234.
90. The RAF lost 1,079 aircraft in France in May and June 1940. Ibid., 192. For a full discussion of the serviceability issues afflicting the RAF during the Battle of France, see ibid., chaps .4–5.
91. Fraser, *And We Shall Shock Them*, 121–24.
92. Guedalla, *Middle East*, 98; Playfair et al., *Mediterranean and Middle East*, 1:281.
93. Bickers, *Desert Air War*, 43–44.

Chapter 6

1. *London Gazette*, 4 Mar. 1941, 1303; ibid., 24 Nov. 1942, 5149.
2. "Report on Operations in Libya by Lt. General R.N. O'Connor, from September 1940 to April 1941 (written when Prisoner-of-war in Italy)," n.d., TNA WO 106/2148, 27.
3. Collishaw, *Air Command*, 249. The language in his official report was more guarded, "It appeared to the Germans and Italians at the time that the British would be able to advance upon Tripoli without much difficulty," but Collishaw's contemporary interest in continuing the advance to Tripoli was confirmed by Tedder. See Air Commodore Raymond Collishaw, "Brief Report on Royal Air Force Operations in the Western Desert from the Outbreak of War with Italy—the Capture of Cyrenaica to the Time of the Enemy Counter Offensive," 19 Apr. 1941, TNA AIR 23/6475, 9; and Tedder, *With Prejudice*, 55.
4. Wavell, "Operations in the Middle East from 7th February, 1941 to 15th July, 1941," 3424.
5. Air Chief Marshal Arthur M. Longmore, "Despatch on Air Operations in the Middle East from January 1st, 1941 to May 3rd, 1941," 1 Nov. 1941, 2nd supplement to *London Gazette*, 17 Sept. 1946, 4675 (also in TNA AIR 23/809).
6. Buckingham, *Tobruk*, 142–43.
7. Wavell, "Operations in the Middle East from 7th February, 1941 to 15th July, 1941," 3424.
8. A. P. Wavell to C.I.G.S., 10 Feb. 1941; and C.I.G.S. to A. P. Wavell, 11 Feb. 1941, both quoted in Connell, *Wavell*, 326–27.
9. Longmore, *From Sea to Sky*, 257.
10. Tedder, *With Prejudice*, 59–60.
11. Air Marshal A. W. Tedder to Air Chief Marshal Sir W. R. Freeman, 11 Mar. 1941, TNA AIR 20/2792. See also his critical comments about Collishaw's desire to advance to Tripoli in Tedder, *With Prejudice*, 55.
12. For various appraisals of this decision, see Barnett, *Desert Generals*, 60–65; Correlli Barnett, "'The Desert Generals': An Address by Correlli Barnett, British Commission for Military History Annual General Meeting," 5 Feb. 2005, British Commission for Military History; Barr, *Pendulum of War*, 5–8; and Buckingham, *Tobruk*, 141–42.
13. Collishaw, "Brief Report on Royal Air Force Operations in the Western Desert," 12; Longmore, "Despatch on Air Operations in the Middle East from January 1st, 1941

to May 3rd, 1941," 4673–74; AHB, *The Middle East Campaigns*, vol. 1, *Operations in Libya and the Western Desert, September 1939 to June 1941*, TNA AIR 41/44, 97–99; Wavell, "Operations in the Middle East from 7th February, 1941, to 15th July, 1941," 3423–44.

14. Maughan, *Tobruk and El Alamein*, 3–12; Playfair et al., *Mediterranean and Middle East*, 2:2–4.

15. For the background to the Greek deployment, see Playfair et al., *Mediterranean and Middle East*, vol. 1, chaps. 12, 18, 20; Higham, *Diary of a Disaster;* and Raugh, *Wavell in the Middle East*, chap. 7.

16. Playfair et al., *Mediterranean and Middle East*, 2:1.

17. Wavell, "Operations in the Middle East from 7th February, 1941, to 15th July, 1941."

18. Ibid.; Playfair et al., *Mediterranean and Middle East*, 1:371–72, 388–89, 2:1–2. The British deployment to Greece was based on helping an ally, but the concomitant U.S. support for such a mission was a major part of the British calculation.

19. Wavell, "Operations in the Middle East from 7th February, 1941, to 15th July, 1941," 3423–44; Playfair et al., *Mediterranean and Middle East*, 2:2–4.

20. Bernd Stegemann, "The Italo-German Conduct of the War in the Mediterranean and North Africa," in Schreiber, Stegemann, and Vogel, *Germany and the Second World War*, 658–59, 673–74.

21. AHB, *Middle East Campaigns*, 1:99–108; Playfair et al., *Mediterranean and Middle East*, 2:9–15.

22. AHB, *Middle East Campaigns*, 1:99–108; Playfair et al., *Mediterranean and Middle East*, 2:9–15; Stegemann, "Italo-German Conduct of the War," 654–78.

23. Lt. Gen. P. Neame, "Operations in Cyrenaica from 27th February, 1941, when Lt.Gen. P. Neame assumed command until his capture on 7th April 1941," n.d. [ca. May 1941], TNA CAB 106/767; Group Capt. L. O. Brown, "Report on Operations Carried out by the R.A.F. Cyrenaica during Enemy Advance," 22 Apr. 1941, TNA AIR 23/6486.

24. Collishaw, "Brief Report on Royal Air Force Operations in the Western Desert," 9; AHB, *Middle East Campaigns*, 1:103–105.

25. "Report on Naval Operations in Support of the Army off the Western Desert, 7th December 1940–31st May 1941," 1 Jan. 1942, TNA DEFE 2/822, phase IV, sec. N.

26. AHB, *Middle East Campaigns*, 1:103–5.

27. "Report on Naval Operations in Support of the Army off the Western Desert," phase IV, sec. N. For additional details, see "HMS *Terror*," uboat.net, http://uboat.net/allies/warships/ship/5460.html, accessed 7 Mar. 2015.

28. "Report on Naval Operations in Support of the Army off the Western Desert," phase IV, sec. N.

29. "Detail of Work Carried Out, 22 February 1941," app. J to ORB, No. 3 RAAF Squadron, Feb. 1941, NAA Digital Record, http://naa12.naa.gov.au/SearchNRetrieve/Interface/ViewImage.aspx?B=1158595&S=1, p. 228, accessed 24 Jan. 2013. The ORB entry for the engagement recorded that the Ju 88 was damaged but not seen to crash, while appendix J recorded the enemy aircraft as destroyed. Christopher Shores confirmed the German aircraft was destroyed. Shores, Massimello, and Guest, *Mediterranean Air War*, 134.

30. ORB, No. 3 RAAF Squadron, Feb. 1941, NAA Digital Record, accessed 24 Jan. 2013.

31. AHB, *Middle East Campaigns*, 1:103–105.

32. Collishaw, "Brief Report on Royal Air Force Operations in the Western Desert," 9.

33. Ibid., 9–10.

34. The intelligence indicated that the reinforcements comprised "two Italian Infantry Divisions, two Italian Motorized Arty. Regts., and German Armd. Troops estimated at maximum of one Armd. Bde. Gp," and Axis forces "can probably maintain up to one Inf. Div, and Armd. Bde. along the coast road in about three weeks." Telegram, Commander-in-Chief, Middle East to the War Office, 2 Mar. 1941, TNA CAB 65/22/11.

35. Ibid.

36. Ibid.

37. Ibid.

38. AHB, *Middle East Campaigns*, 1:106–107.

39. The flight of No. 6 Squadron at Agedabia established reserve airfields at Antelat and Msus, while No. 3 RAAF Squadron was prepared to fall back from Benina to Got es Sultan. Brown, "Report on Operation Carried out by the R.A.F. Cyrenaica during Enemy Advance," 16–17; AHB, *Middle East Campaigns*, 1:108–9.

40. Hinsley, *British Intelligence in the Second World War*, 388–91.

41. "RAF Reconnaissance Reports Supplied to the Army, February–March 1941," app. 25 to AHB, *Middle East Campaigns*, vol. 1.

42. The Oberkommando des Heeres was Nazi Germany's army high command. It was led by Generalfeldmarschall Walther von Brauchitsch until December 1941.

43. Stegemann, "Italo-German Conduct of the War," 673–74.

44. Playfair et al., *Mediterranean and Middle East*, 2:15–16; Raugh, *Wavell in the Middle East*, 187–88.

45. "RAF Reconnaissance Reports Supplied to the Army, February–March 1941."

46. "Counter Offensive from Tripolitania," 24 Mar. 1941, in WD, General Headquarters, Joint Planning Staff, Middle East, Mar. 1941, TNA WO 169/914.

47. Telegram, Prime Minister to A. P. Wavell, 26 Mar. 1941, in War Cabinet, *Principal War Telegrams and Memoranda*, 3:73.

48. Telegram, A. P. Wavell to Prime Minister, 27 Mar. 1941, ibid., 77.

49. Playfair et al., *Mediterranean and Middle East*, vol. 2, chaps. 1–2.

50. Wavell, "Operations in the Middle East from 7th February, 1941, to 15th July, 1941," 3425.

51. Hinsley and Bennett noted that Ultra (the Allied code word for the intelligence gained from the decryption of the top-secret German Enigma machine) provided some useful intelligence but was not yet able to offer the quality of information available later in the war. See Hinsley, *British Intelligence in the Second World War*, 380–99; and Bennett, *Ultra and Mediterranean Strategy*, 36–40.

52. A recent study on the Battle of Mersa Brega makes a convincing case that Wavell and Neame had a number of options to reinforce the forward British positions that would have had a good chance of stopping the initial German success on 31 March and possibly forestalling Rommel's entire offensive. See N. Murphy, "'Lost' Battle of Mersa El Brega."

53. For details of the army during this period, see Gen. A. P. Wavell, "Report on the Action of the 2nd Armoured Division during the Withdrawal from Cyrenaica, March–April 1941," 11 July 1941, TNA CAB 66/17/32; Neame, "Operations in

Cyrenaica from 27th February, 1941"; Wavell, "Operations in the Middle East from 7th February, 1941, to 15th July, 1941," 3423–44; and Playfair et al., *Mediterranean and Middle East*, vol. 2, chap. 3.

54. Buckingham, *Tobruk*, 350.

55. HQ RAF ME Fortnightly Op Sum 1, "Period 24th March to 6th April, 1941," app. 92 to ORB, RAF Middle East, Air Staff, HQ Unit, June 1941, AIR 24/1075; RAF ME Fortnightly Op Sum 12, "Period 7th April to 20th April, 1941," app. 85 to ibid.; Brown, "Report on Operation Carried out by the R.A.F. Cyrenaica during Enemy Advance," 15–16.

56. Brown, "Report on Operation Carried out by the R.A.F. Cyrenaica during Enemy Advance," 17.

57. RAF ME Fortnightly Op Sum 1, "Period 24th March to 6th April, 1941"; ORB, HQ RAF ME, appendixes, Mar.–Apr. 1941, TNA AIR 24/1073.

58. Details of these attacks may be found in the daily operational summaries in ORB— Appendices, RAF HQ ME, Mar.–Apr. 1941, TNA AIR 24/1073. See also Brown, "Report on Operation Carried out by the R.A.F. Cyrenaica during Enemy Advance."

59. "British Operational Air Losses in the Desert, 7 February–18 June 1941," app. 32 to AHB, *Middle East Campaigns*, vol. 1.

60. Brown, "Report on Operation Carried out by the R.A.F. Cyrenaica during Enemy Advance"; ORB, RAF HQ Middle East—Appendices, Mar.–Apr. 1941, TNA AIR 24/1073. See also Playfair et al., *Mediterranean and Middle East*, 2:30.

61. Playfair et al., *Mediterranean and Middle East*, 2:30; "I Bersaglieri in Africa Settentrionale," http://digilander.libero.it/avantisavoiait/I%20Bersaglieri%20 in%20Africa.htm, accessed 27 Jan. 2013.

62. Brown, "Report on Operation Carried out by the R.A.F. Cyrenaica during Enemy Advance"; ORB—Appendices, RAF HQ Middle East, Mar.–Apr. 1941, TNA AIR 24/1073; Col. H. B. Latham, "An Account of the Operations Carried out by the 2nd Support Group in Cyrenaica from March 31st to April 7th 1941," n.d., TNA CAB 106/619, 7; Playfair et al., *Mediterranean and Middle East*, vol. 2, chap. 2 (esp. pp. 24, 31).

63. WD, 3rd Armoured Brigade, Apr. 1941, TNA WO 169/1278. See also the attached app. D, "Report by Lieutenant A. C. Doyle, R.T.R.," 22 Apr. 1941. Doyle was the officer in charge of the supply column sent from divisional headquarters.

64. Shores, Massimello, and Guest, *Mediterranean Air War*, 144.

65. Longmore, *From Sea to Sky*, 272.

66. For an overview and introduction to the British deployment to Greece and the German invasion, see Playfair et al., *Mediterranean and Middle East*, vol. 2, chaps. 4–5. See also Detlef Vogel, "German Intervention in the Balkans," in Schreiber, Stegemann, and Vogel, *Germany and the Second World War*, 497–526.

67. Playfair et al., *Mediterranean and Middle East*, vol. 2, chaps. 9–10; Gerhard Schreiber, "Politics and Warfare in 1941," in Schreiber, Stegemann, and Vogel, *Germany and the Second World War*, 589–618.

68. For details on the campaign in Italian East Africa, see Playfair et al., *Mediterranean and Middle East*, vol. 1, chaps. 22–23. For the German perspective, see Stegemann, "Italo-German Conduct of the War," 643–53.

69. Owen, *Desert Air Force*, 52.

70. Air Vice-Marshal A. C. Maund to Air Commodore R. Collishaw, 8 Apr. 1941, HQ RAF ME (Deputy Air Commander-in-Chief's Files)—Formation of Western Desert Air Command, Apr.–Oct. 1941, TNA AIR 23/902.

71. RAF ME Fortnightly Op Sum 13, "Period 21st April to 4th May, 1941," app. 39 to ORB, RAF Middle East, Air Staff, HQ Unit, June 1941, AIR 24/1075, 7.

72. Air Commodore R. Collishaw, "Brief Report on the Royal Air Force Operations from the Time of Our Retreat through Cyrenaica—including the Operation Battleaxe," 12 Aug. 1941, TNA AIR 23/6474, 1.

73. Ibid.

74. RAF ME Fortnightly Op Sum 12, "Period 7th April to 20th April, 1941," app. 85 to ORB, RAF Middle East, Air Staff, HQ Unit, June 1941, AIR 24/1075; RAF ME Fortnightly Op Sum 13, "Period 21st April to 4th May, 1941," app. 39 to ibid.

75. Quoted in Stegemann, "Italo-German Conduct of the War," 692. See also translated enemy document quoted in AHB, *Middle East Campaigns*, 1:141; and Gundelach, *Die Deutsche im Mittelmeer*, 135–37.

76. Collishaw, "Brief Report on the Royal Air Force Operations from the Time of Our Retreat through Cyrenaica," 3; RAF ME Fortnightly Op Sum 12, "Period 7th April to 20th April, 1941"; RAF ME Fortnightly Op Sum 13, "Period 21st April to 4th May, 1941."

77. Playfair et al., *Mediterranean and Middle East*, 2:30; Gundelach, *Die Deutsche im Mittelmeer*, 119–24.

78. Neame made these comments in his report, which was written while he was a prisoner of war. This document did not circulate in the United Kingdom until sometime in 1944. It would have a direct influence on army-RAF relations in the way that the Wavell report did, but it does reflect the mindset of the senior army leaders at the time of the defeat. See Neame, "Operations in Cyrenaica from 27th February," 5, 14.

79. 9th Australian Division, "Report on Operations in Cyrenaica, March–October, 1941 including the Defence of Tobruch," n.d., TNA WO 201/353, 4.

80. Wavell, "Report on the Action of the 2nd Armoured Division during the Withdrawal from Cyrenaica," 8. This is not the original version of the report, but one amended by Wavell based on his telegram of 20 June 1941. The revisions are clearly marked in the text.

81. Ibid.

1. The mechanical defects of A.F.V.s of the 3rd Armoured Brigade, and in particular among the cruiser tanks of the 5th R.T.R

2. The shortage of transport, which tied Divisions to the dumps, with all the inevitable anxieties which their existence caused

3. The false air reports on the 3rd April about the enemy being at Msus

4. The frequent changes of orders and regrouping consequent on these air reports, which resulted in the disintegration of formations and units

5. The failure of the petrol supply, due to the decision to change the line of withdrawal

6. The complete breakdown of signal communications, partly due to the loss of vehicles and partly to lack of opportunities of charging batteries

7. Lack of tactical reconnaissances, particularly in the latter stages

8. Lack of topographical knowledge, and the consequent failure to appreciate that the sceleidima escarpment afforded neither good positions nor good tracks. See ibid., app. B, 14–15.

83. AHB, *Middle East Campaigns*, 1:133.

84. Tedder became acting air officer commanding-in-chief Middle East in early May 1941, when Longmore was recalled to England. He was confirmed in this position on 1 June 1941. The Brigadier General Staff was responsible for matters related to operations and intelligence, including coordination with the air force. Ibid., 134.

85. Winston S. Churchill, "Note by the Minister of Defence on Report on the Acton of the 2nd Armoured Division," 11 July 1941, TNA CAB 66/17/32, 2.

86. Portal wrote to the secretary of state for air, Sir Archibald Sinclair, to recommend addressing Wavell's report at the cabinet level as it "may be quoted against the R.A.F. in the future." Chief of the Air Staff to Secretary of State for Air, 6 Aug. 1941, TNA AIR 8/585.

87. Brown also wrote an initial report immediately after the battle. Brown, "Report on Operation Carried out by the R.A.F. Cyrenaica during Enemy Advance"; Air Commodore L. O. Brown, "Report on Certain Aspects of the Air Operations in Cyrenaica," 19 July 1941, TNA AIR 8/585; Brig. A. F. Harding and Air Commodore L. O. Brown, "On Certain Aspects of the G.H.Q M.E. Report on the Action of the 2nd Armoured Division during the Withdrawal from Cyrenaica, March–April 1941," 25 July 1941, TNA CAB 66/18/24.

88. Harding and Brown, "On Certain Aspects of the G.H.Q M.E. Report on the Action of the 2nd Armoured Division."

89. The war diary of the 3rd Armoured Brigade indicated that a convoy carrying 8,000 gallons of petrol had left the dump before it was destroyed on 3 April. Unfortunately, this was one of the convoys destroyed by air attack on 4 April. WD, 3rd Armoured Brigade, Apr. 1941; "Report by Captain the Hon. A. H. P. Hore-Ruthven 2nd Bn. Rifle Brigade Concerning the Situation at Msus on 3 April 1941," attachment to app. 31 (a copy of the Harding and Brown report) of AHB, *Middle East Campaigns*, vol. 1. The Hore-Ruthven report does not appear as an appendix to the version of the report reproduced in the Cabinet Papers.

90. Harding and Brown, "On Certain Aspects of the G.H.Q M.E. Report on the Action of the 2nd Armoured Division," 3–4.

91. Brown, "Report on Certain Aspects of the Air Operations in Cyrenaica," 2.

92. Ibid., 3–4. For details on this episode, see "Report on Operations in Libya by Lt. General R. N. O'Connor, from September 1940 to April 1941 (written when Prisoner-of-war in Italy)," n.d., TNA WO 106/2148, 40–46; and Playfair et al., *Mediterranean and Middle East*, 2:20–21, 29, 34.

93. Brown, "Report on Certain Aspects of the Air Operations in Cyrenaica," 4–5.

94. Ibid., 5–6.

95. Telegram, C.-in-C. Middle East to War Office, 26 July 1941, TNA AIR 8/585.

96. Citino, *Death of the Wehrmacht*, 124.

97. The epithet "Royal Absent Force" was first been bestowed on the RAF at Dunkirk, when the army felt it had been abandoned to its fate and not provided with sufficient air cover to prevent enemy attacks. The name reappeared in Greece, where it was inscribed in the diary of a British soldier captured by the Germans. "Rare As

Fairies" was bestowed by Anzac troops in Greece. See Sadler, *El Alamein*, 45. For Dunkirk, see Franks, *Air Battle for Dunkirk;* for Greece, see Behrendt, *Rommel's Intelligence in the Desert Campaign*, 55.

98. Quoted in Stockings and Hancock, "Reconsidering the Luftwaffe in Greece," 772. Stockings and Hancock demonstrated that the Luftwaffe was not the decisive factor in the British defeat but rather pointed out that it was natural for the army to seek to shift the blame for the disaster onto the RAF and at the same time use the perceived failure to again lobby for subordinating that service to its control. Fortunately, the interservice report on Greece concluded that an air force controlled by the army would have made no difference to the outcome of the campaign, and these demands went nowhere. See also AHB, *The Middle East Campaigns*, vol. 6, *The Campaign in Greece, 1940–1941*, TNA AIR 41/28.

Chapter 7

1. Collishaw, *Air Command*, 251.

2. AHB, *The Middle East Campaigns*, vol. 1, *Operations in Libya and the Western Desert, September 1939 to June 1941*, TNA AIR 41/44, 146.

3. RAF ME Fortnightly Op Sum 12, "Period 7th April to 20th April, 1941," app. 85 to ORB, RAF Middle East, Air Staff, HQ Unit, June 1941, AIR 24/1075; RAF ME Fortnightly Op Sum 13, "Period 21st April to 4th May, 1941," app. 39 to ibid.

4. ORB, HQ 204 Group RAF, Apr. 1941, TNA AIR 25/815.

5. Collishaw, *Air Command*, 251.

6. Air Commodore Raymond Collishaw, "Brief Report on Royal Air Force Operations in the Western Desert from the Outbreak of War with Italy—the Capture of Cyrenaica to the Time of the Enemy Counter Offensive," 19 Apr. 1941, TNA AIR 23/6475, 13–14; AHB, *Middle East Campaigns*, 1:161; Collishaw, *Air Command*, 251.

7. Collishaw, *Air Command*, 251.

8. Buckingham, *Tobruk*, 215–39; Playfair et al., *Mediterranean and Middle East*, 2:37–38.

9. Bernd Stegemann, "The Italo-German Conduct of the War in the Mediterranean and North Africa," in Gerhard Schreiber, Stegemann, and Vogel, *Germany and the Second World War*, 681–84.

10. Playfair et al., *Mediterranean and Middle East*, 2:38.

11. Stegemann, "Italo-German Conduct of the War," 683.

12. Kitchen, *Rommel's Desert War*, 90–93; Stegemann, "Italo-German Conduct of the War," 683–85; Playfair et al., *Mediterranean and Middle East*, 2:38; Buckingham, *Tobruk*, 250–69.

13. HQ RAF ME Daily Op Sums, Apr. 1941, in ORB—Appendices, RAF Middle East, Air Staff, HQ Unit, TNA AIR 24/1073.

14. Gundelach, *Die Deutsche im Mittelmeer*, 134–36.

15. Air Commodore R. Collishaw to Air Marshal A. W. Tedder, 23 Apr. 1941, TNA AIR 23/1391; ORB, RAF Middle East, Air Staff, HQ Unit, Apr. 1941, TNA AIR 24/1051.

16. Message, RAF Liaison Section Tobruch to 204 Group, 25 Apr. 1941, in App. K, "Air Situation at Tobruch," attached to Maj. Gen. L. Morshead, "Operations 9 Aust Div—Cyrenaica," 27 Apr. 1941, app. to WD, 9th Australian Division, Apr. 1941, Australian War Memorial 52, 1/5/20.

17. Message, TOBFORT to DESFORCE, 25 Apr. 1941, ibid.

18. App. M, Maj. Gen. W. Beresford-Peirse to Maj. Gen. L. Morshead, 26 Apr. 1941, attached to Morshead, "Operations 9 Aust Div—Cyrenaica"; Message, DESFORCE to TOBFORT, 25 Apr. 1941, in App. K, "Air Situation at Tobruch," ibid.

19. HQ RAF ME Daily Op Sums, Apr. 1941.

20. Quoted in AHB, *Middle East Campaigns*, 1:128–29.

21. App. K, "Air Situation at Tobruch," attached to Morshead, "Operations 9 Aust Div—Cyrenaica"; 9th Australian Division, "Report on Operations in Cyrenaica, March–October 1941, including the Defence of Tobruch," n.d., TNA WO 201/353.

22. HQ RAF ME Op Sum, 1 May 1941, in ORB—Appendices, HQ RAF ME, TNA AIR 24/1074; Playfair et al., *Mediterranean and Middle East*, 2:155–56; Stegemann, "Italo-German Conduct of the War," 686–92; Maughan, *Tobruk and El Alamein*, chap. 6; Gundelach, *Die Deutsche im Mittelmeer*, 139; Ministero della Difesa, *La Prima Controffensiva Italo-Tedesca*, Schizza, n.13. The German casualty figures are taken from Rommel's report to the German army high command cited in Stegemann, "Italo-German Conduct of the War," 693. The Italian figures come from the British official history, Playfair et al., *Mediterranean and Middle East*, 2:156. The Australian figures are from Maughan, *Tobruk and El Alamein*, 235.

23. Air Commodore R. Collishaw, "Brief Report on the Royal Air Force Operations from the Time of Our Retreat through Cyrenaica, including the Operation Battleaxe," 12 Aug. 1941, TNA AIR 23/6474, 1–4; AHB, *Middle East Campaigns*, 1:140–41, 143.

24. Terraine, *Right of the Line*, 337–38.

25. Tedder, *With Prejudice*, 82.

26. Ibid., 81–82.

27. Furse, *Wilfrid Freeman*, 177–78.

28. "The Middle East Command of the Royal Air Force, May 1941–January 1943. Draft for Despatch by Marshal of the Royal Air Force Lord Tedder, G.C.B." n.d., TNA AIR 20/5532, 1. Noted on the cover of this document in pencil: "prepared by S/L J.N. White. Lord Tedder never wrote a despatch as A.O.C.-in-C. M.E. therefore this draft was never used although it was submitted to him."

29. For this correspondence, see "Middle East: Correspondence with Air Vice-Marshal Tedder," Vice Chief of the Air Staff Files, TNA AIR 20/2791, 20/2792.

30. HQ RAF ME Op Sum 331, "Period 24 hours ending 1800 hours 7th May 1941," ORB—Appendices, RAF Middle East, Air Staff, HQ Unit, TNA AIR 24/1074; Shores, Massimello, and Guest, *Mediterranean Air War*, 78.

31. HQ RAF ME Op Sum 342, "Period 24 hours ending 1800 hours 18th May 1941," in ORB—Appendices, RAF Middle East, Air Staff, HQ Unit, TNA AIR 24/1074.

32. Collishaw, "Brief Report on the Royal Air Force Operations from the Time of Our Retreat through Cyrenaica," 2.

33. Stegemann, "Italo-German Conduct of the War," 687–90.

34. Translated enemy document quoted in AHB, *Middle East Campaigns*, 1:141. See also Gundelach, *Die Deutsche im Mittelmeer*, 135–37.

35. Quoted in AHB, *Middle East Campaigns*, 1:153.

36. Collishaw, "Brief Report on the Royal Air Force Operations from the Time of Our Retreat through Cyrenaica," 1–4; ORB, 204 Group, Apr.–May 1941, TNA AIR

25/815; HQ RAF ME Daily Op Sums, Apr.–May 1941, in ORB—Appendices, RAF Middle East, Air Staff, HQ Unit, TNA AIR 24/1074; AHB, *Middle East Campaigns*, 1:146, 153–54.

37. HQ RAF ME Daily Op Sums, Apr.–June 1941, in ORB—Appendices, RAF Middle East, Air Staff, HQ Unit, TNA AIR 24/1074 & 1075; Collishaw, "Brief Report on the Royal Air Force Operations from the Time of Our Retreat through Cyrenaica," 3; AHB, *Middle East Campaigns*, 1:143–44.

38. Collishaw, "Brief Report on the Royal Air Force Operations from the Time of Our Retreat through Cyrenaica," 3.

39. Ibid., 1–3; HQ RAF ME Op Sum 346, "Period 24 hours ending 1800 hours 22nd May 1941," ORB—Appendices, RAF Middle East, Air Staff, HQ Unit, TNA AIR 24/1074; Shores, Massimello, and Guest, *Mediterranean Air War*, 191–92.

40. Quoted in Stegemann, "Italo-German Conduct of the War," 692. See also Gundelach, *Die Deutsche im Mittelmeer*, 139–40.

41. At this point in the war, the British were able to read Luftwaffe Enigma messages. Hinsley, *British Intelligence in the Second World War*, 396–97.

42. Wavell, "Operations in the Middle East from 7th February, 1941, to 15th July, 1941," 3441.

43. Collishaw, "Brief Report on the Royal Air Force Operations from the Time of Our Retreat through Cyrenaica," 4.

44. Ibid., 4–5.

45. Playfair et al., *Mediterranean and Middle East*, 2:160.

46. Collishaw, "Brief Report on the Royal Air Force Operations from the Time of Our Retreat through Cyrenaica," 4.

47. AHB, *Middle East Campaigns*, 1:156; Playfair et al., *Mediterranean and Middle East*, 2:160–62; Stegemann, "Italo-German Conduct of the War," 697–700; Jentz, *Tank Combat in North Africa*, 132–33.

48. HQ RAF ME Op Sum 340, "Period 24 hours ending 1800 hours 16th May 1941," ORB—Appendices, RAF Middle East, Air Staff, HQ Unit, TNA AIR 24/1074; AHB, *Middle East Campaigns*, 1:155; Gundelach, *Die Deutsche im Mittelmeer*, 142–43.

49. Playfair et al., *Mediterranean and Middle East*, 2:162; Jentz, *Tank Combat in North Africa*, 140.

50. HQ RAF ME Op Sum 341, "Period 24 hours ending 1800 hours 17th May 1941," ORB—Appendices, RAF Middle East, Air Staff, HQ Unit, TNA AIR 24/1074; ORB, 204 Group, May 1941, ibid., 25/815.

51. HQ RAF ME Op Sum 343, "Period 24 hours ending 1800 hours 19th May 1941," ORB—Appendices, RAF Middle East, Air Staff, HQ Unit, TNA AIR 24/1074; ORB, 204 Group, May 1941; AHB, *Middle East Campaigns*, 1:156.

52. Playfair et al., *Mediterranean and Middle East*, 2:162; Hinsley, *British Intelligence in the Second World War*, 398. Hinsley also referred to the battle as a failure.

53. Quoted in Connell, *Wavell*, 478. "Tiger cubs" refers to the special "Tiger" convoy that Churchill dispatched to the Middle East to provide reinforcements for an upcoming attack. The convoy arrived in Egypt on 12 May with its precious cargo of eighty-two cruiser, 135 "I," and twenty-one light tanks as well as forty-three Hurricanes. These reinforcements would allow the RAF and 7th Armoured Division to be rebuilt in time for Operation Battleaxe. See Playfair et al., *Mediterranean and Middle East*, 2:107–19, 162.

54. Rommel, *Rommel Papers*, 136–37.

55. Playfair et al., *Mediterranean and Middle East*, 2:163; Stegemann, "Italo-German Conduct of the War," 700; Gundelach, *Die Deutsche im Mittelmeer*, 142–43. RAF aircraft were not available to support the army during this battle due to the commitment of squadrons to the Crete operation. HQ RAF ME Op Sum 351, "Period 24 hours ending 1800 hours 27th May 1941," ORB—Appendices, RAF Middle East, Air Staff, HQ Unit, TNA AIR 24/1074.

56. Detlef Vogel, "German Intervention in the Balkans," in Schreiber, Stegemann, and Vogel, *Germany and the Second World War*, 527–33.

57. On 11 May the RAF contingent on Crete consisted of six Hurricanes and "approximately fourteen very old Blenheim Is and Gladiators." AHB, *The Middle East Campaigns*, vol. 7, *The Campaign in Crete, May 1941*, TNA AIR 41/29, 19–22.

58. Tedder, *With Prejudice*, 101.

59. The range difference was even more marked to locations on the western part of the island: Derna to Suda Bay—410 miles; Mersa Matruh to Suda Bay—684 miles. Distances calculated on Google maps.

60. The spikes were effective at denying the enemy use of the airfield by puncturing aircraft tires. ORB, HQ 204 Group, May 1941.

61. Ibid.; ORB, RAF Middle East, Air Staff, HQ Unit, May 1941, TNA AIR 24/1051; AHB, *Middle East Campaigns*, vol. 7 (esp. apps.); Tedder, *With Prejudice*, 101–105; Shores, Massimello, and Guest, *Mediterranean Air War*, 194–207.

62. Vogel, "German Intervention in the Balkans," 549–50.

63. Ibid., 550.

64. Wavell to Gen. Sir John Dill, 27 May 1941, TNA AIR 8/545.

65. AHB, *Middle East Campaigns*, 7:70–72.

66. Tedder to Air Chief Marshal Sir W. R. Freeman, 3 June 1941, TNA AIR 20/2792.

67. Tedder to CAS, 30 May 1941, ibid., 23/1395.

68. An unknown commentator underlined this passage in the report and wrote, "Infamous libel!" Collishaw, "Brief Report on the Royal Air Force Operations from the Time of Our Retreat through Cyrenaica," 4.

69. Raymond Collishaw, "A Brief History of the Crete Campaign, 1941," n.d., Collishaw Correspondence File, III-15, The Beatrice Hitchens Memorial Collection of Aviation History, Western Archives, Western University, London, Ont.

70. Tedder to Freeman, 3 June 1941.

71. Tedder to Freeman, 29 May 1941, TNA AIR 20/2792.

72. Ibid.

73. Telegram, CAS Personal from Tedder, 23 May 1941, TNA AIR 23/1395.

74. "HQ RAF ME Daily Operational Summaries, April–June 1941," in ORB—Appendices, RAF Middle East, Air Staff, HQ Unit, TNA AIR 24/1074, 24/1075.

75. See correspondence between Tedder, Freeman, and Portal in TNA AIR 20/2791 and AIR 23/1395, and especially Tedder to Freeman, 29 May, 3 June 1941, and telegram, CAS Personal from Tedder, 23 May 1941. For the Tedder–Mountbatten discussion, see Tedder, *With Prejudice*, 107–108. The fallout over the perceived lack of RAF air support over Greece and Crete would continue to resonate for months. New Zealand prime minister Peter Fraser, advised that his forces had not received the necessary air support in Greece and Crete, appealed directly to Churchill in October to receive assurances that his country's forces would not again be

committed to battle without adequate air cover. See ibid., 176–77.
76. Quoted in Orange, *Tedder*, 127.
77. Tedder to Air Chief Marshal Sir W. R. Freeman, 11 Mar. 1941, TNA AIR 20/2792.
78. Tedder to Freeman, 29 May 1941.

Chapter 8

1. Telegram, General Wavell to War Office, 7 June 1941, TNA WO 106/2161; Western Desert Force Operation Instruction 11 [op order for Battleaxe], 12 June 1941, TNA WO 201/2482, 3; W. G. F. Jackson, *The Battle for North Africa* (New York: Mason, Charters, 1975), 159.
2. Playfair et al., *Mediterranean and Middle East*, 2:163.
3. Telegram, Prime Minister to General Wavell, 28 May 1941, TNA PREM 3/287–1.
4. Telegram, Prime Minister to General Wavell, 9 June 1941, TNA AIR 8/582.
5. Telegram, Tedder from CAS, 9 June 1941, ibid.
6. Playfair et al., *Mediterranean and Middle East*, 2:166; AHB, *The Middle East Campaigns*, vol. 1, *Operations in Libya and the Western Desert, September 1939 to June 1941*, TNA AIR 41/44, 161, 165–66. The composition of 204 Group at the start of Operation Battleaxe was as follows: Nos. 1 SAAF, 2 SAAF, 73, and 274 Squadrons (Hurricane); No. 250 Squadron (Tomahawk); Nos. 14 and 113 Squadrons (Blenheim); No. 24 SAAF Squadron (Maryland); No. 6 (Hurricane), No. 39 (Maryland) Army Co-operation Squadrons; and Nos. 37, 38, 70, and 148 (Wellingtons) Squadrons.
7. The approximate strength of serviceable aircraft for the RAF was fifty heavy bombers, fifty-five medium bombers, eighty-four single-engine fighters, and fourteen twin-engine fighters. Playfair et al., *Mediterranean and Middle East*, 2:166; AHB, *Middle East Campaigns*, 1:165–66. Gundelach gives the Luftwaffe strength as forty-six Ju 87s, eleven Ju 88s, nine Me 110s, twenty-six Me 109s, and eleven reconnaissance aircraft. This figure is used here as it is based on the most recent research. The British official history provides higher numbers—fifty-nine bombers/dive bombers and sixty single/twin-engine fighters, while the RAF AHB report provides a lower figure of eighty German aircraft—ten bombers, twenty-nine dive bombers, twenty-four single-engine fighters, and seventeen twin-engine fighters. Details of the Italian air strength (114 aircraft as of 1 May 1941) are not available. Gundelach, *Die Deutsche Luftwaffe im Mittelmeer*, 143–44; Playfair et al., *Mediterranean and Middle East*, 2:166; AHB, *Middle East Campaigns*, 1:161, 165–66.
8. Gundelach, *Die Deutsche Luftwaffe im Mittelmeer*, 143–45.
9. Playfair et al., *Mediterranean and Middle East*, 2:107–19, 162.
10. Telegram, C.I.G.S. from General Wavell, 28 May 1941, TNA AIR 8/582.
11. Telegram, C.I.G.S. from General Wavell, 31 May 1941, ibid.
12. Telegram, C.I.G.S. from General Wavell, 7 June 1941, ibid.
13. Ibid.
14. AHB, *Middle East Campaigns*, 1:163–65; HQ RAF ME Daily Op Sums, June 1941, in ORB—Appendices, RAF Middle East, Air Staff, HQ Unit, TNA AIR 24/1075.
15. Telegram, CAS from Tedder, 10 June 1941, TNA AIR 8/582.
16. HQ RAF ME Daily Op Sums, June 1941; ORB, 204 Group, June 1941, TNA AIR 25/815.

17. Air Commodore R. Collishaw, "Brief Report on Royal Air Force Operations in the Western Desert from the Outbreak of War with Italy—the Capture of Cyrenaica to the Time of the Enemy Counter Offensive," 19 Apr. 1941, TNA AIR 23/6475, 11–12.

18. "Report on Air Co-Operation with the Army during Operations in the Western Desert and Libya, December 1940–February 1941," May 1941, TNA AIR 2/7447.

19. Air Commodore R. Collishaw, "Brief Report on the Royal Air Force Operations from the Time of our Retreat through Cyrenaica—including the Operation Battleaxe," 12 Aug. 1941, TNA AIR 23/6474, 7.

20. Telegram, CAS from Tedder, 9 June 1941, TNA AIR 23/1395.

21. Telegram, For CAS Personal from TEDDER, 23 May 1941, ibid.

22. Telegram, Personal for CAS from TEDDER, 25 May 1941, ibid.; Telegram, Private and Personal for CAS from TEDDER, 27 May 1941, ibid.

23. Telegram, Private and Personal for CAS from TEDDER, 27 May 1941.

24. Telegram, Private and Personal for Tedder from CAS, 28 May 1941, TNA AIR 23/1395.

25. Tedder to Freeman, 3 June 1941, ibid., 20/2792.

26. Telegram, CAS to Tedder, 11 June 1941, ibid., 23/1395.

27. This point was emphasized to the author in personal correspondence with Sebastian Cox, head of the RAF Historical Branch, 25 Oct. 2013.

28. The quotations in this paragraph are found in Telegram, Tedder to C.A.S, 11 June 1941, TNA AIR 23/1395.

29. Telegram, CAS from Tedder, 21 June 1941, ibid., 8/582.

30. Collishaw, "Brief Report on the Royal Air Force Operations from the Time of Our Retreat through Cyrenaica," 7.

31. Raymond Collishaw, "Personal Impressions during the Decade Ending 1924," 3rd Course, RAF Staff College, 23 Sept. 1924, TNA AIR 1/2387/228/11/40. This is a course paper he wrote detailing his war experiences,

32. Raymond Collishaw, "Notes on Experiences," n.d., [ca. 1940], CWM 19770669-025, 41.

33. Collishaw, "Brief Report on Royal Air Force Operations in the Western Desert," 11–12.

34. Ibid., 13.

35. Tedder, *With Prejudice*, 123.

36. The author is very grateful to Sebastian Cox, head of the RAF Historical Branch, for sharing his knowledge and guidance on the political dimensions of RAF relations with the army during this period.

37. Bernd Stegemann, "The Italo-German Conduct of the War in the Mediterranean and North Africa," in Schreiber, Stegemann, and Vogel, *Germany and the Second World War*, 700.

38. Lt. Gen. N. Beresford-Peirse, "The Battle of Capuzzo, 15–17 June, 1941," n.d. [ca. Aug. 1941], TNA WO 201/2482.

39. "Note on the Remainder of the Plan for Operation 'Battleaxe,'" 16 June 1941, TNA WO 106/2161.

40. Playfair et al., *Mediterranean and Middle East*, 2:168; Stegemann, "Italo-German Conduct of the War," 702.

41. Beresford-Peirse, "Battle of Capuzzo"; "Notes on Action 7 Armd Div 14–17 Jun 41," n.d., TNA WO 201/357; "Report by Comd 4 Ind Div on Operations in the Western

Desert 15–18 June 1941," n.d., ibid.; Stegemann, "Italo-German Conduct of the War," 702–703.

42. Telegram, General Wavell to War Office, 17 June 1941, TNA WO 106/2161.

43. Beresford-Peirse, "Battle of Capuzzo"; "Notes on Action 7 Armd Div 14–17 Jun 41"; "Report by Comd 4 Ind Div on Operations in the Western Desert 15–18 June 1941."

44. Telegram, General Wavell for War Office, 18 June 1941, TNA WO 106/2161.

45. The breakdown of casualties was as follows: Western Desert Force—122 men killed, 588 wounded, and 259 missing; Germans—88 men killed, 336 wounded, and 168 missing; Italians—95 men killed, 355 wounded, and 235 missing. British figures given in Playfair et al., *Mediterranean and Middle East*, 2:171. Axis figures from Ministero della Difesa, *La Prima Controffensiva Italo-Tedesca*, 183.

46. Playfair et al., *Mediterranean and Middle East*, 2:171; Stegemann, "Italo-German Conduct of the War," 703.

47. HQ RAF ME Op Sum 371, "Period 24 hours ending 1800 hours 16th June 1941," ORB—Appendices, RAF Middle East, Air Staff, HQ Unit, TNA AIR 24/1075; "No. 204 Group Operation Order No. 4," 14 June 1941, app. D to ORB, 204 Group, June 1941, TNA AIR 25/815.

48. Shores, Massimello, and Guest, *Mediterranean Air War*, 222.

49. HQ RAF ME Op Sum 371, "Period 24 hours ending 1800 hours 16th June 1941"; HQ RAF ME Op Sum 372, "Period 24 hours ending 1800 hours 17th June 1941," in ORB—Appendices, RAF Middle East, Air Staff, HQ Unit, TNA AIR 24/1075; ORB, 204 Group, June 1941, TNA AIR 25/815; Beresford-Peirse, "Battle of Capuzzo"; AHB, *Middle East Campaigns*, 1:168–69.

50. German and Italian sources cited in AHB, *Middle East Campaigns*, 1:169. These numbers are confirmed in Gundelach, *Die Deutsche Luftwaffe im Mittelmeer*, 144–45. The after-action reports of the Western Desert Force as well as the 7th Armoured and 4th Indian Divisions did not miss any opportunity to criticize the RAF, but they made no reference to any casualties from air attacks on 16 June. See Beresford-Peirse, "Battle of Capuzzo"; "Notes on Action 7 Armd Div 14–17 Jun 41"; "Report by Comd 4 Ind Div on Operations in the Western Desert 15–18 June 1941."

51. HQ RAF ME Op Sum 372, "Period 24 hours ending 1800 hours 17th June 1941"; ORB, 204 Group, June 1941, TNA AIR 25/815; AHB, *Middle East Campaigns*, 1:169; Brown, *Eagles Strike*, 44.

52. "Note for C.I.G.S. on Progress of Operation 'Battleaxe,'" 16 June 1941, TNA WO 201/2161. This file also contains the series of telegrams dispatched from Egypt to London during the course of the battle.

53. Telegram, CAS to Air Chief Marshal Tedder, 17 June 1941, TNA AIR 23/1395.

54. Telegram, C.I.G.S. to General Wavell, 17 June 1941, TNA AIR 8/582.

55. Message, Air Marshal Tedder to Air Commodore Collishaw, 17 June 1941, app. 23 to ORB, 204 Group, June 1941, TNA AIR 24/1075.

56. Message, Air Marshal Tedder to Air Ministry, 17 June 1941, TNA AIR 8/582.

57. Collishaw, "Brief Report on the Royal Air Force Operations from the Time of Our Retreat through Cyrenaica," 9; HQ RAF ME Op Sum 373, "Period 24 hours ending 1800 hours 18th June 1941," in ORB—Appendices, RAF Middle East, Air Staff, HQ Unit, TNA AIR 24/1075; ORB, 204 Group, June 1941, TNA AIR 25/815; Wavell, "Operations in the Middle East from 7th February, 1941, to 15th July, 1941," 3442–43; Brown, *Eagles Strike*, 42–45.

58. Collishaw, "Brief Report on the Royal Air Force Operations from the Time of Our Retreat through Cyrenaica," 8; HQ RAF ME Op Sum 373, "Period 24 hours ending 1800 hours 18th June 1941"; ORB, 204 Group, June 1941, TNA AIR 25/815.

59. AHB, *Middle East Campaigns*, 1:169–70; Shores, Massimello, and Guest, *Mediterranean Air War*, 224–27; HQ RAF ME Op Sum 373, "Period 24 hours ending 1800 hours 18th June 1941."

60. "4 Ind. Div. Report on Operations 15–17 Jun 41. Report by C.R.A. [Comd, Royal Artillery]," app. B to "Report by Comd 4 Ind Div on Operations in the Western Desert 15–18 June 1941" n.d., TNA WO 201/357.

61. Tedder mentioned Wavell's complaint in a message to London, while Beresford-Peirse, Creagh, and Messervy each discussed the attack without providing context. See Message, Tedder to Air Ministry, 17 June 1941; Beresford-Peirse, "Battle of Capuzzo"; "Notes on Action 7 Armd Div 14–17 Jun 41"; and "Report by Comd 4 Ind Div on Operations in the Western Desert 15–18 June 1941."

62. AHB, *Middle East Campaigns*, 1:169–71; Brown, *Eagles Strike*, 42–45; Shores, Massimello, and Guest, *Mediterranean Air War*, 224–28.

63. Stegemann, "Italo-German Conduct of the War," 703. This comment is based in part on Gundelach, *Die Deutsche Luftwaffe im Mittelmeer*, 145–46.

64. Playfair et al., *Mediterranean and Middle East*, 2:169.

65. Telegram, C.I.G.S. from General Wavell, 18 June 1941, TNA AIR 8/582.

66. Telegram, General Wavell to C.I.G.S., 10 June 1941, TNA WO 106/2161.

67. Telegram, General Wavell to War Office, 16 June 1941, ibid.

68. Hinsley, *British Intelligence in the Second World War*, 399; Gundelach, *Die Deutsche Luftwaffe im Mittelmeer*, 144–45.

69. Telegram, C.I.G.S. from General Wavell, 18 June 1941.

70. Telegram, CAS from Tedder, 21 June 1941, TNA AIR 8/582.

71. Stegemann, "Italo-German Conduct of the War," 703.

72. Telegram, CAS from Tedder (six parts), 21 June 1941, TNA WO 106/2161; Playfair et al., *Mediterranean and Middle East*, 2:171; AHB, *Middle East Campaigns*, 1:172; Shores, Massimello, and Guest, *Mediterranean Air War*, 218–28; Brown, *Eagles Strike*, 45–46.

73. Letter, Lt. Gen. N. Beresford-Peirse, "Subject: Battle of Capuzzo 14–17 Jun 41," 6 Aug. 1941, TNA WO 201/357.

74. Maj. Gen. Michael O'Moore Creagh, "Lessons from Recent Operations," n.d., TNA WO 201/357.

75. "HQ 4th Indian Division—Operations in the Western Desert, 15–17 June 1941," 30 June 1941, TNA WO 201/357.

76. Godfrey, *British Army Communications in the Second World War*, 101, 105, 106, 114.

77. AHB, *Middle East Campaigns*, 1:175.

78. "R.A.F. Co-operation—Operation Battle Axe," 12 June 1941, app. C to Western Desert Force Operations Instructions 11, TNA WO 201/2482.

79. App. A to ibid.

80. Telegram, CAS from Tedder, 21 June 1941, TNA WO 106/2161.

81. Collishaw, "Brief Report on the Royal Air Force Operations from the Time of Our Retreat through Cyrenaica," 8.

82. Telegram, CAS from Tedder, 21 June 1941, TNA WO 106/2161.

83. Telegram, CAS from Tedder, 21 June 1941, TNA AIR 8/582; Collishaw, "Brief Report on the Royal Air Force Operations from the Time of Our Retreat through Cyrenaica," 7–9.
84. Telegram, CAS from Tedder, 21 June 1941, TNA WO 106/2161.
85. Air Chief Marshal Charles Portal, untitled note for Prime Minister, 29 June 1941, TNA CAB 20/633.

Chapter 9

1. Churchill, *Second World War: The Grand Alliance*, 343.
2. John Colville, Diary, 18 June 1941, quoted in Churchill, *War Papers*, 814.
3. Telegram, Prime Minister to A. P. Wavell, 21 June 1941, quoted in Connell, *Wavell*, 504.
4. Playfair et al., *Mediterranean and Middle East*, 2:246.
5. Tedder to Air Chief Marshal Sir W. R. Freeman, 7 July 1941, TNA AIR 20/2792.
6. Telegram, Tedder to Portal, 9 July 1941, TNA AIR 23/1395.
7. Air Marshal A. M. Tedder to Air Commodore R. Collishaw, 10 July 1941, TNA AIR 23/1391.
8. Terraine, *Right of the Line*, 352.
9. Biographical information on Slessor is taken from Slessor, *Central Blue*; Slessor, *Air Power and Armies*; Orange, *Slessor*; and Meilinger, "Slessor and the Genesis of Air Interdiction."
10. Phillip S. Meilinger, foreword to Slessor, *Air Power and Armies*, n.p.
11. Ibid., introduction.
12. Ibid.
13. Phillip S. Meilinger, "Trenchard, Slessor, and Royal Air Force Doctrine before World War II," in Meilinger, ed., *The Paths of Heaven: The Evolution of Airpower Theory* (Maxwell Air Force Base, Ala.: Air University Press, 1997), 66.
14. Bechthold, "Question of Success."
15. Hall, *Learning How to Fight Together*, 9.
16. Ibid. See also Omissi, *Air Power and Colonial Control*; and Ritchie, *RAF, Small Wars, and Insurgencies in the Middle East*.
17. Waldie, "Relations between the Army and the RAF," 296.
18. Hall, *Strategy for Victory*, 22–24.
19. AHB, *Air Support*, RAF Air Publication 3235 (London, 1955), TNA AIR 10/5547, 17–19; Hall, *Strategy for Victory*, 42.
20. Gen. the Viscount Gort, "Second Despatch on Operations of the British Expeditionary Force, France and Belgium, 1 February 1940 to 31 May 1940," *Supplement to the London Gazette*, 17 Oct. 1941, 5932. See also Hall, *Learning How to Fight Together*, 11.
21. Hall, *Learning How to Fight Together*, 11. For a complete discussion of the development of army-air matters during the Battle of France, see AHB, *Air Support*, chap. 2; Hall, *Strategy for Victory*, chap. 3; Ellis, *War in France and Flanders*, esp. chap. 22; Richards, *Royal Air Force*, chap. 5; and Terraine, *Right of the Line*, chaps. 12–15.
22. "Air Support for the Army: Memorandum by Secretary of State for War," 23 Sept. 1940, TNA AIR 20/3706.
23. Ibid.
24. W.P. (41) 69, Annex 1, 26 Mar. 1941, TNA CAB 66/15.

25. This debate may be followed in the following documents: COS (41) 83 (O), War Cabinet, COS Committee, "The Air Programme. Memorandum by the Chief of the Air Staff," 21 May 1941, TNA CAB 80/57; COS (41) 89 (O), War Cabinet, COS Committee, "Army Air Requirements: Memorandum by the Chief of the Imperial General Staff," 30 May 1941, TNA CAB 80/57; COS (41) 119 (O), War Cabinet, COS Committee, "Army-Air Requirements: Memorandum by the Chief of the Air Staff," 26 June 1941, TNA CAB 80/58; COS (41) 129 (O), War Cabinet, COS Committee, "Army-Air Requirements: Memorandum by the Chief of the Air Staff," 26 June 1941, TNA CAB 80/58; COS (41) 242 (O), War Cabinet, COS Committee, "Army Air Requirements: Memorandum by the Chief of the Imperial General Staff," 22 Oct. 1941, TNA CAB 80/60; and COS (41) 119 (O), War Cabinet, COS Committee, "Army-Air Requirements: Memorandum by the Chief of the Air Staff," 2 Nov. 1941, TNA CAB 80/60. See also P. M. McCallum, "Army-Air Co-operation," TNA CAB 101/136, 1–24.
26. AHB, *Air Support*, 26; Hall, *Strategy for Victory*, 91–93.
27. Air Vice-Marshal J .C. Slessor to Vice CAS, 6 May 1941, TNA AIR 39/16.
28. Ibid.
29. John Colville, Diary, 20 June 1941, quoted in Churchill, *War Papers*, 826.
30. Churchill to General Ismay, 20 June 1941, quoted ibid.
31. "Opportunity cost" is an economics and business phase that describes a "benefit, profit, or value of something that must be given up to acquire or achieve something else. Since every resource (land, money, time, etc.) can be put to alternative uses, every action, choice, or decision has an associated opportunity cost." "Opportunity Cost," BusinessDictionary.com, http://www.businessdictionary.com/definition/opportunity-cost.html, accessed 3 Oct. 2013.
32. Telegram, Tedder to CAS, 21 June 1941, TNA WO 106/2161.
33. Churchill to General Smuts, 30 June 1941, quoted in Churchill, *War Papers*, 872.
34. Churchill to General Auchinleck, 19 July 1941, quoted ibid., 962.
35. Gen. John Dill to Lt. Gen. Claude Auchinleck, 26 June 1941, quoted in Kennedy, *Business of War*, 134.
36. Ibid., 136.
37. Ibid.
38. Harriman and Abel, *Special Envoy*, 69.
39. It should be noted that the use of the navy in such a bombardment role would have required the RAF to provide significant support in the form of air cover for the ships at a time when there were already too few aircraft to perform the myriad of other assigned roles.
40. This cable was sent on 5 July. Harriman and Abel, *Special Envoy*, 68–69.
41. Ibid., 71.
42. Orange, *Tedder*, 145. For a full discussion of Harriman and Lyttelton, see Harriman and Abel, *Special Envoy*, 68–71; Tedder, *With Prejudice*, 135; and Orange, *Tedder*, 144–45.
43. COS (41) 417, 6 July 1941: Annex I, "Copy of Telegram from Commander-in-Chief, Middle East to War Office (Auchinleck to Churchill)," 4 July 1941, TNA CAB 80/29.
44. Ibid.
45. Auchinleck's proposal suggested that separate squadrons be devoted to army, navy, and air force missions. Minutes of D.D Plans (O) in response to ibid.

46. AHB, *The Middle East Campaigns*, vol. 2, *Operations in Libya and the Western Desert, June 1941 to January 1942*, TNA AIR 41/25, 13.

47. Telegram, Prime Minister to C-in-C, ME, 6 July 1941, quoted in McCallum, "Army-Air Co-operation," 25.

48. Telegram, C-in-C, ME to Prime Minister, 15 July 1941, quoted ibid., 25–26.

49. Tedder, *With Prejudice*, 138.

50. Churchill, *Second World War: The Grand Alliance*, 405.

51. "War Cabinet, Defence Committee (Operations): Minutes," 1 Aug. 1941, quoted in Churchill, *War Papers*, 1022.

52. Ibid., 1023–24.

53. Ibid., 1024. See also Tedder, *With Prejudice*, 139.

54. "War Cabinet, Defence Committee (Operations):Minutes," 1 Aug. 1941, quoted in Churchill, *War Papers*, 1024.

55. Churchill, *Second World War: The Grand Alliance*, 405.

56. Connell, *Wavell*, 267–69.

57. Tedder, *With Prejudice*, 138–43 (quotation, 143).

58. Churchill, *Second World War: The Grand Alliance*, 430.

59. Ibid., 427–30 (quotation, 430).

60. The full text of this statement is quoted by Churchill in his memoirs. See ibid., 498–500.

61. Colville, *Churchillians*, 146.

62. Auchinleck received a copy of the directive on 29 August 1941. He immediately recognized its importance and added a handwritten annotation, "Keep as history!" Tedder recalled in his memoirs that he received it in early September. Memorandum, Churchill to Auchinleck, 29 Aug. 1941, Reference GB 133/AUC/304, Papers of Field Marshal Sir Claude Auchinleck, AUC/182, John Rylands University Library, The University of Manchester; Churchill, *Second World War: The Grand Alliance*, 498–500; Tedder, *With Prejudice*, 169. Both Tedder and Churchill quoted extensively from the directive.

63. Winston S. Churchill, "A Note by the Minister of Defence," 7 Oct. 1941, TNA AIR 8/983. Though this copy of the directive is dated 7 October, the original was drafted by Churchill in early August, sent to the Middle East in late August or early September, and widely circulated to high commanders in October.

64. Churchill, "Note by the Minister of Defence"; Tedder, *With Prejudice*, 169; Hall, *Strategy for Victory*, 108.

65. Churchill, "Note by the Minister of Defence."

66. Hall, *Strategy for Victory*, 107–8.

67. Alanbrooke, *War Diaries*, 157 (13 May 1941).

68. Winston Churchill, House of Commons Debates, "Defense of Crete," 10 June 1941, *Hansard*, vol. 372, cc.157, http://hansard.millbanksystems.com/commons/1941/jun/10/defence-of-crete, accessed 16 June 2013.

69. Ibid.

70. Gen. A. P. Wavell, "Report on the Action of the 2nd Armoured Division during the Withdrawal from Cyrenaica, March–April 1941," 11 July 1941, TNA CAB 66/17/32; Brig. A. F. Harding and Air Commodore L. O. Brown, "On Certain Aspects of the G.H.Q M.E. Report on the Action of the 2nd Armoured Division during the Withdrawal from Cyrenaica, March–April 1941," 25 July 1941, TNA CAB 66/18/24.

71. Winston S. Churchill, "Note by the Minister of Defence on Report on the Acton of the 2nd Armoured Division," 11 July 1941, TNA CAB 66/17/32, 2.

72. Winston S. Churchill to Air Chief Marshal Sir Charles Portal, 19 Aug. 1941, quoted in Churchill, *War Papers*, 1085.

73. Winston S. Churchill to Air Chief Marshal Sir Charles Portal, 27 Aug. 1941, quoted ibid., 1117.

74. Tedder to Freeman, 4 Oct. 1941, TNA AIR 20/2792.

75. Ibid.

76. Ibid.

77. See "Minutes of Meeting to Consider Options in the Western Desert, Held at G.H.Q. Middle East, on 3rd October, 1941," TNA AIR 20/2792; and Tedder to Freeman, 4 Oct. 1941.

78. Tedder to Freeman, 4 Oct. 1941.

79. Eighth Army, under the command of Lt. Gen. Sir Alan Cunningham, was formed in September 1941 based on the Western Desert Force. ORB, 253 Wing, July–Aug. 1941, TNA AIR 26/351; Middle East: Army Cooperation (Aug.–Oct. 1941), TNA AIR 20/2996.

80. Hall, *Strategy for Victory*, 109. Hall reproduced this complete directive in the appendix to his book.

81. Hall, *Learning How to Fight Together*, 15.

82. Orange, *Coningham*, 79.

83. Tedder, *With Prejudice*, 169–70.

84. Ibid., 394.

85. Churchill, *Second World War: The Grand Alliance*, 500.

86. All quotations from B. L. Montgomery, "Some Notes on High Command in War," 2nd ed., Italy, Sept. 1943, TNA AIR 8/984, n.p. This is a reissue of the original, first released in January 1943. The only change was the addition of a new introduction by Montgomery.

87. Gen. Elwood R. Quesada and Gen. William W. Momyer, two U.S. Air Force officers who served in North Africa and were leaders in developing American tactical air doctrine, believed that Coningham was the key figure in the creation of this Allied tactical air doctrine and his force of personality ensured that it would be adopted. For a full discussion, see Kohn and Harahan, *Air Superiority in World War II and Korea*, 30–35.

88. "Talk by Air Vice-Marshal Sir A. Coningham to assembled British and American General and Senior Officers," Tripoli, 16 Feb. 1943, TNA AIR 8/984.

89. Ibid.

90. For a full discussion of the North African Campaign and its role as the genesis of Allied tactical-air-support doctrine, see Bechthold, "Question of Success." Brad Gladman argued that the lessons learned by the British and their American partners in North Africa led to the creation of "the best system of air/land warfare ever seen," which would become one of the Allies' "great tools for victory." See Gladman, *Intelligence and Anglo-American Air Support*, 1–18 (quotations, 2, 18).

Chapter 10

1. Collishaw, *Air Command*, 255.

2. AHB, *Air Support*, RAF Air Publication 3235 (London, 1955), TNA AIR 10/5547, 50.

3. AHB, *The Middle East Campaigns*, vol. 1, *Operations in Libya and the Western Desert, September 1939 to June 1941*, TNA AIR 41/44, 176.
4. Orange, *Tedder*, 126.
5. Orange, "Tedder, Arthur William, first Baron Tedder," accessed 20 June 2013.
6. Harold Denny, "Noted Air Chief Will Leave Egypt," *New York Times*, 29 Aug. 1941, 5.
7. Collishaw, *Air Command*, 94–95.
8. Conroy, *Best of Luck*, 51–52.
9. Letter, Frank Woolley, n.d., Raymond Collishaw Fonds, LAC, MG 30-E280, vol. 1, p. 4. This letter appears to have been written to a friend of R. V. Dodds who was inquiring about Collishaw on Dodds's behalf.
10. Ibid., 3.
11. Orange, "Getting Together," 6, 8–9; Orange, *Tedder*, 126–27.
12. Raymond Collishaw, "Personal Impressions during the Decade Ending 1924," 3rd Course, RAF Staff College, 23 Sept. 1924, TNA AIR 1/2387, pt. 1.
13. Coningham, "Development of Tactical Air Forces," 212.
14. Ibid., 225. Hill made these comments following Coningham's address. He referred specifically to Coningham's early handling of the Desert Air Force, but his remarks may be even more applicable to the period when Collishaw was in command.
15. Tedder to Air Chief Marshal Sir W. R. Freeman, 7 July 1941, TNA AIR 20/2792.
16. U.S. War Department Field Service Regulations FM 100-20, *Command and Employment of Air Power* (Washington: Department of the Army, 21 July 1943), U.S. Air Force Historical Research Agency, Maxwell Air Force Base, Ala., reel A1927, frames 1720–36, copy held by Laurier Centre for Military Strategic and Disarmament Studies, Wilfrid Laurier University, Waterloo, Ont.
17. Greenfield, *Army Ground Forces and the Air–Ground Battle Team*, 47.
18. Collishaw, *Air Command*, 254.
19. Ibid.
20. ORB, 14 Group, TNA AIR 25/250; App. to ORB, 14 Group, TNA AIR 25/253.
21. A survey of RAF Staff College graduates of the 1924 class shows that Collishaw was in the middle in terms of age, and a number of his classmates who went on to the highest ranks in the RAF were as old or older than him. Of the fourteen members of the 1924 class of the RAF Staff College who achieved the rank of air commodore or above, three retired during the war (plus one who left the RAF but served with British intelligence), two died, and eight served through the end of the war. Seven men were younger than Collishaw, and six were the same age or older. Both men who died and two who retired during the war were the same age or older, and the other retiree was younger. Two officers who served in significant roles until the end of the war were older than Collishaw. Data for this survey was found at Air of Authority—A History of RAF Organisation, http://www.rafweb.org, accessed 24 June 2013.
22. See Orange, "Dowding, Hugh Caswall Tremenheere, first Baron Dowding," accessed 20 Sept. 2013; Wright, *Dowding and the Battle of Britain;* Orange, *Dowding of Fighter Command*.
23. Collishaw, *Air Command*, 254–55.
24. Collishaw's correspondence with Dodds is collected in his extensive personal papers at Library and Archives Canada as well as the Directorate of History and

Heritage, both in Ottawa. Additional material is housed in the Canadian War Museum archives as well as in The Beatrice Hitchens Memorial Collection of Aviation History, Western Archives, Western University, London, Ontario. For Dodds's career, see Halliday, "Air Historian—Part II."

25. Collishaw, *Air Command*, 255. Ironically, though he considered his time in the Western Desert as the most important of his career, his efforts as an historian were largely focused on issues related to the First World War.

Bibliography

Archives

Australian War Memorial, Canberra, Australia
AWM 52—Second World War Diaries
Canadian War Museum, Ottawa, Ontario, Canada
Air Vice Marshal Raymond Collishaw Fonds
A. L. Bocking Fonds
Kenneth Edgar Clayton-Kennedy Fonds
Lloyd S. Breadner Fonds
Directorate of History and Heritage, National Defence Headquarters, Ottawa, Ontario, Canada
Air Marshal L. S. Breadner Papers
E. R. Grange Biography File
Fred Hitchens Papers
Robert Leckie Biography File
Raymond Collishaw Biography File
RCAF Official History Volume 3 Files
William Avery Bishop Collection
Library and Archives Canada, Ottawa, Ontario, Canada [LAC]
MG 30-E280—Raymond Collishaw Fonds
RG 9—Records of the Department of Militia and Defence
National Archives of Australia, Australia
AWM 64—Operations Record Book, No. 3 Squadron RAAF
The National Archives, Kew, United Kingdom [TNA]
ADM 199—Admiralty: War History Cases and Papers, Second World War
ADM 273—Admiralty: Royal Naval Air Service, Registers of Officers' Services
AIR 1—Air Ministry: Air Historical Branch: Papers (Series I)
AIR 2—Air Ministry and Ministry of Defence: Registered Files
AIR 5—Air Ministry: Air Historical Branch: Papers (Series II)
AIR 8—Air Ministry and Ministry of Defence: Department of the Chief of the Air Staff: Registered Files
AIR 10—Ministry of Defence and Predecessors: Air Publications and Reports
AIR 20—Air Ministry and Ministry of Defence: Papers Accumulated by the Air Historical Branch
AIR 23—Air Ministry and Ministry of Defence: Royal Air Force Overseas Commands: Reports and Correspondence
AIR 24—Air Ministry and Ministry of Defence: Operations Record Books, Commands
AIR 25—Air Ministry and Ministry of Defence: Operations Record Books, Groups
AIR 26—Air Ministry: Operations Record Books, Wings
AIR 27—Air Ministry: Operations Record Books, Squadrons

AIR 28—Air Ministry and Ministry of Defence: Operations Record Books, Royal Air Force Stations

AIR 39—Air Ministry: Army Cooperation Command: Registered Files

AIR 41—Air Ministry and Ministry of Defence: Air Historical Branch: Narratives and Monographs

AIR 54—South Africa Air Force: Operations Record Books

AIR 75—Marshal Sir John Slessor: Papers

AVIA 15—Ministry of Aircraft Production and Predecessor and Successors: Registered Files

CAB 65—War Cabinet and Cabinet: Minutes (WM and CM Series)

CAB 66—War Cabinet and Cabinet: Memoranda (WP and CP Series)

CAB 80—War Cabinet and Cabinet: Chiefs of Staff Committee: Memoranda

CAB 101—War Cabinet and Cabinet Office: Historical Section: War Histories (Second World War), Military

CAB 106—War Cabinet and Cabinet Office: Historical Section: Archivist and Librarian Files: (AL Series)

CAB 120—Cabinet Office: Minister of Defence Secretariat: Records

DEFE 2—Combined Operations Headquarters

PREM 3—Prime Minister's Office: Operational Correspondence and Papers

WO 106—War Office: Directorate of Military Operations and Military Intelligence, and Predecessors: Correspondence and Papers

WO 216—War Office: Office of the Chief of the Imperial General Staff: Papers

WO 169—War Office: British Forces, Middle East: War Diaries, Second World War

WO 201—War Office: Middle East Forces; Military Headquarters Papers, Second World War

WO 277—War Office: Department of the Permanent Undersecretary of State, C.3. Branch: Historical Monographs

U.S. Air Force Historical Research Agency, Maxwell Air Force Base, Alabama

A1927 (microfilm reel)—U.S. War Department Field Service Regulations FM 100-20, *Command and Employment of Air Power*

Western Archives, Western University, London, Ontario, Canada

The Beatrice Hitchens Memorial Collection of Aviation History

Primary Sources

Alanbrooke, Field Marshal Lord. *War Diaries, 1939–1945: Field Marshal Lord Alanbrooke.* Edited by Alex Danchev and Daniel Todman. London: Weidenfeld and Nicholson, 2001.

Bishop, William A. *Winged Warfare.* New York: Doran, 1918.

Cathcart-Jones, Owen. *Aviation Memories, including Australia and Back and Other Record Flights.* London: Hutchinson, 1934.

Churchill, Winston S. *The Churchill War Papers.* Compiled by Martin Gilbert. Vol. 3, *The Ever-Widening War 1941.* New York: W. W. Norton, 2000.

Ciano, Galeazz. *The Ciano Diaries, 1939–1943: The Complete, Unabridged Diaries of Count Galeazz Ciano Italian Minister for Foreign Affairs, 1936–1943.* Edited by Hugh Gibson. Garden City, N.Y.: Doubleday, 1946.

Collishaw, Raymond. *Air Command: A Fighter Pilot's Story.* With R. V. Dodds. London: William Kimber, 1973.

———. "Memories of a Canadian Airman." *Roundel* 16, no. 4 (May 1964): 4–10; 16, no. 5 (June 1964): 18–24; 16, no. 6 (July/August 1964): 20–24.

Colville, John. *The Churchillians*. London: Weidenfeld and Nicolson, 1981.

Coningham, Arthur. "The Development of Tactical Air Forces." *RUSI Journal* 91, no. 562 (1946): 211–26.

Conroy, Dennis. *The Best of Luck: In the Royal Air Force, 1935–1946*. Bloomington, Ind.: Trafford, 2003.

Cross, Kenneth. *Straight and Level*. London: Grub Street, 1993.

Cunningham, Viscount. *A Sailor's Odyssey: The Autobiography of Admiral of the Fleet Viscount Cunningham of Hyndhope*. London: Hutchinson, 1951.

De Guingand, Francis. *Operation Victory*. London: Hodder and Stoughton, 1947.

Douglas, Sholto. *Years of Combat: The First Volume of the Autobiography of Sholto Douglas*. London: Collins, 1963.

Drummond, P. R. M. "The Air Campaign in Libya and Tripolitania." *RUSI Journal* 88, no. 552 (1943): 249–66.

Elmhirst, Thomas. "Mobile Air Forces." *RUSI Journal* 96, no. 583 (1951): 457–61.

Embry, Basil. *Mission Completed*. London: Methuen, 1957.

Fonck, Rene. *Ace of Aces: The Combat Memoir of the Foremost Allied Fighter Pilot*. Translated by Martin H. Sabin and Stanley M. Ulanoff. New York: Doubleday, 1967.

Graziani, Rodolfo. *Africa Settentrionale, 1940–1941*. Rome: Danesi, 1948.

Halton, Matthew. *Ten Years to Alamein*. S. J. Reginald Saunders, 1944.

Harriman, W. Averell, and Elie Abel. *Special Envoy to Churchill and Stalin, 1941–1946*. New York: Random House, 1975.

Horrocks, Brian. *A Full Life*. London: Collins, 1960.

Ironside, Edmund. *High Road to Command: The Diaries of Major-General Sir Edmund Ironside, 1920–1922*. Edited by Lord Ironside. London: Leo Cooper, 1972.

Kennedy, John. *The Business of War: The War Narrative of Major-General Sir John Kennedy, GCMG, KCVO, KBE, CB, MC*. London: Hutchinson, 1957.

Lloyd, Hugh. "Allied Air Power in the Mediterranean, 1940–45." *RUSI Journal* 92, no. 568 (1947): 554–66.

Longmore, Arthur. *From Sea to Sky, 1910 to 1945*. London: Geoffrey Bles, 1946.

Montgomery, Bernard Law. *The Memoirs of Field Marshal Montgomery*. Cleveland, Ohio: World, 1958.

Morley-Mower, Geoffrey. *Messerschmitt Roulette: The Western Desert, 1941–42*. St. Paul, Minn.: Phalanx, 1993.

Noonan Steven P., ed. *Canadian Forces Joint Publication CFJP 01: Canadian Military Doctrine*. Ottawa: Canadian Department of National Defence, 2009.

North, John, ed. *The Alexander Memoirs, 1940–1945: Field-Marshal Earl Alexander of Tunis*. London: Cassell, 1962.

Roberts, G. P. B. *From the Desert to the Baltic*. London: William Kimber, 1987.

Rochford, Leonard H. *I Chose the Sky*. London: William Kimber, 1977.

Rommel, Erwin. *The Rommel Papers*. Edited by B. H. Liddell Hart. 1957. Reprint, London: Arrow Books, 1987.

Rosier, Frederick, and David Rosier. *Be Bold*. London: Grub Street, 2011.

Slessor, John. *The Central Blue: The Autobiography of Sir John Slessor, Marshal of the RAF*. New York: Frederick A. Praeger, 1957.

Tedder, Arthur. "Air, Land, and Sea Warfare." *RUSI Journal* 91, no. 561 (1946): 59–68.

———. *With Prejudice: The War Memoirs of Marshal of the Royal Air Force Lord Tedder, GCB*. London: Cassell, 1966.

Udet, Ernst. *Ace of the Iron Cross*. New York: Doubleday, 1970.

War Cabinet. *Principal War Telegrams and Memoranda, 1940–1943: Middle East*. 6 vols. Millwood, N.Y.: KTO, 1976.

Wavell, Archibald P. "Operations in the Middle East from 7th February, 1941, to 15th July, 1941." *Supplement to the London Gazette*, 3 July 1946, 3423–44.

———. "Operations in the Middle East from August, 1939, to November, 1940." *Supplement to the London Gazette*, 13 June 1946, 2997–3006.

———. "Operations in the Western Desert from December 7th, 1940, to February 7th, 1941." *Supplement to the London Gazette*, 26 June 1946, 3261–69.

———. *The Good Soldier*. London: Macmillan, 1948.

Wilson, Field Marshal Lord. *Eight Years Overseas, 1939–1947*. London: Hutchinson, 1948.

Secondary Sources

Addison, Paul, and Angus Calder, eds. *Time to Kill: The Soldier's Experience of War in the West, 1939–1945*. London: Pimlico, 1997.

Agar-Hamilton, J. A. I., and L. C. F. Turner. *Crisis in the Desert, May–June 1942*. Cape Town, South Africa: Oxford University Press, 1952.

———. *The Sidi Rezegh Battles, 1941*. Cape Town, South Africa: Oxford University Press, 1957.

Angelucci, Enzo, and Paolo Matricardi, *World War II Airplanes*, 2 vols. New York, Rand McNally, 1978.

Atkinson, Rick. *An Army at Dawn: The War in North Africa, 1942–1943*. New York: Henry Holt, 2002.

Ball, Simon. *The Bitter Sea: The Struggle for Mastery in the Mediterranean, 1935–1949*. London: Harper, 2009.

Barnett, Correlli. *The Desert Generals*. 1960. Reprint, London: Pan Books, 1983.

Barr, Niall. *Pendulum of War: The Three Battles of El Alamein*. London: Jonathan Cape, 2004.

Bashow, David L. "Four Gallant Airmen: Clifford Mackay McEwen, Raymond Collishaw, Leonard Joseph Birchall, and Robert Wendell McNair." In *Intrepid Warriors: Perspectives on Canadian Military Leaders*, edited by Bernd Horn, 155–98. Toronto: Dundurn Group and Canadian Defence Academy Press, 2007.

———. *Knights of the Air: Canadian Fighter Pilots in the First World War*. Toronto: McArthur, 2000.

Baynes, John. *The Forgotten Victor: General Sir Richard O'Connor, KT, GCB, DSO, MC*. London: Brassey's, 1989.

Bechthold, B. Michael. "A Question of Success: Tactical Air Doctrine and Practice in North Africa, 1942–43." *Journal of Military History* 68, no. 3 (July 2004): 821–51.

———. "The Development of an Unbeatable Combination: U.S. Close Air Support in Normandy." *Canadian Military History* 7, no. 4 (Autumn 1998): 7–20.

Behrendt, Hans-Otto. *Rommel's Intelligence in the Desert Campaign*. London: William Kimber, 1985.

Bennett, Ralph. *Ultra and Mediterranean Strategy*. New York: William Morrow, 1989.

Bharucha, P. C. *The North African Campaign, 1940-1943*. Calcutta, India: Combined Inter-Services Historical Section, India and Pakistan, 1956.

Bickers, Richard Townshend. *The Desert Air War 1939-1945*. London: Leo Cooper, 1991.

———. *Von Richthofen: The Legend Evaluated*. London: Airlife, 1996.

Bierman, John, and Colin Smith. *The Battle of Alamein: Turning Point, World War II*. New York: Viking, 2002.

Bishop, William Arthur. *The Courage of the Early Morning: A Frank Biography of Billy Bishop, the Great Ace of World War I*. Toronto: D. McKay, 1966.

Boog, Horst, ed. *The Conduct of the Air War in the Second World War: An International Comparison*. Providence, R.I.: Berg, 1992.

Bowyer, Chaz. *RAF Operations, 1918-38*. London: William Kimber, 1988.

Boyne, Walter J., ed. *Air Warfare: An International Encyclopedia*. Vol. 1, *A-L*. Santa Barbara, Calif.: ABC CLIO, 2002.

———. *Air Warfare: An International Encyclopedia*. Vol. 2, *M-Z*. Santa Barbara, Calif.: ABC CLIO, 2002.

Bradford, George R. *Rommel's Afrika Korps: El Agheila to El Alamein*. Mechanicsburg, Pa.: Stackpole Books, 2008.

Brown, James Ambrose. *Eagles Strike: The Campaigns of the South African Air Force in Egypt, Cyrenaica, Libya, Tunisia, Tripolitania, and Madagascar, 1941-1943*. Cape Town: Purnell, 1974.

Browne, John Gilbert. *The Iraq Levies, 1915-1932*. London: Royal United Services Institute, 1932.

Bryant, Arthur. *The Turn of the Tide: Based on the War Diaries of Field Marshal Viscount Alanbrooke*. London: Collins, 1957.

Buckingham, William F. *Tobruk: The Great Siege, 1941-42*. Stroud, Gloustershire, U.K.: History, 2008.

Buckley, John. *Air Power in the Age of Total War*. Bloomington: Indiana University Press, 1999.

Bungay, Stephen. *Alamein*. London: Aurum, 2002.

Burt, R. A. *British Battleships, 1919-1939*. London: Arms and Armour, 1993.

Butler, J. R. M. *Grand Strategy*. Vol. 2, *September 1939-June 1941*. London: Her Majesty's Stationery Office, 1957.

Caravaggio, Angelo N. "The Attack at Taranto: Tactical Success, Operational Failure." *Naval War College Review* 59, no. 3 (Summer 2006): 103-27.

Carrington, C. E. "Army/Air Co-operation, 1939-1943." *Journal of the Royal United Services Institute* (December 1970): 37-41.

Carver, Michael. *Dilemmas of the Desert War: A New Look at the Libyan Campaign, 1940-1942*. Bloomington: Indiana University Press, 1986.

———. *El Alamein*. London: Batsford, 1962.

———. "O'Connor, Sir Richard Nugent (1889-1981)." *Oxford Dictionary of National Biography*. Oxford: Oxford University Press, 2004; online ed., January 2011, http://dx.doi.org/10.1093/ref:odnb/31511.

———. *Tobruk*. London: Batsford, 1964.

Ceva, Lucio. "The North African Campaign, 1940-43." *Journal of Strategic Studies* 13, no. 1 (1990): 84-104.

Churchill, Winston S. *The Second World War: The Grand Alliance*. Boston: Houghton Mifflin, 1950.

———. *The Second World War: Their Finest Hour*. Boston: Houghton Mifflin, 1949.

Citino, Robert M. *Death of the Wehrmacht: The German Campaigns of 1942*. Lawrence: University Press of Kansas, 2007.

Clayton, Tim, and Phil Craig. *The End of the Beginning: From the Siege of Malta to the Allied Victory at El Alamein*. New York: Free Press, 2007.

Clodfelter, Mark A. "Molding Airpower Convictions: Development and Legacy of William Mitchell's Strategic Thought." In *The Paths of Heaven: The Evolution of Airpower Theory*, edited by Phillip S. Meilinger, 79–114. Maxwell Air Force Base, Ala.: Air University Press, 1997.

Cole, Christopher. *McCudden, VC*. London: Tempus, 2001.

Collier, Basil. *The Defence of the United Kingdom*. London: Her Majesty's Stationery Office, 1957.

Connell, John. *Auchinleck: A Biography of Field-Marshal Sir Claude Auchinleck*. London: Cassell, 1959.

———. *Wavell: Scholar and Soldier*. London: Collins, 1964.

Cook, Tim. *Shock Troops: Canadians Fighting the Great War, 1917–1918*. Toronto: Viking Canada, 2008.

Cooling, Benjamin Franklin, ed. *Case Studies in the Development of Close Air Support*. Washington, D.C.: Office of Air Force History, 1990.

Coombes, David. *Morshead: Hero of Tobruk and El Alamein*. Melbourne: Oxford University Press, 2001.

Cooper, E. L., and A. J. M. Sinclair. "War Neuroses in Tobruk: A Report of 207 Patients from the Australian Imperial Force Units in Tobruk, 1 August 1942, Medical Association Journal of Australia." In *Combat Stress in the 20th Century: A Commonwealth Perspective*, edited by Terry Copp and Mark Osborne Humphries, 163–76. Kingston, Ont.: Canadian Defence Academy Press, 2010.

Copp, Terry, ed. *Montgomery's Scientists: Operational Research in Northwest Europe: The Work of No. 2 Operational Research Section with 21 Army Group June 1944 to July 1945*. Waterloo, Ont.: Laurier Centre for Military Strategic and Disarmament Studies, 2000.

Cosgrove, Edmund. *Canada's Fighting Pilots*. Toronto: Dundurn, 2003.

Cull, Brian, and Don Minterne. *Hurricanes over Tobruk: The Pivotal Role of the Hurricane in the Defence of Tobruk, January–June 1941*. London: Grub Street, 1999.

Dean, Maurice. *The Royal Air Force and Two World Wars*. London: Cassell, 1979.

Dodds, Ronald V. *The Brave Young Wings*. Stittsville, Ont.: Canada's Wings, 1980.

———. "Britain's First Strategic Bombing Force: No. 3 (Naval) Wing." *Roundel* 15, no. 6 (July–August 1963).

Douglas, W. A. B. *The Creation of a National Air Force: The Official History of the Royal Canadian Air Force*. Vol. 2. Toronto: University of Toronto Press, 1986.

Drew, George A. *Canada's Fighting Airmen*. Toronto: Maclean, 1930.

Dunning, Chris. *Courage Alone: The Italian Air Force, 1940–1943*. Aldershot, Hants, U.K.: Hikoki, 1998.

Edmonds, James. *Military Operations: France and Belgium, 1918*. Vol. 1. London: Macmillan, 1935.

Ellis, L. F. *The War in France and Flanders, 1939–1945*. London: Her Majesty's Stationery Office, 1954.

Elmhirst, Thomas. "Mobile Air Forces." *RUSI Journal* 96, no. 583 (1951): 457–61.

English, Allan D. *The Cream of the Crop: Canadian Aircrew, 1939–1945*. Montreal: McGill-Queen's University Press, 1996.

———. "The RAF Staff College and the Evolution of British Strategic Bombing Policy, 1922–1929." *Journal of Strategic Studies* 16, no. 3 (1993): 408–31.

Fennell, Jonathan. *Combat and Morale in the North African Campaign: The Eighth Army and the Path to El Alamein*. Cambridge: Cambridge University Press, 2011.

Fergusson, Bernard, and Judith M. Brown. "Wavell, Archibald Percival, first Earl Wavell (1883–1950)." *Oxford Dictionary of National Biography*. Oxford: Oxford University Press, 2004; online ed., January 2011, http://dx.doi.org/10.1093/ref:odnb/36790.

Forty, George. *The First Victory: General O'Connor's Desert Triumph, Dec 1940–Feb 1941*. London: Guild, 1990.

Francis, Martin. *The Flyer: British Culture and the Royal Air Force, 1939–1945*. Oxford: Oxford University Press, 2008.

Franks, Norman. *Air Battle for Dunkirk, 26 May–3 June 1940*. London: Grub Street, 2006.

Franks, Norman, and Andy Saunders. *Mannock: The Life and Death of Major Edward Mannock, VC, DSO, MC, RAF*. London: Grub Street, 2008.

Fraser, David. *And We Will Shock Them: The British Army in the Second World War*. London: Hodder and Stoughton, 1983.

Friedman, Norman. *British Carrier Aviation: The Evolution of the Ships and Their Aircraft*. London: Conway Maritime, 1988.

Furse, Anthony. *Wilfrid Freeman: The Genius behind Allied Survival and Air Supremacy, 1939–1945*. Staplehurst, Kent: Spellmount, 1999.

Gibbs, N. H. *Grand Strategy*. Vol. 1, *Rearmament Policy*. London: Her Majesty's Stationery Office, 1976.

Gladman, Brad W. "Air Power and Intelligence in the Western Desert Campaign, 1940–43." *Intelligence and National Security* 13, no. 4 (1998): 144–62.

———. *Intelligence and Anglo-American Air Support in World War Two: The Western Desert and Tunisia, 1940–43*. New York: Palgrave Macmillan, 2009.

Godfrey, Simon. *British Army Communications in the Second World War: Lifting the Fog of Battle*. London: Bloomsbury Academic, 2013.

Gokay, Bulent. *A Clash of Empires: Turkey between Russian Bolshevism and British Imperialism, 1918–1923*. London: I. B. Tauris, 1997.

Gollin, Alfred. *The Impact of Air Power on the British People and their Government, 1909–1914*. Basingstoke: Macmillian, 1989.

Gooch, John. *Mussolini and His Generals: The Armed Forces and Fascist Foreign Policy, 1922–1940*. Cambridge: Cambridge University Press, 2007.

Gooderson, Ian. *Air Power at the Battlefront: Allied Close Air Support in Europe, 1943–1945*. London: Frank Cass, 1998.

Greene, Jack, and Alessandro Massignani. *Rommel's North Africa Campaign: September 1940–November 1942*. Conshohocken, Pa.: Combined Publishing, 1994.

Greenfield, Kent Roberts. *Army Ground Forces and the Air-Ground Battle Team, Including Organic Light Aviation*. Army Ground Forces Historical Section Study 35. Washington, D.C.: U.S. Army, Office of the Chief of Military History, 1948.

Greenhous, Brereton. "Close Air Support Aircraft in World War I: The Counter Anti-Tank Role." *Aerospace Historian* 21 (Summer 1974): 87–93.

———. "Evolution of a Close Ground-Support Role for Aircraft in World War I." *Military Affairs* 39, no. 1 (February 1975): 22–28.

———. *The Making of Billy Bishop: The First World War Exploits of Billy Bishop, VC.* Toronto: Dundurn, 2002.

Gudmundsson, Bruce I., ed. *Inside the Afrika Korps: The Crusader Battles, 1941–1942.* London: Greenhill Books, 1999.

Guedalla, Philip. *Middle East, 1940–1942: A Study in Air Power.* London: Hodder and Stoughton, 1944.

Gundelach, Karl. *Die Deutsche Luftwaffe im Mittelmeer, 1940–1945.* Frankfurt: Lang, 1981.

Gunn, Roger. *Raymond Collishaw and the Black Flight.* Toronto: Dundurn, 2012.

Gustavsson, Hakan, and Ludovico Slongo. *Desert Prelude: Early Clashes, June–November 1940.* Petersfield, Hampshire, U.K.: Stratus/MMP Books, 2010.

———. *Desert Prelude: "Operation Compass."* Petersfield, Hampshire: Stratus/MMP Books, 2010.

Hackett, J. W. "Wilson, Henry Maitland, first Baron Wilson (1881–1964)." *Oxford Dictionary of National Biography.* Oxford: Oxford University Press, 2004; online ed., January 2011, http://dx.doi.org/10.1093/ref:odnb/36956.

Hall, David Ian. "From Khaki and Light Blue to Purple: The Long and Troubled Development of Army/Air Co-operation in Britain, 1914–1945." *Journal of the Royal United Services Institute* (October 2002): 78–83.

———. *Learning How to Fight Together: The British Experience with Joint Air-Land Warfare.* Maxwell Air Force Base, Ala.: Air University Air Force Research Institute, 2009.

———. *Strategy for Victory: The Development of British Tactical Air Power, 1919–1943.* Westport, Conn.: Praeger Security International, 2008.

Halliday, Hugh. "The Air Historian—Part II." *Canadian Air Force Journal* 4, no. 4 (Fall 2011): 22–30.

Hallion, Richard P. *Strike from the Sky: The History of Battlefield Air Attack, 1911–1945.* Shrewsbury, Eng.: Airlife, 1989.

Halpern, Paul G. *The Mediterranean Fleet, 1919–1929.* Farnham, Surrey: Navy Records Society and Ashgate, 2011.

Hamilton, Archibald Milne. *Road through Kurdistan: The Narrative of an Engineer in Iraq.* London: Faber, 1937.

Hamilton, Nigel. *Monty: The Making of a General, 1887–1942.* London: Hamish Hamilton, 1981.

Harris, J. P. *Douglas Haig and the First World War.* Cambridge: Cambridge University Press, 2008.

Hartmann, Bernard. *Panzers in the Sand: The History of Panzer-Regiment 5.* Vol. 1, *1935–1941.* Mechanicsburg, Pa.: Stackpole Books, 2010.

Hastings, Max. "Slessor, Sir John Cotesworth (1897–1979)." *Oxford Dictionary of National Biography.* Oxford: Oxford University Press, 2004; online ed., January 2011, http://dx.doi.org/10.1093/ref:odnb/31692.

Hezlet, Arthur. *Aircraft and Sea Power.* New York: Stein and Day, 1970.

Higham, Robin. *Armed Forces in Peacetime: Britain, 1918–1940: A Case Study.* London: G. T. Foulis, 1962.

———. *Diary of a Disaster: British Aid to Greece, 1940–1941.* Lexington: University Press of Kentucky, 1986.

———. *The Military Intellectuals in Britain, 1918–1939*. 1966. Reprint, Westport, Conn.: Greenwood, 1981.

———. "The Ploesti Ploy: British Considerations and the Idea of Bombing the Roumanian Oilfields, 1940–41." *War and Society* 5, no. 2 (1987): 57–71.

———. *Unflinching Zeal: The Air Battles over France and Britain, May–October 1940*. Annapolis: Naval Institute Press, 2012.

Hinsley, F. H. *British Intelligence in the Second World War*. Vol. 1, *Its Influence on Strategy and Operations*. London: Her Majesty's Stationery Office, 1979.

Hodgson, John Ernest. *With Denikin's Armies: Being a Description of the Cossack Counter-Revolution in South Russia, 1918–1920*. London: Temple Bar, 1932.

Hone, Thomas C., Norman Friedman, and Mark D. Mandeles. *American & British Aircraft Carrier Development, 1919–1941*. Annapolis: Naval Institute Press, 1999.

Hughes, Thomas Alexander. *Overlord: General Pete Quesada and the Triumph of Tactical Air Power in World War II*. New York: Free Press, 1995.

Hunt, C. W. *Dancing in the Sky: The Royal Flying Corps in Canada*. Toronto: Dundurn, 2009.

Hyde, H. Montgomery. *British Air Policy between the Wars, 1918–1939*. London: William Heinemann, 1976.

Ireland, Bernard. *The War in the Mediterranean, 1940–1943*. Arms and Armour, 1993. Reprint, Barnsley, South Yorkshire: Leo Cooper, 2004.

Ishoven, Armand van. *The Fall of an Eagle: The Life of Fighter Ace Ernst Udet*. London: William Kimber, 1979.

Jackson, Robert. *At War with the Bolsheviks: The Allied Intervention into Russia, 1917–20*. London: Tom Stacey, 1972.

———. *Strike from the Sea: A Survey of British Naval Air Operations, 1909–69*. London: Arthur Barker, 1970.

Jacobs, W. A. "Air Support for the British Army, 1939–1943." *Military Affairs* (December 1982): 174–82.

James, Barrie G. *Hitler's Gulf War: The Fight for Iraq, 1941*. Barnsley, South Yorkshire: Pen and Sword Books, 2009.

James, John. *The Paladins: A Social History of the RAF up to the Outbreak of World War II*. London: Macdonald, 1990.

James, T. C. G. *The Growth of Fighter Command, 1936–1940*. London: Cass, 2002.

Jentz, Thomas L. *Tank Combat in North Africa: The Opening Rounds—Operations Sonnenblumme, Brevity, Skorpion, and Battleaxe, February 1941–June 1941*. Atglen, Pa.: Schiffer, 1998.

Jones, H. A. *The War in the Air: Being the Story of the Part Played in the Great War by the Royal Air Force*. Vol. 4. 1934. Reprint, London: Naval and Military Press, 2002.

———. *The War in the Air: Being the Story of the Part Played in the Great War by the Royal Air Force*. Vol. 6. 1937. Reprint, London: Naval and Military Press, 2002.

Jordan, David. "The Royal Air Force and Air/Land Integration in the 100 Days, August-November 1918." *Royal Air Force Air Power Review* 11, no. 2 (Summer 2008): 12–29.

Keegan, John, ed. *Churchill's Generals*. London: George Weidenfeld and Nicolson, 1991.

Kelly, Saul. *The Lost Oasis: The Desert War and the Hunt for Zerzura*. London: John Murray, 2002.

Kennett, Lee. "Developments to 1939." In Cooling, *Case Studies in the Development of Close Air Support*, 13–70. Washington, D.C.: Office of Air Force History, 1990.

Kilduff, Peter. *Red Baron*. Newton Abbot, U.K.: David and Charles, 2007.

Kitchen, Martin. *Rommel's Desert War: Waging World War II in North Africa, 1941–1943*. Cambridge: Cambridge University Press, 2009.

Knox, MacGregor. *Hitler's Italian Allies: Royal Armed Forces, Fascist Regime, and the War of 1940–1943*. Cambridge: Cambridge University Press, 2000.

———. *Mussolini Unleashed, 1939–1941: Politics and Strategy in Fascist Italy's Last War*. Cambridge: Cambridge University Press, 1982.

Kohn, Richard H., and Joseph P. Harahan, eds. *Air Superiority in World War II and Korea: An Interview with Gen. James Ferguson, Gen. Robert M. Lee, Gen. William Momyer, and Lt. Gen. Elwood R. Quesada*. Washington, D.C.: Office of Air Force History, 1983.

Kopisto, Lauri. "The British Intervention in South Russia, 1918–1920." Ph.D. dissertation, University of Helsinki, 2011.

Laffin, John. *Swifter than Eagles: A Biography of Marshal of the Royal Air Force Sir John Maitland Salmond GCB, CMG, CVO, DSO*. Edinburgh: William Blackwood and Sons, 1964.

Latimer, Jon. *Alamein*. Cambridge, Mass.: Harvard University Press, 2002.

Lee, David. "Longmore, Sir Arthur Murray (1885–1970)." *Oxford Dictionary of National Biography*. Oxford: Oxford University Press, 2004; online ed., January 2012, http://dx.doi.org/10.1093/ref:odnb/34593.

Levine, Alan J. *The War against Rommel's Supply Lines, 1942–43*. 1999. Reprint, Mechanicsburg, Pa.: Stackpole Books, 2008.

Lewis, Walter David. *Eddie Rickenbacker: An American Hero in the Twentieth Century*. Baltimore: The Johns Hopkins University Press, 2005.

Lloyd, Hugh. "Allied Air Power in the Mediterranean, 1940–45." *RUSI Journal* 92, no. 568 (1947): 554–66.

Long, Gavin. *To Benghazi*. Australia in the War of 1939–1945, Series 1 (Army). 1952. Reprint, Canberra: Australian War Memorial, 1961.

Macfie, A. L. "The Chanak Affair (September–October 1922)." *Balkan Studies* 20, no. 2 (1979): 309–41.

Macksey, Kenneth. *Beda Fomm: The Classic Victory*. London: Ballantine Books, 1971.

MacLaren, Roy. *Canadians in Russia, 1918–1919*. Toronto: Macmillan, 1976.

Mason, R. A. *History of the Royal Air Force Staff College, 1922–1972*. Bracknell, U.K.: RAF Staff College, 1972.

Maughan, Barton. *Tobruk and El Alamein*. Australia in the War of 1939–1945, Series 1 (Army). Canberra: Australian War Memorial, 1965.

McCaffery, Dan. *Air Aces: The Lives and Times of Twelve Canadian Fighter Pilots*. Toronto: James Lorimer, 1990.

———. *Billy Bishop: Canadian Hero*. Toronto: James Lorimer, 2002.

McKee, Alexander. *El Alamein: Ultra and the Three Battles*. London: Souvenir, 1991.

McMillan, Richard. *Mediterranean Assignment*. Garden City, N.Y.: Doubleday, Doran, 1943.

Mearsheimer, John J. "Assessing the Conventional Balance: The 3:1 Rule and Its Critics." *International Security* 13, no. 4 (Spring 1989): 54–89.

Meilinger, Phillip S. "Air Power and Joint Operations during World War II." In *Airwar: Essays on Its Theory and Practice*, 129–51. London: Taylor and Francis, 2003.

———. *Air War: Theory and Practice*. London: Frank Cass, 2003.

———. "Alexander P. De Seversky and American Airpower." In *The Paths of Heaven: The Evolution of Airpower Theory*, edited by Phillip S. Meilinger, 239–78. Maxwell Air Force Base, Ala.: Air University Press, 1997.

———. "John C. Slessor and the Genesis of Air Interdiction." *Journal of the Royal United Services Institute* (August 1995): 43–48.

Melhorn, Charles. *Two-Block Fox: The Rise of the Aircraft Carrier, 1911–1929*. Annapolis: Naval Institute Press, 1974.

Mets, David R. "A Glider in the Propwash of the Royal Air Force?: General Carl A. Spaatz, the RAF, and the Foundations of American Tactical Air Power." In Mortensen, *Airpower and Ground Armies*, 30–63.

Ministero della Difesa Stato Maggiore Esercito. *In Africa Settentrionale: La Preparazione Al Conflitto l'Avanzata Su Sidi El Barrani, Ottobre 1935–Settembre 1940*. Rome: Ufficio Storico, 1955.

———. *La Prima Controffensiva Italo-Tedesca in Africa Settentrionale (15 Febbraio–18 Novembre 1941)*. Rome: Ufficio Storico, 1974.

———. *La Prima Offensiva Britannica in Africa Settentrionale*. Rome: Ufficio Storico, 1979.

Montgomery, Archibald. *The Story of the Fourth Army in the Battles of the Hundred Days, August 8th to November 11th, 1918*. 1919. Reprint, London: Naval and Military Press, 2008.

Morewood, Steven. *British Defense of Egypt, 1935–1940: Conflict and Crisis in the Eastern Mediterranean*. London: Frank Cass, 2004.

Morrow, John H. *The Great War in the Air: Military Aviation from 1909 to 1921*. Washington, D.C.: Smithsonian Institute Press, 1993.

Mortensen, Daniel R., ed. *Airpower and Ground Armies: Essays on the Evolution of Anglo-American Air Doctrine, 1940–1943*. Maxwell Air Force Base, Ala.: Air University Press, 1998.

———. *A Pattern for Joint Operations: World War II Close Air Support in North Africa*. Washington, D.C.: Office of Air Force History and U.S. Army Center of Military History, 1987.

Moseley, Ray. *Mussolini's Shadow: The Double Life of Count Galeazzo Ciano*. New Haven, Conn.: Yale University Press, 1999.

Murphy, Norman Kenneth. "The 'Lost' Battle of Mersa El Brega, Libyan Desert, 31 March 1941." Ph.D. dissertation, University of Hull, 2011.

Murphy, W. E. *Official History of New Zealand in the Second World War, 1939–45: The Relief of Tobruk*. Wellington: War History Branch, 1961.

Murray, Williamson, and Allan R. Millett, eds. *Military Innovation in the Interwar Period*. Cambridge: Cambridge University Press, 1996.

Neillands, Robin. *The Desert Rats: 7th Armoured Division, 1940–1945*. London: Weidenfeld and Nicolson, 1991.

———. *Eighth Army: The Triumphant Desert Army that Held the Axis at Bay from North Africa to the Alps, 1939–45*. New York: Overlook, 2004.

Nicholson, G. W. L. *The Canadian Expeditionary Force, 1914–1919: Official History of the Canadian Army in the First World War*. Ottawa: Queen's Printer, 1962.

Olsen, John Andreas, ed. *A History of Air Warfare*. Washington, D.C.: Potomac Books, 2010.

Omissi, David E. *Air Power and Colonial Control: The Royal Air Force, 1919–1939.* Manchester: Manchester University Press, 1990.

———. "Technology and Repression: Air Control in Palestine, 1922–36." *Journal of Strategic Studies* 13, no. 4 (1990): 41–63.

Orange, Vincent. *Churchill and His Airmen: Relationships, Intrigue, and Policy Making, 1914–1945.* London: Grub Street, 2013.

———. *Coningham: A Biography of Air Marshal Sir Arthur Coningham.* London: Methuen, 1990.

———. "Dowding, Hugh Caswall Tremenheere, first Baron Dowding (1882–1970)." *Oxford Dictionary of National Biography.* Oxford: Oxford University Press, 2004; online ed., May 2008, http://dx.doi.org/10.1093/ref:odnb/32884.

———. *Dowding of Fighter Command: Victor of the Battle of Britain.* London: Grub Street, 2008.

———. "Getting Together: Tedder, Coningham, and Americans in the Desert and Tunisia, 1940–43." In Mortensen, *Airpower and Ground Armies,* 1–29.

———. *Slessor: Bomber Champion, the Life of Marshal of the Royal Air Force Sir John Slessor, GCB, DSO, MC.* London: Grub Street, 2006.

———. "Tedder, Arthur William, first Baron Tedder (1890–1967)." *Oxford Dictionary of National Biography.* Oxford: Oxford University Press, 2004; online ed., January 2011, http://dx.doi.org/10.1093/ref:odnb/36446.

———. *Tedder: Quietly in Command.* London: Frank Cass, 2004.

Orpen, Neil. *South African Forces World War 2: War in the Desert.* Cape Town: Purnell, 1971.

Owen, Roderic. *The Desert Air Force.* London: Hutchinson, 1948.

———. *Tedder.* London: Collins, 1952.

Parkinson, Roger. *The War in the Desert.* London: Hart-Davis, MacGibbon, 1976.

Paxton, Robert O. *Vichy France: Old Guard and New Order.* 1972. Reprint, New York: Columbia University Press, 2001.

Pengelly, Colin. *Albert Ball V.C.: The Fighter Pilot Hero of World War I.* London: Pen and Sword Books, 2010.

Petracarro, Domenico. "The Italian Army in Africa, 1940–1943: An Attempt at Historical Perspective." *War and Society* 9, no. 2 (October 1991): 103–27.

Philpott, Ian M. *The Royal Air Force: An Encyclopedia of the Inter-War Years.* Vol. 1, *The Trenchard Years—1918–1929.* Barnsley, South Yorkshire: Pen and Sword Aviation, 2005.

———. *The Royal Air Force: An Encyclopedia of the Inter-War Years.* Vol. 2, *Rearmament—1930–1939.* Barnsley, South Yorkshire: Pen and Sword Aviation, 2008.

Pitt, Barrie. *The Crucible of War: Western Desert, 1941.* London: Book Club Associates, 1980.

Playfair, I. S. O., G. M. S. Stitt, C. J. C. Molony, and S. E. Toomer. *The Mediterranean and Middle East.* Vol. 1, *The Early Successes against Italy (to May 1941).* London: Her Majesty's Stationery Office, 1954.

———. *The Mediterranean and Middle East.* Vol. 2, *The Germans Come to the Help of Their Ally (1941).* London: Her Majesty's Stationery Office, 1956.

———. *The Mediterranean and the Middle East.* Vol. 4, *The Destruction of the Axis Forces in North Africa.* London: Her Majesty's Stationery Office, 1966.

Powers, Barry D. *Strategy without Slide-Rule: British Air Strategy, 1914–1939.* London: Croom Helm, 1976.

Price, Alfred. "Air Power Taken to Its Limits and Beyond: The Battle of Amiens." *Royal Air Force Air Power Review* 4, no. 4 (2001): 118–36.

Probert, Henry. *High Commanders of the Royal Air Force.* London: Her Majesty's Stationery Office, 1991.

R.A.F. *Middle East: The Official Story of Air Operations in the Middle East, from February 1942 to January 1943.* London: His Majesty's Stationery Office, 1945.

Ralph, Wayne. *William Barker, VC: The Life, Death, and Legend of Canada's Most Decorated War Hero.* Mississauga, Ont.: John Wiley and Sons Canada, 2007.

Raugh, Harold E. *Wavell in the Middle East, 1939–1941: A Study in Generalship.* London: Brassey's, 1993.

Reynolds, Clark G. *Command of the Sea: The History and Strategy of Maritime Empires.* New York: Morrow, 1974.

Richards, Denis. "Portal, Charles Frederick Algernon, Viscount Portal of Hungerford (1893–1971)." *Oxford Dictionary of National Biography.* Oxford: Oxford University Press, 2004; online ed., January 2011, http://dx.doi.org/10.1093/ref:odnb/31561.

———. *Royal Air Force.* Vol. 1, *The Fight at Odds.* London: Her Majesty's Stationery Office, 1953.

Ritchie, Sebastian. *The RAF, Small Wars, and Insurgencies in the Middle East, 1919–1939.* Shrivenham, U.K.: Air Historical Branch, 2011.

Robbins, Guy. *The Aircraft Carrier Story, 1908–1945.* London: Cassell, 2001.

Roskill, S. W. *The War at Sea, 1939–1945.* Vol. 1, *The Defensive.* London: Her Majesty's Stationery Office, 1954.

Sadkovich, James J. "Anglo-American Bias and the Italo-Greek War of 1940–1941." *Journal of Military History* 58, no. 4 (October 1994): 617–42.

———. "German Military Incompetence through Italian Eyes." *War in History* 1, no. 1 (1994): 39–62.

———. "Of Myths and Men: Rommel and the Italians in North Africa, 1940–1942." *International History Review* 13, no. 2 (May 1991): 284–313.

———. "Re-Evaluating Who Won the Italo-British Naval Conflict, 1940–42." *European History Quarterly* 18 (1988): 455–71.

———. "Understanding Defeat: Reappraising Italy's Role in World War II." *Journal of Contemporary History* 24, no. 1 (January 1989): 27–61.

Sadler, John. *El Alamein: The Story of the Battle in the Words of the Soldiers.* Stroud, Gloucestershire: Amberley, 2010.

Schreiber, Gerhard, Bernd Stegemann, and Detlef Vogel. *Germany and the Second World War.* Vol. 3, *The Mediterranean, South-East Europe, and North Africa, 1939–1941.* Oxford: Oxford University Press, 1995.

Scoullar, J. L. *Official History of New Zealand in the Second World War, 1939–45.* Wellington: War History Branch, 1955.

Segrè, Claudio G. *Italo Balbo: A Fascist Life.* Berkeley: University of California Press, 1987.

Sela, Avraph. "The 'Wailing Wall' Riots (1929) as a Watershed in the Palestine Conflict." *Muslim World* 84, nos. 1–2 (1994): 60–94.

Shores, Christopher. *Above the Trenches: A Complete Record of the Fighter Aces and Units of the British Empire Air Forces, 1915–1920.* Stoney Creek, Ont.: Fortress, 1990.

———. *Dust Clouds in the Middle East: The Air War for East Africa, Iraq, Syria, Iran, and Madagascar, 1940–42*. London: Grub Street, 1996.

Shores, Christopher, Brian Cull, and with Nicola Malizia. *Air War for Yugoslavia, Greece, and Crete, 1940–41*. London: Grub Street, 1987.

Shores, Christopher, Norman Franks, and Russell Guest. *Above the Trenches: Supplement*. London: Grub Street, 1996.

Shores, Christopher, Giovanni Massimello, and Russell Guest. *A History of the Mediterranean Air War, 1940–1945*. Vol. 1, *North Africa—June 1940-January 1942*. London: Grub Street, 2012.

Shores, Christopher, and Hans Ring. *Fighters over the Desert: The Air Battles in the Western Desert, June 1940 to December 1942*. New York: Arco, 1969.

Simpson, Michael. *A Life of Admiral of the Fleet Andrew Cunningham: A Twentieth-Century Naval Leader*. London: Routledge, 2004.

Slessor, John. *Air Power and Armies*. 1936. Reprint, Tuscaloosa: University of Alabama Press, 2009.

Sluglett, Peter. *Britain in Iraq: Contriving King and Country, 1914–1932*. 2nd ed. London: I. B. Tauris, 2007.

Smith, Adrian. *Mick Mannock, Fighter Pilot: Myth, Life, and Politics*. New York: Palgrave, 2001.

Smith, John T. *Gone to Russia to Fight: The RAF in South Russia, 1918–1920*. Stroud, Gloucestershire: Amberley, 2010.

Smith, Malcolm. "The Allied Air Offensive." *Journal of Strategic Studies* 13, no. 1 (1990): 67–83.

Smith, Peter. *Massacre at Tobruk: The British Assault on Rommel, 1942*. 1987. Reprint, Mechanicsburg, Pa.: Stackpole Books, 2008.

Smith, Peter C. *Close Air Support*. London: Crown, 1990.

Snowie, J. Allan. *Collishaw & Company: Canadians in the Royal Naval Air Service, 1914–1918*. Bellingham, Wash.: Nieuport, 2010.

Stephens, Alan. "The True Believers: Airpower between the Wars." In *The War in the Air*, edited by Alan Stephens, 29–68. Maxwell Air Force Base, Ala.: Air University Press, 2001.

Stephens, G. R. *Fourth Indian Division*. Toronto: McLaren and Sons, 1948.

Stephens, W. G. *Official History of New Zealand in the Second World War: Bardia to Enfidaville*. Wellington: War History Branch, 1962.

Stevenson, David. *With Our Backs to the Wall: Victory and Defeat in 1918*. Cambridge, Mass.: Belknap Press of Harvard University Press, 2011.

Stockings, Craig. *Bardia: Myth, Reality, and the Heirs of Anzac*. Sydney: University of New South Wales Press, 2009.

Stockings, Craig, and Eleanor Hancock. "Reconsidering the Luftwaffe in Greece, 1941." *Journal of Military History* 75, no. 3 (July 2012): 747–73.

Sturtivant, Ray. *British Naval Aviation: The Fleet Air Arm, 1917–1990*. Annapolis: Naval Institute Press, 1990.

Sullivan, Alan. *Aviation in Canada, 1917–1918*. Toronto: Rous and Mann, 1919.

Sullivan, Brian. "The Italian Soldier in Combat, June 1940–September 1943: Myths, Realities, and Explanations." In Addison and Calder, *Time to Kill*, 177–205.

Sutherland, Jon. *Air War Malta: June 1940 to November 1942*. Barnsley, South Yorkshire: Pen and Sword Books, 2008.

Sutherland, Jon, and Dianne Canwell. *Air War East Africa: The RAF Versus the Italian Air Force*. Barnsley, South Yorkshire: Pen and Sword Aviation, 2009.

Sweet, John Joseph Timothy. *Iron Arm: The Mechanization of Mussolini's Army, 1920–1940*. 1980. Reprint, Mechanicsburg, Pa.: Stackpole Books, 2007.

Swettenham, J. A. *Allied Intervention in Russia, 1918–1919; and the Part Played by Canada*. Toronto: Ryerson, 1967.

Sykes, Claud W. *Richthofen: The Red Knight of the Air*. Bristol: Cerberus, 2005.

———. *Air Power in War*. London: Hodder and Stoughton, 1947.

Terraine, John. *The Right of the Line: The Royal Air Force in the European War, 1939–1945*. London: Hodder and Stoughton, 1985.

———. *To Win a War: 1918, the Year of Victory*. New York: Doubleday, 1981.

Thetford, Owen. *British Naval Aircraft since 1912*. London: Putnam, 1958.

The Tiger Kills: The Story of the Indian Divisions in the North African Campaign. 1944. Reprint, [London]: Military Library Research Service, 2004.

Till, Geoffrey. *Air Power and the Royal Navy, 1914–1945: A Historical Survey*. London: Jane's, 1979.

Titterton, G. A. *The Royal Navy and the Mediterranean*. Vol. 1, *September 1939–October 1940*. 1952. Reprint, London: Whitehall History in association with Frank Cass, 2002.

———. *The Royal Navy and the Mediterranean*. Vol. 2, *November 1940–December 1941*. 1952. Reprint, London: Whitehall History in association with Frank Cass, 2002.

Tjepkema, Andy. "Coningham: The Architect of Ground-Air Doctrine." *Air Clues* 45, no. 6 (1991): 205–11.

Tolppanen, Bradley P. "Getting the Air Force on Side: The Development of Tactical Air Support Doctrine by the Royal Air Force in the Western Desert, 1941–1943." M.A. thesis, University of New Brunswick, 1994.

Toppe, Alfred. *Desert Warfare: German Experiences in World War II*. 1952. Reprint, Fort Leavenworth, Kans.: Combat Studies Institute, U.S. Army Command and General Staff College, 1991.

Townshend, Charles. *When God Made Hell: The British Invasion of Mesopotamia and the Creation of Iraq*. London: Faber and Faber, 2010.

Tucker, Gilbert Norman. *The Naval Service of Canada, its Official History*. Vol. 1, *Origins and Early Years*. Ottawa: King's Printer, 1962.

Ullman, Richard H. *Anglo-Soviet Relations, 1917–1921*. 3 vols. Princeton, N.J.: Princeton University Press for the Center of International Studies, 1961–72.

Vernay, G. L. *The Desert Rats: The 7th Armoured Division in World War II*. London: Hutchinson, 1954. Reprint, New York: Greenhill, 2002.

Wahlert, Glenn. *The Western Desert Campaign, 1940–41*. 2nd ed. Canberra: Army History Unit, 2009.

Waldie, Derek J. P. "Relations between the Army and the RAF, 1918–1939." Ph.D. dissertation, King's College, 1980.

Walker, Ronald. *Official History of New Zealand in the Second World War: Alam Halfa and El Alamein*. Wellington: War History Branch, 1967.

Westrop, Mike. *A History of No. 10 Squadron Royal Naval Air Service in World War 1*. Atglen, Pa.: Schiffer Military History, 2004.

Wilmot, Chester. *Desert Siege: Tobruk, a Great Example of Australian Courage*. 1944. Reprint, Victoria: Penguin Books Australia, 2003.

Winton, Harold R. *To Change an Army: General Sir John Burnett-Stuart and British Armoured Doctrine, 1927–1938.* Lawrence: University Press of Kansas, 1988.

Wise, Sydney F. "The Black Day of the German Army: Australians and Canadians at Amiens, August 1918." In *1918: Defining Victory. Proceedings of the Chief of Army's History Conference Held at the National Convention Centre, Canberra, 29 September 1998*, edited by Peter Dennis and Jeffrey Grey, 1–32. Canberra: Army History Unit, Department of Defence, 1999.

———. *Canadian Airmen and the First World War. The Official History of the Royal Canadian Air Force.* Vol. 1, *The Creation of a National Air Force.* Toronto: University of Toronto Press, 1980.

Woodward, Llewellyn. *British Foreign Policy in the Second World War.* London: Her Majesty's Stationery Office, 1962.

Woolven, Robin. "Mitchell, Sir William Gore Sutherland (1888–1944)." *Oxford Dictionary of National Biography.* Oxford: Oxford University Press, 2004; online ed., January 2008, http://dx.doi.org/10.1093/ref:odnb/35047.

Wright, Robert. *Dowding and the Battle of Britain.* London: Macdonald, 1969.

Websites

Air of Authority—A History of RAF Organisation. 2015. http://www.rafweb.org.

Judge, J. W. B. "Airfield Creation for the Western Desert Campaign." [Ca.1940s]. 2009. http://www.laetusinpraesens.org/guests/jwbj/jwb1.htm.

"U.K. House of Commons Debates." Hansard, 1803–2005. http://hansard.millbank systems.com/.

The U-boat Wars, 1939–1945 (Kreigsmarine) and 1914–1918 (Kaiserliche Marine), and Allied Warships of World War II. uboat.net. 1995–2016. http://uboat.net/.

Index

Page numbers in *italics* indicate illustrations.